THE FOUNDERS AND THE BIBLE

THE FOUNDERS AND THE BIBLE

Carl J. Richard

ROWMAN & LITTLEFIELD
Lanham • Boulder • New York • London

Published by Rowman & Littlefield
A wholly owned subsidiary of The Rowman & Littlefield Publishing Group, Inc.
4501 Forbes Boulevard, Suite 200, Lanham, Maryland 20706
www.rowman.com

Unit A, Whitacre Mews, 26-34 Stannary Street, London SE11 4AB

British Library Cataloguing in Publication Information Available

Library of Congress Cataloging-in-Publication Data

Names: Richard, Carl J.
The Founders and the Bible / Carl J. Richard.
Description: Lanham, Maryland : Rowman & Littlefield, 2016. | Includes index.
Identifiers: LCCN 2015035506| ISBN 9781442254640 (cloth : alk. paper) | ISBN 9781442254657 (electronic)
Subjects: LCSH: Religion and politics—United States—History—18th century. | Religion and state—United States—History—18th century. | Founding Fathers of the United States—Religious life. | United States—Religion—To 1800. | United States—Politics and government—Philosophy.
Classification: LCC BL2525 .R53 2016 | DDC 200.973/09033—dc23
LC record available at http://lccn.loc.gov/2015035506

∞ ™ The paper used in this publication meets the minimum requirements of American National Standard for Information Sciences Permanence of Paper for Printed Library Materials, ANSI/NISO Z39.48-1992.

Printed in the United States of America

For Eran Shalev, the best of brothers

CONTENTS

PREFACE

While American historians have used the term "framers" in a fairly consistent manner—to refer to the delegates of the Constitutional Convention—they have not displayed the same consistency in their employment of the word "founders." Often, they have focused on the six most famous leaders of the early American republic (the first four presidents, joined by Benjamin Franklin and Alexander Hamilton), implying that their views were typical of their class and generation. By contrast, this book is based on a study of approximately thirty prominent American political leaders of the late eighteenth and early nineteenth centuries, a number that is large enough to reveal both shared beliefs and theological differences among the political class of that era, yet small enough to avoid a voluminous and tedious descent into the idiosyncrasies of relatively minor figures. While my list of founders excludes loyalists, who opposed American independence and thus cannot be considered the founders of a new nation, it includes Anti-Federalists, who opposed the replacement of the nation's first constitution, the Articles of Confederation, with the current one. To exclude the Anti-Federalists would be to neglect some of the most important leaders of the American Revolution, such as Samuel Adams and Patrick Henry, as well as the fifth president of the United States, James Monroe.

In addition to discussing the founders' use of the Bible in their political rhetoric, this book also examines the theological and moral principles they derived from scripture. Focusing exclusively on the numerous scriptures the founders cited and the various biblical figures to whom they alluded while neglecting to examine the ideas that they derived from the Bible—ideas that were both central to their worldviews and crucial to the rebellion they led and the political system they created—would leave a stunted and distorted impression of biblical influence.

This book discusses the relationship between the biblical heritage and the classical and Whig traditions in the founders' thought. The term "classics" refers to ancient Greek and Roman writings, both in their original languages and in translation. The Whigs referred to in this book were seventeenth-century British political philosophers, such as James Harrington, Algernon Sidney, and John Locke, who supported balanced government in opposition to absolute monarchy and who emphasized the natural rights of individuals.

The focus of this book on the influence of the Bible on late eighteenth- and early nineteenth-century American political leaders is not meant to suggest that the Bible did not have an equally powerful impact on other eras, nations, and classes. But these biblical influences have been addressed in numerous other books. Hence I refer to them only as they relate to the founders.

I would like to thank my dear friends and admired colleagues E. Christian Kopff, Dolores Egger Labbe, Glenn Moots, and Eran Shalev, who read this manuscript and provided valuable insights. Additionally, I would like to express gratitude to my editor, Jon Sisk, for his unfailing enthusiasm and encouragement. I would also like to thank the Guilbeau Charitable Trust at the University of Louisiana at Lafayette for its 2013 summer research award, which helped me to complete this work. As always, I would like to thank my precious wife, Debbie, my other half, for her unceasing prayers and support. As Proverbs 31:10–12 states regarding the good wife, "Her value is far above rubies. The heart of her husband safely trusts in her, so that he shall have great gain. She does him good and not harm all the days of her life."

INTRODUCTION

The American founders resist all efforts at appropriation for twenty-first-century agendas, whether political or religious, by their diversity of thought. As a case in point, a thorough study of the founders' relationship with the Bible reveals that the more extreme claims of some modern Christians and secularists are equally invalid.

The claim that "all of the founders were Christians" holds true only if one adopts an uncommonly broad definition of Christianity. Four of the most important founders—Thomas Paine, Thomas Jefferson, Benjamin Franklin, and John Adams—rejected crucial biblical doctrines concerning the origin and authority of scripture, the divinity of Jesus, and the means of salvation. The first three men also rejected biblical teaching regarding human nature. Three other crucial founders—George Washington, the later James Madison, and James Monroe—wrote so little about the Bible, Jesus, and salvation that no honest historian can make confident assertions about them. This means that of the first five presidents of the United States, only one of them (James Madison) can be termed a biblically orthodox Christian with any degree of assurance, and then only during the early part of his life. Furthermore, even fairly orthodox founders sometimes possessed unorthodox opinions: Samuel Adams's postmillennialism, his belief that Jesus would return only after humans created the utopia of the Millennium, contradicted biblical teachings regarding both human nature and the end times, and Benjamin Rush's universalism, his belief that all souls would eventually arrive in heaven, conflicted with numerous scriptures that declare hell is eternal.

But the attempt to convert the founders into twenty-first-century secularists is even more problematic. Such efforts invariably focus obsessively on the four unorthodox founders, engage in bouts of wild speculation about the three mysterious ones, and steadfastly ignore the far larger number of fairly orthodox founders, a list that includes Samuel Adams, Fisher Ames, Elias Boudinot, Charles Carroll, John Dickinson, Christopher Gadsden, Alexander Hamilton, John Hancock, Patrick Henry, John Jay, Henry Laurens, William Livingston, the early James Madison, John Marshall, George Mason, Charles Pinckney, Edmund Randolph, Benjamin Rush, Roger Sherman, Charles Thomson, James Wilson, and John Witherspoon. Samuel Adams entered the Revolutionary movement, and became its most important organizer, as a result of the Great Awakening—a religious revival movement that inspired him with a passionate desire to establish an independent America as a "Christian Sparta," a nation both deeply pious and profoundly republican. Patrick Henry, the Revolution's greatest orator, dressed in parson's gray, modeled the style of his powerful and influential speeches on the sermons of his favorite revivalist preacher, and filled those orations with biblical references. Benjamin Rush, a signer of both the Declaration of Independence and the Constitution, was so devout that he could scarcely write a sentence without referring to his faith; he even selected his wife based on her taste in sermons. Daily reading of the Book of Psalms gave this Philadelphia physician the courage to risk his life treating the victims of a yellow fever epidemic rather than flee the city, as some other doctors did. Charles Thomson, who served as the secretary of the Continental Congress throughout its entire existence, spent his retirement years composing a well-regarded translation of the Bible.[1]

The image of even the least orthodox founders as modern secularists is a false conception that wrenches them from the historical and cultural context in which they lived. The founders were steeped in a culture that revered the Bible as the Word of God. Many were raised by devout parents who named them after biblical figures, and several were closely related to ministers. At least two founders, James Madison and John Adams (who married a preacher's daughter), seriously considered a career in the ministry before deciding on law, and a third, John Witherspoon, was one of the most prominent clergymen in America. Like most children of their day, the founders probably learned to read by means of the Bible, the latter testament of which they then studied in the original

Greek at their grammar schools and colleges. Most attended church services regularly, where they listened to sermons that lasted for hours, addresses that mingled numerous scriptures with classical learning. Many married devout wives. They lived in a society filled with biblical place names and expressions, a society rocked by the Great Awakening, which constituted one of the primary causes of the American Revolution, uniting Americans of different denominations and regions around the same biblical themes (the danger of corruption and the existence of a divine mission) that had motivated the Puritans over a century earlier.

Although biblical allusions performed important rhetorical functions in political speeches, the founders' continual use of such references cannot be dismissed as a cynically employed means of manipulating the masses. They continued to study the Bible closely in their retirement years, long after it ceased to possess any political utility for them. Even Thomas Jefferson loved the psalms and carried a pocket Bible.

Although a few of the founders rejected important biblical doctrines, they were almost unanimous in asserting the Bible's central role in promoting the social morality they deemed essential to the survival and success of the new republic. Thus, most not only urged their own children to read scripture and to attend church services in which it was recited but also worked to disseminate biblical knowledge more broadly. Elias Boudinot, who served as president of the Continental Congress, later established the American Bible Society, which distributed Bibles to the poor. While John Jay, the nation's first Supreme Court chief justice, served as the organization's president, Charles Cotesworth Pinckney, a signer of the Constitution and a two-time presidential nominee of the Federalist Party, served as one of its vice presidents, in which capacity he boldly defied slaveholders' attacks on the organization for dispensing Bibles to African Americans, a policy the slaveholders held as responsible for the Denmark Vesey slave revolt. Both Benjamin Rush and Samuel Adams urged the continued reading of the Bible in public schools. Rush started a Sunday school movement and founded the Philadelphia Bible Society. George Washington consistently supported the preaching of the gospel to Native Americans, not merely for reasons of national interest but also for what he sincerely regarded as their own good. Even Thomas Jefferson endorsed adult Bible reading for moral reasons and contributed a large sum to the American Bible Society.

The Bible furnished the founders with a treasure trove of virtues and vices, illustrated in vivid stories that were intimately familiar to nearly all Americans. Thus, they drew moral and political lessons from scripture and attempted to persuade their fellow citizens to act on these lessons. Equally familiar to rich and poor, male and female—unlike the Greco-Roman classics, the founders' other chief literary inheritance from Europe, the detailed knowledge of which was largely restricted to affluent males—the Bible facilitated communication by providing a common collection of stories, knowledge, and ideas.

Even the least orthodox founders (with the sole exception of Thomas Paine in his later years) considered the Bible a source of wisdom, and they valued the lessons they derived from it. They employed biblical references and analogies in private letters as frequently as in public documents because scripture formed an important part of their stock of knowledge, their way of making sense of the world. Its influence in their society was too pervasive to permit them to ignore or dismiss it, even had they wished to do so. Instead, they grappled with the Bible unceasingly, and while the end result of that lifelong engagement by the unorthodox founders included the discarding of some important doctrines, it also produced a deepening of scripture's rhetorical, moral, and spiritual imprint on their minds.

That imprint not only influenced the founders' self-perceptions but also proved crucial to the outcome of national debates. In the colonial period Benjamin Franklin viewed himself as an American Solomon, dispensing practical advice in the form of proverbs as Poor Richard. In 1776, as the leading orator for independence in Congress, John Adams considered himself a latter-day Moses, leading his people from Egyptian-style bondage at the hands of Britain to freedom and independence (although most Americans bestowed that appellation on George Washington). In the same year Thomas Paine succeeded in persuading Americans to declare their independence largely by convincing them that God condemned monarchy in 1 Samuel 8.

Contrary to popular belief, none of the founders was a deist—at least not as the term is generally used. Deism was an eighteenth-century philosophy that contended that God had created the universe and the physical laws that governed it but declined to intervene in its affairs, a formulation that combined the biblical concept of an omniscient, omnipotent, and just Creator with the Epicurean doctrine of divine noninterference. All of the founders—even Thomas Paine, who attacked the Bible publicly, and Thomas Jefferson, who assaulted portions of it privately, in their later years—rejected this philosophy, continually claiming that God not only invested each individual with inalienable rights but also intervened in the affairs of individuals, societies, and nations to enforce those rights, as well as to advance other goods necessary to human happiness. The only difference between the orthodox and unorthodox founders concerning divine intervention was that the latter rejected the idea that God intervened through miracles, asserting instead that He intervened solely through natural causes.

Too many historians have overstated the influence of deism in late eighteenth- and early nineteenth-century American society, partly because they have taken at face value the jeremiads of orthodox clergymen who needed dragons to slay in their sermons. As a rhetorical form, the jeremiad centered on dire warnings of divine judgment resulting from a serious violation of the society's covenant with God. While there was no shortage of bad behavior in American society to which preachers could point, the form required for its full dramatic power a less prosaic and more sinister threat to the covenant than mere bad behavior by unruly individuals. "British corruption and tyranny" furnished such a danger during the Revolutionary period, but afterward another threat was needed. Hence preachers exaggerated the danger to Christianity posed by a small number of deists, an exaggeration that reached its height after the Reign of Terror in France stoked the fear that French-style "atheism and infidelity" might cross the Atlantic Ocean and lead to the mass guillotining of American Christians. This fear, both shared and exploited by some political leaders, was sincere but preposterous. In 1801 Congregationalist clergymen actually persuaded some Bostonians to hide their Bibles from the mild-mannered president-elect Thomas Jefferson, who would surely confiscate them.[2]

Although it is only natural that historians, relying heavily on the two great bodies of literature that dominated the period (sermons and political pamphlets), should echo the conviction of the clergymen and their political allies that deism was popular enough to constitute a serious alternative to Christianity in the early American republic, the facts prove otherwise. Far more significant evidence of the temper of the times than the exaggerated claims made in sermons and political speeches was the torrent of abuse that fell on Thomas Paine after he published *The Age of Reason* and the fact that so far were Americans from taking up Paine's call for a "natural religion" devoid of biblical influence that they soon launched a Second Great Awakening. In short, like most of their leaders, the vast majority of late eighteenth- and early nineteenth-century Americans were Christian in belief, if not always in act, and there was never any prospect that a significant number of them would abandon the Bible for deism. Even the small Unitarian and Universalist denominations that arose in New England during the early republican period attached themselves firmly to scripture, merely departing from orthodox interpretation regarding a particular issue or two.

As a result of the founders' unanimous belief in an interventionist God, all except Thomas Paine believed in the efficacy of prayer and therefore frequently called for public and private prayer both in times of crisis and in periods of peace and prosperity. The most famous such appeal was Benjamin Franklin's emotional speech urging daily prayer at the Constitutional Convention, a plea he based on his personal experience that "God governs in the affairs of men." In the original manuscript for the speech Franklin underscored the whole sentence once, and "God" twice.

The founders' conception of what they termed divine "Providence" extended to their own personal lives. It comforted them amid misfortunes and motivated them to sacrifice everything for the cause of liberty in a revolution against the greatest power on earth and in the establishment of a sound and durable republic. As the Declaration of Independence noted, "a firm reliance on the protection of Divine Providence" was the chief source of their willingness to sacrifice their lives and fortunes. Even after Paine wrote a tome attacking the Bible, he continued to assert a strong belief in its most important concept: the existence of an omniscient, omnipotent, benevolent God who intervened on behalf of individuals and nations. Indeed, Paine credited his own survival of the French Revolution to divine protection, a claim that flatly contradicted a central tenet of deism. The founders overcame their greatest misfortunes, such as the death of a fiancée (Charles Carroll) or a small child (John Marshall and John Jay), by interpreting them as God's way of teaching wisdom, fortitude, compassion, humility, and the futility of a life focused on fleeting earthly pleasures rather than on eternity.

The founders considered the United States a new Israel—a nation chosen by God to accomplish a sacred purpose. They believed that the

United States was destined by the Almighty to advance the cause of freedom by erecting a model republic that would provide a haven for the world's oppressed. This belief in a divine mission gave them a sense of identity and purpose and the courage to face the enormous trials of their day. They believed that God led them to victory, against staggering odds, over Great Britain in the Revolutionary War. Many of them considered the U.S. Constitution another divine gift, with the usually reticent James Madison going so far as to call it "a miracle" in a private letter to Jefferson. Yet many of the founders also worried that the same intervening God might punish the nation for its greatest violation of the covenant of liberty: its institution of slavery.

The founders considered Christian morality superior to all other ethical systems, past and present, due to its promotion of humility, benevolence, and forgiveness, and they believed religion and morality, defined largely in Judeo-Christian terms, were vital to the survival and success of any republic. Despite his rejection of portions of the Bible, Thomas Jefferson was particularly emphatic regarding the superiority of Christian ethics, which was why he invested so much time in distilling its essence in his own abbreviated Bible. Even Thomas Paine, the sole founder who denied the superiority of Christian morality, defined virtue precisely as Jesus had (the fulfillment of duty to God and to one's neighbor) while almost comically refusing to acknowledge the obvious source of this principle. Except for Jefferson and Paine, the founders were adamant that the widespread belief in an omniscient God who rewarded virtue and punished vice was essential to republican government, and even Jefferson conceded that while such a belief might not be essential, it provided a powerful inducement to virtue. Despite their private doubts regarding certain biblical doctrines, both Benjamin Franklin and John Adams reacted with great fury when anyone assaulted the Bible publicly because they viewed popular belief in it as one of the chief pillars of the republic and dreaded its collapse.

The founders also shared crucial beliefs in the biblical concepts of human equality before God, free will, and the existence of an afterlife that included rewards and punishments. The founders' belief in spiritual equality was derived from the biblical concept of a single creation, which contrasted sharply with contemporary, racist, European theories of separate creations of different human species on various continents. It led the founders to abolish slavery throughout the North and to end the foreign slave trade, though they were unable to end the institution in the South, where it was more deeply entrenched socially and economically. John Witherspoon and William Livingston were instrumental in abolishing slavery in New Jersey, as were Benjamin Rush, Thomas Paine, and Benjamin Franklin in Pennsylvania and John Jay and Alexander Hamilton in New York. Despite being a slaveholder himself, Jefferson succeeded in persuading Congress to prohibit slavery in the Northwest Territory (the land north of the Ohio River) as a first step toward his goal of ending it nationally. George Washington freed and provided for his own slaves in his will. Many of the founders used scriptural arguments to condemn slavery and denounced all efforts to employ biblical passages in its favor. Despite living in a Calvinist nation, they also cited biblical references against predestination and in support of free will, a belief that imbued them with a strong sense of responsibility for the outcome of events. All of the founders, even the least orthodox, expressed a belief in an afterlife characterized by divine rewards and punishments that was clearly based on biblical teaching. This belief provided the founders with priceless consolation for the deaths of their loved ones and motivated them to hazard all for their fellow citizens. Alexander Hamilton's confidence in the existence of such an afterlife led him to sacrifice his life rather than return Aaron Burr's gunfire in their famous duel.

What separated the few unorthodox founders from their brethren was not their conception of God, but rather their conception of man. Like the European deists, the unorthodox founders adopted the biblical conception of a just, omniscient, and omnipotent God wholeheartedly—so wholeheartedly, in fact, that they rejected those biblical accounts they believed violated the conception of a just deity. As a result, they emphasized God's role as Creator, using terms such as "Nature's God" and "Supreme Architect of the Universe," while denying His authorship of scripture. But in the Western world the historical and cultural source of the conception of God as Creator was Genesis 1:1, the first verse of the Bible, and this role had been emphasized by Jewish and Christian theologians for millennia. If a reference to the deity as "Nature's God" had possessed a strong deistic connotation, the Continental Congress (made up largely of orthodox Christians like John Witherspoon, Samuel Adams, and Benjamin Rush) would never have approved its inclusion in the Declaration of Independence. Rather, as a term that united the orthodox and unorthodox, it was ideally suited to a document whose purpose was to unite all

Americans in the patriot cause. To imply, as some historians do, that the mere use of such a term marked a founder as a deist is sheer nonsense. Likewise, the unorthodox founders' emphasis on the rationality of God did not depart from a long-standing tradition, beginning with the earliest Jewish and Christian theologians, resting on the marvelous nature of the divine creation.[3]

Instead, what distinguished the few unorthodox founders from the orthodox majority was their conception of humanity. In contrast to the biblical concept of original sin—the belief that humans, although retaining a small portion of man's original goodness, vested in the conscience, were fundamentally crippled by the inheritance of a powerful propensity for wickedness due to the sin of their progenitor, thus necessitating a Redeemer—the unorthodox founders possessed a strong confidence in the ability of human reason not only to improve society but also, and more remarkably, to fathom the thought of an omniscient God. While the more orthodox founders considered it irrational and presumptuous for a severely limited creature such as man to expect that his flawed reason, operating on a small fund of knowledge and experience, could ascertain what a Being of unlimited knowledge, experience, and wisdom would and would not do (and, upon such a faulty basis, assault a book that had been considered the Word of God by countless generations), the unorthodox founders possessed no such qualms. While the unorthodox founders viewed man primarily as a rational animal, the orthodox considered him a rationalizing one, a being expert at employing his God-given reason to justify any behavior, no matter how abhorrent, that advanced his perceived (often misperceived) self-interest.

The orthodox majority, joined by the unorthodox John Adams and the generally reticent Washington and Madison, strongly espoused a view of human nature that was fundamentally biblical. This pessimistic conception of human nature encouraged them to oppose British claims to unchecked power during the Revolutionary era and led them to establish elaborate systems of checks and balances in both state and federal constitutions thereafter.

Even the founders' shared advocacy of religious freedom, variously defined but always including the right to worship freely in the manner of an individual's own choosing, was based on the Bible's emphasis on the importance of the individual's relationship with an omniscient God who cared deeply about His creatures' inner beliefs. No government had the authority to interpose itself between the individual and his Creator, the founders frequently declared. Furthermore, they often noted that both Jesus Himself and His disciples in the early church never compelled anyone to express any belief, relying solely on the power of the Holy Spirit to attract people to the faith according to their own free will.

In the following chapters I will discuss the educational system, familial influences, church experience, and social conditions that immersed the founders in the Bible; their lifelong engagement with scripture; their biblically infused political rhetoric; their powerful belief in a divine Providence that protected them and guided the nation; their belief in the superiority of Christian ethics and the necessity of religion in republican government; their belief in spiritual equality, free will, and an afterlife; their religious differences; the influence of their biblical conception of human nature on their formulation of state and federal constitutions; and their use of biblical precedent to advance religious freedom. I will conclude by summarizing the manner in which the subsequent generation of Americans carried these themes to new heights while, in the process, transforming American society.

I

A PEOPLE OF THE BOOK

The founders were steeped in a biblical culture that pervaded their schools, homes, churches, and society. The curricula of their primary schools, grammar schools, and colleges included Bible reading; in the latter two institutions they studied the New Testament in the original Greek. Most were raised by devout parents who inculcated biblical principles in the home, and many married pious wives. Many possessed living relatives who were clergymen or were descended from them. Most attended church services regularly throughout their lives, listening to sermons that lasted for hours and that quoted scripture extensively. Their society had recently been electrified by the Great Awakening, a religious revival movement that united Americans for the first time, breaching denominational and regional walls by reintroducing biblical themes that had been central to Puritanism. When stated in Whig form, these themes, especially the dangers of corruption and the existence of a collective mission from God, led directly to the American Revolution.

SCHOOL

The Bible provided not only one of the principal motives for the settlement of the American colonies but also the chief impetus for colonial education. Historians estimate that three-quarters of the American colonists were Center (or Reformed) Protestants, in the tradition of Martin Luther and John Calvin. These included the Congregationalists of New

England and the Presbyterians of the Middle Colonies, many of whom immigrated to America to escape persecution by the Church of England, as well as many "low-church Anglicans," who possessed Calvinist views. Center Protestant theology inculcated a strong belief in the importance of literacy, teaching that salvation came solely through faith in Jesus, which, in turn, came primarily through reading scripture. As a result, by 1750, the literacy rate in New England was 70 percent among men and 45 percent among women, and in the South it was almost 60 percent among free men and 40 percent among free women, rates that were somewhat higher than in London and considerably higher than in the English countryside or on the European continent.[1]

The Puritans, many of whose leaders had caught the Puritan fever while attending Cambridge University and who boasted an unusually high percentage of university graduates, established the first public schools in America so that even the poorest children could learn to read the Bible. Indeed, they required competence in the scriptures for full membership in their Congregational Church. A 1642 Massachusetts law, widely copied throughout New England, penalized both parents and masters of apprentices who failed to ensure their children's ability "to read and understand the principles of religion." Since a shortage of wealth made the establishment of private schools, and the work obligations of parents made home schooling, extremely difficult, five years later the colony passed another law, also widely copied in the other New England colonies, that required towns of fifty or more people to establish public schools. The preamble to the law famously began, "It being one chief project of that old deluder, Satan, to keep men from the knowledge of the Scriptures, as in former times by keeping them in an unknown tongue, so in these latter times by persuading from the use of tongues." Pupils of the new schools included girls as well as boys.[2]

The Bible was not only the chief motivational force behind colonial American literacy but also the principal means by which it was achieved. Primers taught the skill of reading through the employment of biblical passages with which the learner was already familiar, having heard them in church. Students then progressed to collections of psalms (Psalters) and then to the Bible itself, a traditional progression endorsed by John Locke in *Some Thoughts Concerning Education*. As the educational historian Lawrence Cremin observed, "Doubtless many a colonial youngster learned to read by mastering the letters and syllables phonetically and then hearing Scriptural passages again and again, with the reader pointing to each word until the relationship between the printed and oral passages became manifest."[3]

In the late seventeenth century Boston printer and bookseller Benjamin Harris published the *New England Primer*, which was widely used in both elementary and grammar schools. It listed the books of both testaments and included the Lord's Prayer, the Apostle's Creed, and the Ten Commandments. It taught the alphabet through rhymed couplets that often focused on biblical figures:

A. In Adam's Fall
  We sinned all. . . .
J. Job feels the Rod
  Yet blesses God. . . .
P. Peter denies
  His Lord and Cries.
Q. Queen Esther comes in royal State
  To Save the Jews from dismal Fate.
R. Rachel doth mourn
  For her first born.
S. Samuel anoints
  Whom God appoints. . . .
U. Uriah's beauteous wife
  Made David seek his life. . . .
Z. Zacchaeus he did climb the Tree
  His Lord to see.

The *Primer* also featured "The Dutiful Child's Promise," which included the vows, "I will fear God. . . . I will honour my Father & Mother. . . . I will as much as in me lies keep all God's Holy Commandments." A single Philadelphia firm sold 37,100 copies of the *New England Primer* from 1749 to 1766. John Adams used it as a young teacher in 1756. Thomas Dilworth's *New Guide to the English Tongue* (1740), the most popular speller of the eighteenth century, also combined spelling with religious and moral precepts.[4]

The Society for the Propagation of the Gospel in Foreign Parts, formed in London in 1710, established schools and distributed Bibles and prayer books in the southern and middle colonies, not only among colonists but also among Native Americans. The society's instructors taught children to read scripture and led them in morning and evening prayers.

Like the Massachusetts law, a Pennsylvania statute of 1682 mandated that parents teach all of their children to read and write "so that they may be able to read the Scriptures," but few parents required such a law to compel them to fulfill what they considered an essential duty. As the historian Bernard Bailyn noted, colonial Americans considered educational institutions essential, "schools to train the young in purity and loyalty; colleges to educate the educators, to produce a proper ministry and mission, and to provide benefits which otherwise would be sought by the ambitious young from proselytizing rivals." Even denominational schisms benefited literacy by multiplying educational efforts.[5]

The 1642 Massachusetts law also stipulated that towns of one hundred or more residents must establish grammar schools, masculine institutions of secondary education that focused on the study of Greek and Latin, but even in these institutions competence in Bible reading was required for admission, and Saturday afternoons were set aside for religious instruction. Some grammar schools required children to give an account of the Sunday sermon the following day. Each day typically began with the master leading his pupils in prayer and concluded with one of the older students reciting the Lord's Prayer in Latin, thus combining piety with linguistic instruction. Similarly, at the Boston Latin School, students were required to translate "a Psalm or something divine" into Latin. Even the grammar schools of the Quakers (who were officially known as the Society of Friends), whose denomination emphasized direct revelation by God to the individual believer, featured Bible reading. Since most grammar school masters were recent college graduates who were preparing for a career in the ministry, they took the religious component of the grammar school curriculum seriously.[6]

At the time the founders were educated, teachers at nearly all grammar schools required their students to study the New Testament in the original Greek. James Madison's early training under Donald Robertson and the Reverend Thomas Martin was so thorough that although he arrived at the College of New Jersey (now Princeton) in 1769 only two weeks before final examinations in the Greek New Testament and other subjects, he passed them all. Nathan Tisdale, an instructor in Lebanon, Connecticut, for most of the second half of the eighteenth century, who attracted children from every North American colony and the British West Indies, also taught the Greek New Testament in addition to the classics.[7]

Grammar school masters often wielded considerable influence on impressionable children through their classical erudition and Christian piety. Benjamin Rush attended the academy of his uncle, the Reverend Samuel Finley, in Nottingham, Maryland. The academy, which quickly acquired a reputation for excellence, was designed chiefly to prepare young men for the ministry but also produced several state governors and prominent physicians. It prepared Rush so well that he was admitted into Princeton at age fourteen. In his autobiography (1800) Rush recalled Finley, who later served as president of the College of New Jersey:

> Many of the remarks that he made upon passages in the Bible, which then passed hastily through my mind, occurred to me many years afterwards, and I hope not without some effect. . . . The Instructions of the Sunday evening were usually closed by delivering in a plain way some of the most striking and intelligible evidences of the truth of the Christian Religion. Many of his arguments upon these occasions, tho' clothed in a simple language, were the same which are to be met with in the most logical writers upon that subject, and to the impressions they made upon my understanding I ascribe my not having at any time of my life ever entertained a doubt of the divine origin of the Bible. I wish this mode of fortifying the reason of young people in the principles of Christianity were more general. The impressions which are made upon their fears or their faith by sermons and creeds soon wear away, but arguments fixed in the understanding are indelible. They operate upon the judgment, and this process of mind we know to yield as necessarily to the impressions of truth as vision in a sound eye succeeds the impression from the rays of light.

Rush added regarding Finley's students, "I never met with one of them who did not admire, esteem, and love him. . . . I endeavoured to show my gratitude to him by adopting and educating his youngest son, who is now a respectable physician and citizen of South Carolina." In fact, Rush decided to go into medicine rather than law because Finley warned him that law "was full of temptations." Rush declared, "I now rejoice that I followed Dr. Finley's advice. I have seen the hand of heaven clearly in it." Rush was later present to close Finley's eyes when he died.[8]

All but one of the American colleges established during the colonial period were denominational, and most college trustees were ministers. In 1636, only six years after landing in the wilderness in Massachusetts, the Puritans founded Harvard College, the first institution of higher learning in the American colonies. Its principal purpose was to train ministers—not only in theology but also in logic, rhetoric, and science—although almost half of the graduates went into medicine, law, and other professions. The College of William and Mary (1693) was established for the training of Anglican ministers, and Yale College (1701) was formed for Connecticut Puritans who believed that Harvard had become too unorthodox. All three colleges required biblical orthodoxy of their faculty members and instituted strict rules of moral and religious conduct for students.[9]

As a result of the Great Awakening, Presbyterians established the College of New Jersey (Princeton, 1746), Anglicans King's College (Columbia, 1754), Baptists the College of Rhode Island (Brown, 1764), members of the Dutch Reformed Church Queen's College (Rutgers, 1766), and Congregationalists Dartmouth College (1769, originally for Native Americans). Only Benjamin Franklin's College of Philadelphia (the University of Pennsylvania, 1751) was officially nondenominational, though dominated by Anglicans and Presbyterians.[10]

College entrance requirements demanded the ability to translate the Greek New Testament into English. Harvard required it of John Adams when he entered in the 1750s. In 1774, when Alexander Hamilton entered King's College, one of the requirements was the ability to read the Greek gospels. When John Jay entered King's College in 1760, he was even required to translate the first ten chapters of the Gospel of John from Greek into Latin.[11]

Bible reading, both in English and in Greek, continued in college. According to a promotional pamphlet, students at Harvard were pressed to consider that the main end of their studies was "to know God and Jesus Christ, which is eternal life, and therefore to lay Christ in the bottom, as the only foundation of all sound knowledge and learning." Thus, every student was required to read scripture twice per day so that he would "be ready to give an account of his proficiency therein, both in theoretical observations of the language and in logic, and in practical and spiritual truths, as his tutor shall require, according to his ability." He also had to eschew profanity and association with dissolute company. Every afternoon Harvard students studied Greek, Hebrew, and even Aramaic (for the books of Daniel and Ezra). This surpassed the requirements of most colleges, which did not require Aramaic and mandated Hebrew only for graduate students pursuing a divinity degree. Until 1763, Greek reading at Harvard was confined almost exclusively to the New Testament. Even at Franklin's nondenominational College of Philadelphia, the Bible was read in the institution's English School, and Franklin himself proposed that scriptural readings accompany the college's morning and evening prayers. As in England, students at nearly every American college were required to attend such prayer sessions, as well as Sunday worship services. Senior theses often focused on religious subjects. Commencement ceremonies always opened and closed with prayers.[12]

While some college students, teenagers freed from parental supervision for the first time, were rowdy, others were sober and pious. While at Princeton, James Madison, who was the son of devout parents, as well as the cousin of the first Episcopalian bishop in Virginia, chose to copy passages regarding the Gospels of Matthew and Luke and the Acts of the Apostles from William Burkitt's *Expository Notes* (1724), a commentary on the New Testament, into his commonplace book. (Students at nearly all American schools were required to keep commonplace books, notebooks in which they copied the passages from their studies that most interested them. Since the choice of what was copied was left to the individual student, they serve as intriguing windows into young pupils' minds.) Madison had fallen under the sway of the president of the college, the Presbyterian minister John Witherspoon. Witherspoon served as Madison's personal tutor during his senior year and for the six months he remained following graduation to pursue further studies in the Hebrew language, ethics, and theology. Madison seriously considered a career in the ministry, calling divinity "the most sublime of all Sciences," and urged his friend William Bradford, who had decided against a ministerial career, to keep that option open later in life. Young Madison wrote that "I have sometimes thought there could not be a stronger testimony in favor of Religion or against temporal Enjoyments even the most rational and manly than for men who occupy the most honorable and gainful departments and are rising in reputation and wealth publicly to declare their unsatisfactoriness by becoming fervent Advocates in the cause of Christ & if you wish you may give your Evidence in this way."[13]

Alexander Hamilton's patron and guide as a youth in the West Indies was Hugh Knox, a Presbyterian minister and author of theological tracts who impressed upon Hamilton the dangers of excessive drinking and the value of education and hard work. As part of Hamilton's move to the mainland, Knox transferred mentorship of the boy to his friends Elias

Boudinot and William Livingston, both devout Presbyterians, the former a future president of the Continental Congress, the latter a future governor of New Jersey and signer of the Constitution. Hamilton attended King's College, where, his roommate Robert Troup later recalled, he was attentive to public worship. Hamilton was never cited for violating any rule at a college that required attendance at a two-hour prayer meeting every morning, at afternoon and evening prayers, and at two worship services on Sundays. Both Troup and Boudinot, at whose house Hamilton lived for a while, also remembered his "habit of praying upon his knees both night and morning." Troup recalled being "often powerfully moved by the fervor and eloquence of his prayers." Hamilton read widely in religious literature and expressed a firm belief in the fundamentals of Christianity as identified in the New Testament. In fact, Troup claimed that "the arguments with which he was accustomed to justify his belief have tended, in no small degree, to confirm my own faith in revealed religion."[14]

It is important to note that all of these American colleges, despite their denominational founding and trustees, admitted all qualified students, and religious instruction there, aside from theology courses taken only by future ministers of the denomination, was nonsectarian. By accepting students from all colonies and denominations and instructing them in a combination of Whig politics and a generalized Protestant Christianity that focused on nonsectarian Bible study, American colleges proved a crucial instrument in forging a shared sense of identity and purpose among future political leaders that was crucial to the undertaking and success of the American Revolution.[15]

HOME

The founders received biblical training in the home as well as at school. Indeed, it was in the home that moral lessons derived from scripture were not merely taught but lived.

Benjamin Franklin descended from Puritans on each side of his family. According to family tradition, during the reign of Queen Mary, his great-great grandfather had been compelled to hide his English Bible and post a lookout at the door when removing it to read to the rest of the family. Franklin's maternal grandfather, Peter Folger, was one of the earliest settlers of New England, a man Cotton Mather called "a godly and learned Englishman." Franklin's father Josiah left England for religious freedom. Although Benjamin was named partly after an uncle, his parents almost certainly also named him, the last of their ten sons, in imitation of the biblical patriarch Jacob, who had given that name to the last of his twelve sons, the child of his old age (Genesis 35:18). Josiah often played a violin and sang psalms at home after work. In fact, Benjamin's epitaph for his parents included the following lines: "He was a pious and prudent man, / She a discreet and virtuous woman." When Benjamin was only four years old, his uncle composed for him a set of instructions for leading a Christian life in the form of an acrostic poem that spelled out their common name:

> Be to thy parents an Obedient son;
> Each Day let Duty constantly be Done;
> Never give Way to sloth or lust or pride
> If free you'd be from a Thousand Ills beside.
> Above all Ills be sure to Avoide the Shelfe;
> Man's Danger lyes in Satan, sin, and selfe.
> In vertue, Learning, Wisdome progress make.
> Nere shrink at suffering for thy saviour's sake;
> Fraud and Falsehood in thy Dealings Flee;
> Religious Always in thy station be;
> Adore the Maker of thy Inward part;
> Now's the Accepted time, Give him thy Heart.
> Keep a Good Conscience, 'tis a constant Frind;
> Like Judge and Witness This Thy Acts Attend.
> In Heart with bended knee Alone Adore
> None but the Three in One Forevermore.

Even the substitution of "I" for "J" in the fourth letter of "BENJAMIN" was somewhat biblical, since there is no *j* in Hebrew (though *y* would have been closer to the Hebrew letter *yod*). At the age of five the younger Benjamin began reading the Bible. When his intelligence seemed to destine him for the clergy, or, as he put it, as his father's tithe to the church, his uncle gave him a volume of sermons with which to set up shop. However, precisely because Benjamin was the last of ten sons, his father lacked the funds to give him a college education, a requirement for the Congregational clergy, so he removed Benjamin even from grammar school in less than a year and set him to study arithmetic and writing.[16]

Nevertheless, the precocious boy read most of his father's theological books, as well as John Bunyan's *Pilgrim's Progress* and Cotton Mather's *Bonifacius*, both of which he loved. Regarding the latter book, whose subject was Christian virtue, Franklin later wrote, "If I have been, as you seem to think, a useful citizen, the public owes the advantage of it to that book. . . . [Due to it,] I have always set a greater value on the character of a doer of good than on any other kind of reputation." In fact, Franklin's first pen name, "Silence Dogood," was a tribute to Mather; he derived the "Silence" from Mather's sermon, "Silentiarius: The Silent Sufferer," and the "Dogood" from the subtitle of *Bonifacius*, "Essays to Do Good." The Junto that Franklin organized, which later became the American Philosophical Society, was based on Mather's proposal of voluntary associations to promote religion and morality in *Bonifacius*. Many of the group's early discourses concerned ethics, a subject that remained dear to Franklin's heart throughout his life.[17]

Patrick Henry and Samuel Adams were also raised by devout parents. Like Franklin, Henry was named after a pious uncle (in his case, an Anglican minister). Patrick's father, John, well educated at college in Aberdeen before immigrating to America, taught the boy himself. Known for his love of both Horace and the Bible, John's biblical instruction must have been deep. His defense of the doctrine of eternal punishment in an argument with his friends was based on an examination of the original Greek wording of the relevant New Testament passages. Adams's mother rocked him to sleep with hymns, used the Bible to teach him the alphabet, made certain that he learned the Lord's Prayer at an early age, and supervised his daily biblical reading.[18]

Benjamin Rush's parents were equally pious. In his autobiography Rush wrote regarding his mother Susanna, who raised him and his siblings alone after his father died when Rush was only five, "She had no superior in kindness, generosity, and attention to the morals and religious principles of her children." Her last words were "Sweet Jesus!" Rush's father, John, was fond of religious books, and none more than the Bible itself. Rush recalled, "I have heard one of his apprentices who lived six years in his family say that he never saw him but once out of temper. His death was peaceful and happy. The last words he uttered were, 'Lord! Lord! Lord!'" Rush then quoted these lines from William Cowper's "On the Receipt of My Mother's Picture" (1798):

My boast is not that I derive my birth
From loins enthroned and rulers of the earth,
But higher far my proud pretensions rise,
The son of parents passed into the skies.[19]

Charles Cotesworth Pinckney's father was so devout that he bequeathed funds for the hiring of a minister to preach a sermon each May and October on the "Greatness and Goodness of God." On these occasions the family hosted a dinner for all of the local clergy of various denominations.[20]

In addition to parents, pious wives and sisters served as powerful models of biblical principles in the home. Just three years before George Mason drafted the influential Virginia Declaration of Rights, he recorded in his family Bible regarding his wife, "On Tuesday, the ninth of March 1773, about three o'clock in the morning, died at Ganston Hall, of a slow fever, Mrs. Ann Mason, in the thirty-ninth year of her life, after a painful and tedious illness of more than nine months, which she bore with truly Christian patience and resignation, in faithful hope of eternal happiness in the world to come. She, it may be truthfully said, led a blameless and exemplary life. She retained unimpaired her mental faculties to the last and, spending her last moments in prayer for those around her, seemed to expire without the usual pangs of dissolution." Mason added that she "was charitable to the poor and pious to her Maker; her virtue and religion were unmixed with hypocrisy or ostentation."[21]

In 1793 Benjamin Rush wrote regarding his sister, whose service as his nurse during a yellow fever epidemic caused her death, "Yesterday my sister Wallace breathed her last. She had previously weakened her constitution (naturally delicate) by great fatigue in nursing me and waiting upon the poor who crowded my house at all hours of the day and night. . . . She died as she had lived for nine years past, believing and rejoicing in God her Saviour. . . . No person ever wept in our parlor or entry (and many, many tears were shed in both) with whom she did not weep. Her whole soul was made up of sympathy and kindness. In her last illness she was composed and patient as an angel. She repeated several passages from the Psalms expressive of the love and goodness of God the day before she died."[22]

In addition to being taught prayers by his mother at a young age, which resulted in his reciting the Lord's Prayer for company before dinner, Thomas Jefferson also received tutelage from his older sister Jane, whom he loved deeply. Jane taught him to sing the psalms, which may be why he always loved that book more than any other in the Old Testament.[23]

Samuel Adams's sister maintained a journal in which she noted the clergymen she heard preach and the content of their sermons. His wife, Elizabeth, wrote in her will, "I commend my soul into the hands of my blessed Lord and Saviour Jesus Christ," and declared that she depended "absolutely, entirely, and exclusively on his atonement and finished work of righteousness for the pardon of my sins and acceptance with God to eternal life."[24]

George Washington's wife, Martha, attended church regularly and read her Bible daily, including her children and grandchildren in these devotions. On her deathbed in 1802 she talked to her children at length about "the Christian faith and its obligations."[25]

Although Alexander Hamilton once joked that he wanted a wife who was only moderately religious, he married Elizabeth Schuyler, whose nickname was "the Saint." Her son James recalled that every morning at breakfast she required one of the younger boys to read either a chapter in the Bible or a portion of Oliver Goldsmith's history of Rome, thereby mingling Christian and classical education. She probably played a role in her husband's return to piety in his later years.[26]

Edmund Randolph, the nation's first attorney general, was born into a family of skeptics but was converted to orthodox Christianity by the example of his wife, Elizabeth. In an autobiography written for his children Randolph recalled regarding his wife, "I cannot answer for myself that I should have been brought to examine the genuineness of holy writ if I had not observed the consolatory influence which it brought upon the life of my dearest Betsey."[27]

The grandson of a clergyman, John Marshall, one of the most important Supreme Court chief justices in American history, recalled the piety of his wife, Mary, in his eulogy for her. He declared, "She was educated with a profound reverence for religion, which she preserved to her last moment. This sentiment among her earliest and deepest impressions gave character to her whole life. Hers was the religion taught by the Saviour of man. She was cheerful, mild, benevolent, serious, humane, intent on self-improvement and the improvement of those who looked to her precept or example."[28]

John Adams's wife Abigail was the daughter of a minister. Her belief in divine Providence sustained her during the numerous years in which her husband was away serving his country as a congressman and a diplomat. In 1773 she wrote to John regarding the dangerous Revolutionary conflict then brewing, "You cannot be, I know, nor do I wish to see you, an Inactive Spectator, but if the sword be drawn, I bid adieu to all domestic felicity and look forward to that Country where there is neither war nor rumors of war [Matthew 24:6] in a firm belief that through the Mercy of its King we shall both rejoice there together." After her eleven-year-old-son, the future president, John Quincy Adams, departed for France with his father in 1778, she wrote to remind him, "Adhere to those religious Sentiments and principles which were early instilled in your mind and remember that you are accountable to your Maker for all your words and actions." After John Quincy barely survived another ocean voyage the following year, Abigail used the occasion to make a point, writing to her son, "You have seen how inadequate the aid of Man would have been if the winds and seas had not been under the particular Being who stretched out the Heavens as a span [Isaiah 42:5], who holdeth the ocean in the hollow of his hand [Isaiah 40:12], and rideth upon the wings of the wind [2 Samuel 22:11]. . . . The only sure and prominent foundation of virtue is Religion. Let this important truth be engraven upon your Heart, and that the foundation of Religion is Belief in the one [and] only God and a just sense of attributes as a Being infinitely wise, just, and good, to whom you owe the highest Reverence." She added that this deity "superintends and governs all nature, even to clothing the lilies of the field [Matthew 6:28–30] . . . but more particularly regards man, whom he created in his own image and breathed life into an immortal spirit [Genesis 2:7] capable of a happiness beyond the grave, for the attainment of which he is bound to the performance of certain duties, which all tend to the happiness and welfare of society, and are comprised in one short sentence expressive of universal benevolence, 'Thou shalt love thy Neighbor as thyself' [Leviticus 19:18]." When Abigail became a grandmother in 1794, she urged her daughter to accustom her children "to a constant attendance upon public worship, and enforce it by your own example and precept." She added, "It is a duty for which we are accountable to the Supreme Being." When her daughter passed away in 1813, Abigail wrote, "My own loss is not to be estimated by words and can only be alleviated by the consoling belief that my Dear Child is partaking of the Life and immortality brought to Light by him who endured the cross and is gone before to prepare a place for those who Love him and express his commandments." Although Abigail, like her husband, became a Unitarian in later years, she quoted scriptures, in contradiction to the usual deist practice of relying on reason alone, to justify her opposition to the doctrine of the Holy Trinity and continued to declare, in contradiction to deist belief, that Jesus "shall come to Judge the World in righteousness, all power being given him by the Father." Whatever unorthodox opinions John Adams himself adopted, his closeness to so strong a Christian presence in his household and in the rearing of his children must partly account for his continual expressions of reverence for the Bible and his lifelong anger at anyone who publicly assaulted it.[29]

The founders' family Bibles served not only as sources of spiritual and moral edification but also as historical records of the births, baptisms, and marriages of family members, a function that denoted its special status among all the books of the household. For instance, George Mason's family Bible recorded his own birth in 1725, his marriage in 1750, the baptisms of his children, and the death of his wife in 1773.[30]

CHURCH

The period before the American Revolution witnessed a surge in church construction. From 1696 to 1760 the number of churches in New England alone more than quadrupled, far outpacing population growth.[31]

In the founders' era, speeches constituted one of the most popular forms of entertainment, and the sermon was one of the most common types of oratory. Like the political speeches and courtroom orations of the period, lengthy sermons touched on a multitude of subjects, both biblical and secular. Among the most learned members of the community, American ministers linked the old oral culture with the new literary one, often promoting classical and Whig ideas alongside biblical precepts. Churches served as community centers, gathering places where news was exchanged, youthful friendships started, and courtships begun. Recognizing churches' special status as community centers, governments often used them to disseminate proclamations.[32]

Most of the founders attended church services regularly and listened attentively to sermons filled with scriptural references. Considered in isolation, this regularity of church attendance provides no evidence of belief, but it does suggest that sermons constituted one source of the biblical knowledge the founders often displayed in their private letters and public speeches.

In 1811 John Adams noted, "I have been a church-going animal for seventy-six years, from the cradle." In fact, while serving in the Continental Congress during the Revolution, Adams attended services at many different churches in Philadelphia, a city famous for its large number of denominations. One day in 1774 he visited a Presbyterian church and enjoyed the sermon regarding the Lord's Supper, although he still thought his own "Congregational Way best." More surprisingly, he attended a Catholic Mass at St. Mary's Church the same afternoon, where he "heard a good, short moral Essay upon the Duty of Parents to their Children, founded in Justice and Charity, to take care of their Interests, temporal and spiritual." He reported to his wife Abigail regarding that church, "But how shall I describe the Picture of our Saviour in a Frame of Marble over the Altar at full Length upon the Cross, in the Agonies, and the Blood dropping and streaming from his Wounds? The Musick, consisting of an organ and a Choir of singers, went all afternoon, excepting sermon Time, and the Assembly chanted most sweetly and exquisitely. Here is every Thing which can lay hold of the Eye, Ear, and Imagination." In 1777 Adams even visited the Church of the Scottish Seceders, a small group that had split from the Presbyterian Church. In his retirement years in Quincy, Massachusetts, he attended services twice every Sunday.[33]

Adams's surprised appreciation of the Mass was not an isolated occurrence. While most of the founders were Protestant, they were also broad-minded men who were willing to find wisdom wherever they could. In 1787, while visiting Philadelphia, Edmund Randolph, the governor of Virginia, and other state officials attended a Mass there. Despite George Mason's comment that this was done "more out of Compliment than Religion & more out of Curiosity than compliment," and despite Mason's reference to the sermon as "a loose & trivial one" delivered by a foreign priest with bad pronunciation, Mason, like Adams before him, was startled by his own appreciation of the Mass. He wrote, "Altho' I have been in a Roman Catholic Chapel before, I was struck with the Solemnity of the Apparatus & could not help remarking how much everything was calculated to warm the Imagination & captivate the Senses. No wonder that this should be the popular Religion of Europe. The Church music was exceedingly fine." Mason's only suggestion for improvement was to substitute for the annoying "Tinkling of a little Bell" during the blessing of the sacrament "some more solemn & deep-toned Instrument."[34]

A lifelong member of a small, rural church, George Washington was an Anglican/Episcopalian vestryman. Yet, like Adams, he took advantage of his time in Philadelphia during the Revolution to attend the services of other denominations. One Sunday in 1774 he visited a Quaker meeting in the morning, following it with an Anglican service in the afternoon. Two weeks later he attended a Presbyterian service in the morning and a Catholic Mass in the afternoon. Thirteen years later, once again in Philadelphia to serve as president of the Constitutional Convention, he returned to St. Mary's Church for another Catholic Mass. During the early portion of his presidency in New York, he mostly attended Anglican services but repeated the pattern of visiting the churches of other denominations when traveling. While in Portsmouth, Maine, during a presidential tour of New England, he attended an Episcopalian service in the morning and visited a Congregational one in the afternoon. While visiting York, Pennsylvania, in 1791, he wrote in his diary, "There being no Episcopal Minister present in the place, I went to hear the morning Service performed in the Dutch Reformed Church—which, being in that language, not a word of which I understood, I was in no danger of becoming a proselyte to its religion by the eloquence of the Preacher."[35]

Between 1767 and 1785 Thomas Jefferson was a vestryman at two different Anglican churches and a regular attendee at their services. While Jefferson was vice president, according to the U.S. Senate chaplain Thomas Clagger, he "attended prayers every morning," as well as a course of sermons delivered by Clagger. While president, Jefferson attended multidenominational services in the Hall of the House of Representatives regularly and even assisted in singing Psalm 100: "Make a joyful noise unto the Lord, all you lands. Serve the Lord with gladness. Come before His presence with singing. Know that the Lord is God; it is He who has made us and not we ourselves; we are His people, the sheep of His pasture. Enter His gates with thanksgiving and His courts with praise; be thankful to Him and bless His name. For the Lord is good; His mercy is everlasting, and His truth endures to all generations." After Jefferson retired, he worshipped regularly at multidenominational services conducted at the Albemarle County Courthouse. He explained in 1822, "The court-house is the common temple one Sunday in the month to each [denomination]. Here Episcopalian and Presbyterian, Methodist and Baptist meet together, join in hymning their Maker, and listen with attention and devotion to each others' preachers." To a lover of tolerance like Jefferson, it was a beautiful sight.[36]

Benjamin Rush was such a connoisseur of sermons that he selected his wife based on her taste in them. In his autobiography he wrote regarding Julia (whom he met in 1776, when she was only sixteen) and John Witherspoon, "She said he was the best preacher she had ever heard. Such a declaration I was sure could only proceed from a soundness of judgment and correctness of taste seldom to be met in a person of her age, for there was nothing in Dr. Witherspoon's sermons to recommend them but their uncommon good sense and simplicity of style. From this moment I determined to offer her my hand."[37]

Rush was impressed with the sermons he heard while traveling in France in 1769. He wrote, "The preachers in general here are much more animated than in any other country. Their sermons abound with the boldest strokes of rhetoric, as frequent apostrophes or addresses to the Deity, or to particular virtues, or in some cases the very walls of the churches in which they are preaching. The subjects of all the sermons I heard were chiefly moral. One reason why the French preachers excel the English is that they almost always commit their sermons to memory and never carry a written word into the pulpit with them."[38]

Samuel Adams, who married his pastor's daughter, attended Congregational worship services regularly. After Adams died, the Reverend William Bentley wrote in his diary that Adams had possessed "the severity of Cato in his manners and the dogmatism of a priest in his religious observances."[39]

Even an irregular churchgoer like Benjamin Franklin recognized the power of clergymen to shape minds. As Poor Richard in 1747, he wrote:

> O, formed Heaven's Dictates nobly to rehearse,
> Preacher Divine! Accept the grateful Verse.
> Thou hast the Power the hardened Heart to warm,
> To grieve, to raise, to terrify, to charm;
> To fix the Soul on God, to teach the Mind
> To know the Dignity of Humankind;
> By stricter Rules well-governed Life to scan,
> And practice o'er the Angel in the Man.

As a result of his appreciation of the power of clergymen to reform minds, Franklin encouraged the building of churches. When Franklin was attempting to persuade the Anglican minister Samuel Johnson to accept the presidency of the College of Philadelphia, and Johnson worried that he might be stepping on the toes of preexisting churches by establishing a new one there, Franklin reassured him, "Your tenderness of the church's peace is truly laudable; but, methinks, to build a new church in a growing place is not properly dividing but multiplying, and will richly be a means of increasing the number of those who worship God in that way." After urging his biblically named daughter, Sarah, to be "attentively dutiful and tender" to her "good Mama," remembering the promise that accompanied the commandment (Exodus 20:12: "Honor your father and mother, so that your days may be long upon the earth"), Franklin added, "Go constantly to Church, whoever preaches. The Acts of the Devotion in the [Anglican] common Prayer book are your principal Business there; and if properly attended to, will do more towards mending the Heart than Sermons generally can do. For they were composed by Men of much greater Piety and Wisdom than our common Composers of Sermons can pretend to be. And therefore I wish you would never miss the Prayer Days. Yet I do not mean that you should despise Sermons even of the Preachers you dislike, for the Discourse is often much better than the Man, as sweet and clear Waters come to us thro' very dirty Earth." He wrote to the Reverend Thomas Coombe Jr. regarding the latter's growing fame, "That which you are acquiring as an Orator gives me Pleasure as your Friend, and it will give you yourself the most solid Satisfaction if you find that by your Eloquence you can turn many to Righteousness. Without that effect, the Preacher or the Priest, in my Opinion, is not merely a sounding Brass or a tinkling Cymbal, which are innocent Things; he is rather like the Cunning-man in the Old Bailey who conjures and tells Folks their Fortunes to cheat them of their Money." In this statement Franklin referred to Daniel 12:3 ("Those who are wise shall shine as the brightness as the firmament, and those who turn many to righteousness as the stars forever and ever") and to 1 Corinthians 13:1 ("Though I speak with the tongues of men and of angels, if I have not love, I am like a sounding brass or a tinkling cymbal").[40]

Not content with making generous financial contributions to individual churches, as well as to Philadelphia's sole synagogue, Franklin also played an important role in establishing the American Catholic and Episcopalian clergies on sound footing after the Revolutionary War. In 1784 Franklin's strong recommendation of John Carroll, with whom he had traveled on a mission to seek the aid of French Canadians during the war, was instrumental in the Vatican's selection of him as the first Catholic bishop in America. At about the same time Franklin, by then a member of an Episcopalian church himself, helped the new American offshoot of the Church of England get off the ground by securing the ordination of two American bishops in England. This increased the number of Episcopalian bishops in America to three, the number required to render the ordination of future bishops self-sustaining.[41]

Like Franklin, Benjamin Rush praised the high calling of the minister. In his earliest extant letter he wrote that although he considered himself more suited to medicine than divinity, he considered the latter the higher calling: "We are employed, it's true, in a necessary calling, but a calling that enforces to us the weakness and mortality of human nature. This earthly frame, a minute fabric, a center of wonders, is forever subject to Diseases and Death. The very air we breathe too often proves noxious, our food often is armed with poison, the very elements conspire the ruin of our constitutions, and Death forever lies lurking to receive us. Now how inglorious must this study appear when set in competition with Divinity—the one employed in advancing temporal happiness, the other eternal—one applying remedies to a fading, mortal Body, the other employed in healing the sickness of a Soul immortal and everlasting. Every pursuit of life must dwindle into naught when Divinity appears."[42]

Through publication, the sermons of popular preachers sometimes outlived not only the preaching but also the preachers themselves. Sermons were one of the most popular forms of literature in late eighteenth- and early nineteenth-century America, constituting 10 percent of all pamphlets and often selling well enough to merit second printings. To cite one colony as an example, sermons and other religious works dominated the smaller book collections of eighteenth-century Maryland and composed at least one quarter of the contents of even the colony's larger libraries. Published sermons played a key role in fomenting the American Revolution.[43]

SOCIETY

The founders lived in a profoundly Christian society. They received biblical names like Benjamin, Samuel, John, Thomas, and James from parents who bore such names as Josiah, Abiah, and Peter. Their brothers possessed names like Jacob, their sisters Rebecca and Rachel. They married women with biblical names, such as Martha, Abigail, Elizabeth, and Deborah. Although they generally selected classical and Whig pseudonyms for their political essays, when it came to naming what they cherished most, their children, they chose biblical names like Sarah and Hannah. Granted, most of these names had become so common in Protestant families (as saint names, the New Testament names were also common in Catholic families) that they often occasioned little thought about their biblical origins, but that is partly the point: the founders lived in a culture that was so steeped in Christianity that many of its biblical elements had begun to operate at a subconscious level.

The founders were surrounded by communities with names derived from the Old Testament, such as Ararat, Bethel, Bethlehem, Ebenezer, Eden, Eleazer, Elisha, Ephrata, Gaza, Goshen, Hebron, Jericho, Joppa, Mizpah, Mt. Carmel, Mt. Gilboa, Mt. Hermon, Mt. Horeb, Mt. Moriah, Mt. Nebo, Mt. Olive, Mt. Tabor, Naomi, New Canaan, Newark, Pisgah, Rehoboth, Salem (an Anglicization of *shalem*, which is a variant of *shalom*, the Hebrew word for "peace," as well as another name for Jerusalem), Sharon, Shiloh, Siloam, Zarephath, and Zion. Providence was, of course, named after an important biblical concept, and Philadelphia (Greek for "brotherly love") derived its name from Revelation 3:7–10, in which Jesus praises the church located in a city of that name in Asia Minor.[44]

Then as now, the founders lived in a society filled with biblical expressions, including the following: my brother's keeper (Genesis 4:9); man does not live by bread alone (Deuteronomy 8:3); the apple of his eye (Deuteronomy 32:10); a voice crying in the wilderness (Isaiah 40:3); nothing new under the sun (Ecclesiastes 1:9); sparing the rod (Proverbs 13:24); pride goes before destruction (Proverbs 16:18); my cup overflows (Psalms 23:5); a man after his own heart (1 Samuel 13:14); how the mighty have fallen (2 Samuel 1:19); the handwriting on the wall (Daniel 5:5); into the lion's den (Daniel 6:16); sowing the wind and reaping the whirlwind (Hosea 8:7); the meek shall inherit the earth (Matthew 5:5);

blessed are the peacemakers (Matthew 5:9); the salt of the earth (Matthew 5:13); a city on a hill (Matthew 5:14); don't hide your lamp under a bushel (Matthew 5:15); turn the other cheek (Matthew 5:39); one hand does not know what the other is doing (Matthew 6:3); you cannot serve two masters (Matthew 6:24); casting your pearls before swine (Matthew 7:6); the blind leading the blind (Matthew 15:14); render unto Caesar what is Caesar's (Matthew 22:21); better for him if he had never been born (Matthew 26:24); the spirit is willing but the flesh is weak (Matthew 26:41); those who live by the sword die by the sword (Matthew 26:52); washing one's hands of the whole affair (Matthew 27:24); a prophet is honored everywhere except in his own country (Mark 6:4); walking on water (Mark 6:49); lambs among wolves (Luke 10:3); casting the first stone (John 8:7); a doubting Thomas (John 20:25); being all things to all people (1 Corinthians 9:22); the love of money is the root of all sorts of evil (1 Timothy 6:10); and fighting the good fight (1 Timothy 6:12). The difference was that the founders and their contemporaries were far more capable of identifying the scriptural sources of these expressions than the average American today.

In the 1730s and 1740s the colonies were rocked by a religious revival movement that later became known as the Great Awakening. The emotional brand of religion associated with this movement began in the 1690s among Lutherans and Moravians in Germany. From there it reached the pulpit of Theodorus Frelinghuysen, a Dutch Reformed minister in New Jersey in the 1720s. By the 1730s it had spread to the Presbyterians of New Jersey and Pennsylvania, led by William Tennent, who established the famous "log college" of Neshaminy Creek, Pennsylvania, for the training of Presbyterian revivalist ministers. Tennent's pupils went on to establish small academies of their own. Meanwhile, Jonathan Edwards launched what later became known as the "Little Awakening" in 1734–1735 in Northampton, Massachusetts. Edwards doubled the size of his congregation, necessitating the construction of a new meetinghouse. Edwards's own house soon replaced the local tavern as the favorite meeting place of the youth, an instance of the Spirit replacing spirits.[45]

The young Anglican minister George Whitefield brought the Great Awakening to its peak. Inspired by Edwards's account of the revival in Northampton, Whitefield sought to save souls by preaching the gospel throughout Britain and the American colonies. Like his friend John Wesley, the founder of Methodism, Whitefield despised the cold rationalism then seeping into his church. Replacing the logical and theological style with a more direct and dramatic simplicity, he attracted large audiences.[46]

Whitefield's first stop on his grand tour of the American colonies in 1739–1740 was Philadelphia, where he was the guest of Benjamin Franklin, who often hosted visiting preachers. Whitefield whipped the six to ten thousand Philadelphians who came to see his outdoor sermons into a frenzy. Although Franklin did not intend to contribute anything to Whitefield's cause, a Georgia orphanage, because he thought it better to bring the orphans to Philadelphia, Franklin found himself donating his copper coins in the first collection plate, his silver in the second, and finally emptying his pocket of the remaining gold coins into the third. Another Philadelphian, having heard of Whitefield's persuasive powers, had taken care not to bring any money with him, lest he be persuaded to give it all away. But Whitefield's sermon so overwhelmed the man that he begged a friend to lend him the money to contribute. The friend, who was indeed a Friend (a Quaker), must have been the only person in Philadelphia unmoved by Whitefield, for he replied sternly, "At any other time, Friend Hopkinson, I would lend to thee freely; but not now, for thee seems to be out of thy right senses."[47]

Franklin aptly summarized Whitefield's impact on Philadelphia in his own *Pennsylvania Gazette*: "The Alteration in the Face of Religion here is altogether surprizing. Never did the People show so great a Willingness to attend Sermons nor the Preachers greater Zeal and Diligence in performing the Duties of their Function. Religion is become the Subject of most Conversations. No Books are in Request but those of Piety and Devotion; and instead of idle Songs and Ballads, the People are everywhere entertaining themselves with Psalms, Hymns and Spiritual Songs. All of which, under God, is owing to the successful Labours of the Reverend Mr. Whitefield." Franklin later wrote, "From being thoughtless or indifferent about religion, it seemed as if all the world were growing religious, so that one could not walk thro' the town in an evening without hearing psalms sung in different families of every street." A printer at the time, Franklin advertised and sold collections of Whitefield's sermons, as well as Bibles, Psalters, and other religious works, and even collected money to print German-language Bibles for poor immigrants. In 1747 Franklin confided to his brother John regarding Whitefield, "He is a good Man, and I love him." He was so impressed with the preacher that he wrote to him suggesting that the two men organize the establishment of a colony in the Ohio River valley: "What a glorious Thing it would be to settle in that fine Country a large, Strong Body of Religious and Industrious People!" Franklin added, "God would bless us with Success if we undertook it with a sincere Regard to his Honour, the Service of our gracious King, and (which is the same thing) the Publick Good." Many years later, on hearing of Whitefield's death, Franklin wrote, "I knew him intimately upwards of 30 years. His Integrity, Disinterestedness, and indefatigable Zeal in prosecuting every good Work I have never seen equaled, I shall never see exceeded."[48]

After leaving Pennsylvania on his tour of the colonies in 1739, Whitefield journeyed to Georgia, then moved northward, like a conquering general, blazing a trail through the colonies. Some who had not been to church in years came out to see him. In New Brunswick, New Jersey, seven thousand people heard him. By the time Whitefield reached Massachusetts, the Reverend Benjamin Coleman claimed that the people were ready to receive him as "an angel of God and Messenger of Jesus Christ." Whitefield addressed four thousand people in a Boston meetinghouse. Another twenty thousand citizens, the largest crowd ever assembled in America, thronged the Boston Common to hear him. They wept when Whitefield spoke of his imminent departure for England. Jonathan Edwards then hosted him at his church. Many congregations, like John Seccomb's, felt a "great shaking among the Dry Bones" (a reference to God's resurrection of a field of skeletons representing Israel in Ezekiel 37) whereby "the Bible hath appeared to some to be a new Book." Youth groups met to pray, sing, and encourage one another, in imitation of the early church as depicted in the Acts of the Apostles.[49]

Whitefield undertook numerous other journeys to America, including seven other visits to Philadelphia by 1770. In 1765 Benjamin Rush wrote regarding Whitefield's preaching at his church, "Mr. Whitefield when he came down from the pulpit and began to speak to the communicants seemed as if he had come from Heaven and glowed with all the seraphic love of a Gabriel. When he spoke of the dying love of a Mediator in instituting the Feast of his Supper the night in which he was betrayed, when he traced the Son of God through all his sufferings and beheld him wounded for our sins and bruised for our iniquities [Isaiah 53:5], his soul catched fire at the thoughts, and earth seemed scarce able to contain him. 'Twas a Heaven upon Earth, I believe, to many souls, for I think I never saw more attention and solemnity in a place of worship in my life before." Americans loved Whitefield so much, it was claimed, that even Calvinists were willing to tolerate the appointment of an Anglican bishop over America if Whitefield was selected as the bishop. Numerous itinerant preachers toured the colonies in imitation of the revivalist.[50]

The Great Awakening helped bring about the American Revolution in three ways. First, as we have seen, it led to the establishment of a host of colleges. These colleges, which taught Whig principles along with Protestant Christianity, trained most of the founders. Second, as the first intercolonial movement, the Great Awakening united Americans by reminding them of a shared biblical tradition, thereby dissolving denominational and regional walls. The resultant formation of a national consciousness was crucial not only to the success of the Revolution but also to its very undertaking. No colony would have rebelled against the greatest power on earth without the assurance of assistance from the other colonies. The Revolution's leaders would never have undertaken the war effort if they had not possessed a strong sense that it was a collective movement. Third, the Great Awakening revived two biblical themes, the danger of corruption and the concept of a divine mission, that had been central to American Puritanism and thus were deeply rooted in native soil.

The Great Awakening helped revive throughout America both the Puritan fear of British corruption and the Puritan belief in a collective, divine mission to form a purer society, the two motivational forces behind the establishment of the New England colonies a century earlier. When the parliamentary acts of the 1760s reawakened among the descendants of those who had fled religious persecution the belief that Britain was hopelessly corrupt, it was plain to many Americans that they must resist, not merely to defend their natural rights of life, liberty, and property but also to save their very souls. In 1772 Samuel Adams, who has justly been called "the Father of the American Revolution" for his able leadership of the Boston Sons of Liberty, asked, "Is it not High Time for the People of this Country explicitly to declare whether they will be Freemen or Slaves? . . . The Salvation of our Souls is interested in the Event. For whenever Tyranny is establish'd, Immorality of every Kind comes in like a Torrent. It is in the Interest of Tyrants to reduce the People to Ignorance and Vice. . . . For this Reason it is always observable that those who are combin'd to destroy the People's Liberties practice every Art to poison their Morals." A year later Benjamin Franklin maintained that the British government's claim to unlimited power over the colonists amounted to the contention that it could not only kill the colonist's bodies but also "damn their souls to all Eternity by compelling them, if it pleases, to worship the Devil." This was a reference to Matthew 10:28, in which Jesus warns, "Do not fear those who kill the body but are unable to kill the soul, but rather fear Him [God] who is able to destroy both soul and body in hell." The British government, in claiming unbounded powers, was claiming what rightly belonged to God alone. As such, it was a false idol that could be worshipped only at the peril of the colonists' souls. In 1776 John Witherspoon preached a sermon in which he declared, "There is not a single instance in history in which civil liberty was lost and religious liberty preserved entire. If therefore we yield up our temporal property, we at the same time deliver the conscience into bondage."[51]

While "Old Light" opponents of revivalism (including most Anglican ministers, two-thirds of whom returned to England during the Revolutionary War), often remained loyal to Britain, "New Light" revivalist clergymen were among the first, the most ardent, and the most influential of patriots. Dubbed the "black regiment" by Boston loyalist Peter Oliver in reference to their clerical garb, these ministers were crucial to preparing the American public for independence, in an age in which rebellion was considered the darkest act of villainy and rebels were summarily hanged, by convincing Americans that God favored the Revolution. After the Boston Massacre, the loyalist Thomas Hutchinson complained, "Our pulpits are filled with such dark-covered expressions, and the people are led to think they may as lawfully resist the king's troops as any foreign enemy." March 18, the anniversary of the repeal of the Stamp Act, was celebrated each year with sermons and prayers. In 1774 the loyalist Daniel Leonard observed, "When the clergy engage in political warfare, they become a most powerful engine, either to support or overthrow the state. What effect must it have had upon the audience to hear the same sentiments and principles which they had before read in a newspaper delivered on Sundays from the sacred desk, with a religious awe, and the most solemn appeals to heaven from lips which they had been taught from their cradles to believe could utter nothing but eternal truths." John Adams reported to his wife Abigail from Philadelphia, where he was serving in the Continental Congress, "The Clergy of all Denominations here Preach Politicks and War. . . . They are a Flame of Fire." Thomas Jefferson noted approvingly that sermons advocating resistance to British tyranny ran through Virginia "like a shock of electricity." John Todd led Virginia Presbyterians in support of the patriot movement, while John Witherspoon rallied those in Pennsylvania. Previously pacifistic, Virginia Baptists embraced the patriot cause, enlisting as soldiers and sending preachers to the army camps. A British colonial official reported that clergymen were so deeply involved in the conflict that it had become "at the Bottom very much a Religious war." John Adams later recalled, "The Revolution was in the minds and hearts of the people, a change in their religious sentiments of their duties and obligations."[52]

Many Calvinist dissenters believed that in fighting against the corrupt Parliament they were also fighting against the Anglican establishment, which they considered a form of "popery." Many feared that Parliament's Quebec Act, which granted religious toleration and territory in the Ohio River valley to French Canadian Catholics, was a prelude to ecclesiastical repression in the American colonies.[53]

The revival of these Puritan fears was accompanied by the revival of the Puritan sense of divine mission. The religious mission of the Puritans to turn New England into the world's incubator for a purer form of Protestantism—into what John Winthrop called "a city upon a hill" based on Jesus's statement in Matthew 5:14, "You are the light of the world; a city that is set on a hill cannot be hidden"—was gradually transformed into the political mission of all Americans to convert the United States into its model of republicanism. Rarely was this concept ever stated as baldly as John Adams did in 1780 when he wrote, "America is the City set upon a Hill," but the idea was in the air everywhere. The transition to this secularized version of the Puritan mission was greatly smoothed by the theological and moralistic tone of political rhetoric, which conflated tyranny with sin, liberty with virtue, and military victories on behalf of the latter with salvation.[54]

Of course, evangelical Protestantism was not the only source of the fear of corruption and of the missionary spirit that produced the American Revolution. Taught in every grammar school and college, many classical texts were equally concerned with the duty to resist tyranny as a source of corruption. Steeped in a Greco-Roman literature whose perpetual theme was the steady encroachment of tyranny upon liberty, the founders became virtually obsessed with spotting the early warning signs of impending tyranny so that they might avoid the fate of their classical heroes. They learned from the political horror stories of their favorite Greek and

Roman historians that liberty was as precarious as it was precious—precarious because cunning individuals were constantly conspiring against it, precious because virtue could not survive its demise. Tyranny was the worst fate not so much because it deprived one of liberty as because it deprived one of virtue. The corrupting effects of living in tyranny—the dehumanizing sycophancy and the degrading collaboration required to avoid the tyrant's disfavor—were more abhorrent and disgusting than the oppression itself. The founders feared that if the cunning prime ministers of Britain could ever convince the American public to accept even the smallest unconstitutional tax, Americans would eventually lose not only the power but also the will to resist. They would then be no more than slaves, subject to the whims of distant masters. To stay within the British Empire would be to witness the recreation of that horrifying degradation and depravity that the historian Tacitus had so vividly described in imperial Rome. But to leave the empire and start anew would be to embrace the exciting possibility of creating a republic so elevated and virtuous as to inspire future Plutarchs to immortalize the nation. The fear of witnessing another Roman Empire was as essential to producing the Revolution as the hope of creating another Roman republic. As Jefferson astutely noted in the Declaration of Independence, humans are not, by nature, rebels. Only genuine fear of the dire consequences of persisting in their current situation, joined with real hope in the possibility of achieving a better fate, can inspire people to disrupt their lives and undertake the arduous sacrifices and hazard the frightful dangers characteristic of revolutions.[55]

The thesis that affluent Americans, who constituted a large proportion of college graduates, were all classical republicans, while ordinary Americans were all evangelical Christians, is far too simplistic. It ignores the fact that most colleges were led by clergymen like Witherspoon and included Christian as well as classical training, and the fact that even less affluent Americans imbibed classical principles not only from translations, newspapers, and speeches but also from sermons, since most clergymen were college graduates who liked to show off their erudition. Classical and Christian influences merged in the minds of many, quite probably most, Americans of every class. Hence it is often impossible for the historian to determine whether an individual patriot's fear of corruption and hope of creating a better society stemmed more from Protestant sermons or classical histories. To the founders, there was but one worthy tradition—the tradition of liberty—and they would not have understood the modern historian's need to distinguish between the classical, biblical, and other traditions and measure the influence of one against the other.

The conjunction of Christian and classical influences can be seen most clearly in the lives of the patriots' leading organizer and greatest orator. An avid reader of Jonathan Edwards, Samuel Adams had been energized by the Great Awakening while a student at Harvard in the 1730s. By the 1760s, long before most other Americans, Adams had come to the conclusion that America must separate from Britain in order to escape its corruption. His dream was to construct a "Christian Sparta," a nation that would combine Christian piety with classical republican frugality, self-discipline, courage, and patriotism.[56]

Patrick Henry, almost universally acknowledged as the greatest orator of the Revolution, claimed that he was "first taught what an orator should be" by his favorite preacher, the Presbyterian revivalist Samuel Davies, who attracted hundreds of churchgoers. Davies's style was systematic, thoughtful, solemn, and dignified, but also plain, direct, daring, emotional, and extemporaneous, centering on repetition, rhythm, and well-timed pauses. It stood in sharp contrast to the older style of preaching, which consisted of the reading of sermon manuscripts that were elaborate, learned, polished, and theological. As a boy, Henry repeated Davies's sermons to his mother each Sunday, a practice that strengthened his memory and improved his rhetorical skills. He heard Davies's sermons for twelve impressionable years, from age eleven to twenty-three, at which point Davies left to become president of the College of New Jersey. Henry admired Davies's powerful, rich, and well-modulated voice, his elegant diction, and his dramatic yet restrained delivery. Henry's own political orations and speeches to juries often employed scriptural references. When Charles Thomson, the secretary of the Continental Congress, first saw Henry in 1774, he recalled, "He was dressed in a suit of parson's gray, and from his appearance, I took him for a Presbyterian clergyman," so uncommon among political leaders was Henry's simple garb. Edmund Randolph recalled regarding Henry's "liberty or death" speech, delivered in St. John's Church in Richmond, "In the sacred place of meeting, the church, the imagination had no difficulty to conceive, when he launched forth in solemn tones various causes of scruples against oppressors that the British King was lying prostrate from the thunder of heaven. . . . This enchantment was spontaneous obedience to the working of the soul." Recalling the same speech, St. George Tucker even likened Henry's effect to that of God Himself, writing, "Imagine that you saw the handwriting on the wall of Belshazzar's palace [Daniel 5]. Imagine that you had heard a voice from heaven uttering the words, 'We must fight,' as the doom of Fate, and you may have some idea of the speaker." Henry declared, "An appeal to arms and the God of Hosts is all that is left us!" "The God of Hosts" was a common Old Testament expression denoting the Almighty's power in war. Judge Archibald Stuart described Henry as rising "on the wings of the Tempest to seize upon the Artillery of Heaven and direct it against his adversaries." Yet Henry had also received a rigorous classical training from his father and, as an adult, made it a rule to read Livy's *History of Rome* each year. In his famous Stamp Act Speech, Henry even compared George III to Julius Caesar and hinted that the king might suffer the same fate.[57]

While both evangelical Protestantism and classical republicanism were traditional, communal, and moralistic, a third ideology that contributed to the American Revolution, derived from the British Whigs, looked more to the future than to the past and concerned itself more with individual rights and contractual obligations than with moral duties. But even this ideology, though conflicting somewhat with its fellow contributors to the Revolution, often melded with them in the minds of patriots. The influential sermons of patriot ministers generally appealed to natural rights as well as to the need to escape British corruption. As the historian Mark Noll has written, "So deep was the mutual compatibility of late Puritan Christianity and Whig ideology that over the course of the Revolutionary period it became increasingly difficult to discern where one left off and the other began." While the belief that a society's level of justice (now significantly recast in Whig terms as "liberty") depended on its degree of piety and virtue was both biblical and classical, the belief that its level of piety and virtue depended on its degree of civil liberty was a new doctrine. The early Christian Church, which grew rapidly under the persecution of Roman emperors, would have been mystified by this latter doctrine. Nevertheless, while introducing a new emphasis on civil liberty, Whig ideology fit neatly with the biblical tradition in a crucial way: the narrative it told was one of an enduring struggle between good and evil that good was destined to win.[58]

Whig ideology was able to merge so easily with Protestant Christianity because the former was a descendant of the latter. Most of the British

Whig authors were themselves Protestant dissenters whose support for classical theories of checks and balances was based on the biblical doctrine of a fundamentally selfish human nature and whose emphases on hard work and frugality also found support in the Bible. Even those Whigs, like John Locke, who were biblically unorthodox were heavily influenced by Protestant reformers; Locke cited seven different Calvinists in his *Two Treatises on Civil Government*. Even the Whig emphasis on individual rights, especially when joined to the notion of corresponding duties, was somewhat biblical. While the Book of Acts portrays the ideal of the Christian Church as a community of selfless individuals who voluntarily share their worldly possessions, the Bible as a whole also teaches the crucial principle of individual accountability before God the Judge. If the concept of individual rights had not accorded so well with numerous scriptures that left no doubt that eternal salvation was an individual affair—that God will judge individuals, not families, societies, or nations, on the last day—it is doubtful that it would ever have succeeded among a pious populace. It was this biblical theme that led Martin Luther and his Protestant successors, including early Americans, to posit the authority of the individual to interpret scripture for himself. This individualistic element distinguished the Bible from the traditions of other ancient cultures, such as the classical civilizations of Greece and Rome, which viewed religious obligation almost exclusively in social terms. Thus, while the Whig emphasis on individual liberty was indeed new, it did not constitute a rejection of the biblical tradition but a mere emphasis of its individualistic elements.[59]

When the relationship between these two intellectual forces is viewed in this light, one is not surprised to discover that while most historians have tended to focus their attention on the Whig influence on the founders, the documents tell a different story. After conducting an extensive survey of American political literature from 1760 to 1805, a survey that actually excluded a vast body of political sermons, the political scientist Donald Lutz reported that authors cited the Bible more frequently than the works of any European writer or school of thought, including those of the British Whig and Enlightenment traditions. In fact, biblical references accounted for one-third of all citations. The Book of Deuteronomy alone was cited twice as much as the works of John Locke; the epistles of the apostle Paul were cited as much as the writings of the French Enlightenment author Montesquieu.[60]

It is also crucial to note that the Whig dichotomy between liberty and tyranny merely supplemented and did not displace the traditional biblical conception of good versus evil in American culture. Americans continued not only to define personal morality in Judeo-Christian terms but also to insist that the prevalence of this moral code in society was crucial to the survival and success of government.

The marriage between evangelical Protestantism and its secular partners, classical republicanism and Whig ideology, was not altogether easy, since their emphases conflicted in some ways. But the offspring they produced, the United States of America, was, in the words of John Adams, a "spirited infant."[61]

2

A LIFELONG PASSION

Given the founders' immersion in the Bible as children due to its ubiquity in their homes, schools, churches, and society, it is not surprising that nearly all of them maintained a deep, lifelong interest in the Bible. For many of the founders, even the less orthodox ones, this interest reached the level of passion. The fact that they exhibited this passion in private diaries and letters and that it continued long after their political careers ended testifies to its genuineness; although socially and politically useful, their public references to the Bible were not mere formalities or exercises in political opportunism. Many of the founders took advantage of the greater leisure time afforded by retirement from political office to study the Bible, just as they did the Greco-Roman classics, the other works that had filled their youth. Indeed, throughout their lives, many of the founders promoted the spread of biblical knowledge among their children, among their grandchildren, and in American society at large because they deemed Christian faith crucial to fostering the morality they considered essential to the survival and success of the new republic.

LIFELONG STUDY

Long after the founders left college, where the Bible formed a part of the curriculum, they continued to study scripture. Shortly after graduating from Harvard, John Adams embraced the combination of Christian and classical study then considered most likely to improve the mind. He wrote in his diary, "I am resolved not to neglect my Time as I did last year. I am resolved to rise with the Sun and to study the Scriptures on Thursday, Friday, Saturday, and Sunday mornings and to study some Latin author the other three mornings. Noons and Nights I intend to read English Authors. This is my fixt Determination, and I will set down every neglect and every compliance with this Resolution. May I blush whenever I suffer one hour to pass unimproved. I will rouse up my mind and fix my Attention. I will stand collected within myself and think upon what I read and what I see. I will strive with all my soul to be something more than Persons who have had less Advantages than myself." In 1761, while acting as an attorney for Daniel Prat, who sued Thomas Colson for violating the terms of apprenticeship by failing to teach him to read, Adams summarized his Protestant argument on the importance of Bible reading: "No Priest or Pope has any Right to say what I shall believe, and I will not believe one Word they say if I think it is not founded in Reason and in Revelation. Now how can I judge what my Bible justifies unless I can read my Bible?" Adams added that Bible reading was as useful in the fulfillment of a person's civic obligation to vote wisely, as it was necessary to the performance of his religious and moral duties: "A Man who can read will find in his Bible, in the common sermon Books that common People have by them, and even in the Almanack and the News Papers, Rules and observations that will enlarge his Range of Thought and enable him the better to judge who has and who has not that Integrity of Heart and that Compass of Knowledge and Understanding which form the Statesman." More than half a century later, on Christmas Day in 1813, Adams wrote to Thomas Jefferson, asking, "Do you know anything of the Prophecy of Enoch? Can you give me a comment on the 6th, the 9th, the 14th verses of the epistle of Jude?" The first two of these verses refer to fallen angels; the last quotes Enoch regarding the coming of the Messiah, which Jude identifies as the Second Coming of Christ. Three years later Adams declared, "For fifty years I have neglected all Sciences but Government & Religion," adding that while he had now relinquished the former preoccupation, "the latter still occupies my thoughts." Study of the Bible and sermon literature occupied much of the quarter century of his retirement.[1]

Jefferson continued reading the Bible as well. In 1787 he ordered a copy of the Septuagint, the Greek translation of the Old Testament, and a Greek New Testament. Thereafter he ordered many different Greek,

Latin, and English New Testaments, including the first Greek New Testament printed in America. In 1800, while awaiting the final outcome of his own presidential election, he ordered Scotcherd's Pocket Bible, calling it "an edition which I have long been wishing to get to make part of a portable library which the course of my life has rendered convenient." While president, Jefferson often passed the time in the evenings by studying the Bible. In 1813, after joining John Adams in praising Cleanthes's "Hymn to Jupiter," Jefferson added, "Yet in the contemplation of a being so superlative [as God], the hyperbolic flights of the Psalmist may often be followed with approbation, even with rapture; and I have no hesitation in giving him the palm over all the Hymnists of every language, and of every time." Jefferson then commented on the merits and flaws of numerous translations of the psalms. Adams replied in full agreement, writing, "The Psalms of David, in Sublimity, beauty, pathos, and Originality, or, in one Word, poetry, are superior to all the Odes, Hymns, and Songs in any language. . . . Could David be translated as well [as some of the Greek and Latin authors] his superiority would be universally acknowledged."[2]

Like Jefferson, George Washington was an active man who desired portable scripture that could accompany him anywhere. In 1771 Washington ordered a combination Anglican Book of Common Prayer and translation of the psalms in metrical verse. He specified that it must be compact enough to carry in his pocket.[3]

Benjamin Franklin read popular vernacular parables that can be traced back to ancient, extra-biblical, Jewish sources and rewrote them in the style of the King James Version of the Bible. These included a parable against persecution in which God rebukes Abraham for driving a guest out into the wilderness because the man is an idol worshipper who refuses to worship the Almighty: "Have I borne with him these hundred ninety and eight Years, and nourished him, and clothed him, notwithstanding his Rebellion against me, and couldst not thou, that art thyself a Sinner, bear with him one Night?" Abraham goes out into the wilderness, finds the man, returns him to his tent for the evening, and presents him with many gifts upon his departure the next morning. Franklin concludes the parable as follows: "And God spoke again unto Abraham, saying, 'For this thy Sin shall thy Seed be afflicted four Hundred Years in a strange Land. But for thy Repentance will I deliver them; and they shall come forth with Power and Gladness of Heart, and with much Substance.'" In Franklin's retelling of an equally ancient Jewish parable, Reuben refuses to lend his new ax to any of his brothers. When Reuben's ax falls into a river, none of his angry siblings will lend him his own, except for Judah, who forgives his brother. When the story is reported to their father, Jacob, by their brother Joseph, it becomes the basis for Jacob's famous prophecy regarding Judah (Genesis 49:10): "He shall rule over his Brethren, nor shall the Scepter depart from his house, nor a Lawgiver from between his Feet, until Shiloh comes." According to Luke's genealogy (Luke 3:26), Jesus was a descendant of Judah whose rule would one day fulfill that prophecy. In retelling these ancient parables that had become better known in vernacular English, Franklin used the King James style, so familiar to all of his readers, to present tales that not only imparted moral lessons but also ended with the unexpected twist of adding to the biblical narrative by identifying the previously hidden cause of the events related in it.[4]

In 1781, while serving as an American commissioner to France, Franklin proposed to have a sermon of the Reverend Samuel Cooper that he liked translated into French and printed in Geneva. Cooper's sermon did not provide scriptural citations, but Franklin's knowledge of the Bible was sufficient that he offered to provide them himself. Franklin wrote to the clergyman, "It was not necessary in New England, where everybody reads the Bible and is acquainted with Scripture Phrases, that you should note the Texts from which you took them. But I have observed in England, as well as in France, that Verses and Expressions taken from the sacred Writings and not known to be such appear very strange and awkward to some Readers, and I shall therefore in my Edition take the Liberty of marking the quoted Texts in the Margin."[5]

In his retirement years during the 1790s Patrick Henry devoted himself to the study of the Bible. Each morning after rising, his first act was to read scripture in the dining room. Once, when one of his neighbors came upon him while he was reading the Bible, he held it aloft and declared, "This book is worth all the books that were ever printed, and it has been my misfortune that I have never found time to read it with the proper attention and feeling till lately. I trust in the mercy of Heaven that it is not yet too late." Whenever possible, he took communion at his Episcopalian church and, in obedience to Paul's warning about the seriousness and introspection with which the Lord's Supper should be approached (1 Corinthians 11:27–29), he always prepared himself by fasting and spent the rest of the day in quiet reflection.[6]

Like Henry, Alexander Hamilton employed much of the additional time afforded by retirement from politics in studying the Bible, a book from which he drew consolation for personal and political disasters, such as the death of his son Philip in a duel; the madness of his oldest daughter, Angelica; and the end of his political career amid the ascendancy of the Democratic-Republican Party. Hamilton's son John later recalled regarding his father's interest in horticulture at this time, "His religious feelings grew with his growing intimacy with the marvelous works of nature, all pointing in their processes and their results to a great pervading, ever active Cause. Thus his mind rose from the visible to the invisible, and he found intensest pleasure in studies higher and deeper than all speculation. His Bible exhibits on its margins the care with which he perused it. . . . He now united the habit of daily prayer, in which exercise of faith and love the Lord's Prayer was always a part. The renewing influences of early pious instruction and habit appear to have returned in all their force on his truest sensibilities." The night before Hamilton was fatally wounded in a duel, he recited the Lord's Prayer with John, who was then twelve years old.[7]

Benjamin Rush never stopped reading the Bible and reflecting on its contents. In 1791 he penned fifteen pages of notes on "Diseases of the Old and New Testaments," though he never got around to writing the actual essay for which he had taken the notes. The purpose of the essay was not only scientific but also to "establish the truth and excellency of the Scriptures." Two years later the sight of Jean-Pierre Blanchard's balloon ride in Philadelphia led Rush to contemplate its connection to biblical prophecies regarding the Millennium:

> The first command to man "to subdue the earth" [Genesis 1:28], like every other command, must be fulfilled. The earth certainly includes water and air as well as dry land. The first and last have long ago yielded to the dominion of man. It remains for him only to render the air subservient to his will. This I conceive will sooner or later be affected by the improvement and extension of the principles of balloons. . . . Above all, who knows but that they may be the vehicles which shall convey the inhabitants of our western world to Jerusalem to pay their annual homage to the Saviour of the World during the period of the millennium? Should this be the case, the 8th verse of the

> 60th chapter of Isaiah will be intelligible. I refer you to the whole of the chapter, particularly to the verses which succeed the above, in which there seems to be an evident relation to the conversion and ingathering of the inhabitants of this western part of our globe.

Isaiah 60:8 states regarding millennial pilgrimages to the Holy Lands, "Who are these that fly as a cloud and as the doves to their windows?"[8]

While risking his life to treat victims of yellow fever in Philadelphia in 1793, in stark contrast to those physicians who fled the city, Rush agonized over the possibility that he would never see his family again but comforted himself by reading the psalms every day. When the threat passed, he wrote to his wife, "In a former letter I mentioned to you that I had wept one evening over the 102nd psalm. Last night I felt great satisfaction in reading the 103rd psalm. I beg of you to read it over and over and to join with me in praising God for the wonderful deliverance he has wrought for me." He then quoted Song of Solomon 2:11–12: "The winter is gone. The flowers appear upon the earth; the time of the singing birds is come, and the voice of the turtle is again heard in our land." A couple of weeks later, he noted, "I have this morning been rebuked, humbled, and comforted by reading the 37th psalm." In 1796 he considered writing another essay that he called "an attempt to explain sundry passages in the Old and New Testaments by the principles of medicine and the laws of animal economy." He added, "It will contain many new arguments in favor of Christianity and will I hope render infidelity, at least among physicians, as much a mark of ignorance as it is of impiety or immorality. Should it please God to bless this work to the benefit of any of his creatures, I shall be thankful. What an honor to be employed by Him in any way, but chiefly in promoting the knowledge, the love, and the future enjoyment of Himself." In 1811 Rush expressed enthusiasm about Adam Clarke's commentary on the Bible. In a letter to Thomas Jefferson he cited Clarke's remarks on Genesis 1:24 ("And God said, 'Let the earth bring forth the living creature after his kind, cattle and creeping things and beasts of the earth after his kind, and it was so'"). Clarke discussed the incredible size and attributes of the "colossal mammoth," a subject Rush knew would interest Jefferson. Rush noted that Clarke concluded the passage with the exultation, "How wondrous are the works of God!"[9]

John Dickinson, whose *Letters from a Farmer in Pennsylvania* constituted one of the most important pamphlets of the American Revolution, spent his final years studying the Bible and taking extensive notes on it under such headings as "Notes on the Bible," "The New Covenant commonly called the New Testament," "Alterations of the Old Testament," and "The Gospel According to Matthew." He compared and contrasted various translations of the Bible.[10]

Henry Laurens, the president of the Continental Congress after John Hancock, was equally fond of Bible reading. His friend, the historian David Ramsay, recalled, "In the performance of his religious duties Mr. Laurens was strict and exemplary. The emergency was great which kept him from church either forenoon or afternoon, and very great indeed which kept him from his regular monthly communion. With the bible he was intimately acquainted. Its doctrines he firmly believed, its precepts and history he admired, and was much in the habit of quoting and applying portions of it to present circumstances. He not only read the scriptures diligently to his family but made all his children read them also. His family bible contained in his own handwriting several of his remarks on passing providences."[11]

Three founders went further in their biblical scholarship. Charles Thomson labored for years to produce a well-regarded translation of the Bible in 1808 and a *Synopsis of the Four Evangelists* seven years later. Roger Sherman, a signer of both the Declaration of Independence and the Constitution, published *A Sermon on the Duty of Self-Examination Preparatory to Receiving the Lord's Supper* in 1789. A deacon in his Congregational church, Sherman possessed a library that was filled with Bibles, concordances, and sermon collections. As a member of Congress, he opposed meetings and travel on the Sabbath and argued that the maximum number of lashes administered for military discipline should be set at forty, the limit established for criminals by Deuteronomy 25:3. Oliver Ellsworth, a signer of the Constitution and the second chief justice of the U.S. Supreme Court, helped write *A Summary of Christian Doctrine and Practice*.[12]

PROMOTING THE BIBLICAL EDUCATION OF FUTURE GENERATIONS

The founders were determined that their own progeny, and future generations of Americans in general, should receive the same biblical instruction they had received. Unlike the founders' dedication to the spread of classical learning, which was largely restricted to boys, their determination to increase biblical knowledge applied equally to girls. Another difference between the founders' efforts on behalf of biblical training and their advocacy of classical education was that they never had to construct elaborate rhetorical defenses of the former as they did for the latter because there were almost no public critics of Bible study.[13]

In *Letters on Education* (1765), a manual of advice on parenting and children's education originally addressed to a Scottish gentleman but later published, John Witherspoon advised, "You should, in your general deportment, make your children perceive that you look upon religion as absolutely necessary." Parents should not be afraid to speak of heaven and hell: "Many parents are much more ready to tell their children such or such a thing is mean and not like a gentleman than to warn them that they will thereby incur the displeasure of their Maker. . . . The care of our souls is represented in Scripture as the one thing most needful. He makes a miserable bargain who gains the whole world and loses his soul [Matthew 16:26]. It is not the native beauty of virtue, or the outward credit of it, or the inward satisfaction arising from it, or even all these combined together, that will be sufficient to change our natures and govern our conduct, but a deep conviction that unless we are reconciled to God, we shall without doubt perish everlastingly." Witherspoon argued that the best way to demonstrate the importance of Christian piety to children was not by words but by deeds, especially the faithful keeping of the Sabbath.[14]

Witherspoon contributed much to the dissemination of biblical knowledge and scriptural principles by training both future ministers and future political leaders at Princeton. In his "Lectures on Eloquence" (1782) Witherspoon included a section for preachers since a good portion of his students were destined for the ministry. He first declared, "Preaching the gospel of Christ is a truly noble employment, and the care of souls [is] a very important trust." Witherspoon then claimed that the qualities most important in a preacher were piety, simplicity, accuracy, vehemence, propriety, and extensive knowledge. Regarding simplicity, he stated, "If I heard a lawyer pleading in such a style and manner as was more adapted to display his own talents than to carry his client's cause, it would considerably lessen him in my esteem, but if I heard a minister acting the same part, I should not be satisfied with contempt, but hold him in detestation." Witherspoon was universally admired for both his piety and his erudition.

He taught a future president, a future vice president, three future Supreme Court justices, twelve future members of the Continental Congress, five future delegates to the Constitutional Convention, and fourteen future members of the state ratifying conventions. Equally significant, he taught thirty-one future Continental Army officers. George Washington paid twenty-five pounds sterling per year so that a friend's son could study under him.[15]

Samuel Adams's house was one in which prayers were spoken before every meal, passages from the Bible were read before bedtime, and the Sabbath was scrupulously observed. He named his daughter Hannah, thereby reversing the original relationship between the biblical mother and the prophetic son whom she dedicated to the Lord after initially being unable to bear a child (1 Samuel). In 1780 Adams wrote to his beloved daughter, praising her devotion to her parents but also adding, "Be equally attentive to every Relation in which all-wise Providence may lead you, and I will venture to predict for my dear Daughter an unfailing source of Happiness in the reflection of her own Mind. If you carefully fulfill the various Duties of Life from a Principle of Obedience to your heavenly Father, you shall enjoy that Peace which the World cannot give nor take away. . . . If this has any Influence on your Mind, you know you cannot gratify me as much as by seeking most earnestly the Favor of Him who made & supports you, who will supply you with whatever his infinite Wisdom sees best for you in this World, and above all, who has given us his Son to purchase for us the Reward of Eternal Life." He wrote to his son-in-law, "Religion in a Family is at once its brightest Ornament & its best Security. The first Point of Justice, says a Writer I have met with, consists in Piety, nothing certainly being so great a Debt upon us as to render to the Creator & Preserver those Acknowledgments which are due to Him for our being and the hourly Protection which he affords us."[16]

Applying this lesson to society at large, Adams championed public education as a means of instructing the poor in biblical principles. In 1779 he claimed, "It gives me the greatest Concern to hear that some of our Gentlemen in the Country begin to think the Maintenance of Schools too great a Burden. . . . If Virtue and Knowledge are diffused among the People, they will never be enslaved. This will be their great Security. . . . I hope your Countrymen will never depart from the Principles & Maxims which have been handed down to us from our wise forefathers." Eleven years later he urged, "Let Divines and Philosophers, Statesmen and Patriots, unite their endeavours to renovate the Age, by impressing the Minds of Men with the importance of educating their little boys and girls—of inculcating in the Minds of youth the fear and love of the Deity and universal Philanthropy; and in subordination to these great principles, the Love of their Country—of instructing them in the Art of self-Government, without which they never can act a wise part in the Government of Societies, great or small—in short, of leading them in the Study and Practice of the exalted Virtues of the Christian system, which will happily tend to subdue the turbulent Passions of Men." As the new governor of Massachusetts in 1794, Adams wasted no time in writing to the legislature in support of a system of training youth that "will impress their minds with a profound reverence of the Deity, universal benevolence, and warm attachment and affection towards their country." He added, "It will excite in them a just regard to Divine Revelation, which informs them of the original character and dignity of Man; and it will inspire them with a sense of true honor, which consists in conforming as much as possible their principles, habits, and manners to that original character." In 1797 he again wrote to the legislature emphasizing the importance of instilling "Piety, Religion, and Morality" in the youth through the schools.[17]

Benjamin Franklin also advocated the study of scripture. In 1755 he advised the daughter of a friend to "go constantly to Meeting or Church," "live like a Christian," and "spend your spare Hours in sober Whisk, Prayers, or learning to cipher." He added advice concerning her future marriage, "As to Division, I say with Brother Paul [1 Corinthians 1:10], 'Let there be no Divisions among ye.'" In 1766 he bought an expensive, gilded Bible for his daughter. In 1782, concerned that the archaic language of the King James Version of the Bible might prevent some Americans from reading it (though Franklin himself often quoted verbatim from the KJV), he called for more modern translations. As a sample of what he had in mind, he put forth his own translation of Job 1:6–11. Although Franklin was entirely serious about his call for new translations, he could not help but add a few comic touches to his own version, as in Job 1:11, in which he has Satan speak to God regarding Job in the manner of an eighteenth-century politician: "Withhold his pensions, and you will soon find him in the opposition."[18]

Patrick Henry also encouraged the spread of biblical knowledge within his family and in American society generally. In 1786 he wrote to his daughter Anne, who had just been married, "Sermons and other well-written productions will not fail to enlarge your understanding, to render you a more agreeable companion, and to exalt your virtue." He added regarding a hypothetical woman, "Besides, in those hours of calamity to which families must be exposed, where will she find support if it be not in the just reflections upon that all-ruling Providence which governs the universe whether animate or inanimate?" A decade later he wrote to another daughter, Elizabeth, "Amongst all the handsome things I hear said of you, what gives me the greatest pleasure is to be told of your piety and steady virtue." Henry served actively as a trustee for Hampden Sydney College, a Presbyterian academy that taught both the classics and the Bible. After bequeathing all of his property, Henry concluded his will as follows: "This is all the inheritance I can give to my dear family. The religion of Christ can give them one which will make them rich indeed."[19]

Named after Elijah (Elias is the Greek New Testament name for the prophet) and baptized by George Whitefield, Elias Boudinot led daily prayers for his family and servants. In 1816 he established the American Bible Society, which published Bibles and distributed them to the poor. It was the realization of a forty-three-year dream to unite "the people of God, of all denominations, in the United States, in carrying on the great work of disseminating the Gospel of Jesus Christ throughout the habitable world." When selected the organization's first president, he declared it the highest possible honor this side of the grave and contributed the then massive sum of $10,000 to it. He was also a leading figure in the establishment of Princeton Theological Seminary. Capping a lifetime of charitable contributions to the poor, in his will he bequeathed $200 to the New Jersey Bible Society "for the purchase of spectacles to be given by them to poor old people, it being in vain to give a Bible to those who cannot obtain the means of reading it." He left $2,000 to the United Brethren of Moravians "for the purpose of endeavoring to civilize and gospelize the Indian nations or any others destitute of a gospel ministry." A young Cherokee subsequently adopted Boudinot's name and translated part of the New Testament into the tribal language. President of the Presbyterian General Assembly at the time of his death in 1821, Boudinot also bequeathed it a large sum for the purchase of books for ministers and left another to his own particular church to distribute to widows and orphans. In his will he wrote regarding his daughter Susan, "I do . . . beseech and entreat her to make the fear and the love of God the great object of her constant attention and pursuit. . . . And I do more especially press it upon her, under every circumstance of life, to consider that day more than lost in which she does not seek, earnestly seek, communion with her Heavenly Father under the special influences of his Holy Spirit. And she may be positively assured that this may be done even amidst the common and ordinary business of life as in the most profound and secret retirement, assisted by the ordinances of His Gospel. I would also earnestly recommend her habitually living under a prevailing sense of God's overruling providence, which, however wonderful, regards the smallest things of those who love and fear him, even to the numbering of the hairs on their heads [Matthew 10:30]."[20]

John Jay, who later served as president of the American Bible Society and as a member of the American Board of Commissioners of Foreign Missions, was determined that his children read the Bible. In 1784, while still in Paris after helping to negotiate the treaty that ended the Revolutionary War, Jay wrote to his son Peter, who was staying with his aunt, "She also tells me that you love your Books, that you daily read in the Bible, and have learned by Heart some Hymns in the Book I sent you. These Accounts give me great pleasure, and I love you for being such a good Boy. The Bible is the best of all Books, for it is the word of God, and teaches us the way to be happy in this world and in the next. Continue therefore to read it and to regulate your Life by its precepts." His son William later recalled, "The Scriptures were pre-eminently his study and were the subjects of his daily and careful perusal. . . . Every morning immediately before the breakfast, the family, including the domestics, were summoned to prayers and the call was repeated precisely at nine at night, when he read to them a chapter in the Bible and concluded with prayers." A. H. Stevens, a frequent visitor at the house, recalled the Jays "uniting in thanksgiving, confession, and prayer." In 1814 Jay took extensive notes on the Book of Genesis under the heading of "Jacob and Esau," finally concluding, "The Scriptures give us to understand that the works of neither of them had any influence on the Election of Jacob or the Rejection of Esau, but it strongly intimates that Regard was had to the *Faith* of Jacob and the *Infidelity* of Esau" (emphasis in original). Jay gave a copy of this manuscript to his son Peter and instructed him to distribute copies to each of his siblings. In his will Jay declared, "While my children lament my departure, let them recollect that in doing them good I was only the agent of their heavenly Father and that he never withdraws his care and consolations from those who diligently seek him." Jay's last words were, "The Lord is better than we deserve." One of his sons inscribed this epitaph on his tombstone: "He was in his life and death an example of the virtues, the faith, and the hopes of a Christian."[21]

In 1810 Charles Cotesworth Pinckney played a leading role in establishing the Bible Society of Charleston, which became an auxiliary of the American Bible Society in 1817, at which point Pinckney became one of the national society's vice presidents. Even after Pinckney retired from public life at age seventy, he remained active in the organization, hosting meetings in his home. In the 1820s he disregarded the fierce criticisms of slaveholders who blamed the society for the Denmark Vesey slave revolt, insisting that the society continue distributing Bibles to African Americans.[22]

John Marshall urged his progeny to study the Bible. He wrote to his grandson and namesake regarding happiness, "Its inseparable companion is a quiet conscience. Of this, Religion is the surest and safest foundation. The individual who turns his thoughts frequently to an omnipotent, omniscient, and all perfect being, who feels his dependence on, and his infinite obligations to, that being will avoid that course of life which must harrow up the conscience."[23]

Benjamin Rush was equally fervent in urging his children to listen attentively to biblically based sermons and to read the Bible. While apart from his wife on a Sabbath in 1791, he informed her that their son Richard "asked for permission to stay home this afternoon." Rush added, "I told him I had no more right to excuse him from going to church than I had to grant him permission to lie or steal. After this explanation of the obligation of public worship, he went without a single objection." Five years later, before their son John set sail on a long voyage in which he served as a surgeon on a ship departing for India, Benjamin and Julia Rush wrote a series of instructions under four headings, the first of which was "Morals": "1. Be punctual in committing your soul and body to the protection of your Creator every morning and evening. Implore at the same time his mercy in the name of his Son, our Lord and Saviour Jesus Christ. 2. Read your Bible frequently, more especially on Sundays. 3. Avoid swearing and even an irreverent use of your Creator's name. Flee youthful lusts. 4. Be courteous and gentle in your behavior to your fellow passengers and respectful and obedient to the captain of the vessel.

5. Attend public worship regularly every Sunday when you arrive at Calcutta."[24]

Rush's promotion of biblical knowledge went far beyond his own family. He proposed the establishment of public schools, which were then a rare commodity outside of New England, in Pennsylvania as a means of both practicing Christian charity and instilling biblical values in poor children. In "A Plan for the Establishment of Public Schools and the Diffusion of Knowledge in Pennsylvania" (1786) Rush argued that the Bible should be read in the new schools just as it was in the state's private and in New England's public schools. He emphasized "the tremendous advantages of making children early and intimately acquainted with the means of acquiring happiness both here and hereafter," adding, "There is no book of its size in the world that contains half so much useful knowledge for the government of states or the direction of the affairs of individuals as the Bible." Rush went on to say, "The first impressions upon the mind are the most durable. They survive the wreck of the memory and exist in old age after the ideas acquired in middle life have been obliterated. Of how much consequence then must it be to the human mind in the evening of life to be able to recall those ideas which are most essential to its happiness, and these are to be found chiefly in the Bible. The great delight which old people take in reading the Bible, I am persuaded, is derived chiefly from its histories and precepts being associated with the events of childhood and youth, the recollection of which forms a material part of their pleasures."[25]

The following year Rush issued another appeal for public schools in Philadelphia centered on the Bible. He wrote, "We shall render an acceptable service to the Divine Being in taking care of that part of our fellow creatures who appear to be the more immediate objects of his compassion and benevolence. . . . Above all, let both sexes be carefully instructed in the principles and obligations of the Christian religion. This is the most essential part of education—this will make them dutiful children, teachable scholars, and afterwards good apprentices, good husbands, good wives, honest mechanics, industrious farmers, peaceable sailors, and in everything that relates to this country, good citizens." Rush ended his appeal by quoting Psalms 41:1–2: "Blessed is he that considereth the poor; the Lord will deliver him in time of trouble. The Lord will preserve him and keep him alive upon the earth; he will not deliver him into the will of his enemies." In "Thoughts upon Female Education," written in the same year, Rush proposed schools for girls that also focused on biblical training. Rush wrote, "Our pupils should be furnished with some of the most simple arguments in favor of the truth of Christianity." The Bible should be read every day in these schools, and "such questions should be asked, after reading it, as are calculated to imprint upon their minds the interesting stories contained in it." Such instruction could and should start very young. Rush added, "The female breast is the natural soil of Christianity, and while women are taught to believe its doctrines and obey its precepts, the wit of Voltaire and the style of Bolingbroke will never be able to destroy its influence upon our citizens." He concluded, "Christianity exerts the most friendly influence upon science as well as upon the morals and manners of mankind. . . . It is certain that the greatest discoveries in science have been made by Christian philosophers and that there is the most knowledge in those countries where there is the most Christianity. . . . [Therefore] parents or schoolmasters who neglect the religious instruction of their children and pupils reject and neglect the most effectual means of promoting knowledge in our country." In 1789, in an essay offering advice to farmers who intended to settle in the West, Rush listed the items necessary for survival there, then added, "There is one more article that must not be left behind if a farmer wishes to prosper in a new country, and that is the Bible." In 1807, when delivering a public lecture on diseases of domestic animals, he planned to touch on "the precepts of the Old and New Testaments which inculcate tenderness to and care of them."[26]

In 1791 Rush advocated the continued use of the Bible as the primary text in teaching children to read. Rush based his view on these propositions: "I. That Christianity is the only true and perfect religion, and that in proportion as mankind adopts its principles and obeys its precepts, they will be wise and happy. II. That a better knowledge of this religion is to be acquired by reading the bible than in any other way. III. That the bible contains more knowledge necessary to man in his present state than any other book in the world." Rush claimed that biblical principles were most effectively instilled at an early age, adding, "The interesting events and characters recorded and described in the Old and New Testaments are accommodated above all others to seize upon all the faculties of the minds of children. The understanding, the memory, the imagination, the passions, and the moral powers are all occasionally addressed by the various incidents which are contained in these books, insomuch that not to be delighted with them is to be devoid of every principle of pleasure that exists in a sound mind. . . . The Bible contains more truths than any other book in the world." Rush again contended that biblical principles, once acquired in childhood, were sure to be revived in old age: "There is a wonderful property in the memory which enables it in old age to recover the knowledge it had acquired in early life after it had been apparently forgotten for forty or fifty years. Of how much consequence, then, must it be to fill the mind with that species of knowledge in childhood and youth which, when recalled in the decline of life, will support the soul under the infirmities of age and smooth the avenues of approaching death? The Bible is the only book which is capable of affording this support to old age, and it is for this reason that we find it resorted to with so much diligence and pleasure by such old people as have read it in early life." Rush then quoted Deuteronomy 6:5–7: "And thou shalt love the Lord thy God with all thy heart and with all thy soul and with all thy might. And these words which I command thee this day shall be in thine heart. And thou *shalt teach them diligently unto thy children* and shalt talk of them when thou sittest in the house and when thou walkest by the way, and when thou liest down and when thou risest up" (emphasis in original). Rush attributed the positive cultural attributes of other nations and sections of the United States to biblical education: "The industry and habits of order which distinguish many of the German nations are derived from their early instruction in the principles of Christianity by means of the Bible. The moral and enlightened character of the inhabitants of Scotland and of the New England states appears to be derived from the same cause." He approved the naming of children after biblical figures: "I conceive there may be some advantage in bearing scripture names. It may lead the persons who bear them to study that part of the scripture in which their names are mentioned with uncommon attention, and perhaps it may excite a desire in them to possess the talents or virtues of their ancient namesakes."[27]

Rush promoted biblical education at both his alma mater, the College of New Jersey, and the new institution of higher learning he helped establish, Dickinson College. In 1784 he proudly noted that the seal of the latter institution consisted of a Bible, a telescope, and a liberty cap, an emblem that combined religion, science, and politics. When the college's cornerstone was laid in 1799, Rush wrote, "May it become in a more especial manner the nursery of the Church of Christ, and many precious streams issue from it to make glad the cities of our God!" Three years later he wrote to Ashbel Green, acting president of the College of New Jersey:

> I cannot omit this opportunity of expressing to you the great pleasure I have derived by learning from my son James that instruction in the evidences of the Christian religion has at length become a part of the education of a young man at the Jersey College. I have often publicly as well as privately advised it. Three-fourths of all the infidelity of the gentlemen of our country I believe has arisen from the neglect of it. To perfect the plan now happily introduced into the College, it only remains to pass a law to oblige candidates for degrees to undergo an examination in theological science as well as in the sciences which relate only to our existence in this world. . . . Would not a few lectures upon Jewish antiquities, as far as they relate to the connections between the Old and New Testaments, be useful? Infidelity generally makes its first approaches by attacking the supposed absurdities and cruelties of the Jewish worship. By explaining them properly and showing the relation of every part of it to the New Testament institutions, much evil might be prevented in the minds of young men. The antidote would be administered before the poison would have time to produce its effect.

In 1804 Rush expressed his delight at the fact that the college was requiring students to recite lessons from the Bible and other religious works: "In this way only they will be prepared in future life to resist the flimsy declamations of infidel writers, as well as to regulate their conduct by a system of morals which they never can cease to believe are of divine origin."[28]

Rush was one of the founders of the Sunday school movement. A couple of months before the first nonsectarian Sunday school in America began in Philadelphia in 1791, he explained, "The Bible is the only book that is to be read in them. The schools will be under the direction of persons of all religious denominations." Rush envisioned the Sunday school as a means of educating poor children in reading, writing, and scripture. He also endorsed commentaries on the Bible, such as Elhanan Winchester's *Lectures on the Prophecies*. He wrote to Winchester, "You have made the Old and New Testaments intelligible books and added greatly to our obligations to love and admire them. To pry into the meaning of the prophecies is certainly a duty. Our Saviour condemns his disciples for being slow of heart in believing all that the Scriptures say concerning him [Luke 24:25] and commends Abraham for beholding his day far off and rejoicing in the great events which were to follow [John 8:56]. Perhaps a great part of the errors in principle and lukewarmness in practice of all sects of Christianity arise chiefly from their ignorance of the literal meaning and extent of the prophecies which relate to the kingdom of our Lord and Saviour Jesus Christ." Finally, Rush was the founder and vice president of the Philadelphia Bible Society, which distributed Bibles to the city's poor.[29]

In 1801, a decade after Rush's essay on the subject, the Federalist leader Fisher Ames also endorsed the use of the Bible as a school book. He wrote regarding scripture, "Its morals are pure, its examples captivating and noble. The reverence for the sacred book that is thus early impressed lasts long."[30]

George Washington supported the preaching of the gospel to Native Americans both for their own good and in order to increase their friendship with the United States. As early as 1779, Washington declared to the Delaware chiefs, "You do well to wish to learn our arts and ways of life, and above all, the religion of Jesus Christ. These will make you a greater and happier people than you are." Nine years later Washington called an effort to preach the gospel to Native American tribes a "laudable" undertaking and referred to "an event so long and so earnestly desired as that of converting the Indians to Christianity and consequently to civilization." While president in 1789, he instructed his commissioners to the southern tribes, "You will also endeavour to obtain a stipulation for certain missionaries to reside in the nation, provided the General Government should think proper to adopt the measure—these men to be precluded from trade or attempting to purchase any lands. . . . The object of this establishment will be the happiness of the Indians, teaching them great duties of religion and morality, and to inculcate a friendship and attachment to the United States." The same year he wrote to the Moravian Society for Propagating the Gospel, "Be assured of my patronage in your laudable undertakings," namely, "the disinterested endeavours of your society to civilize and Christianize the Savages of the Wilderness," adding, "I pray Almighty God to have you always in his holy keeping." Four years later Washington permitted a group of Moravians and Quakers to accompany his commissioners to the northwestern tribes.[31]

Thomas Jefferson encouraged adult Bible reading because of its moral effects. As early as 1767 and often thereafter, he recommended the study of the New Testament to young men who sought his educational advice. In 1809 he wrote regarding Americans, "We all agree in the obligation of the moral precepts of Jesus, & nowhere will they be found delivered in greater purity than in his discourses." In 1814 he contributed the then hefty sum of $50 to the American Bible Society, writing, "There never was a more pure and sublime system of morality delivered to man than is to be found in the four evangelists." Although Jefferson objected to various Bible societies' missions to China partly because he feared they would disturb the peace of an alien culture, he also opposed them because he believed that American missionaries' obligation to provide biblical instruction in the United States took precedence over any duty to do so in other nations. He asked, "While we have so many around us, within the same social pale, who need instruction and assistance, why carry to a distance and to strangers what our neighbors need?" For this reason Jefferson also contributed what were then considered substantial sums to the construction of Episcopalian, Presbyterian, Baptist, and Catholic churches.[32]

It is true that Jefferson famously argued against children's Bible reading in *Notes on the State of Virginia* (1782). Jefferson wrote, "Instead, therefore, of putting the Bible and Testament into the hands of children at an age when their judgments are not sufficiently matured for religious inquiries, their memories may be stored with the most useful facts from Grecian, Roman, European, and American history." But Jefferson applied this prohibition only to children. Furthermore, ever the moralist, Jefferson immediately added, "The first elements of morality too may be instilled in their minds." While Jefferson believed that children's rational capacity was too weak to engage successfully in religious inquiry, he believed that their moral sense was formed at an early age. Thus, he did not oppose the teaching of moral principles to children via Bible stories and select scriptural passages.[33]

In fact, Jefferson himself engaged in just such a practice. In 1825, a year before his death, when asked by a friend to write a letter of advice as a memorial to a baby boy the friend had named after Jefferson, Jefferson concluded the touching letter with his favorite translation of his favorite psalm, Nahum Tate and Nicholas Brady's translation of the fifteenth psalm (1696), under the heading "The portrait of a good man by the most sublime of poets, for your imitation":

> Lord, who's the happy man that may to Thy blest courts repair,
> Not stranger-like to visit them, but to inhabit there?
> 'Tis he whose every thought and deed by rules of virtue moves,
> Whose generous tongue disdains to speak the thing his heart disapproves.
> Who never did a slander forge, his neighbor's fame to wound,
> Nor hearken to a false report by malice whispered round.
> Who vice, in all its pomp and power, can treat with just neglect;
> And piety, though clothed in rags, religiously respect.
> Who to his plighted vows and trust has ever firmly stood,
> And though he promise to his loss, he makes his promise good.
> Whose soul in usury disdains his treasure to employ.
> Whom no rewards can ever bribe the guiltless to destroy.
> The man who, by his steady course, has happiness insur'd,
> When earth's foundations shake, shall stand, by Providence secur'd.

A year earlier, when asked by an editor for an essay on ethics, Jefferson replied simply, "Nothing is more moral, more sublime, than David's description of the good man in his 15th Psalm."[34]

The fact that even so biblically unorthodox a founder as Thomas Jefferson not only possessed a deep affection for portions of the Bible but also was willing to contribute a large sum toward its dissemination is compelling evidence of the almost universal reverence that the Bible commanded in eighteenth- and nineteenth-century American society. With the exception of Thomas Paine, even those founders who rejected some biblical doctrines believed that scripture served a crucial purpose in fostering the virtue that was essential to any republic.

3

HEROES AND VILLAINS

The founders' lifelong study of the Bible furnished them with a rich source from which to draw moral and political lessons that they then applied to contemporary problems, both personal and political. The founders' political rhetoric was suffused with biblical references intended to persuade their fellow citizens to pursue favored courses of action. The greatest instance of success in this regard was Thomas Paine's use of God's curse on the Israelites for demanding a king in 1 Samuel 8 to convince many Americans that the Almighty abhorred monarchy and favored republics, a conviction that was instrumental in bringing about American independence.

The founders employed biblical references for the same purposes that they used classical allusions: to communicate, to impress, and to persuade. The Bible facilitated communication by furnishing a common set of stories, knowledge, and ideas, a literature select enough to provide common ground yet rich enough to address a wide range of human problems from a variety of perspectives. Biblical stories and the lessons they imparted proved a vital source of unity in a nation whose people were separated from one another by vast stretches of terrain and divided by an ever increasing multiplicity of denominations. Scriptural references also allowed the founders to impress audiences with their own piety and virtue and to appropriate the support of divine authority for their arguments and causes. Finally, the Bible supplied them with an invaluable resource in making sense of the confusing events of their day.

In the late eighteenth and early nineteenth centuries the political utility of the Bible differed from that of the Greco-Roman classics. While a detailed knowledge of the classics was largely restricted to affluent males, who could afford to attend exclusively male grammar schools and colleges, nearly all Americans, rich and poor, male and female, read the Bible. As a result, scriptural references were far less useful to a politician as a means of proving his status as "a gentleman" than classical allusions, but they were far more valuable in communicating ideas to a wide audience. Furthermore, while most Americans respected classical authors, they did not consider their works sacred and infallible, as they did the Bible. Therefore, while politicians could not prove their erudition through biblical citations, they hoped that such references would incline their audiences to consider them pious and virtuous and thus be persuaded by their arguments.

The founders' recognition of the political utility of the Bible is no more an indication of any insincerity in their professions of admiration for it than their recognition of the political usefulness of the classics is proof of the falsity of their claims of reverence for classical works. In both cases the founders' private letters and diary entries reveal the same admiration as their public pronouncements, and the founders continued to read and comment on the revered texts in their retirement years, long after they ceased to derive any political benefit from them. Even those founders who rejected fundamental biblical doctrines tended to view the Bible as a source of wisdom and to value the moral and political lessons they learned from its rich collection of stories.

THE IMPORTANCE OF BIBLICAL HEROES

While the founders turned chiefly to the classics for exemplars of patriotism and other civic virtues, they turned to the vivid stories of the Bible for heroes who personified such private virtues as charity, love, forgiveness, piety, righteousness, faith, humility, wisdom, loyalty, truthfulness, sobriety, and industriousness. Although many of these virtues were not directly related to politics, nearly all served important civic ends. No wonder that the founders considered the Bible an invaluable resource for fostering the virtue necessary to all republics.

JESUS, THE CHIEF ROLE MODEL

Raised in a profoundly Christian culture, most of the founders naturally viewed Jesus as the greatest role model. When Benjamin Franklin appealed for contributions for a new hospital in Philadelphia in 1751, he began the essay with Jesus's assurance to the saved on Judgment Day in Matthew 25:36, "I was sick and ye visited me." Franklin noted, "The great Author of our Faith, whose Life should be the constant Object of our Imitation, as far as it is imitable, shewed the greatest Compassion and Regard for the Sick; he disdained not to visit and minister Comfort and Health to the meanest of the People; and he frequently inculcated the same Disposition in his Doctrine and Precepts to his Disciples." Franklin added that one of the ways in which Jesus inculcated the virtue of charity was by telling the parable of the Good Samaritan (Luke 10:30–37), who paid for the health care of a man who had been beaten nearly to death by thieves.[1]

In 1793, in the midst of a yellow fever epidemic in Philadelphia, Benjamin Rush wrote to his wife Julia, "None of the doctors who have been ill are so far recovered as to be able to attend the sick except your husband. I am thankful for this great privilege. It is meat and drink for me to do my Master's will. He loved human life, and among other errands into our world, he came 'not to destroy men's lives but to save them'" (Luke 9:56). Rush's reference to meat and drink was taken from John 4:34, in which Jesus tells the apostles after ministering to the woman at the well that He does not need the food they have brought because doing the will of His father in heaven is His nourishment.[2]

In 1801 Thomas Jefferson referred to Jesus when he comforted Samuel Adams concerning his recent unpopularity in Massachusetts due to his support for Jefferson. After invoking the Old Testament by calling Adams "the patriarch of liberty," Jefferson added, "When I have been told that you were avoided, insulated, frowned on, I could but ejaculate, 'Father, forgive them, for they know not what they do.'" This, of course, is Jesus's plea for those who mock Him at His crucifixion in Luke 23:34.[3]

OLD TESTAMENT HEROES

The founders also admired the heroes of the Old Testament. As Poor Richard, Benjamin Franklin compared Isaac Newton to Enoch, one of the earliest and most mysterious of the patriarchs, a seventh-generation descendant of Adam and the first biblical figure with the distinction of going to heaven without dying (Elijah was the second). Genesis 5:24 states, "And Enoch walked with God, and he was not, for God took him." Hebrews 11:5 elaborates, "By faith Enoch was changed, that he should not see death, and was not found, because God changed him. For before his transformation, he had this testimony, that he pleased God." As part of Franklin's epitaph for Newton, he wrote:

> Who in the Eye of Heaven like Enoch stood,
> And thro' the Paths of Knowledge walked with God,
> Who made his Fame a Sea without a Shore,
> And but forsook one World to know the laws of more.

In 1765 Franklin noted, "The Patriarch Noah, Founder of the New World after the Flood, is called a Preacher of Righteousness. Righteousness, or Justice, is undoubtedly, of all the Virtues, the surest Foundation on which to erect and establish a new State." Franklin also wrote regarding prosperity, "Ask that blessing [of God] humbly, and be not uncharitable to those who at present seem to want it, but comfort and help them. Remember that Job suffered and was afterwards prosperous."[4]

As the progenitor of the Chosen People, Abraham was another revered figure. When Franklin introduced a new persona to dispense wisdom in *Poor Richard Improved* (1758), he named the old, white-haired character "Father Abraham."[5]

The founders often compared their leaders and nation to Moses and the Israelites at the time of the Exodus. This is a trope that can be traced back to the Puritans, who saw themselves as latter-day Hebrews crossing a great sea to escape Egyptian-style persecution at the hands of an English pharaoh. In 1776, just a few weeks before his impassioned oratory helped secure the passage of an independence resolution by the Continental Congress, John Adams was deeply affected by a sermon in which America was compared to Israel and Britain to Egypt, a sermon that "indicated strongly the Design of Providence that We should be separated from G. Britain." Adams wrote to his wife Abigail, "Is it not a saying of Moses, who am I that I should go in and out before this great People

[Exodus 3:11]? When I consider the great Events which are passed, and those greater which are rapidly advancing, and that I may have been instrumental in touching some Springs and turning some small Wheels which have had and will have such Effects, I feel an Awe upon my Mind which is not easily described." Adams regarded himself as a Moses, an unlikely man exalted by God for a crucial mission, leading his people to freedom and independence. Such a self-image must have provided tremendous motivation in the face of hardship during the long war.[6]

Soon after independence, Benjamin Franklin and Thomas Jefferson expressed a similar view of the commonality of the United States and post-exodus Israel in their proposals for the national seal. Benjamin Franklin described his proposed seal, which was based on Exodus 14:27–28: "Moses standing on the Shore, and extending his Hand over the Sea, thereby causing the same to overwhelm Pharaoh, who is sitting in an open Chariot, a Crown on his Head and a Sword in his Hand. Rays from a Pillar of Fire in the Clouds, reaching to Moses, to express that he acts by Command of the Deity. Motto: Rebellion to Tyrants is Obedience to God." Jefferson's proposal was virtually identical.[7]

Moses was among the most revered of Old Testament heroes. At the Massachusetts ratifying convention the Federalist William Phillips responded to the fear that officials under the proposed new constitution might be corrupt by contending that it was more important that the people themselves exercise virtue. He declared regarding the officials, "If they had the meekness of Moses, the patience of Job, and the wisdom of Solomon, and the people were determined to be slaves, sir, could the Congress prevent them?" In 1786 Benjamin Rush encouraged his fellow trustees of Dickinson College by depicting them all as Moses's Israelites: "The difficulties in the establishment of our College are now nearly at an end. We have passed the Red Sea and the wilderness. A few of us, it is true, have been bitten by fiery serpents in the way, but the consciousness of pure intentions has soon healed our wounds. We have now nothing but the shallow waters of the Jordan before us. One more bold exertion will conduct us in safety and triumph to the great objects of our hopes and wishes." In the 1790s, as part of James Wilson's famous series of lectures on law at the College of Philadelphia, he referred to Moses as "the first and wisest" of legislators.[8]

Federalists often compared the U.S. Constitution to the Sinai Covenant, the sacred pact between God and the Hebrew people introduced through Moses, a comparison that grew ever more popular with time. In 1797 Christopher Gadsden wrote, "As the Israelites were ordered to have the words which Moses commanded them in their hearts and to write them on the posts of their houses and on their gates [Deuteronomy 11:20], so let us imitate this injunction with our constitution, that excellent (I think) heavenly gift also, by having it hung up in the most conspicuous places in our houses." Gadsden added that Washington's Farewell Address deserved a place alongside the Constitution in American homes.[9]

The frequency of the comparison of America to post-exodus Israel only increased after the Revolution. In 1817 Thomas Jefferson wrote regarding European immigration to America, "This refuge, once known, will produce [a] reaction on the happiness even of those who remain there, by warning their task-masters that when the evils of Egyptian oppression become heavier than those of the abandonment of the country, another Canaan is open where their subjects will be received as brothers and secured against like oppressors by a participation in the right of self-government."[10]

George Washington was widely hailed as both the nation's Moses and its Joshua. In the ten weeks after Washington's death in 1799 countless eulogies compared him to many past heroes, but none more than Moses. Among the most frequently cited texts in the Washington eulogies was Deuteronomy 34, which relates the death of Moses and the mourning of the Israelites. Eulogists claimed that God caused the ancestors of Washington and Moses to move to the most fertile region of another continent to escape the scarcity of the former continent. Both were humble and patriotic men. Moses relinquished the luxury of the Egyptian court, and Washington the bliss of Mount Vernon, for their people. Both were passionate men who learned to govern their passions. Both were tested and hardened in the wilderness. Both showed courage when others faltered—Moses when cornered at the Red Sea, Washington during the most hopeless parts of the Revolutionary War—because they trusted God. Their trust was clearly merited because God saved both men repeatedly from certain death. God placed both in the seemingly hopeless situation of attempting to defeat the greatest empire of their day in order to make His own power clear to the world. Just as Moses led the Israelites to safety and freedom through a red sea, so Washington led his people to the same blessings through a sea of blood. Just as Moses was compelled to confront rebels against his authority, so Washington had to overcome a conspiracy against his command by lesser men. Each left a farewell address to guide his grief-stricken nation (Moses's was called the Book of Deuteronomy). The only differences were that Washington possessed more genuine faith than Moses because God spoke directly to Moses and not to Washington, and Washington was even more successful than Moses, who died outside the Promised Land, in contrast to Washington, who conducted his people to it. While Moses died on a mount of hope (Nebo), Washington died on a mount of possession (Vernon). Because of the latter difference, some, like William Henry Hill of South Carolina, contended that Washington was not only a Moses who rescued his people from the hands of their enslavers but also a Joshua who, as president, established them firmly in their Promised Land.[11]

William Livingston compared the love of liberty to the faith exhibited by a host of Old Testament heroes. In 1778 he declared, "The love of liberty is like the faith of the ancient patriarch. 'It subdues kingdoms, works righteousness, obtains promises, stops the mouths of lions, quenches the violence of fire, escapes the edge of the sword; it is made strong out of weakness, it waxes valiant in fight, and, lastly, it turns to flight whole armies of aliens.'" This was a paraphrase of Hebrews 11:32–34, which concerns the mighty deeds of faith performed by Gideon, Barak, Samson, Jephthae, Daniel, David, Samuel, and other prophets. Livingston added, "In a word, the empire of liberty, like the Christian religion, is founded in miracles and subdues all before it by its own intrinsic excellence, whereas the empire of despotism, like the religion of Mahomet, is founded in blood and is propagated only by fire and sword." Livingston's analogy is a prime example of American leaders' fusion of biblical imagery with Whig politics.[12]

Gideon was a model of wisdom and caution. After the rout of British General Edward Braddock's army during the French and Indian War, Benjamin Franklin proposed establishing a militia in Pennsylvania to protect the frontier from the French. He defended his Militia Act's exemption of the Quakers from compulsory military service by referring to Deuteronomy 20:8, in which God allowed the fainthearted to withdraw from the fighting, and by recalling the example of Gideon, who later did the same (Judges 7:3). Franklin argued that allowing the reluctant to refuse combat prevented the spread of fear in an army. He added, "Accordingly, we find that under this military Law, no People in the World fought more gallantly or performed greater Actions than the Hebrew

Soldiery." In opposing a petition to replace the proprietary government of the colony of Pennsylvania under the Penns with a royal government in 1764, John Dickinson cited Gideon as a model of caution. He declared, "It is scarcely possible, in the present case, that we can spend too much time in forming resolutions the consequences of which are to be perpetual. . . . Gideon, though he had conversed with an 'angel of the Lord,' would not attempt to relieve his countrymen, then sorely oppressed by the Midianites, lest he should involve them in greater miseries, until he was convinced by two miracles that he should be successful [Judges 6:11–38]. I do not say we ought to wait for miracles, but I think we ought to wait for something which will be next of kin to a miracle, I mean, some sign of a favourable disposition in the ministry towards us. I should like to see an olive leaf at least brought to us before we quit the ark." This last sentence was a reference to Genesis 8:11, in which Noah's dove returns with an olive leaf, thus signifying the receding of the flood waters and the prospect of safety on disembarking.[13]

In *Common Sense*, Thomas Paine presented Gideon as a biblical Cincinnatus, a man who surrendered power and refused to be king, the chief difference with the Roman hero being that in Gideon's case the motivating factor was piety, not republicanism. Paine wrote regarding the Israelites' offer to make Gideon a hereditary king, "Here was temptation in its fullest extent: not a kingdom only, but an hereditary one. But Gideon in the piety of his soul, replied, 'I will not rule over you, neither shall my son rule over you. The Lord shall rule over you!' [Judges 8:23]. Words need not be more explicit: Gideon doth not decline the honour but denieth their right to give it. Neither doth he compliment them with invented declarations of his thanks, but in the positive style of a prophet charges them with disaffection to their proper Sovereign, the King of Heaven."[14]

In spite of this antimonarchical trope, a few kings of Israel also served the founders as role models. One of these was David. In 1775 Benjamin Franklin wrote regarding Josiah Quincy Jr., who was stricken with tuberculosis, "His Zeal for the Public (like that of David for God's House) will, I fear, eat him up." This was a reference to Psalms 69:9: "Zeal for your house has consumed me." The following year John Witherspoon contrasted American boasting over recent victories in the Revolutionary War with the humility of David, who, in response to Goliath's taunts, made no mention of his own prowess but merely stated, "You come to me with a sword, a spear, and a shield, but I come to you in the name of the

Lord of hosts, the God of Israel's armies, whom you have defied" (1 Samuel 17:45). In an open letter to the American people in 1779, the Continental Congress likened the United States to David and Britain to Goliath. The letter stated, "Americans, without arms, ammunition, discipline, revenue, government, or ally, with 'a staff and sling' only, dared 'in the name of the Lord of Hosts,' to engage a gigantic adversary, prepared at all points, boasting of his strength, and of whom even mighty warriors 'were greatly afraid.'"[15]

Based on David's praise, the founders also admired the Israelite general Abner. In 1814, after listing George Washington's virtues and faults, Thomas Jefferson concluded, "These are my opinions of General Washington, which I would vouch at the judgment seat of God, having been formed on an acquaintance of thirty years. . . . I felt on his death, with my countrymen, that 'verily a great man hath fallen this day in Israel.'" This is David's statement regarding Abner in 2 Samuel 3:38.[16]

David's friend Jonathan personified fidelity. In 1763 John Adams vented his spleen in a letter (never sent) to his friend Jonathan Sewall, whose recently published loyalist essay Adams considered perfidious. Adams wrote the letter in the King James style, full of "thee"s and "thou"s, in order to highlight the irony in having so disloyal a friend named Jonathan. He raged, "Such senseless, such pityful Stuff and Trash I did not expect from thee, friend Jonathan."[17]

Solomon was, of course, a model of wisdom. In 1734 Benjamin Franklin wrote, "I am for taking Solomon's Advice, eating Bread with Joy, and drinking Wine with a merry heart [Ecclesiastes 9:7]. Let us rejoice and bless God that we are neither Oysters, Hogs, nor Dray-Horses, and not stand repining that He has not made us Angels, lest we be found unworthy of that share of Happiness He has thought fit to allow us." In 1763, as "Humphrey Ploughjogger," the commoner-sage, John Adams claimed that instead of writing political screeds in the newspapers, people should "study like King Solomon the Herbs, from the Cedars of Lebanon to the Hyssop in the wall" (1 Kings 4:33), though the Revolutionary crisis soon made it impossible for him to follow Solomon's practice and his own advice. While a student at Princeton considering a ministerial career in the early 1770s, James Madison chose to copy extracts from the ninth through the twentieth chapters of Solomon's Book of Proverbs into his commonplace book.[18]

In the same book of the Bible, Benjamin Franklin found a model in the person of Augur. After doing genealogical research while in London in 1758, Franklin noted, "I am the youngest Son of the youngest Son . . . for five generations, whereby I find that had there originally been any Estate in the Family, none could have stood a worse Chance for it. God, however, has blest me with Augur's Wish, and what is still more with Augur's Temper, for which double Blessing I desire to be ever thankful." This was a reference to Proverbs 30:7–9, in which Augur asks God, "Two things have I required of you; do not deny me them before I die. Remove far from me vanity and lies. Give me neither poverty nor riches; feed me with food convenient for me, lest I be full and deny you and say, 'Who is the Lord?' or lest I be poor and steal, and take the name of my God in vain." Even at a stage in life in which Franklin had risen to considerable wealth, he still envisioned himself as an Augur, a man who had sought and received the quintessentially American blessing of a middle-class status.[19]

Franklin often quoted from and praised the Book of Proverbs. In an essay called "The Way to Wealth" in 1757, he quoted Proverbs 22:7, "The Borrower is a Slave to the Lender." In 1779 he wrote approvingly of Congress's intention to mint copper coins and "to put on one Side some important Proverb of Solomon, some pious, moral, prudential, or economical Precept, the frequent Inculcation of which by seeing it every time one receives a Piece of Money might make an Impression upon the Mind, especially of Young Persons, and tend to regulate the Conduct, such as on some, 'The Fear of the Lord is the Beginning of Wisdom'" (Proverbs 1:7). In 1782, when Henry Laurens congratulated Franklin on having been selected as an American peace commissioner and noted Jesus's blessing of peacemakers in Matthew 5:9, Franklin replied, "The Blessing promised to Peace Makers, I fancy, relates to the next World, for in this they seem to have a greater Chance of being curst." Franklin added that he was nonetheless thankful that he was not the only commissioner and made this reference to Proverbs 11:14: "And as another Text observes, 'In the Multitude of Counsellors there is Safety,' which I think may mean Safety to the Counsellors as well as to the Counselled, because if they commit a Fault in Counselling, the Blame does not fall on one." The following year Franklin quoted Proverbs 3:16–17 in his advice to a friend of his grandson: "You have a great many [years] before you, and their being happy or otherwise will depend much on your own Conduct. If by diligent Study now, you improve your Mind and practice carefully hereafter the Prompts of Religion & Virtue, you will have in your favour the Promise respecting the Life that now is, as well as that which is to come. You will possess true Wisdom, which is nearly allied to Happiness: 'Length of Days are in her right hand, and in her left hand Riches & Honours; all her Ways are Ways of Pleasantness, and all her Paths are Peace!'" This was one of Franklin's favorite proverbs. Decades earlier he had inscribed it in the "little book" dedicated to his own personal moral improvement. Indeed, it is no accident that Franklin referred to the maxims he composed in the guise of Poor Richard as "proverbs." He saw himself as a latter-day, rustic Solomon providing the American public with practical and moral instruction.[20]

Solomon played a prominent role in an exchange of humorous letters between Franklin and the philosopher David Hume. On Franklin's departure from London in 1762, Hume wrote, "I am very sorry that you intend soon to leave our Hemisphere. America has sent us many good things, Gold, Silver, Sugar, Tobacco, Indigo, & c. But you are the first Philosopher and indeed the first Great Man of Letters for whom we are beholden to her; it is our own Fault that we have not kept him. Whence it appears that we do not agree with Solomon that Wisdom is above Gold [Proverbs 16:16]. For we take care never to send back an ounce of the latter which we once lay our Fingers upon." Franklin replied, "Your Compliment of Gold and Wisdom is very obliging to me but a little injurious to your Country. The various Value of everything in every Part of the World arises, you know, from the various Proportions of the Quantity to the Demand. We are told that Gold and Silver in Solomon's Time were so plentiful as to be of no more Value in his Country than the Stones in the Street [2 Chronicles 1:15]. You have here at present just such a Plenty of Wisdom. Your People are therefore not to be censured for desiring no more among them than they have, and if I have any, I should certainly carry it where from its Scarcity it may probably come to a better Market."[21]

In "Thoughts upon Female Education" (1787) Benjamin Rush contrasted the foolishness of "modern writers" with the wisdom of Solomon, the author of Proverbs 31, regarding the proper estimation of women. Rush noted, "The former confine their praises chiefly to personal charms and ornamental accomplishments, while the latter celebrates only the virtues of a valuable mistress of a family and a useful member of society." Rush then contrasted the women thus praised: "The one is perfectly acquainted with all the fashionable languages of Europe; the other 'opens her mouth with wisdom' [verse 26] and is perfectly acquainted with all the uses of the needle, the distaff, and the loom [v. 19]. The business of one is pleasure; the pleasure of the other is business. The one is admired abroad; the other is honored and beloved at home. 'Her children arise up and call her blessed, her husband also, and he praiseth her' [v. 28]. There is no fame in the world equal to this, nor is there a note in music half so delightful as the respectful language with which a grateful son or daughter perpetuates the memory of a sensible and affectionate mother."[22]

The founders also admired the prophets and other faithful Jews of the prophetic era. In 1809, on retiring from political life at the end of his presidential administration, Thomas Jefferson replied to a message from the inhabitants of his Virginia county welcoming him home by quoting from the prophet Samuel's remarks at the time of his own retirement (1 Samuel 12:3): "Of you, then, my neighbors, I may ask, in the face of the world, 'Whose ox have I taken, or whom have I defrauded? Whom have I oppressed, or of whose hand have I received a bribe to blind mine eyes therewith?' On your verdict I rest with conscious security." In 1771 Samuel Adams likened the patriots to the seven thousand faithful Jews to whom God referred when Elijah complained that he was alone (1 Kings 19:18). Adams declared, "We hope and believe, nay we know, that there are more than seven thousand who will never bow the knee to Baal, or servilely submit to Tyranny, temporal or spiritual." In 1816 Benjamin West's painting, *Benjamin Franklin Drawing Electricity from the Sky*, depicted Franklin as a latter-day Elijah surrounded by angels while drawing fire from heaven (1 Kings 18:38). In 1791 Benjamin Rush wrote to Elhanan Winchester, "Go on, my dear sir, with your researches into the true meaning of the Scriptures. Your works, however much neglected or opposed now, will be precious to those generations which are to follow us, and, like the bones of Elisha, will perform miracles after your death." This was a reference to 2 Kings 13:21, in which a deceased man is resurrected when his corpse touches the bones of Elisha after being cast into the prophet's sepulcher. Twenty years later Rush compared himself to Jeremiah, a prophet who was persecuted because of his boldness in speaking the truth. Rush wrote to John Adams, "To the defects in the temper and the conduct of the illustrious reformer [Martin Luther] I heartily subscribe, but I think there is a character in the Old Testament which more nearly accords with mine. It is that of the prophet Jeremiah. I shall give it to you in his own words [Jeremiah 15:10]: 'Woe is me, my mother, that thou hast borne me, a man of strife and a man of contention to the whole earth. I have neither lent on usury nor have men lent to me on usury, yet every one of them doth curse me.'"[23]

Benjamin Franklin was so steeped in the Bible that one wonders whether it influenced some of the tales in his own autobiography. For instance, Franklin's story of his early employment at a printing house, a time in which he proved to his fellow workers by his own example that his practice of drinking water rather than beer with meals was not only more economical but also more productive of good work, is startlingly similar to the story told in Daniel 1:7–16, in which the prophet proves to the chief eunuch of the Persian king that his diet of water and vegetables is superior to the prescribed diet of wine and (non-kosher) meat. Most readers in Franklin's day would have recognized the similarity in the stories and would have been obliged to envision the young Franklin as a Daniel, a (literally) sober, frugal, hardworking, and pious youth.[24]

The founders often referred to Micah 4:4, which prophesied regarding the reign of the Messiah, a reign that Christians equated with the Millennium of Christ's rule: "Every man will sit under his vine and under his fig tree, and none shall make him afraid." In 1779, while in France, Benjamin Franklin wrote to Thomas Viny, who wished to immigrate to America from Europe, "When all the Bustle [of the Revolutionary War] is over, if my short Remainder of Life will permit my Return thither, what a Pleasure it will be to me to see my old Friend and his Children settled there. I hope he will find Vine and Fig trees there for all of them, under which we may sit and converse, enjoying Peace & Plenty, a good Government, good Laws & Liberty, without which Men lose half their Value." Two years later John Jay referred to the same scripture, writing, "I am confident that Liberty and Independence will sooner or later be firmly established and should I live to see that blessed Day, I think if I know my own Heart, I shall return with inexpressible Pleasure to dwell securely and happily under the Shade of my Vine and Fig Tree."[25]

Micah 4:4 was George Washington's favorite verse, the imagery reminding him of the natural pleasures of his beloved estate, Mount Vernon. He used the "vine and fig tree" reference nearly four dozen times during the latter half of his life. Like other Federalists, Washington often cited the millennial verse as something he hoped could be achieved through the Constitution. He claimed, "When the people shall find themselves secure under an energetic government, when foreign nations shall be disposed to give us equal advantages in commerce free from the dread of retaliation, when the burdens of the war shall be in a manner done away with by the sale of western lands, when the seeds of happiness which are sown here shall begin to expand themselves, and when everyone (under his own vine and fig tree) shall begin to taste the fruits of freedom, then all these blessings (for all these blessings will come) will be referred to the fostering influence of the new government." As president in 1790, Washington wrote to a Jewish congregation in Newport, Rhode Island, "May the Children of the Stock of Abraham [Acts 13:26] who dwell in this land continue to merit and enjoy the good will of the other Inhabitants, while every one shall sit in safety under his own vine and fig tree, and there shall be none to make him afraid." In 1797 alone, newly released from the rigors of the presidency and enjoying his retirement, Washington used the phrase "under my own Vine and Fig tree" or "seated in the shade of my Vine and Fig tree" in at least six different letters. The references continued almost until the time of his death. Washington was not prone to quoting literary works of any kind, so his repeated use of the phrase indicates that its imagery touched a strong chord within him, speaking of the peace, rest, and natural beauty that his home represented, blessings that his public service had denied him for so many years. To Washington, Mount Vernon was a foretaste of the Millennium.[26]

NEW TESTAMENT HEROES

Following George Washington's death in 1799, he was eulogized throughout the nation. One hundred thirteen of the 120 scriptural texts cited in published eulogies of Washington were in the Old Testament. There were several reasons for this disparity between the use of the Old and New Testaments in early American political rhetoric. First, since the Old Testament is significantly longer than the New, it furnished political leaders with a great deal more material. Second, while the New Testament focuses on individual salvation, the Old Testament is, to a great extent, the story of a nation. Thus, the latter was more useful in the founders' political discourse than the former, especially since many Americans considered their nation the new Israel. It was only natural to compare Washington to other military and political leaders, of which the Old Testament furnished many, the New Testament virtually none. Third, by the late eighteenth and early nineteenth centuries there was a long American tradition, going back to the early Puritans and other Calvinist settlers, of focusing on the Old Testament. Center Protestant sermons tended to emphasize the holiness and justice of God over His love and mercy. Both sets of qualities were essential—if God were not holy and just, one could not respect Him, and if He were not loving and merciful, one could not love Him—but in tension, since justice involves giving someone his due while mercy involves giving him better than his due. Although both testaments portray God as possessing these qualities, the Old Testament clearly emphasizes the former set, while the New highlights the latter. Therefore, Calvinist ministers, whose sermons provided the template for biblical references employed by early American political leaders, judged the Old Testament particularly useful. While the emphasis would soon change due to the Second Great Awakening, many late eighteenth- and early nineteenth-century preachers and the politicians they influenced were still operating on the basis of a long tradition.[27]

Yet it would be a grave mistake to minimize the New Testament's importance to the founders. First, as heirs to a Christian heritage almost two millennia old, the founders viewed the Old Testament through the prism of the New. Second, as we shall see later, the founders drew from the New Testament beliefs regarding the nature of virtue, the afterlife, and other matters that possessed not only great personal significance but also political implications.

Jesus was not the only New Testament figure whom the founders admired. In 1782 Benjamin Franklin likened himself to Simeon, the elderly Jew who praised God after seeing the Christ child in the temple. He wrote, "I am now entering my 78th Year. Public Business has engrossed fifty of them. I wish now to be, for the little time I have left, my own Master. If I live to see this Peace concluded, I shall beg leave to remind the Congress of their Promise then to dismiss me. I shall be happy to sing with Old Simeon, 'Now letteth thou thy Servant Depart in Peace, for mine Eyes have seen thy Salvation'" (Luke 2:29–30). In a letter to Thomas Jefferson regarding the Constitution, Christopher Gadsden also identified himself with Simeon: "I bless God to have lived to see this important Point in so fair a Way to be accomplish'd & if I live to see it compleatly so, I shall be apt to cry out with old Simeon, 'Now may thy Servant depart in peace, for mine Eyes have seen thy Salvation.'" Jefferson must have liked the reference because he reportedly murmured on his deathbed, "Lord, now letteth thy servant depart in peace."[28]

In the third paragraph of *Letters from a Farmer in Pennsylvania* (1767–1768) John Dickinson used the poor widow Jesus praised for putting all of the money she had (two mites—coins of extremely low value) into the collection plate (Mark 12:42–44) as a metaphor for himself, a humble person overcoming doubts about his own adequacy to contribute to the Revolutionary debate. Dickinson wrote, "As a Charitable but poor Person does not withhold his Mite because he can not relieve all the Distresses of the Miserable, so let not any honest Man suppress his Sentiments concerning Freedom, however small their Influence is likely to be. Perhaps he may touch some Wheel that will have a greater Effect than he expects." Dickinson's mite was only the second most influential pamphlet of the American Revolution (after *Common Sense*). In 1783 George Washington advised his nephew, "Let your heart feel for the affliction and distresses of everyone, and let your hand give in proportion to your purse; remember always the estimation of the Widow's mite."[29]

The woman who anointed the head of Jesus was another role model. In commiserating with John Adams over their political failures, Benjamin Rush noted, "'She did all that she could' [Mark 14:8] was once both the acquittal and the praise of a pious woman in the New Testament, and pronounced too by those lips which must finally decide the merit and demerit of all human actions. They are full of consolation to those who have aimed well." Rush added that he appreciated the response of a friend to his lament that so many of his reform efforts had failed: "Remember that your Saviour at the day of judgment will not say, 'Well done, thou successful, but well done, thou faithful servant' [Matthew 25:21]. You have been faithful, Doctor, and that is enough."[30]

Thomas Jefferson found role models even in Jesus's parables. He considered the Prodigal Son's father an exemplar of forgiveness and the son himself a model of repentance. In writing to a friend who was estranged from his son, Jefferson declared, "Persuaded that a reconciliation with your son would tend much to the quiet of your mind, it would give me particular pleasure to learn that he could see the duty he is under of 'arising and going unto his father and saying, father I have sinned' & c.

and that you had fallen on his neck and kissed him" (Luke 15:18–20). In decrying the raging animosity of political partisans Jefferson identified himself with the Good Samaritan, writing, "Sincerely the friend of all the parties, I ask of none why they have fallen out by the way, and would gladly infuse the oil & wine of the Samaritan into all their wounds" (Luke 10:33–34).[31]

Most of the founders admired Paul. In 1782, when advising preachers in an essay on eloquence, John Witherspoon praised the apostle for possessing the humility to lay aside his impressive rhetorical training in order to preach the gospel in a simple fashion so that it could be understood by ordinary folk and so that God might be exalted rather than Paul. The same year Henry Laurens wrote to Benjamin Franklin regarding the apostle, "He was a very sensible Man and much of a Gentleman, who said, if our hopes are confined to this Life, we should be of all Men the most miserable [1 Corinthians 15:19]. He was an Ambassador too [Ephesians 6:20]. The observation was strong but full of encouragement and with proper Modification may be fairly adopted by every honest Man of the diplomatic Corp[s]." Franklin was the American minister to France at the time.[32]

Early Christians served as models of unity. As "Fabius," John Dickinson compared the unity of the early church with the kind of cohesion he wished to see in the United States, a unity that would be fostered by the more powerful federal government created by the proposed Constitution. He wrote, "How beautifully and forcefully does the inspired Apostle Saint Paul argue upon a sublimer subject. . . . His words are: 'If the foot shall say, because I am not the hand, I am not of the body, is it therefore not of the body?' . . . His meaning is enforced by his description of the benefits of union in these expressions: 'But now there are many members, yet but one body; and the eye cannot say to the hand, I have no need of thee; nor again, the head to the feet, I have no need of you'" (1 Corinthians 12:15, 20–21). Just as Paul had characterized individual Christians as parts of a single organism (the body of Christ) that must work together for the common good, so Dickinson suggested that the American states must join together to form a healthy political organism. In the process Dickinson implicitly compared the Anti-Federalists, with their narrow focus on state interests, to the selfish Christians to whom Paul directed his appeal, both groups denying their connection and obligations to the larger union.[33]

THE MINGLING OF HEROES

Since the founders regarded the sixty-six books of the Bible as a single entity, it is not surprising that they often mingled role models from the Old and New Testaments, just as they regarded the classical tradition as a single entity and thus often combined Greek and Roman heroes that were centuries apart. As Poor Richard, Benjamin Franklin plumbed the depths of the whole Bible to present exemplars of hard work and the divine rewards it received. In 1756 he wrote, "God has often called Men to Places of Dignity and Honour when they have been busy in the honest Employment of their Vocation. Saul was seeking his Father's Asses, and David keeping his Father's Sheep, when called to the Kingdom. The Shepherds were feeding their Flocks when they had their glorious Revelation. God called the four Apostles from their Fishery, and Matthew from the Receipt of Customs, Amos from the Herdsmen of Tekoah, Moses from keeping Jethro's Sheep, and Gideon from the Threshing Floor & c. God never encourages Idleness, and despises not Persons in the meanest Employments."[34]

Benjamin Rush derived models of patriotism from both testaments. In 1773, when attempting to rally the public in the midst of the Revolutionary crisis, Rush declared that patriotism was "both a moral and a religious duty," since it constituted a love of, and a willingness to sacrifice for, future generations. He continued:

> The holy men of old, in proportion as they possessed a religious were endowed with a public spirit. What did not Moses forsake and suffer for his countrymen? What shining examples of Patriotism do we behold in Joshua, Samuel, Maccabeus, and all the illustrious princes, captains, and prophets among the Jews! St. Paul almost wishes himself accursed for his countrymen and kinsmen after the flesh [Romans 9:3–4]. Even our Saviour himself gives a sanction to this virtue. He confined his miracles and gospel at first to his own country. He wept at the prospect of her speedy dissolution [Luke 19:41–44], and even after she had imbrued her hands in his blood, he commanded his Apostles to begin the promulgation of his gospel at Jerusalem [Acts 1:8]. I might go on farther and show that this benevolent virtue sometimes goes beyond humanity and extends itself to the very soil that gives us birth. Joseph charged his brethren with his last breath to inter his bones in his own country [Genesis 50:25].[35]

THE SIGNIFICANCE OF BIBLICAL VILLAINS

In addition to the numerous heroes whom the founders encountered in the Bible, they also discovered a rich collection of villains who served as equally useful object lessons in their political discourse. While the classical political horror stories in which the founders were steeped left them fearful of conspiracies against liberty launched by ambitious individuals, the Bible not only illustrated the nature and consequences of ambition but also highlighted the dangers to society posed by other vices. To Caesar and Catiline were added a plethora of biblical villains.

SATAN, THE CHIEF VILLAIN

The most despised figure in the Bible was, of course, Satan, a frightful figure in whose literal existence many of the founders believed. These founders considered him both the chief opponent of goodness and the principal enemy of freedom. In 1767 John Adams wrote regarding liberty, "The world, the flesh, and the devil have always maintained a confederacy against her, from the fall of Adam to this hour, and will probably continue so till the fall of the Antichrist." In an essay signed "A Puritan," Samuel Adams claimed, "I could not help fancying that the Stamp Act itself was contrived with a design only to inure the people to the habit of contemplating themselves as the slaves of men, and the transition from thence to a subjection to Satan is mighty easy." Adams liked to use serpent imagery when discussing British threats as a way of marking the enemy as Satanic. While he compared the Stamp Act to "Job's Sea Monster," Leviathan (Job 41), a dreadful danger but one whose size provoked preparedness, he worried more about smaller but more insidious threats, such as revenue bills disguised as trade regulation measures, which he likened to serpents: "The lurking Serpent lies concealed, & not noticed by the unwary Passenger, darts its fatal Venom. It is necessary that each Colony should be awake and upon its Guard."[36]

In 1772 Benjamin Franklin, angered by what he considered a slanderous attack on the physician Sir John Pringle by his rival, Sir William Browne, wrote to Browne, "Heretofore, therefore, your Malevolence has done no great Mischief. But for your Life, stir not a Foot farther in this Dangerous Road. When a Man once gives the Devil leave to guide him, there is no knowing how far he may be led." When Franklin wrote to George Washington after the general's victory at Yorktown, he compared George III to a demoniac and Lord North and his cohorts to the possessing demons: "I have heretofore congratulated your Excellency on your Victories over the Enemy's Generals. I can now do the same on your having overthrown their Politicians. Your late Successes have so strengthened the hands of the Opposition in Parliament that they are become the Majority and have compelled the King to dismiss all his old Ministers and their Adherents. The unclean Spirits he was possessed with are now cast out of him; but it is imagined that as soon as he has obtained a Peace, they will return with others worse than themselves, and 'the last State of that Man,' as the Scripture says, 'shall be worse than the first.'" This was a reference to Jesus's statement in Matthew 12:43–45: "When the unclean spirit leaves a man, he goes through dry places, seeking rest, and finds none. Then he says, 'I will return to my house whence I came.' And when he comes, he finds it empty, swept, and clean. Then he goes and brings with himself seven other spirits more wicked than he, and they enter in and dwell there, and the last state of that man is worse than the first."[37]

In 1776 General Charles Lee, who was recovering from gout and fever, wrote to George Washington, "God preserve you, my Dear General, from all disorders, at least until we have trampled Satan under our feet." The following year Thomas Paine compared British General William Howe, who was offering peace proposals, to Satan whispering "the delusion softly" to Eve. (He later used the same analogy of "the serpent that beguiled Eve" to refer to the Federalists whom he claimed persuaded Aaron Burr to oppose Thomas Jefferson for the presidency.) In 1778, on hearing rumors that the supporters of Horatio Gates were trying to secure his replacement of Washington as commander of the Continental Army, Edward Rutledge wrote to John Jay, then president of the Congress, expressing the fear "that a damned, infamous Cabal is forming against our Commander in Chief and that whenever they shall find themselves strong enough, they will strike an important Blow." He added, "I give you this Hint that you may be on your Guard, and I know you will excuse me for doing so when you recollect that there are some Men of our Acquaintance who are in the Possession of all the Qualities of the Devil, his Cunning not excepted." That same year, Governor William Livingston of New Jersey, who was facing reelection, noted, "I stand some chance of seeing my family at last, and perhaps the Devil and the Tories may so manage their cards at the ensuing Election that I may have no avocation to leave it in [the] future." George Mason wrote regarding the new American republic, "I trust that neither the Power of Great Britain nor the Power of Hell will be able to prevail against it." This was a reference to Matthew 16:18, in which Jesus states that the "gates of hell shall not prevail against" the church. In Virginia in 1779 Richard Henry Lee wrote concerning French Admiral d'Estaing and British soldiers, "I am satisfied that nothing else but his being here will prevent our being visited this Fall by these Devils (for I can call by no other name Men desperate in evil) from N. York."[38]

The founders sometimes portrayed their adversaries as sin itself. In 1776 Christopher Gadsden referred to the opponents of his independence resolution in the South Carolina legislature as "the old leaven," a reference to 1 Corinthians 5:6–7 in which the apostle Paul uses the phrase as a metaphor for sin. Urging the Corinthians to expel from their church a member who had committed adultery with his own stepmother, Paul writes, "Do you not know that a little leaven leavens the whole lump? Therefore, purge out the old leaven that you may be a new lump." Paul then referred to the Jewish Feast of Unleavened Bread, on which day Jesus, having taken all of humanity's sin of upon Himself, had lain in the grave, thus taking sin out of the world: "For even Christ, our Passover lamb, is sacrificed for us. Therefore, let us keep the feast, not with the old leaven, neither with the leaven of malice and wickedness, but with the unleavened bread of sincerity and truth." In 1784 Richard Henry Lee used the same phrase when complaining about the British restriction of American trade with their islands in the West Indies: "It is not difficult for an attentive and diligent enquirer to discern the old Leaven working in the British councils. The same men still rule in secret."[39]

During the constitutional debates, Federalists often attempted to link the Anti-Federalists to the devil. Under the pseudonym "America," the Federalist Noah Webster addressed Anti-Federalists as follows: "Obstinacy is the leading trait in your public characters, and, as it serves to give consistency to your actions, even in error, it cannot fail to procure you that share of respect which is paid to the firmness of Satan and his fellow apostates, who, after their expulsion from Heaven, had too much pride to repent and ask for re-admission." Meanwhile, Joseph Barrell claimed that the Anti-Federalist "Vox Populi" (Voice of the People) should have called himself "Vox Diaboli."[40]

The allusions to Satan continued long after the constitutional period. In 1793 Benjamin Rush wrote regarding the French Reign of Terror, "Let us not despair. Chaos existed before the order and beauty of the universe [Genesis 1:2]. The devil, who is the present tenant of our world, will not quit his hold of it till he has done the premises all the mischief that lies in his power, but go he must, sooner or later." Twelve years later Rush contended that distilled liquors "produce not only falsehood but fraud, theft, uncleanliness, and murder." He added, "Like the demoniac mentioned in the New Testament [Mark 5:9], their name is 'Legion,' for they convey into the soul a host of vices and crimes." Near the end of his life, while composing a final statement of advice for his country, James Madison became concerned by the talk of disunion spawned by the Nullification Crisis in South Carolina. Madison mingled classical and Christian symbols of mayhem: "The advice nearest my heart and deepest in my convictions is that the Union of the States be cherished and perpetuated. Let the open enemy of it be regarded as a Pandora with her box opened, and the disguised one as the Serpent creeping with his deadly wiles into Paradise."[41]

JUDAS, THE RUNNER-UP

The second most detested biblical figure was Judas, the betrayer of Jesus. In his famous "Liberty or Death" speech in 1775, Patrick Henry declared regarding "that insidious smile with which our petition has been lately received" by the British government, "Trust it not, sir; it will prove a snare to your feet. Suffer not yourselves to be destroyed with a kiss." This was, of course, a reference to Judas's betrayal of Jesus in the Garden of Gethsemane (Luke 22:48). In 1781 Benjamin Franklin made the inevitable comparison of Benedict Arnold with Judas, though concluding that the former was even more wicked and foolish than the latter: "Judas sold only one Man, Arnold three millions; Judas got for his one Man 30 Pieces of Silver [Matthew 26:15], Arnold not a halfpenny a Head. A miserable Bargainer, Especially when one considers the Quantity of Infamy he has acquired to himself & entailed on his Family."[42]

OLD TESTAMENT VILLAINS

Adam and Eve, whose sin had brought calamity to all of humankind, personified the foolishness inherited by their descendants, who refused to learn from their error. In 1787 John Adams cited the first couple when writing to Thomas Jefferson regarding the human propensity to be ruled by passion rather than learning from the mistakes of others: "Lessons, my dear Sir, are never wanting. Life and History are full. The Loss of Paradise by eating a forbidden apple has been many Thousand years a Lesson to Mankind, but not much regarded."[43]

The builders of Babel exemplified confusion. In his final speech at the Constitutional Convention in 1787, Benjamin Franklin declared regarding the Constitution, "I think it will astonish our enemies who are waiting with confidence to hear that our councils are confounded like those of the builders of Babel, and that our states are on the point of separation—only to meet hereafter for the purpose of cutting one another's throats."[44]

Sodom and Gomorrah were famous for their wickedness and the divine judgment it provoked. In 1778 Thomas Paine compared those Americans who would even consider the British proposal that they join with Britain in waging war against France, then the United States' ally, to the citizens of those infamous cities. Paine wrote, "We are invited to submit to a man who has attempted by every cruelty to destroy us and join him in making war against France, which is already at war against him for our support. Can Bedlam, in concert with Lucifer, form a more mad and devilish request? Were it possible a people could sink into such apostasy they would deserve to be swept from the earth like the inhabitants of Sodom and Gomorrah."[45]

Esau was reviled for showing contempt for his birthright by selling it to his brother Jacob for a bowl of porridge (Genesis 25:29–34), a food early Americans (and the King James Version) referred to as "pottage." The New York constitutional convention of 1776 issued a statement that included these lines: "If then God hath given us freedoms, are we not responsible to him for that as well as other talents? If it is our birth-right, let us not sell it for a mess of pottage, nor suffer it to be torn from us by the hand of violence." In 1811 Thomas Jefferson identified monarchs as Esaus: "A people having no king to sell them for a mess of pottage for himself, no shackles to restrain the power of self-defence, find resources within themselves equal to every trial. This we did during the revolutionary war and this we can do again, let who will attack us, if we act heartily with one another."[46]

Joseph's brothers, who sold him into slavery, were likened to those who would betray their country for financial gain. In 1775 John Adams compared the loyalists to the famous brothers, but added this charitable line: "However, what the sons of Israel [Jacob's other name] intended for ruin to Joseph proved the salvation of his family; and I hope and believe that the whigs will have the magnanimity, like him, to suppress their resentment and the felicity of saving their ungrateful brothers." This was a reference to Genesis 50:20, in which Joseph tells his brothers, "You intended evil for me, but God meant it for good," since Joseph's enslavement ultimately led to his premiership in Egypt, which, in turn, allowed him to feed his whole family in a time of famine.[47]

The founders detested the Egyptians of the Book of Exodus who oppressed their Hebrew slaves. Benjamin Franklin may have been the first American of the Revolutionary era to draw what would become a commonplace American analogy between these Egyptians and the British. After the news of British General James Wolfe's victory over the French at the Battle of Quebec in the French and Indian War reached London, where Franklin was staying, he was shocked to find a few British observers proposing the return of Canada to the French in order to keep the American colonies dependent on British protection. In an essay in the *London Chronicle*, Franklin asked, "Is it not too like the Egyptian Politics practiced by Pharaoh, destroying the young males to prevent the increase of the children of Israel?" The analogy was important because it reflected Franklin's view that the British and Americans were already distinct peoples in 1759. In 1770 Franklin compared the British policy of ordering Americans to pay taxes in coinage while refusing to allow them to print money, a policy that created a shortage of currency in the colonies, to the Egyptian policy of forcing the Hebrews to make bricks without straw (Exodus 5:6–19). As one of the three American commissioners to France in 1778, Franklin was probably responsible for yet another comparison of Britain to Egypt. When recommending the acceptance of the Treaties of Alliance with France as essential to American independence and liberty, the commissioners wrote, "Our People are happy in the Enjoyment of their new Constitutions of Government, [and] Will be so in their extended Trade and Navigation, unfettered by English Acts and Customhouse Officers. They will now never relish the Egyptian Bondage from which they have so happily escaped."[48]

Franklin was far from being the sole employer of this analogy. Samuel Adams compared British officials to the pharaoh of the Book of Exodus but concluded that they were even worse because the pharaoh had at least made a pretense of listening to complaints. He asked, "Are not the Ministry lost to all Sensibility to the people's complaints & like the Egyptian Tyrant, do they not harden their Hearts against the repeated Demands for a redress of Grievances? Does it not fully appear not only that they neither fear God nor regard Man, but that they are not even to be wearied, as one of their ancient predecessors was, by frequent Applications?" By 1776 Adams had begun comparing the king himself unfavorably to the pharaoh: "It is my opinion that his heart is more obdurate, and his Disposition towards the People of America is more unrelenting and malignant, than was that of Pharaoh towards the Israelites in Egypt."[49]

Patrick Henry often employed the Egyptian analogy. In 1775 someone reported concerning a Henry speech that inflamed a group of Virginia volunteers:

> He had no doubt, he said, that that God who in former ages had hardened Pharaoh's heart that he might show forth his power and glory in the redemption of his chosen people had, for similar purposes, permitted the flagrant outrages which had occurred at Williamsburg [Lord Dunmore's seizure of ammunition] and throughout the continent. It was for them now to determine whether they were worthy of this divine interference; whether they would accept the high boon now held out to them by heaven—that if they would, though it might lead them through a sea of blood, they were to remember that the same God whose power divided the Red Sea for the deliverance of Israel still reigned in all his glory, unchanged and unchangeable—was still the enemy of the oppressor and the friend of the oppressed—that he would cover them from their enemies by a pillar of cloud by day and guide their feet through the night by a pillar of fire [Exodus 13:21].

Three years later, worried about those Americans who sought reunification with Britain, Henry wrote to Richard Henry Lee, who was facing opposition to his bid for reelection to Congress, "For God's sake, my dear sir, quit not the councils of your country until you see us forever disjoined from Great Britain. The old leaven still works. The flesh pots of Egypt are still savoury to degenerate palates." The last sentence was a reference to Exodus 16:3, in which the Israelites say to Moses and Aaron in the wilderness, "Would to God that we had died by the hand of the Lord in the land of Egypt, when we sat by the flesh pots and when we ate bread until we were full." In 1782 Edmund Randolph wrote regarding the British smuggling of goods into the United States and their lying about it, "The stratagems used for the insinuation of British goods are doubly wicked, in the attempt to corrupt us with the flesh-pots of Egypt and in fortifying those attempts by the infamous outworks of perjury." Note that American leaders felt no need to explain references to "the old leaven" and "flesh pots" in their letters because they assumed that their readers possessed a thorough knowledge of the Bible.[50]

The Egyptians remained useful villains during the constitutional debates as well. Writing in the *Maryland Journal*, Anti-Federalist Luther Martin declared that the Articles of Confederation, however flawed, was superior to the Constitution, prophesying regarding the latter's ratification, "Should the citizens of America, in a fit of desperation, be induced to commit this fatal act of political suicide . . . the day will come when labouring under more than Egyptian bondage, compelled to furnish their quota of brick, though destitute of straw and mortar, galled with your chains and worn down by oppression, you will, by sad experience, be convinced (when that conviction shall be too late) that there is a difference in evils, and that the buzzing of gnats is more supportable than the sting of a serpent." But in the same journal the Federalist "Unicus" turned the analogy back against an Anti-Federalist essayist: "The Centinel is far more unreasonable than the Egyptian task-masters; they demanded brick without straw, but the Israelites could possibly collect stubble for a substitute. He growls that 'Congress have power to lay and collect taxes, duties, imposts, and excises' without providing even stubble for a substitute." It was unreasonable to expect Congress to fund the federal government without some form of taxation, Unicus insisted.[51]

The founders also criticized unfaithful Israelites of the exodus. Benjamin Rush later recalled that, in 1777, John Adams told him, "I have been distressed to see some of our members [of Congress] disposed to idolize an image which their own hands have molten. I speak of the superstitious veneration which is paid to General Washington." This, of course, was a reference to those Israelites who formed and worshipped the golden calf in the wilderness (Exodus 32:4). The following year William Livingston contended, "The people of America are not yet prepared to enter upon the enjoyment of the blessings of peace and liberty. They were, you know, the fag end of an old rotten monarchical empire, and they have not as yet expiated the political and moral iniquities they contracted by their intimate union with their mother country. They have many things to unlearn, as well as to learn, before they arrive at the full stature of perfect freemen. Some of them, it is true, relish the manna of the wilderness, but too many of them look back with a desire upon the leeks and onions of Egypt." This was a reference to Numbers 11:5, in which the Israelites complain to Moses in the desert, "We remember the fish that we freely ate in Egypt, as well as the cucumbers, the melons, the leeks, the onions, and the garlic." Four years later, Samuel Adams worried that, far from establishing the Christian Sparta he desired, Americans would continue to import British luxury goods and thus continue to be servants of the British pharaoh, a practice that "would gratify those among us who are still hankering after the onions of Egypt and would sacrifice our great cause to the desire of gain." Similarly, Robert R. Livingston worried that some Americans might be so demoralized by the loss of lucrative trade with the British West Indies that they might even consider reunion with Britain. In 1782 he claimed, "The Merchants and Farmers, if excluded at a peace from the advantages which this commerce gave them while connected with England, will consider themselves as losers by the War and pine again for the Fleshpots of Egypt."[52]

As the essayist "K," Benjamin Franklin implicitly likened the Anti-Federalists to those Israelites who rejected Moses and his divinely prescribed Law. He referred to a story "recorded in the most faithful of all histories, the Holy Bible," the account relating the refusal of many Hebrews to accept a constitution that came from God Himself via national heroes: "One would have thought that the appointment of men who had distinguished themselves in procuring the liberty of their nation and had hazarded their lives in openly opposing the will of a powerful monarch, who would have retained that nation in slavery, might have been an appointment acceptable to a grateful people; and that a constitution fram'd for them by the Deity himself might on that account have been secure of a universal welcome reception, yet there were in every one of the thirteen tribes, some discontented restless spirits who were continually exciting them to reject the proposed new government." Note Franklin's reference to thirteen tribes in Israel instead of the biblical twelve, a common form of revisionist accounting by Americans eager to promote the analogy between the United States and Israel that involved splitting the tribe of Joseph into the sub-tribes of Manasseh and Ephraim, Joseph's two sons. Here Franklin constructs an implicit analogy not only between the Law of Moses and the Constitution, both divinely inspired, but also between two sets of national heroes—Moses and Aaron, on the one hand, and Washington and Franklin, on the other—as well as between the Egyptian and British oppressors from which both sets of heroes freed their peoples through divine assistance. Franklin then speculated that some of the Israelite dissenters had been motivated by personal ambition, and others by an excessive regard for the independence of their own tribe, thereby suggesting an analogy between these wicked Israelites and the Anti-Federalists. Franklin shrewdly added that some Israelites undoubtedly complained that Moses's meetings with God, the meetings that resulted in the Law, were secretive—a clear reference to the Anti-Federalist complaint about the secrecy of the deliberations at the Constitutional Convention.[53]

The pagans whom the Israelites encountered when they entered the Promised Land provided other cautionary tales. As punishment for the Gibeonites, who lied to the Israelites in order to obtain a nonaggression treaty with them, the Israelites condemned them to hew wood and draw water for them (Joshua 9). Thus, in 1782, Benjamin Franklin complained about his duty, as American minister to France, to serve as a conduit for funds to other American representatives in Europe, writing, "This has, among other things, made me quite sick of my Gibeonite office, that of drawing water for the Congregation of Israel." At the Connecticut ratifying convention Oliver Ellsworth warned that unless the United States formed a stronger central government, it would suffer the fate of the Canaanites, whom the Israelites conquered: "Witness the Canaanitish nations, whose divided situation rendered them an easy prey."[54]

Samson exemplified the loss of power, seduction by a wicked woman, and self-destruction. In 1771 Samuel Adams compared Thomas Hutchinson to the mighty man, writing regarding the loyalist, "Should he once lose his Reputation which his friends have with the utmost pains been building for him among the Clergy for these thirty years past as a consummate Saint, he must fall like Samson when his Locks were cut off." In 1778 Thomas Paine likened Britain to Samson and America to his hair. Paine wrote to the British that, by waging a foolish war against the

American colonies, they had destroyed their own mystical aura of invincibility, just as Samson deprived himself of his invincibility by revealing his secret to Delilah. Paine claimed, "Unwise as you were in breaking the charm, you were still more unwise in the manner of doing it. Samson only told the secret, but you have performed the operation; you have shaven your own head and wantonly thrown away the locks. America was the hair from which the charm was drawn that infatuated the world." The same year William Livingston conceded that Sarah Yard, who was suspected of aiding the enemy, might be innocent, as many believed, but added, "I also believe that Adam was deceived by Eve and that Delilah got the better of Samson."[55]

At the Massachusetts ratifying convention the Reverend Samuel Stillman sought to calm the fears of Anti-Federalists by saying, "Should Congress ever attempt the destruction of the particular [state] legislatures, they would be in the same predicament with Samson, who overthrew the house in which Philistines were making sport at his expense; them he killed indeed, but he buried himself in the ruins" (Judges 16:23–30). In 1796 Thomas Jefferson wrote to Philip Mazzei regarding the infiltration of the federal government by men Jefferson regarded as supportive of monarchy and aristocracy, "It would give you a fever were I to name to you the apostates who have gone over to these heresies, men who were Samsons in the field and Solomons in the council, but who have had their heads shorn by the harlot England." In Jefferson's mind England was Delilah, seducing Federalist Samsons into "apostasy" and "heresy" against republicanism, and thus destruction. This private letter was published without Jefferson's permission the following year, thereby creating a scandal because some considered George Washington the chief Samson in the field to whom Jefferson referred.[56]

Even as a youth, Jefferson, who had a difficult relationship with his mother, was moved by the image of Samson as a man who foolishly trusted a deceitful woman. Douglas L. Wilson, the editor of Jefferson's literary commonplace book, has written, "At the age of about 16 or 17 he took a long, careful look at [John] Milton's Samson [in the *Samson Agonistes*]. It is evident from the uncharacteristically large number of extracts from a single work that the sufferings of Samson—the futility of strength without wisdom, the sense of being alone, and of being deeply troubled and in despair, of suffering at the hands of a woman—somehow spoke to the young student and were still meaningful in some wise to the grown man who, many years later, decided to preserve them." Particularly striking was this passage regarding women copied by the adolescent:

> Is it for that such outward Ornament
> Was lavish'd on their Sex, that inward Gifts
> Were left for Haste unfinished, judgment scant,
> Capacity not rais'd to apprehend
> Or value what is best
> In Choice, but oftest to affect the Wrong?
> Or was too much of Self-Love mix'd,
> Of Constancy no Root infix'd,
> That either they love Nothing or not long?

This misogynistic reading of the story of Samson owed more to Milton than to the biblical account, which, while certainly portraying Delilah in a negative light, also depicts Samson as little better than a deranged thug.[57]

Samson's nemeses, the Philistines, were useful villains as well. In 1771 Samuel Adams compared the British government to these pagans. He wrote regarding the Stamp Act crisis, "The Sons of Liberty, animated with a zeal for their country then upon the brink of destruction, and resolved at once to save her, or, like Samson, to perish in the ruins, exerted themselves with such vigor as made the house of Dagon [the Philistine god] to shake from its very foundation, and the hopes of the lords of the Philistines, even while their hearts were merry and when they were anticipating the joy of plundering this continent, were at that very time buried in the pit they had dug." In *The Rights of Man*, Thomas Paine replied to Edmund Burke's reference to aristocracy as "the Corinthian capital of polished society" by saying, "Whenever a nation chuse to act a Samson, not blind, but bold, down will go the temple of Dagon, the Lords and the Philistines."[58]

The Israelites who cried out for a king against the will of God in 1 Samuel 8 became crucial villains during the Revolution. In that chapter God details the tyranny that the Israelites will suffer as a result of getting their wish for a monarch, a list of hardships that includes military conscription, the confiscation of their property, corruption, and oppression. In 1651 John Milton used this passage to justify the new republican government established following the overthrow of King Charles I in the English Civil War. The English republican martyr Algernon Sidney did the same. In 1776 Thomas Paine devoted a quarter of *Common Sense*, more space than any other line of argument, to the contention that God hated monarchy, employing 1 Samuel 8 as his principal text. Paine declared:

> Government by kings was first introduced into the world by the Heathens, from whom the children of Israel copied the custom. It was the most prosperous invention the Devil ever set on foot for the promotion of idolatry. . . . The will of Almighty God, as declared by Gideon and the prophet Samuel, expressly disapproves of government by kings. . . . And when a man seriously reflects on the idolatrous homage which is paid to the persons of kings, he need not wonder that the Almighty, ever jealous of his honour, should disapprove a form of government which so impiously invades the prerogative of Heaven. Monarchy is ranked in scripture as one of the sins of the Jews, for which a curse in reserve is pronounced against them.

The Israelites "wanted to be like unto other nations, i.e., the Heathens, whereas their true glory lay in being as much unlike them as possible." Paine hammered home the point: "But where, say some, is the King of America? I'll tell you, friend, he reigns above and doth not make havoc of mankind like the Royal Brute of Great Britain." Between 75,000 and 150,000 copies of Paine's pamphlet were sold, an unprecedented number in that era.[59]

Paine's antimonarchical interpretation of 1 Samuel 8 was crucial to securing American independence. The colonists had been trained from the time they were children to revere the king as a father figure, based on the traditional equation of the nation with the monarch. So deeply ingrained was this worldview that it would take more than Paine's depiction of the king as a monster to secure popular support for independence. It required nothing short of convincing pious Americans that God Himself was a republican. While the classics were marshaled to prove that government without a king not only was possible but also could be gloriously successful, as it had been in the Greek and Roman republics, the Bible was utilized to demonstrate to a Christian society that such a republic was divinely ordained, while monarchy labored under a divine curse. Soon joined by other advocates of independence, Paine argued that the fact that a few kings, like David and Solomon, had won the favor of the Lord as individuals did not negate divine disapproval of the system as a whole, a system that by elevating a single person to heights of power and glory encouraged an idolatrous worship of that monarch. It was ironic, of course, that the antimonarchical interpretation of 1 Samuel 8 should come to the American people most influentially through a man who would later write a book attacking the authority of scripture, but there is no indication that, however Paine's views on the Bible changed, he ever strayed from the sincere belief that monarchy violated the will of God. In *Common Sense*, Paine succeeded in replacing the concept of the divine right of kings with the doctrine of the divine favor of republics.

The Anti-Federalists later used the same argument in opposition to the new constitution's creation of the office of the presidency, which they depicted as establishing a form of monarchy. As "A Countryman," De Witt Clinton, later the governor of New York, noted that the "Israelites did not trust in the promises which were made by their heavenly Father through his holy prophets; they were restless under the government which was appointed over them by the Almighty; they were fickle and fond of changing; they were ambitious and wanted to appear respectable abroad; they must be like all the nations, have a king to judge them . . . and they accepted Saul, the son of Kish, for a king, the history of whose wicked reign I need not relate to you." Clinton added, "O my dear sir, we ought to be much in prayer with God, lest the same temper which seems to prevail too much at this day among many of us should bring down upon our land some heavy judgment, for to me it appears as if there is a rod in soak for us." Under the pseudonym "A Columbian Patriot," Mercy Otis Warren wrote regarding most Americans, "They deprecate discord and civil convulsions, but they are not yet generally prepared with the ungrateful Israelites to ask for a King, nor are their spirits sufficiently broken to yield the best of their olive grounds to his servants [1 Samuel 8:14], and to see their sons appointed to run before his chariots" (verse 11). At the New York ratifying convention Melancton Smith cited 1 Samuel 8 on the folly of the Israelites in blaming "their constitution" and the "Divine Ruler" who imparted it to them for ills that "were brought upon them by their own misconduct and imprudence" and in demanding a king. Smith followed this with Samuel's prophecy regarding the tyranny that would result from monarchy.[60]

Goliath symbolized evil on a massive scale. At the New York ratifying convention the Anti-Federalist Thomas Tredwell likened the proposed new federal constitution to the wicked giant. Tredwell declared, "I have the fullest confidence that the God who has so lately delivered us out of the paw of the lion and the bear will also deliver us from this Goliath, this uncircumcised Philistine." Tredwell's reference was to 1 Samuel 17:36, in which David reassures Saul just before killing the giant, "Your servant slew both the lion and the bear [that came after my father's sheep], and this uncircumcised Philistine will be as one of them, seeing that he has defied the armies of the living God."[61]

Solomon's kingdom was divided shortly after his death because his son Rehoboam followed bad advice and treated his subjects with contempt (1 Kings 12). In 1753, writing for a committee of the Pennsylvania Assembly, Benjamin Franklin complained about the poor government of the colony by its proprietors, the descendants of the beloved William Penn. Franklin implicitly compared Penn to Solomon and Penn's descendants to Solomon's son Rehoboam: "Our sincere Regard for the Memory of our first Proprietor must make us apprehend for his Children, that if they follow the Advice of Rehoboam's Counsellors, they will, like him, absolutely lose at least the Affections of their People." The "at least" constituted a thinly veiled threat, since the policy of Rehoboam had provoked rebellion and secession.[62]

When Solomon's kingdom was divided, the ten northern tribes followed Jeroboam, who instructed his subjects to worship two golden calves (1 Kings 12:28). In 1771 Samuel Adams compared his nemesis, the loyalist Governor Thomas Hutchinson, to Jeroboam and Massachusetts's loyalist clergymen to the corrupt Jewish priests who followed him. Adams wrote that Jeroboam had been "a very wicked governor" whom the people followed because he was "born and educated among them," a clear reference to Hutchinson's popularity as the first native governor since the British had begun appointing the colony's governors nearly a century earlier. Adams asked, "Are we not fallen into an age when some even of the Clergy think it no shame to flatter the idol, and thereby to lay the people, as in the days of Jeroboam, the son of Nebat, under a temptation to commit great wickedness and sin against God?" Adams rather improbably likened the loyalist clergymen's praise of Hutchinson to actual idolatry, thereby converting the governor into both the wicked king and the idol.[63]

In his famous "liberty or death" speech of 1775 Patrick Henry linked those who clung to illusions of peace with Great Britain to the false prophets of Israel who deceived the people with delusions of peace with Babylon. According to Edmund Randolph, "Henry with indignation ridiculed the idea of peace 'when there was no peace' and enlarged on the duty of preparing for war." This was a reference to Jeremiah 6:14 in which the prophet condemns "those who cry, 'Peace, peace,' when there is no peace." Thus, Henry not only portrayed his loyalist adversaries as false prophets but also took on the mantle of Jeremiah, whose fiery tone he emulated.[64]

NEW TESTAMENT VILLAINS

The founders encountered villains in the New Testament as well. For instance, the Pharisees exemplified hypocrisy and legalism. In 1772 Benjamin Franklin published an essay in the *London Chronicle* in which he urged the British government to outlaw the foreign slave trade in its dominions. Noting the English people's happiness over the freeing of the runaway slave James Somersett, Franklin declared, "Pharisaical Britain! To pride thyself in setting free a single Slave that happens to land on thy coasts, while thy Merchants in all thy ports are encouraged by thy laws to continue a commerce whereby so many hundreds of thousands are dragged into a slavery that can scarce be said to end with their lives, since it is entailed on their posterity!" In 1788 Samuel Osgood expressed to his fellow Anti-Federalist Samuel Adams the fear that if the Constitution were adopted, "the Scribes & Pharisees only will be able to interpret it to give it a Meaning." At the New York ratifying convention the Anti-Federalist Thomas Tredwell declared, "It appears to me that in forming this Constitution, we have run into the same error which the Pharisees of old were charged with; that is, while we have secured the tithes of mint, anise, and cumin, we have neglected the weightier matters of the law: judgment, mercy, and faith." While the Constitution catered to "the paltry local interests of some of the individual states," it confounded justice by giving excessive power to the newly established, distant, unaccountable federal courts. Tredwell's statement was a reference to Matthew 23:23, in which Jesus exclaims, "Woe unto you, scribes and Pharisees, hypocrites! For you pay a tithe of mint and anise and cumin, but have omitted the weightier matters of the law: judgment, mercy, and faith." Although the Pharisees followed the letter of the Mosaic Law so strictly that they tithed even the produce of their gardens, their arrogant behavior contradicted the spirit of the Law. The Federalist "A Friend to Honesty" countered that the Anti-Federalists were the real Pharisees because behind their high-sounding arguments against the Constitution lay their real motivation: a desire to escape the payment of state debts. He declared, "O ye Pharisees! Who profess such a religious concern for the welfare of your country, and of posterity, but pay no regard to the injustice and oppression publicly practiced before your eyes against our public creditors and the scandal brought upon us as a nation thereby."[65]

Closely allied with the Pharisees were the experts in the Mosaic Law. After criticizing the "sophisms" of Chief Justice John Marshall and other jurists, Thomas Jefferson wrote, "May we not say then with Him who was all candor and benevolence, 'Woe unto you, ye lawyers, for ye lade men with burdens grievous to bear.'" This reference to Jesus's statement in Luke 11:46 was a rather odd one coming from Jefferson, a former attorney.[66]

The corrupt people who followed Jesus after His miracle of multiplying the loaves and fishes merely because they wanted free meals were exemplars of greed. To these Jesus said (John 6:26), "Very truly, I tell you, you seek me not because you saw the miracles but because you ate of the loaves and were filled." In 1813 John Adams claimed, "The real terrors of both Parties have always been, and now are, the fear that they shall lose the Elections and consequently the Loaves and Fishes, and that their Antagonists will obtain them."[67]

When appealing for contributions for a new hospital, Benjamin Franklin invoked the rich man who was tormented in hell in Luke 16:19–23: "The rich Man is represented as being excluded from the Happiness of Heaven because he fared sumptuously every Day and had Plenty of Things and yet neglected to comfort and assist his poor Neighbour, who was helpless and full of Sores and might perhaps have been revived and restored with small care by the Crumbs that fell from his Table."[68]

The Antichrist was one of the most famous biblical villains. Many Federalists believed that Napoleon was the Antichrist, which was one reason they opposed the War of 1812 against his enemy, Britain, so ardently. Elias Boudinot even published a book, *The Second Advent*, that identified Napoleon as the Antichrist. The book's publication was poorly timed, however, coming in the same year (1815) as Napoleon's final fall from power.[69]

Just as the founders acquainted themselves with the numerous virtues that were vividly portrayed in the Bible's compelling stories, they also encountered numerous vices there. These vices included cruelty, dishonesty, greed, selfishness, folly, infidelity, pride, idolatry, lust, and hypocrisy. However personal these vices were, they would surely bring destruction on the nation's political fabric if practiced by a sufficient number of its citizens. Thus, the founders took care to warn the public against their destructiveness by pointing to universally recognized biblical narratives.

4

DIVINE INTERVENTION

An abundance of documentary evidence found in both the public and the private papers of the founders refutes the popular misconception that "the founders were deists," at least if "deism" is used in the conventional manner to include a belief in divine noninterference. On the contrary, all of the founders embraced the biblical concept of an omniscient, omnipotent, caring God who not only created the universe but also intervened in it. They believed that the Creator invested each individual with inalienable rights and guided the affairs of individuals, societies, and nations to enforce those rights, as well as to advance other goods necessary to human happiness. The work of this "divine Providence" was mysterious. A few of the founders believed that God carried out His will through natural causes alone, but most were willing to speak of miracles. The founders' belief in a caring, intervening God led them to affirm the efficacy of prayer and thus to call for public as well as private prayer. They found ways of reconciling their belief in such a God with the various misfortunes that befell them and their families, friends, and nation, sometimes attributing these hardships to divine judgment against sin and at other times to God's remarkable capacity to bring good out of evil.

CONFIDENCE IN DIVINE PROVIDENCE

The Bible is one long record of divine intervention. Immediately after the sin of Adam and Eve in the Garden of Eden, God, rather than wash His hands of humanity, begins a program of damage control and repair that includes saving a righteous family from the judgment of the Great Flood, establishing a Chosen People through the seed of Abraham, and finally, in the New Testament, assuming human form and dying for humanity's sin. This wise and loving form of divine intervention was as unknown to Greco-Roman religion, whose gods were interventionist but limited in knowledge and capacity (they could be fooled and manipulated), selfish, and capricious, as it was to most of classical philosophy, whose divine entities (the Platonic Good, the Aristotelian Prime Mover, the Stoic World Soul, the Epicurean gods, and the Neoplatonic One) were impersonal forces that did not concern themselves with individuals and their lives.[1]

Immersed in scripture from their childhoods, the founders often expressed confidence in divine Providence. Sometimes these expressions took the form of direct attacks on deism, a philosophy then fashionable in European intellectual circles. Despite the fact that Benjamin Franklin is often labeled a deist, he was one of the attackers. As early as 1732, in an essay "On the Providence of God in the Government of the World," after attempting to prove the existence of a God of great wisdom, goodness, and power, Franklin took direct aim at deism, declaring, "There can be no Reason to imagine he would make so glorious a Universe merely to abandon it." Franklin added that it was unthinkable that the same God who had been so good as to create such a wonderful universe, filled with so many benefits to His creatures, would sit idly by while the virtuous struggled and implored his aid, only to receive the response, "I do not intermeddle in these affairs," or "I cannot help you, 'tis none of my Business, nor do I at all regard these things." Franklin continued, "How is it possible to believe [that] a wise and infinitely Good Being can be delighted in this Circumstance and can be utterly unconcerned what becomes of the Beings and Things he has created? . . . That Being which, from its Power is most able to Act, from its Wisdom knows best how to act, and from its Goodness would almost certainly act best is, in this Opinion, supposed to become the most inactive of all Beings and remain everlastingly Idle." Rather, Franklin was convinced that God "sometimes interferes by His particular providence and sets aside the effects which would otherwise have been produced by . . . causes." Twenty-five years later Franklin reiterated, "The same great Power that made the Universe governs it by his Providence." He insisted, "Without the belief in a Providence that takes Cognizance of, guards and guides, and may favour, particular Persons, there is no Motive to Worship a Deity, to fear its Displeasure, or to pray for its Protection."[2]

In his autobiography Franklin recalled that although he had rebelled against the teaching of his pious parents at the age of fifteen and had briefly become a deist, he had soon became so appalled by the behavior of the deists he knew that he decided that a philosophy that produced such poor results could not be valid. He came to the conclusion that the Bible prohibited certain behaviors because they were bad for people and encouraged others because they were good for them. Recalling this change in his outlook, Franklin wrote, "And this persuasion, with the kind hand of Providence, or some accidental favourable circumstances and situations, or all together, preserved me (thro' this dangerous time of youth and the hazardous situations I was sometimes in among strangers, remote from the eye and advice of my father) without any willful, gross immorality or injustice that might have been expected from my want of religion." Although conceding that he rarely went to church even after he abandoned deism, Franklin continued:

> I never was without some religious principles. I never doubted, for instance, the existence of the Deity, that he made the world and governed it by his providence, that the most acceptable service of God was the doing of good to man, that our souls are immortal, and that all crime will be punished and virtue rewarded either here or hereafter. These I esteemed the essentials of every religion, and being found in all the religions we had in our country, I respected them all. . . . This respect to all, with an opinion that [even] the worst had some good effects, induced me to avoid all discourse that might tend to lessen the good opinion another might have of his own religion; and, as our province increased in people and new places of worship were continually wanted and generally erected by voluntary contribution, my mite for such purpose, whatever might be the sect, was never refused.

In 1790, the final year of his life, Benjamin Franklin repeated, "Here is my Creed. I believe in one God, Creator of the Universe. That he governs the World by his Providence."[3]

Another founder who is often labeled a deist but whose writings contradicted its tenet of divine nonintervention was Thomas Jefferson. In his own day Jefferson was often criticized for his alleged deism or even atheism by his political opponents, and some historians, myself included, have in the past been led to believe that Jefferson was a deist by two of his rhetorical quirks. The first was his use of the term "deism" as a synonym for Unitarian monotheism, as when he referred approvingly to the ancient Hebrews' "Deism, that is, their belief in only one God." Since Jefferson was an ardent monotheist—so ardent that he could not accept the doctrine of the Holy Trinity—he sometimes wrote enthusiastically about "deism," but this praise had nothing to do with the issue of divine intervention. Jefferson's other misleading rhetorical habit was his praise for Epicureanism, one of whose cardinal doctrines was divine nonintervention—misleading because Jefferson's praise of the philosophy focused on its materialist ontology and resultant rejection of miracles, not on its doctrine of divine noninterference. In other words, the principal influence of Epicureanism on Jefferson was in furthering his belief that God worked in the world through natural causes alone.[4]

In 1823 Jefferson was emphatic in refuting the doctrine of divine noninterference. He declared, "When we take a view of the Universe, in its parts general or particular, it is impossible for the human mind not to perceive and feel a conviction of design, consummate skill, and indefinite power in every atom of its composition. . . . It is impossible, I say, for the human mind not to believe that there is, in all this, design, cause and effect, up to an ultimate cause, a fabricator of all things from matter and motion, their *preserver* and *regulator* while permitted to exist in their present forms, and their *regenerator* into new and other forms" (emphases added). Jefferson then elaborated on this reference to the need for a Preserver, Regulator, and Regenerator as well as a Creator: "We see too evident proofs of the necessity of a superintending power to maintain the Universe in its course and order. Stars, well known, have disappeared; new ones have come into view; comets, in their incalculable courses, may run afoul of suns and planets and require renovation under other laws; certain races of animals are become extinct; and were there no restoring power, all existences might extinguish successively, one by one, until all should be reduced to a shapeless chaos."[5]

Other founders also rejected deism for belief in an interventionist Creator. In the Massachusetts Constitution of 1780 John Adams wrote that it was the duty of all people to worship "the Supreme Being, the great creator and *preserver* of the universe" (emphasis added) in the manner of their own choosing. Forty years later he wrote that whenever he considered stars, planets, moons, and comets, "I feel an irresistible impulse to fall on my knees in Adoration of the Power that moves, the Wisdom that *directs*, and the Benevolence that Sanctifies this wonderful whole" (emphasis added). To Adams, God was more than just a First Cause but a wisdom that continually preserved and directed the universe. In his law lectures at the University of Pennsylvania in 1790–1791, attended by President George Washington, Vice President John Adams, and Secretary of State Thomas Jefferson, James Wilson twice referred to God as not only "the Author" but also "the Preserver" of the universe.[6]

In his later years Patrick Henry was a severe critic of deism, including Thomas Paine's attack on the Bible in *The Age of Reason*, which Henry categorized as a deist work. In 1796 Henry wrote to his daughter Elizabeth:

> The view which the rising greatness of our country presents to my eye is greatly tarnished by the general prevalence of deism, which with me is but another name for vice and depravity. I am, however, much consoled by reflecting that the religion of Christ has, from its first appearance in the world, been attacked in main by all the wits, philosophers, and wise ones aided by every power of man, and its triumph has been complete. . . . The puny efforts of Paine are thrown in to prop this tottering fabric, whose foundations cannot stand the test of time. Amongst other strange things said of me, I hear it said by the deists that I am one of their number; and indeed that some good people think I am no Christian. The thought gives me much more pain than the appellation of tory, because I think religion of infinitely higher importance than politics; and I find much cause to reproach myself that I have lived so long and have given no decided proofs of my being a Christian. But, indeed, my dear child, this is a character I prize far above all this world has or can boast.

Henry even penned a reply to *The Age of Reason*, though he destroyed it after reading Richard Watson's *Apology for the Bible*, which he considered a better work than his own. Having paid to have another of his favorite books that refuted deism, Soame Jenyns's *View of the Internal Evidence of the Christian Religion*, reprinted, Henry personally distributed several hundred copies.[7]

Benjamin Rush often attacked deism. As early as 1769, Rush wrote, "The many artful attacks which have been made upon Christianity by the Deistical writers in England, instead of lessening its credibility, have tended rather to establish it by drawing forth some of the most learned publications in its defense which have ever appeared upon any subjects whatever." Thirty years later he singled out the core of the deist philosophy, Epicurus's doctrine of divine noninterference, for refutation. The physician argued that "the continuance of animal life, no less than its commencement [is] the effect of the constant operation of divine power and goodness, [which] leads us to believe that the whole creation is supported in the same manner." The following year he added reprovingly, "Deism [is] derived from partiality to Greek and Roman writers—morality enough supposed to be found in them."[8]

Numerous other expressions of the founders' confidence in divine Providence were equally clear without referring explicitly to deism. In 1776 the Declaration of Independence concluded with a famous example of such an expression: "For the support of this Declaration, with a firm reliance on the protection of divine Providence, we mutually pledge to each other our lives, our Fortunes, & our sacred Honour." The phrase regarding Providence was not written by Thomas Jefferson; it was instead proposed by an unknown delegate from the floor of Congress, which approved its insertion. But it accorded with a firm belief in divine intervention shared by all the founders, including Jefferson. In 1814 Jefferson declared regarding God, "Our efforts are in his hand, and directed by it, and he will give them their effect in his own time."[9]

No other founder so continually espoused the biblical theme of divine intervention than George Washington. From the time that Washington's coat was riddled with bullet holes and he had two horses shot out from under him without his being so much as scratched while serving under British General Edward Braddock at the Monongahela River during the French and Indian War, he possessed a strong conviction that God shielded him. Just a few days after Washington's narrow escape from death, he wrote that he had survived because of "the miraculous care of Providence that protected me beyond all human expectation." More surprisingly, this same belief concerning God's protection of Washington arose among his fellow citizens at precisely the same time. Tales of the Virginian's bravery and survival having spread rapidly throughout the colonies, the revivalist preacher Samuel Davies referred in a sermon to "that heroic Youth, Colonel Washington, whom I cannot but hope Providence has hitherto preserved in so signal a Manner for some important Service to his Country," an opinion that was later hailed as a prophecy.

Washington was quite sincere when he wrote in 1776, "No Man has a more perfect Reliance on the all-wise and powerful dispensations of the Supreme Being than I have, nor thinks his aid more necessary."[10]

From the outset of his military career, Washington saw the hand of Providence in both defeat and victory. In fact, Washington saw it as clearly in Braddock's defeat as in his own survival, writing, "It's true we have been beaten—most shamefully beaten—by a handful of Men who only intended to molest and disturb our March. Victory was their smallest expectation, but see the wondrous works of Providence, the uncertainty of Human things!" The following year Washington wrote with a palpable sense of relief regarding his journey to northwestern Virginia with thirty militiamen, "With this small company of Irregulars, with whom order, regularity, circumspection, and vigilance were matters of derision and contempt, we set out; and by the protection of Providence, reached Augusta Courthouse in 7 days without meeting the enemy; otherwise we must have fallen a Sacrifice thro' the indiscretion of these hooping, halloing Gentlemen-Soldiers."[11]

When Washington learned that the Second Continental Congress had appointed him commander of the Continental Army in 1775, he wrote to his wife Martha from Philadelphia:

> It has been determined in Congress that the whole Army raised for the defence of the American Cause shall be put under my care and that it is necessary for me to proceed immediately to Boston to take upon me the Command of it. You may believe me, my dear Patsy, when I assure you in the most solemn manner that, so far from seeking the appointment, I have used every endeavour in my power to avoid it, not only from my unwillingness to part with you and the Family, but from a consciousness of its being a trust too great for my Capacity. . . . But, as it has been a kind of destiny that has thrown me upon this Service, I shall hope that my undertaking of it is designed to answer some good purpose. . . . I shall rely, therefore, confidently on that Providence which has heretofore preserved & been bountiful to me.

Five days later he reiterated to her, "I go, fully trusting in that Providence which has been more bountiful to me than I deserve." Two months later he wrote to his brother, "I am now to thank you, which I do most sincerely & cordially for your Affectionate wishes & prayers. The goodness of the cause bids me hope for protection & I have a perfect reliance upon that Providence which heretofore has befriended & Smiled upon me." Three years later, his army having survived appalling conditions at Valley Forge, he wrote from there, "Providence has a . . . claim to my humble and grateful thanks for its protection and direction of me."[12]

In 1784, the year after the conclusion of the war, Washington claimed, "I feel now . . . as I conceive a wearied Traveler must do, who, after treading many a painful step, with a heavy burden on his shoulders, is eased of the latter, having reached the Goal to which all the former were directed, and from his House top is looking back, and tracing with a grateful eye the Meanders by which he escaped the quicksands and Mires which lay in his way, and into which none but the All-powerful guide and great disposer of human Events could have prevented his falling."[13]

Five years later, upon becoming the first president of the United States, Washington depended on Providence for support in the monumental task of creating a federal government virtually from scratch. He declared, "I know the delicate nature of the duties incident to the part which I am called to perform, and I feel my incompetence without the singular assistance of Providence to discharge them in a satisfactory manner." To the officials of Wilmington, Delaware, he wrote, "Heaven and my own heart are witnesses for me with how much reluctance I have yielded to that persuasion [to assume the presidency]. But a sense of duty, in my conception, ought to supersede every personal consideration, and the promises of support which I am daily receiving from my fellow citizens, together with a reliance upon that gracious Providence which sustained us through our struggle for Liberty, encourage me (notwithstanding a diffidence in my own abilities) to hope for a happy issue from my present arduous undertaking." In his seventh annual address to Congress in 1795 Washington reported, "I have never met you at any period when more than at present the situation of our public affairs has afforded just cause for congratulation and for inviting you to join me in profound gratitude to the Author of all good for the numerous and extraordinary blessings we enjoy." A year before he died, after expressing concern about the admission of his grandson, George Washington Custis, into a cavalry unit because of his status as an only son, Washington added quickly, "But the same Providence that would watch over and protect him in domestic walks can extend the same protection to him in a Camp, or the field of battle, if he should ever be in one."[14]

Benjamin Rush possessed the same confidence in divine Providence. In 1762, during the French and Indian War, he saw the hand of God in the British capture of Havana, writing to Ebenezer Hazard, "I admire your pious and grateful adorations to the Supreme Being for the success of our forces at Havana. Let you and I (while the wild mob proclaim their enthusiastic joy in frantic acclamations) cry out perpetually in our hearts, 'Glory to God in the Highest' [Luke 2:14]. How apt are we to extol the prudence and moderation of a general and the bravery and resolution of the soldiery, but how little do we eye the finger of God in our most glorious and important events. 'Tis God that steels the gallant soul! 'Tis God that inspires with martial courage. 'Tis God that teaches our hands to war and our fingers to fight! 'Tis God that rules, protects, commands, and governs all. Glory to God in the Highest!" Three years later, he exulted, "Happy the man that by a steady reliance upon divine providence can give his cares to the wind, humbly trusting that the supreme and omnipotent Being who first called him into existence will never withdraw the protection of his almighty arm from him that lives by a lively faith upon his attributes." In 1767 Rush wrote regarding John Witherspoon, who was then considering the presidency of the College of New Jersey, "May that Providence which has formed him with such great endowments, and which I trust directed the eyes of the College towards him, remove all obstructions from out of his way and make the path of duty clear before him." In 1778 Rush credited God with saving him from death by a bilious fever he caught from a patient, a fever that left him incapacitated for eleven days. In 1797 he contended, "The affairs of nations as well as of individuals are under the direction of a wise and just Providence." In his autobiography (1800) Rush recalled, "With all the folly and indiscretions of my life, with all the odium to which my opinions in medicine, politics, and religion exposed me, and with all the pecuniary defalcations which have been mentioned [his expenditure of 10,000 pounds for the patriot effort in the Revolution], I believe I did more business, and with more profit, between the years of 1769 and 1800 than any contemporary physician in Philadelphia. Thus it is [that] the providence of God often blesses men in spite of themselves and finally protects them from the evils to which an adherence to the dictates of their judgments and well meant endeavours to promote knowledge and public happiness expose them." In 1809 Rush wrote in his commonplace book, "This day my wife and daughter Julia returned from Canada. In traveling 1500 miles by land and water, they were not once in any real danger nor even alarmed with any supposed danger, nor was either indisposed a day during their absence. What cause of gratitude and praise to the Giver of all good!"[15]

In a 1776 sermon John Witherspoon declared that divine Providence extended even "to things the most indifferent and inconsiderable." He cited Jesus's statement in Matthew 10:29–30 that a sparrow cannot fall to the ground without God's notice, and that even the hairs on a person's head are numbered. But far more impressive to Witherspoon was God's repeated humiliation of the devil by outwitting him on every front and using the devil's machinations to fulfill His own plans for human salvation, both physical and spiritual. Witherspoon cited as evidence for this conclusion the fact that the wicked Haman was hanged on the same gallows that he had prepared for Mordecai in Esther 7:10. But even more impressive was God's use of the devil's assassination of Jesus as the means for the salvation of souls. Witherspoon declared, "From the New Testament I will make choice of that memorable event on which the salvation of believers in every age rests as its foundation, the death and sufferings of the Son of God. This the great adversary and all his agents and instruments prosecuted with unrelenting rage. When they had blackened him with slander, when they had scourged him with shame, when they had condemned him in judgment and nailed him to the cross, how could they help esteeming their victory complete? But oh the unsearchable wisdom of God! They were but perfecting the great design laid for the salvation of sinners. Our blessed Redeemer by his death finished his work, overcame principalities and powers, and made a show of them openly, triumphing over them in this cross" (Colossians 2:15). God was the master chess player who easily checkmated Satan, not only during the time of Jesus but also repeatedly thereafter, for God then used the devil's persecution of the church as a mechanism for its growth. Witherspoon declared, "Persecution has been but as the furnace to the gold, to purge it of its dross, to manifest its purity, and increase its luster. It was taken notice early that the blood of the martyrs was the seed of Christianity; the more abundantly it was shed, the more plentiful did the harvest grow." Persecution not only purified the church but also led to the flight of believers, thereby spreading Christianity further. Thus, Witherspoon concluded, biblical and subsequent history taught one to have complete faith in divine wisdom, which was infinitely superior to both human wisdom and that of fallen angels.[16]

Benjamin Franklin's confidence in the wisdom and goodness of God was crucial to his trust in Providence. Looking back on his life in his autobiography, Franklin wrote regarding God, "I owe the mentioned happiness of my past life to his divine providence, which led me to the means I used and gave them success. My belief of this induces me to hope, though I must not presume, that the same goodness will still be exercised towards me in continuing that happiness or in enabling me to bear a fatal reverse, which I may experience as others have done—the complexion of my future fortune being known to him only, and in whose power it is to bless us even in our afflictions."[17]

In 1781, while serving as an officer in the Continental Army, Alexander Hamilton wrote to his wife Elizabeth, "I hope my beloved Betsy will dismiss all apprehensions for my safety; unhappily for public affairs, there seems to be little prospect of activity, and if there should be, Heaven will certainly be propitious to any attachment so tender, genuine, as ours. Heaven will restore me to that bosom of my love and permit me to enjoy with new relish the delights which are centered there." Hamilton was mistaken about the prospects for activity; four months later he would play a prominent role in the patriot victory at the Battle of Yorktown. In 1799 George Washington referred to Hamilton's and his own shared belief in divine intervention when writing to him about recent military decisions with which both men disagreed: "But I have the same reliance on Providence which you express, and trust that matters will end well, however unfavourable they may appear at present."[18]

Other founders expressed the same reliance on Providence. In 1775 Samuel Adams wrote to his wife, "I will endeavor by God's Assistance to act my little part well, and trust everything which concerns me to his all-gracious Providence." Five years later he exhorted his daughter's fiancé Thomas Wells to thank God for "the hourly Protection he affords us." In 1794 John Jay wrote to his wife regarding his appointment by President Washington to negotiate a treaty with Britain, "I feel the impulse of duty strongly. . . . I ought to follow its dictates and commit myself to the care and kindness of that Providence in which we both have the highest reason to repose the most absolute confidence." A few days later he expressed the hope that it would "please God to make me instrumental in the continuance of peace and in preventing the effusion of blood and other evils and miseries incident to war." He added, "God's will be done; to whom I resign, in whom I confide. Do the like. Any other Philosophy applicable to this occasion is delusive. Away with it." In 1821 James Monroe declared in his Second Inaugural Address, "With a firm reliance on the protection of Almighty God, I shall forthwith commence the duties of the high trust to which you have called me."[19]

Confidence in divine intervention did not lead to laziness but rather to greater zeal in the fulfillment of duties due to the feeling of hope it inspired. Thus, the founders' expressions of faith in Providence often took the form of admonitions to do one's duty and leave the rest to God. In 1770, while serving as the representative of several colonies in London and under pressure from the government of Lord North to support his colonial policies, Franklin wrote to his sister, "My rule in which I have always found Satisfaction is never to turn aside in Publick Affairs thro' Views of private Interest, but to go straight forward in doing what appears to me right at the time, leaving the Consequences to Providence." In 1773 James Madison expressed the same belief in the importance of both natural and supernatural means when he wrote concerning two acquaintances who were going into the ministry but whom he considered unsuited for the profession, "Nevertheless, it ought to be acknowledged that spiritual events are not limited or proportional always to human means; yet granting this in its great extent, it must be observed that the best human means should ever be employed—otherwise, it would look like a lazy, presumptuous dependence on Providence." In a 1776 sermon John Witherspoon declared, "The blessing of God is only to be looked for by those who are not wanting in the discharge of their own duty. I would neither have you trust in an arm of flesh nor sit with folded hands and expect that miracles should be wrought in your defense; this is a sin which is in scripture styled tempting God." (In Witherspoon's day, "tempting" served as a synonym for "testing.") In 1779 John Jay wrote regarding his losses of property at the hands of the British, "They never have, and I hope they never will, cost me an Hour's Sleep. Perseverance in doing what we think Right, and Resignation to the Dispensations of the Great Governor of the World, offer a Shield against the Darts of these Afflictions to everybody that will use it." The same year George Washington noted, "Everything in the preparatory way that depends upon me is done and doing. To Count D'Estaing [the commander of the allied French fleet] then and that good Providence which has so remarkably aided in our difficulties, the rest is committed."[20]

In the midst of the yellow fever epidemic of 1793, Benjamin Rush wrote, "While I depend upon divine protection and feel that at present, I live, move, and have my being in a more especial manner in God [Acts 17:28], I do not neglect to use every precaution that experience has discovered to prevent taking the infection." The following year George Washington wrote to John Jay in preparation for Jay's peace mission to Britain, "To deserve success, by employing the means with which we are possessed to the best advantage and trusting the rest to the all wise disposer, is all that an enlightened public and the virtuous and well disposed part of the community can reasonably expect." Similarly, in 1798, Washington wrote to reassure his successor John Adams, who was struggling to avoid war with France, "Satisfied, therefore, that you have sincerely wished and endeavoured to avert war, and exhausted to the last drop the cup of reconciliation, we can with pure hearts appeal to Heaven for the justice of our cause, and may confidently trust the final result to the kind Providence which has heretofore, and so often, signally favoured the people of these United States." In 1813 Thomas Jefferson claimed, "My principle is to do whatever is right, and leave consequences to him who has the disposal of them." Three years later John Adams distilled his philosophy as follows: "Be good fathers, sons, brothers, neighbors, friends, patriots and philanthropists, good subjects of the Universe, and trust the ruler with his skies." While the founders considered their own efforts insignificant when compared to God's, they also considered those efforts essential to securing His invaluable aid.[21]

The founders often attributed their own accomplishments and qualities to God. In 1753 Benjamin Franklin credited the Almighty with his invention of the lightning rod: "It has pleased God in his Goodness to Mankind at length to discover to them the Means of securing their Habitations and other Buildings from Mischief by Thunder and Lightning." In his vice presidential inaugural address in 1797 Thomas Jefferson declared, "I know the difficulties of the station to which I am called and feel and acknowledge my incompetence to them. But whatsoever of understanding, whatsoever of diligence, whatsoever of justice or of affectionate concern for the happiness of man it has pleased Providence to place within the compass of my faculties shall be called forth for the discharge of the duties confided to me." In his autobiography Benjamin Rush referred to "the successes which attended the remedies which it pleased

God to make me the instrument of introducing into general practice in the treatment of the fever of 1793."[22]

Even Thomas Paine often expressed a belief in divine Providence, thereby demonstrating that he was not a deist in the most common sense of the term. While his *Age of Reason* (1794–1795) was certainly a fierce attack on the Bible, he also alluded to divine intervention in the universe several times in the book. Like Jefferson, Paine caused confusion by praising deism while defining it simply as Unitarian monotheism. For instance, Paine wrote, "The only true religion is deism, by which I then meant and now mean the belief in one God and an imitation of his moral character, or the practice of what are called virtues." In the same book Paine referred to "the immensity of that Being who *directs* and *governs* the incomprehensible Whole," and he asked, "Does not the creation, the universe we behold, preach to the existence of an Almighty power that *governs* and *regulates* the whole?" (emphases added). Paine's directing, governing, and regulating God was an intervening one, though, like Jefferson, Paine emphasized that God did so through natural causes, not miracles, which he defined as subversions of the physical laws of the universe.[23]

Paine was even clearer in expressing a belief in an intervening God in works he penned both before and after *The Age of Reason*. In 1792 he wrote to the French people, "Man is ever a stranger to the ways by which Providence regulates the order of things. The interference of foreign despots [in republics like France] may serve to introduce into their own enslaved countries the principles they come to oppose." To Paine, God was not some abstract force like the Stoic World Soul but a person who cared for and protected individuals like himself. Ten years later Paine wrote to the American people regarding the French Revolution, "Of those who began that revolution, I am almost the only survivor and that through a thousand dangers. I owe this not to the prayers of priests nor to the piety of hypocrites but to the continued protection of Providence." These statements demonstrate that however much Paine detested some clergymen and other orthodox Christians, he possessed a strong belief in a God very much like that portrayed in the Bible, a personal God who intervened to protect individuals like Paine himself, and there can be little doubt that the source of this belief, however much Paine might deny it, was his own Christian upbringing. In an essay written in 1806, three years before his death, Paine reiterated his own narrow definition of deism as well as his belief in divine intervention. He wrote, "Deism, from the Latin word Deus, God, is the belief in [a single] God," and referred to his own brand of religion as "reposing itself on his [God's] protection, both here and hereafter."[24]

BELIEF IN THE EFFICACY OF PRAYER

An inevitable result of the founders' belief in a caring, intervening God of infinite power was their confidence in the efficacy of prayer. At the age of eighteen in 1772 Alexander Hamilton wrote a letter about his experience of a hurricane that devastated the island of St. Croix, killing thirty people. In the letter, which earned Hamilton his first notoriety after it was published in various newspapers, he cried out, "Oh Lord, help. Jesus, be merciful!" Hamilton continued, "This I did reflect, and thus at every gust of the wind did I conclude till it pleased the Almighty to allay it. . . . But see the Lord relents. He hears our prayer. The Lightning ceases. The winds are appeased. . . . Rejoice at thy deliverance and humble thyself in the presence of thy deliverer." More than two decades later, alarmed by the illness of his infant son John, Hamilton wrote to his wife Elizabeth, "My fervent prayers are not wanting that God will support you & rescue our loved Child." The child recovered. In 1774 John Winthrop told his students in a lecture, "Prayer has a real efficacy on the event." The following year John Adams applauded the Second Continental Congress's decision to call for a day of fasting and prayer on the grounds that "Millions will be upon their Knees at once before their great Creator, imploring his Forgiveness and Blessing, his Smiles on American Councils and Arms." Adams expected a divine response to so great an upwelling of prayer. In 1776 George Washington declared, "I, in behalf of the Noble cause we are Engaged in and of myself, thank with a grateful Heart all those who supplicate the throne of grace for success to the one & preservation of the other. That being from whom nothing can be hid will, I doubt not, listen to our Prayers and protect our Cause and the supporters of it, as far as we merit his favour and Assistance." Seven years later Washington concluded his final statement to his soldiers by promising to pray to "the God of Armies" that "the choicest of heaven's favours, both here and hereafter, attend those who, under the divine auspices, have secured innumerable blessings for others."[25]

In 1788 Richard Henry Lee wrote to Edmund Pendleton, who was shortly to serve as a delegate at the Virginia ratifying convention, "I pray, sir, that God may bless the convention with wisdom, maturity of counsel, and constant care of the public liberty and that he may have you in his holy keeping." In 1799 John Marshall, writing for the House of Representatives, declared regarding the sending of envoys to France, against whom the United States was engaged in an undeclared naval war, "We offer up our fervent prayers to the Supreme Ruler of the universe for the success of their embassy and that it may be productive of peace and happiness to our common country." Decades later he wrote from Richmond to his friend and fellow Supreme Court justice Joseph Story, then in Boston, regarding a cholera epidemic, "That Providence may protect us, especially Boston and Richmond, is the sincerest prayer of your truly affectionate, J. Marshall." In 1802 James Monroe wrote, "That this genuine liberty, protected by elective governments, founded on the sovereignty of the people, may be preserved and handed down as a blessing to our latest posterity is the object of my most fervent prayer to the Supreme Ruler of the World."[26]

Benjamin Rush spent the summer of 1793 risking his life caring for the victims of a yellow fever epidemic, the whole time praying, requesting prayer, and praising God for the answered prayer of his continued survival. On August 25 he wrote to his wife, "Continue to commit me by your prayers to the protection of that Being who so often manifested his goodness to our family by the preservation of my life." Five days later he reported, "I am preparing to set off for my daily round of duty, and feel heartily disposed to say with Jabez, 'O that the hand of the Lord may be with me' [1 Chronicles 4:10], not only to preserve my life but to heal my poor patients." On September 8 he claimed, "The fear of death from the disease has been taken from me, and I possess perfect composure in the rooms of my patients. Help me to praise God for this and all his inestimable blessings to me. Let it be the business of our future lives (if we should be reunited here) to record and to celebrate the goodness of our God." The next day he reported, "Still alive and in good health after five hours' comfortable sleep. 'Be merciful unto me, O God! Be merciful unto me, for my soul trusteth in you; yea, in the shadow of thy wings do I make my refuge, until these calamities be overpast.' Psalm 57th." On September 10 he wrote, "Thank God! I am still in good health. 'I will sing of thy power, O Lord. Yea, I will sing aloud of thy mercy in the morning, for thou hast been' and thou are still 'my defense and refuge in the day of trouble.' Psalm 59th." Two days later, he noted, "Alive and in good health after a most comfortable night's rest. 'O bless our God, ye people, and make the voice of his praise to be heard, which holdeth our soul in life, and suffered not our feet to be moved.' Psalm 66, 8, 9." The next day he quoted Psalms 68:19: "Blessed be the Lord, who daily loadeth us with benefits, even the God of our salvation." On September 18 he requested, "Continue to pray without ceasing [2 Thessalonians 5:17], not only for me but for a distressed and desolated city." Two days later he reported, "Through the prayers of my friends, purified and accepted through the mediation of a gracious Redeemer, I am again in good health." On September 21 he urged, "Continue to pray for our poor, devoted, and desolated city. Indeed, I have thought that all good Christians should sit, walk, eat, and even sleep with one hand constantly lifted up in a praying attitude to the Father of mercies to avert his judgments from us."

When the epidemic finally ended, Rush wrote to his wife on November 4, "In the midst of my dangers and distresses at all times [I] derived consolation from reflecting that I lived every moment in your remembrance and was constantly carried by you to the throne of heaven for my preservation. I derived comfort in the near prospect of death likewise from reflecting upon your extraordinary prudence, your good sense, and pious dispositions, all of which qualified you in an eminent degree to educate our children in a proper manner in case I had been taken from you. This idea, connected with an unshaken faith in God's promises to widows and fatherless children, sometimes suspended for a while my ardent and natural attachment to you and the children and made me at times willing to part with you, provided my death would have advanced the great objects to which I had devoted myself."[27]

Thomas Jefferson often closed his letters with promises to pray for the recipient and his nation. In 1791 Jefferson wrote to the Marquis de Lafayette, expressing his concern for the success of the French Revolution: "God bless you, my dear friend, and prosper those endeavors about which I never wrote to you because it would interrupt them, but for the success of which, and for your own happiness, nobody prays more sincerely than Your affectionate friend & servt. Th. Jefferson." A decade later Jefferson wrote to the directors of the new Dutch republic, "We pray God to keep you, Citizen Directors, under his Holy protection." The same year he also declared, "I offer my sincere prayers to the Supreme Ruler of the Universe that He may long preserve our country in freedom and prosperity." In 1809 he replied to a group of Democratic-Republicans from New London, Connecticut, who had written to applaud his administration, soon to be concluded, "I thank you, fellow citizens, for your kind expressions of regard for myself and prayers for my future happiness, and I join in supplications to that Almighty Being who has heretofore guarded our councils, still to continue his gracious benefactions towards our country and that yourselves may be under the protection of his divine favor." The following month he replied to a similar group from Massachusetts, "I sincerely supplicate the overruling Providence which governs the destinies of men and nations to dispense His choicest blessing on yourselves and our beloved country." Since such an end to letters was far from obligatory, there is no reason to suspect any insincerity on Jefferson's part.[28]

The same year, when James Madison received letters from a host of people, ranging from Benjamin Rush to the Ursuline nuns in New Orleans, promising to pray for him after his presidential inauguration, rather than merely thanking his correspondents, which would have sufficed, he offered his own prayers for them in return. Since the nation faced a crisis with Great Britain, whose navy was seizing American ships and impressing American sailors, Madison also informed the Republican Committee of New York that he was "devoutly praying" for "the divine blessing . . . of preserving to our Country the advantages of peace without relinquishing its rights or its honor."[29]

Alone in this, as in so much else, Thomas Paine opposed prayer. In 1803 he lectured a disapproving Samuel Adams, "A man does not serve God when he prays, for it is himself he is trying to serve. . . . Instead of buffeting the Deity with prayers, as if I distrusted him or must dictate to him, I reposed myself on his protection [while in France], and you, my friend, will find, even in your last moments, more consolation in the silence of resignation than in the murmuring wish of a prayer." Three years later he called prayer "an attempt to dictate to the Almighty in the government of the world." Paine's opposition to prayer contrasted sharply with the admonitions of both Jesus and the apostle Paul to "pray unceasingly" (Luke 18:1; 1 Thessalonians 5:17), not only with requests but also with expressions of thanksgiving and the confession of sin. Yet it is important to note that Paine's unbiblical argument against prayer—that God was already intervening without need of requests—was based on a conception of an omniscient, interventionist God that was itself profoundly biblical and that flatly contradicted deism.[30]

CALLS FOR PRAYER

Given the founders' belief in the efficacy of prayer, Thomas Paine excepted, it is not surprising that they often called for both collective and individual prayer. While a call for prayer could be politically useful, as a means for a leader to display his piety, there is no reason to doubt the sincerity of the callers, whose own private papers invariably reveal a personal belief in the efficacy of prayer.

Indeed, Benjamin Franklin was already urging the public to pray before he entered politics. In 1749, in the guise of Poor Richard, Franklin urged his readers to begin and close each day in prayer:

> Waked by the Call of Morn, on early Knee
> Ere the World thrust between thy God and thee,
> Let thy pure Orations, ascending, gain
> His ear, and Succour of his Grace obtain,
> In Wants, in Toils, in Perils of the Day,
> And strong Temptations that beset thy Way.
> Thy best Resolves then in his Strength renew
> To Walk in Virtue's Paths and Vice Eschew. . . .
> To Him entrust thy Slumbers, and prepare
> The fragrant Incense of thy Evening Prayer.
> But first tread Back the Day, with Search severe,
> And Conscience, chiding or applauding, hear.
> Review each Step: Where, acting, did I err?
> Omitting, where? Guilt either Way infer.
> Labour this Point, and while thy Frailties last,
> Still each following Day correct the last.

The emphasis on critical self-analysis in the latter part of the poem is a clear reminder of Franklin's Puritan heritage.[31]

When the First Continental Congress met in Philadelphia in 1774, while Boston was occupied by British troops, Thomas Cushing, a Massachusetts representative, moved that the Congress be opened with a prayer. The motion was opposed by John Jay and Edward Rutledge, not out of any disbelief in the efficacy of prayer in securing divine assistance, but because they feared that the prayer might become a source of dissension among the various denominations represented in the assembly. According to John Adams, "Mr. S[amuel] Adams arose and said he was no Bigot, and could hear a Prayer from a Gentleman of Piety and Virtue who was at the same Time a Friend to his Country. He was a Stranger in Philadelphia but he had heard that Mr. [Jacob] Duché (Dushay, they pronounced it) deserved that Character, and therefore he moved that Mr. Duché, an episcopal Clergyman, might be desired to read the Prayers to the Congress tomorrow morning." The proposal by Samuel Adams, an ardent Congregationalist, to have prayers recited by an Episcopalian minister was an olive branch that had an immediate effect. The motion was seconded and passed. After reading several prayers the following morning, Reverend Duché also recited the thirty-fifth psalm, which begins, "Plead my cause, O Lord, with them that strive with me; fight against them that fight with me." John Adams recorded, "I never saw a greater Effect upon an audience. It seemed as if Heaven had ordained that Psalm to be read on that Morning. After this Mr. Duché, unexpected to every Body, struck out onto an extemporary Prayer, which filled the Bosom of every Man present. I must confess I never heard a better Prayer or one so well pronounced. . . . [He] prayed with such fervour, such Ardor, such Earnestness and Pathos, and in Language so elegant and sublime—for America, for the Congress, for The Province of Massachusetts Bay, and especially the Town of Boston. It has had an excellent Effect upon every Body here." Ironically, Duché, like most Anglican ministers, later sided with the British and became a loyalist refugee.[32]

In 1783 Patrick Henry proposed to the Virginia House of Delegates "that a prayer should be composed adapted to all persuasions" and that a chaplain be appointed to read the prayer daily at the start of each session. The House of Delegates had possessed a chaplain from 1777 through 1780, but the proposal of an opening prayer was a novel one. The measure passed the following day.[33]

Benjamin Franklin's emotional call for daily prayer at the Constitutional Convention reflected the same belief in an intervening God. On June 28, 1787, after complaining about the frustrating lack of progress made at the convention thus far, Franklin, who was ill, asked his colleague James Wilson to read to the delegates a speech he had prepared in which he urged daily prayer at the convention. Franklin's speech included this passage:

> In this situation of this Assembly, groping as it were in the dark to find political truth, and scarce able to distinguish it when presented to us, how has it happened, Sir, that we have not hitherto once thought of humbly applying to the Father of lights to illuminate our understandings? In the beginning of the contest with Great Britain, when we were sensible of the danger, we had daily prayer in this room for the divine protection. Our prayers, sir, were heard, and they were graciously answered. All of us who were engaged in the struggle must have observed frequent instances of a Superintending providence in our favor. To that kind providence we owe this happy opportunity of consulting in peace on the means of establishing our future national felicity. And have we now forgotten that powerful friend? Or do we imagine that we no longer need his assistance? I have lived, Sir, a long time, and the longer I live the more convincing proofs I see of this truth—that *God* [underscored twice in Franklin's manuscript] *governs in the affairs of men* [underscored once]. And if a sparrow cannot fall to the ground without his notice, is it probable that an empire can rise without his aid? We have been assured, Sir, in the sacred writings that "except the Lord build the House they labour in vain that build it." I firmly believe this, and I also believe that without his concurring aid we shall succeed in this political building no better than the Builders of Babel. We shall be divided by our little partial local interests; our projects will be confounded; and we ourselves shall become a reproach and a bye-word down to future ages. And what is worse, mankind may hereafter from this unfortunate instance despair of establishing Governments by Human Wisdom and leave it to chance, war, and conquest.
>
> I therefore beg leave to move that henceforth prayers imploring the assistance of Heaven, and its blessings on our deliberations, be held in this Assembly every morning before we proceed to our business, and that one or more of the Clergy of this City be requested to officiate in that service.

Although Franklin's proposal had the support of Roger Sherman and Edmund Randolph, Alexander Hamilton and others expressed the concern that to introduce prayer by a clergyman at that late date would fuel popular rumors that the convention was in disarray. Franklin and his supporters retorted "that the past omission of a duty could not justify a further omission." Since it was late in the day and the delegates were tired, adjournment was called without the motion receiving a vote. In any case, not only did Franklin's underscored statement that "God governs in the affairs of men" contradict a fundamental tenet of deism, but his speech as a whole demonstrated a close familiarity with scripture. The reference to the falling sparrow is taken from Matthew 10:29, the quotation concerning the building of the house is from Psalms 127:1, and the reference to Babel is from Genesis 11.[34]

Benjamin Rush proposed prayer at the Pennsylvania ratifying convention. Rush moved that a committee be appointed to select a minister to open the convention with a prayer. According to the *Pennsylvania Herald*:

> This was considered by several gentlemen as a new and unnecessary measure which might be inconsistent with the religious sentiments of some of the members, as it was impossible to fix on a clergyman to suit every man's tenets, and it was neither warranted by the example of the General Assembly or of the convention that framed the government of Pennsylvania. To these observations Dr. Rush replied that he hoped there was liberality sufficient in the meeting to unite in prayers for the blessing of Heaven upon their proceedings without considering the sect or persuasion of the minister who officiated; and with respect to precedent, he remarked that it might be taken from the conduct of the first and every succeeding Congress, who certainly deserved our imitation. "That the convention who framed the government of Pennsylvania did not preface their business with prayer is probably the reason," added the Doctor, "that the state has ever since been distracted by their proceedings."

Rush's proposal failed not because of any doubt on the part of most delegates concerning the efficacy of prayer but because of the fear of introducing denominational rivalry into the proceedings. Unlike the Pennsylvania convention, the Massachusetts ratifying convention did institute daily prayer, as led by "the clergy in Boston of every denomination . . . in turn."[35]

The founders' calls for prayer were not restricted to the meetings of august bodies but, according to a centuries-old tradition, included the designation of days for public prayer and fasting or thanksgiving. In 1743, on the occasion of Pennsylvania's attempt to raise a militia to defend the colony against a potential attack by Spain, which was then at war with Britain, Benjamin Franklin proposed that the colony designate a day of prayer and fasting "to promote reformation and implore the blessing of Heaven in our undertaking." Since past leaders of the colony, mostly Quakers who believed in a strict separation of church and state, had never called for such a day, there were no local exemplars to follow, so Franklin was selected to draft the proclamation due to the Boston native's familiarity with New England models.[36]

On May 24, 1774, after Parliament's passage of the Coercive (or Intolerable) Acts, the Virginia House of Burgesses called for a public day of prayer and fasting to coincide with the British closing of the port of Boston under that law. The House designated June 1 "a day of fasting, humiliation, and prayer, devoutly to implore the Divine interposition for averting the heavy calamity which threatens destruction to our civil rights and the evils of civil war; to give us one heart and one mind firmly to oppose, by all just and proper means, every injury to American rights; and that the minds of his majesty and his parliament may be inspired from above with wisdom, moderation, and justice to remove from the loyal people of America all cause of danger from a continued pursuit of measures pregnant with their ruin." When this call to prayer was published two days later, the royal governor, Lord Dunmore, angered by what he regarded as an insult to the king and parliament, dissolved the assembly, which then convened at the Raleigh Tavern and called on the colonies to consider the establishment of a Continental Congress. The Coercive Acts also prompted John Dickinson, in "Letters to the Inhabitants of the British Colonies," to call on his fellow Americans to pray, repent, and forgive in order to secure divine favor: "Let us, therefore, in the first place, humbling ourselves before our gracious Creator, devoutly beseech his divine Protection on us, his afflicted servants, most unreasonably and cruelly oppressed. Let us seriously reflect on our manifold transgressions, and by a sincere repentance, and an entire amendment of our lives, strive to recommend ourselves to divine favour. In the next place, let us cherish and cultivate sentiments of brotherly love and tenderness among us. . . . Let us mutually excuse and forgive each other our weaknesses and prejudices (for who is free from weakness and prejudices?)."[37]

The Continental Congress issued numerous calls for days of prayer and fasting or thanksgiving throughout the Revolutionary War, as did the individual states. Governors like Samuel Adams, John Jay, and John Hancock (who was the son, grandson, and great grandson of clergymen) continued the practice during the Confederation period. In his first year as president (1789) George Washington designated a national day of prayer and thanksgiving to commemorate the adoption of the U.S. Constitution. In 1795 Washington called for another such day to commemorate the suppression of the Whiskey Rebellion, a frontier revolt against the whiskey tax. In 1798 his successor, John Adams, designated a day of prayer and fasting as the nation faced the prospect of war with France. As president, James Madison called for days of prayer four times during the War of 1812, just as he had called for such a day as a Virginia legislator in 1785, though he later decided that such proclamations violated the principle of the separation of church and state.[38]

NATURAL RIGHTS ENDOWED AND ENFORCED BY AN OMNIPOTENT CREATOR

While the founders believed that God was prepared to bestow many different blessings on those who turned to Him in prayer, they were also convinced that He was most eager to grant and defend liberty. This belief was crucial because it instilled in the founders the courage necessary to face the many dangers, sacrifices, and hardships of the Revolutionary era.

Thomas Jefferson's famous summary of patriot sentiment at the time of the Revolution ("We hold these truths to be self-evident, that all men are created equal, that they are endowed by their Creator with certain inalienable Rights, that among these are Life, Liberty, and the pursuit of Happiness") was a product of the intermingling of biblical, classical, and Whig traditions. While the doctrine of natural rights was a modern Whig formulation of the classical theory of natural law, the concept of individual rights (coupled with duties) received valuable support from the biblical doctrine of individual accountability before God, and the theory of natural law received equally crucial support from the biblical concept of a universal moral order. Even more important, the biblical concept of an omniscient and omnipotent God who was willing and able to endow and enforce rights was essential to the viability of this theory.[39]

Based on some intimations from the Pythagoreans, in the fourth century BC, Plato (*Meno*, 77c–78b; *Phaedo*, 63c–68b) and Aristotle (*Rhetoric*, 1.1375a.25–b.1–8) advanced the theory of natural law, the belief in a universal code of ethics inherent in nature and comprehensible to humans either through a form of intuition (knowledge arising from the preexistence of the soul, in Plato's formulation) or through reason acting on experience (Aristotle's version). Epicurus (Diogenes Laertius, *Lives of the Eminent Philosophers*, 10.122–35) supported Aristotle's position on this issue. Both Cicero and the Stoics assumed a middle ground, believing that while an understanding of natural law was embedded in human nature through a sort of intuition, humans could access it only with the help of moral training (reason acting on sensory information).[40]

Although the writers of the Old Testament, the apostle Paul, and other early Christians embraced the concept of a universal moral order wholeheartedly, their belief in original sin left them far more pessimistic than the classical philosophers concerning the ability of humans to understand it fully through either reason or intuition ("conscience" in Judeo-Christian terminology). Paul and Augustine maintained that while reason and conscience still acted as guides to ethics, both had been so badly damaged by the fall of Adam as to become insufficient for the task. Humans were unable to lead ethical lives without scripture to teach them true morality and without the infusion of God's grace via the Holy Spirit to help them to adhere to it. Furthermore, the classical association of the universal moral order with nature rather than with the perfect and unchanging Creator was problematic for both Jews and Christians because they believed that nature had been corrupted from its original, perfect form into a scene of chaos and violence by the fall of Adam.[41]

Nevertheless, the theory of natural law persisted through the Middle Ages and the Protestant Reformation, though it was still subordinated to the revealed law. While restricting the category of revealed law to scripture alone, in opposition to the inclusion of church teachings by Thomas Aquinas and other Catholic theologians, the Protestant reformers agreed with these theologians that original sin rendered revealed law superior to natural law as a guide to ethics. Martin Luther concluded that while revelation did not contradict reason, it certainly transcended it. Even those moral tenets that sinful humans might deduce from nature without the aid of revelation they could hardly follow without the aid of the Holy Spirit. John Calvin agreed. He considered scripture essential since reason alone would not necessarily have deduced from nature all of the Ten Commandments. Furthermore, Calvin claimed that Plato had been naïve in assuming that to know the good was to do the good—that virtue required only wisdom. That simplistic formulation overlooked the importance of willpower, which only the Holy Spirit could supply.[42]

In the seventeenth century British Whigs contributed a revolutionary emphasis on the natural rights of individuals, a deduction from natural law rarely pursued by the ancients. John Locke, the most influential of the Whigs, argued that men did not surrender their natural rights to government when forming the social contract, only their prerogative of enforcing natural law. If a government threatened natural rights, its citizens were morally obligated to uphold natural law by opposing the government that violated it. Since such citizens resisted tyranny on behalf of law, they were in no sense rebels.[43]

Like other Christians before them, the founders added to the classical concept of a universal moral order comprehensible to humans through reason and intuition the biblical concept of an omniscient and omnipotent God who was the author, as well as the judge and enforcer, of this moral code. The inclusion of an omniscient and omnipotent judge and enforcer was essential to the success of the theory of natural rights. Without such a Being, the theory was essentially meaningless since there would be no certain penalty for even the most outrageous violations of these rights.

As early as 1764, in *Rights of the British Colonies*, James Otis, the first leader of the Boston patriots, contended, "Parliaments are in all cases to declare what is for the good of the whole; but it is not the declaration of parliament that makes it so. There must be in every instance a higher authority, viz. God. Should an act of parliament be against any of his natural laws, which are immutably true, their declaration would be contrary to eternal truth, equity, and justice, and consequently void." The following year, in his "Dissertation on the Canon and the Feudal Law," John Adams contended, "Liberty must at all hazards be supported. We have a right to it, derived from our Maker. . . . Consenting to slavery is a sacrilegious breach of trust, as offensive in the sight of God as it is derogatory to our own honor or interest or happiness." In 1766 John Dickinson lectured the Committee of Correspondence in Barbados:

> Kings or parliaments could not give the rights essential to happiness, as you confess those invaded by the Stamp Act to be. We claim them from a higher source—from the King of kings [Revelation 17:14] and Lord of all the earth. They are not annexed to us by parchments and seals. They are created in us by the decrees of Providence, which establish the laws of our nature. They are born with us, exist with us, and cannot be taken from us by any human power, without taking our lives. In short, they are founded on the immutable maxims of reason

> and justice. It would be an insult to the divine Majesty to say that he has given or allowed any man or body of men a right to make me miserable. If no man or body of men have such a right, I have a right to be happy. If there can be no happiness without freedom, I have a right to be free. If I cannot enjoy freedom without security of property, I have a right to be thus secured.

In his famous *Letters from a Farmer in Pennsylvania* (1767–1768) Dickinson asserted, "While Divine Providence that gave me existence in a land of freedom permits my head to think, my lips to speak, and my hand to move, I shall so highly and gratefully value the blessing received as to take care that my silence and inactivity shall not give implied assent to any act degrading to my brethren from the birthright wherewith heaven itself 'hath made us free'" (Galatians 5:1). Dickinson added a confident note to his fellow Americans: "Almighty God himself will look down upon your righteous contest with gracious approbation. . . . You are assigned by divine Providence in the appointed order of things the protectors of unborn ages, whose fate depends on your virtue."[44]

That same year Samuel Adams wrote that "the only true basis of all government" was "the laws of God and nature, for government is an ordinance of Heaven, designed by the all-benevolent Creator for the general happiness of his rational creature, man." He noted proudly that the people of Boston were "tenacious of those sacred rights and liberties wherewith God hath made them free." Adams's habit of using the archaic "hath" from the King James Version of the Bible when discussing natural rights reflected his religious understanding of those rights. Adams understood the Almighty to be their enforcer, whether in this life or in the hereafter. In 1770 he claimed, "When the Body of the People or any single Man is deprived of their Right, or under the Exercise of a Power without Right, and have no Appeal on Earth, then they have a Liberty to appeal to Heaven." Four years later he wrote regarding the imminent arrival of British troops in the wake of the Tea Party, "I never suffer my Mind to be ever much disturbed with Prospects. Sufficient for the Day is the Evil thereof [Matthew 6:34]. It is our Duty at all Hazards to preserve the Publick Liberty. Righteous Heaven will graciously smile on every manly and rational Attempt to secure that best of all his Gifts to Man from the ravishing Hand of lawless and brutal Power." Indeed, Adams even claimed that God punished those who failed to fight for their rights. In 1776 he contended, "If Heaven punishes Communities for their Vices, how sore must be the Punishment of that Community who think the Rights of human Nature not worth struggling for and patiently submit to Tyranny?" In "A Summary View of the Rights of British America" (1774) Thomas Jefferson also emphasized the Creator's role in granting and defending rights. Jefferson declared, "The God who gave us life gave us liberty at the same time; the hand of force may destroy but cannot disjoin them."[45]

In 1775, the year in which the Revolutionary War began, the country was awash in patriotic pronouncements about God-given natural rights. Alexander Hamilton wrote concerning natural law, "Upon this law depends the rights of mankind; the supreme being gave existence to man, together with the means of preserving and beatifying that existence. He endowed him with rational faculties by the help of which to discern such things as were consistent with his duty and interest and invested him with an inviolable right to personal liberty and personal safety. . . . Natural liberty is a gift of the beneficent Creator to the whole human race, and civil liberty is founded in that. . . . The sacred rights of mankind are not to be rummaged for among old parchments or musty records. They are written, as with a sunbeam, in the whole volume of human nature by the divinity itself and can never be erased or obscured by mortal power." In his "Declaration of the Causes and Necessity of Taking Up Arms," approved by the Continental Congress the same year, Thomas Jefferson wrote, "We do then most solemnly before God and the world declare that, regardless of every consequence, at the risk of every distress, the arms we have been compelled to assume we will use with perseverance, exerting to the utmost energies all those powers which our creator hath given us to preserve that liberty which he committed to us in sacred deposit." A then orthodox Thomas Paine contended, "Political as well as religious freedom is the gift of God through Christ. . . . Political liberty is the visible pass which guards the religious. It is the outwork by which the church militant is defended, and the attacks of the enemy are frequently made through this fortress." Richard Henry Lee claimed, "The cause of Liberty must be within the protection of Heaven because the Creator wills the happiness of his Creatures; & having joined the faculty of reasoning with our natures, he has made us capable of discerning that the true dignity and happiness of human nature are only to be found in a state of freedom." In a speech James Wilson declared regarding the British tradition of liberty, "The government of Britain, sir, was never arbitrary government: our ancestors were never inconsiderate enough to trust those rights which God and nature had given them unreservedly into the hands of their princes."[46]

In 1779 Benjamin Franklin claimed, "I admire the spirit with which the Irish are at length determined to claim some share of that freedom of commerce which is the right of all mankind but which they have been so long deprived of by the abominable selfishness of their fellow subjects. To enjoy all the advantages of the climate and situation in which God and nature have placed us is as clear a right as that of breathing, and can never be justly taken from men but as punishment for some atrocious crime." Two years later, South Carolina patriot Christopher Gadsden declared, "Our cause is good, the cause of humanity itself, and as it would be blasphemy in the highest degree to think a Good Being would create human nature to make it unhappy, and to countenance its being deprived of those natural rights without which our existence would not be tolerable, our cause may, therefore, justly be called the cause of God also. These were my sentiments at the time of the Stamp Act, the beginning of our dispute; they have continued to be so ever since and, with the Blessing of God, I am ready and willing to undergo anything Heaven may still think proper to call me to suffer in support of it." In his famous law lectures of 1790–1791 James Wilson referred to "that law, which God has made for man in his present state, that law which is communicated to us by reason and conscience, the divine monitors within us, and by the sacred oracles, the divine monitors without us." He added, "It should always be remembered that this law, natural or revealed, made for men or for nations, flows from the same divine source: it is the law of God. . . . Human law must rest its authority, ultimately, upon the authority of that law which is divine. . . . The principle object of the institution of government . . . [was] to acquire a new security for the recovery of those rights to the enjoyment or acquisition of which we were previously entitled by the immediate gift or by the unerring law of our all-wise and all-beneficent Creator." In an essay Wilson cited the Book of Genesis for the assertion that "the general property of man in animals, in the soil, and in the productions of the soil, is the immediate gift of the bountiful Creator of all." In 1795 Thomas Jefferson wrote regarding the success of Dutch republicans, with the help of the French, in driving out the stadtholder William IV and establishing a more democratic system: "It proves there is a god in heaven, and he will not slumber without end on the iniquities of [such] tyrants, or would-be tyrants, as their Stadtholder. This ball of liberty, I believe most piously, is now so well in motion that it will roll around the globe. At least the enlightened part of it, for light and liberty go together. It is our glory that we first put it into motion." At the approach of the fiftieth anniversary of the Declaration of Independence in 1826, John Jay wrote regarding the Almighty, "The most effectual means of securing the continuance of our civil and religious liberties is always to remember with gratitude the source from which they flow."[47]

MISFORTUNE

It is a testimony to the genuineness and power of the founders' faith that it overcame all misfortune. They sometimes considered hardship a form of divine judgment against sin but at other times regarded it as intended for the good of its recipients.

As early as 1756 John Adams interpreted a devastating Lisbon earthquake and the Seven Years' (or French and Indian) War as signs of God's wrath against human arrogance. The young man wrote in his diary, "God Almighty has exerted the Strength of his tremendous Arm which shook one of the finest, richest, and most populous Cities in Europe into Ruin and Desolation by an Earthquake. The greatest Part of Europe and the greatest Part of America have been in violent Convulsions, and [God has] admonished the Inhabitants of both, that neither Riches nor Honours, nor the solid Globe itself, is a proper Basis on which to build our hopes of Security. . . . Is it not then the highest Frenzy and Distraction to neglect these Expostulations of Providence and continue a Rebellion against that Potentate who alone has Wisdom enough to perceive, and Power enough to procure for us, the only certain means of Happiness, and goodness enough to prompt him to both?" A few weeks later, after copying scriptures all morning, Adams wrote, "A World in Flames, and a whole System trembling in Ruins to the Center, has nothing terrifying in it to a man whose Security is builded on the adamantine Basis of good Conscience and confirmed Piety. . . . Have I hardiness enough to contend with omnipotence? Or have I cunning enough to elude infinite Wisdom, or Ingratitude enough to Spurn infinite Goodness? The Situation that I am in, and the Advantages that I enjoy, are thought to be the best for me by him who alone is a competent Judge of Fitness and Propriety. Shall I then complain? Oh Madness, Pride, Impiety." In 1774, when Massachusetts was occupied by British troops in the wake of the Coercive Acts and Adams was informed of a sermon that alleged "that the Judgments of God upon the Land were in consequence of the Mobs and Riots which had prevailed in the Country," he agreed with this assessment but also suggested additional rampant sins, such as bribery, corruption, and theft, as possible "other Causes" of divine displeasure.[48]

Benjamin Rush considered the various setbacks of the Revolutionary War divine punishment for the state governments' injury of widows, orphans, and other poor people by financing the war through inflation. In 1779 he claimed, "I believe the injustice which has been committed under the sanction of law to helpless members of our community is one of the principal reasons why the Supreme Being has so long kept back from us the blessings of peace and why he has made this summer so big with all the calamities of war." Rush later called Philadelphia's yellow fever epidemic of 1793 "the judgment of God upon our city."[49]

Benjamin Franklin possessed an equally strong belief that the Almighty punished sin. In 1757 Franklin alleged that God punished the stingy with poverty: "Proportion your Charity to the Strength of your Estate, or God will proportion your Estate to the Weakness of your Charity." In 1764, a few months after receiving the news that a group of whites had massacred twenty innocent Native Americans in Lancaster County, Pennsylvania, in retribution for the actions of another tribe, Franklin published an essay in which he expressed concern that the massacre would bring down God's wrath on all of Pennsylvania. He lamented, "The Wickedness cannot be covered; the Guilt will lie on the whole land till Justice is done on the Murderers. The Blood of the Innocent will cry to Heaven for Vengeance." This was a reference to Genesis 4:10, in which God tells Cain, "The voice of your brother's blood cries out to me from the ground." Franklin closed the same essay with the plea, "Let all good Men join heartily and unanimously in support of the Laws, and in strengthening the Hands of Government, that Justice may be done, the Wicked punished, and the Innocent protected; otherwise, we can, as a People, expect no Blessing from Heaven, there will be no Security for our Persons or Properties, Anarchy and Confusion will prevail over all, and Violence without Judgment dispose of everything."[50]

In a 1783 letter to the states, George Washington warned that if they failed to raise the funds necessary to pay their war debts and their soldiers, they risked divine wrath. Washington asked, "In what part of the Continent shall we find any Man or body of Men who would not blush to stand up and propose measures purposely calculated to rob the Soldier of his Stipend and the Public Creditor of his due? And were it possible that such a flagrant instance of Injustice could ever happen, would it not excite the general indignation and tend to bring down upon the Authors of such measures the aggravated vengeance of Heaven?"[51]

In 1786 John Jay lamented that since Americans were "doing wrong," he expected "evils and calamities." In his 1795 thanksgiving proclamation as governor of New York, Jay declared, "The great Creator and Preserver of the Universe is the Supreme Sovereign of Nations and does . . . reward or punish them by temporal blessings or calamities, according as their national conduct recommends them to his favour and beneficence or excites his displeasure and indignation."[52]

John Marshall, future chief justice of the Supreme Court, believed that God sometimes punished nations by sending them unjust judges. At the Virginia ratifying convention he declared, "I have always thought from my earliest youth till now that the greatest scourge an angry Heaven ever inflicted upon an ungrateful and sinning people was an ignorant, a corrupt, or a dependent judiciary."[53]

The common requirement of religious oaths for officeholders, as well as for witnesses in court, was predicated on the widespread belief in a God who punished perjury. While some leaders defended the Constitution's lack of a religious test for federal officeholders on the basis of the right of conscience, others declared such a test unnecessary since the oaths of office mandated in that document, oaths that in those days were generally accompanied by the kissing of a Bible (for Jews, a Torah), included the phrase "do solemnly swear in the presence of almighty God before whom I expect to answer for my conduct" (or something similar), and ended with "So help me God," assumed the existence of a divine being who punished perjury. At the Connecticut ratifying convention, Oliver Wolcott declared regarding the absence of a religious test in the Constitution, "I do not see the necessity of such a test as some gentlemen wish for. The Constitution enjoins an oath upon all the officers of the United States. This is a direct appeal to that God who is the Avenger of Perjury. Such an appeal to Him is a full acknowledgment of His being and providence." James Madison agreed, writing, "Is not a religious test as far as it is necessary or would operate involved in the oath itself? If the person swearing believes in the supreme Being who is invoked and in the Penal consequences of offending him, either in this or a future world or both, he will be under the same restraint from perjury as if he had previously subscribed a test requiring this belief."[54]

But the founders did not attribute all misfortune to divine wrath. On the contrary, they believed that God often used hardship to promote the greater good of the afflicted.

Some founders believed that misfortune taught wisdom. In 1766 the fiancée of Charles Carroll, who became the only Catholic signer of the Declaration of Independence a decade later, passed away. Though Carroll was devastated, the following March he was able to write, "It has pleased God to teach me by this severe visitation that no happiness but what results from virtue is permanent and secure. Happy is that man who makes a right use of such trials. . . . He can draw some consolation from the affliction itself."[55]

In 1768 Benjamin Rush was philosophical about the fact that his stint in medical school in Scotland had prevented him from courting and marrying Polly Fisher. He claimed, "Heaven hath ordered it so in order to enable me to provide more honorably for my dear sisters and their sons, whose only hopes of happiness in this world are now fixed on me." Nine years later he wrote to Elizabeth Ferguson, who was betrayed and abandoned by her husband, "Divine providence I believe has something in store for you to which your present afflictions may appear hereafter to have been as necessary an introduction as the unnatural conduct of Benjamin's brothers was to the deliverance of his father Jacob's family. The present war, so prolific of distress, is fruitful likewise in proofs of a general and particular providence." In one of his essays the physician also argued that the increase in bodily ailments that accompanied the aging process was actually merciful because it diminished the reluctance with which the elderly faced death. In 1806 Rush wrote to a former medical student who was suffering from a heart condition, "Continue, my dear friend, to trust in the power and to depend upon the mercy of your God. Disease and death have often been conquered by him, and where they have been permitted to prevail in this world, it is only to furnish a more glorious opportunity for the Saviour of mankind to display his power and mercy in the world to come in vanquishing sin and death. Believe in Him—and whatever may be the issue of your disease, you will be safe and happy."[56]

John Witherspoon devoted much of a 1776 sermon to explaining the wisdom of God in the infliction of hardship. Witherspoon contended that God often limited the damage caused by the wicked. He added, "Whatever be the nature of the afflictions with which he visits either persons, families, or nations, whatever be the disposition or intention of those whose malice he employs as a scourge, the design on his part is to rebuke men for iniquity, to bring them to repentance, and to promote their holiness and peace. The salutary nature and sanctifying influence of affliction in general is often taken notice of in scripture, both as making a part of the purpose of God and the experience of his saints. Heb. 12:2: 'Now no affliction for the present seemeth to be joyous but grievous. Nevertheless, afterwards it yieldeth the peaceable fruit of righteousness unto them which are exercised thereby.'" Witherspoon continued, "Both nations in general and private persons are apt to grow remiss and lax in a time of prosperity and seeming security, but when their earthly comforts are endangered or withdrawn, it lays them under a kind of necessity to seek for something better in their place. Men must have comfort from one quarter or another. When earthly things are in a pleasing and promising condition, too many are apt to find their rest and be satisfied with them as their only portion. But when the vanity and passing nature of all created comfort is discovered, they are all compelled to look for something more durable as well as valuable."[57]

The same year, in fact the day before the Declaration of Independence was approved, John Adams wrote to his wife, Abigail, concerning the benefits of misfortune. He declared that wartime hardship "will have this good Effect at least: it will inspire us with many Virtues which we have not and correct many Errors, Follies, and Vices which threaten to disturb, dishonour, and destroy us." Forty years later, having since lost Abigail, Adams claimed that the grief produced by hardship "drives Men into habits of serious Reflection, sharpens the Understanding, and softens the heart." He added that men could not become truly great until they had "been tossed and buffeted by the Vicissitudes of Life, forced upon profound Reflection by Grief and disappointments, and taught to command their Passions and Prejudices." Hardship taught "Patience and Resignation."[58]

John Jay connected even divine punishment with reformation and redemption, contending that the hardships of the Revolutionary War would purify the nation. In a 1776 pamphlet Jay suggested that the war might partly be intended "to punish the guilt of this country and bring us back to a sense of duty to our Creator." To Jay, punishment and correction went hand in hand; punishment was not a crazed and pointless lashing out by a reckless deity, but rather a sort of discipline applied carefully by a loving father to bring about repentance and redemption. In 1797 Jay contended, "Every scourge of every kind by which nations are punished or corrected is under the control of a wise and benevolent Sovereign."[59]

William Livingston believed that misfortune prevented an arrogant complacency. In 1778 he wrote regarding Revolutionary War victories, "Heaven hath indeed smiled upon us—but some drops of bitterness hath been kindly mingled in the cup of joy, lest the draught should intoxicate and lull us to sleep. Our successes encourage the most sanguine hopes; our losses forbid the least presumption."[60]

George Washington also believed that God intended the misfortunes of the Revolutionary War to achieve necessary ends. In 1778 he consoled a loyalist friend who had tried to get to England but was refused passage because he would not take the required oaths against his fellow Americans that the British demanded. Washington wrote, "The determinations of Providence are always wise, [though] often inscrutable, and though its decrees appear to be hard upon us at times, are nevertheless meant for gracious purposes; in this light I cannot help but viewing your late disappointment, for if you had been permitted to have gone to England, unrestrained even by the rigid oaths which are administered on these occasions, your feelings as a husband, Parent & c. must have been considerably wounded in the prospect of a long, perhaps lasting, separation from your nearest relatives." That same year, when some Americans were angered by the failure of their new French ally to achieve any success against the British navy, Washington was philosophical, writing to Jonathan Trumbull, "The violent gale which dissipated the two fleets when on the point of engaging and the withdrawing of the Count D'Estaing may appear to us as real misfortunes, but with you I consider storms and victory under the direction of a wise providence which no doubt directs them for the best of purposes and to bring round the greatest degree of happiness to the greatest number of his people." Soon after he claimed, "Ours is a kind of struggle designed, dare I say, by Providence to try the patience, fortitude, and virtue of Man; none therefore that are engaged in it will suffer themselves, I trust, to sink under difficulties or be discouraged by hardships." Regarding disunity and profiteering in a time of war, he wrote, "Alas! We are not to expect that the path is to be strewed with flowers. That great and good Being who rules the Universe has disposed matters otherwise and for wise purposes, I am persuaded." But two years later Washington was less philosophical about profiteering, in the process drawing a clear distinction between providential hardships and man-made evils. He wrote regarding crop failure, "I look upon every dispensation of Providence as designed to answer some valuable purpose and hope I shall possess a sufficient degree of fortitude to bear without murmuring any stroke which may happen either to my person or estate from that quarter." But he quickly contrasted such acts of God, which must be endured, with acts of human wickedness such as profiteering, which must be opposed. In 1781 Washington declared, "Our affairs are brought to an awful crisis that the hand of Providence, I trust, may be more conspicuous in our deliverance."[61]

Washington believed that God was always ready to care for and console those who suffered hardship. He wrote to Jonathan Trumbull following the death of the latter's wife, "Although calamities of this kind are what we should be prepared to expect, yet few, upon their arrival, are able to bear them with a becoming fortitude. Your determination, however, to seek assistance from the great disposer of all human events is highly laudable, and is the source from whence the truest consolation is to be drawn." He wrote to Henry Knox on the death of his son, "I sincerely condole with Mrs. Knox on the loss you have sustained. In determining to submit patiently to the decrees of the Allwise disposer of Human events, you will find the only true and substantial comfort under the greatest of calamities." He wrote to the future architect of the nation's capital, Pierre Charles L'Enfant, "While I sincerely condole with you on the loss of your good father, you will permit me to remind you, as an inexhaustible source of consolation, that there is a good Providence which will never fail to take care of his children."[62]

Washington considered submission to Providence an essential duty even when God's ways were mysterious. In 1790 he wrote to his former general, Henry Lee, on the death of Lee's wife and son, "As the ways of Providence are as inscrutable as just, it becomes the children of it to submit with resignation & fortitude to its decrees, as far as the feelings of humanity will allow, and your good sense will, I am persuaded, enable you to do this." In 1797 he wrote to the courageous but failed Polish freedom fighter Thaddeus Kosciuszko, "I beg you to be assured that no one has a higher respect and veneration for your character than I have, or one who more sincerely wished, during your arduous struggle in the cause of liberty and your country, that it might be crowned with success. But the ways of Providence are inscrutable, and Mortals must submit." The following year he wrote to his second cousin, William Augustine Washington, regarding the death of William's wife, "These are the decrees of an Allwise Providence, against whose dictates the skill or foresight of man can be of no avail; it is incumbent upon him, therefore, to submit with as little repining as the sensibility of his nature will admit." In 1799, just six months before his own death, Washington noted regarding the death of Patrick Henry, "At any time I should have received the account of this Gentleman's death with sorrow. In the present crisis of our public affairs, I have heard it with deep regret. But the ways of Providence are inscrutable and not to be scanned by short-sighted man, whose duty is submission, without repining at its decrees." Washington's repeated references to the inscrutable nature of divine Providence demonstrate that he was no deist—not only because he believed in an intervening God but also because he lacked the deists' supreme confidence in the ability of human reason to comprehend fully the ways of an omniscient deity, a confidence that led them to declare, with complete assurance, which parts of the Bible were "rational" and which were not.[63]

Benjamin Franklin believed that God sometimes allowed affliction as an opportunity for people to demonstrate charity. In 1781, at the height of the Revolutionary War, Franklin urged American ship captains to avoid interference with British ships carrying relief aid from the citizens of Dublin to the British West Indian victims of a hurricane. While Franklin acknowledged that divine Providence had allowed the hurricane, he also contended that "the principles of Humanity require of Us to assist our fellow Creatures, tho Enemies, when distressed by the Hand of God, and by no means to Impede the Benevolence of those who Commiserate their distresses and would alleviate them." He assured American captains that compliance with his request would not only give them "the present and lasting Satisfaction of having gratified your own humane and pious feelings as Men and as Christians, but will undoubtedly recommend yourselves to the Favor of God, of the Congress, of your Employers, and of your Country." Like Benjamin Rush, Franklin also believed that God intended the afflictions of old age as a means of preparing humans to accept death. According to Franklin's physician, on his deathbed he acknowledged "his grateful sense of the many blessings he had received from the Supreme Being who had raised him from small and low beginnings to such high rank and consideration among men, and made no doubt that his present afflictions were kindly intended to wean him from a world in which he was no longer fit to act the part assigned him."[64]

In 1800 Thomas Jefferson noted that God often brought about good through misfortune. He claimed, "When great evils happen, I am in the habit of looking out for what good may arise from them as consolations to us, and Providence has in fact so established the order of things that most evils are the means of producing some good. The yellow fever will discourage the growth of great cities in our nation & I view great cities as pestilential to the morals, the health, and the liberties of man." He later argued, much like Rush and Franklin, that the grief produced by life's hardships, such as the loss of loved ones and the ailments of the aging body, "prepares us to loose ourselves [from life] without repugnance."[65]

Alexander Hamilton possessed a similar view of divine wisdom in allowing misfortune. In an 1804 letter Hamilton wrote to a young friend, "Arraign not the dispensations of Providence. They must be founded in wisdom and good, and when they do not suit us, it must be because there is some fault in ourselves which deserves chastisement, or because there is a kind intent to correct in us some vice or failing, of which perhaps we may not be conscious, or because the general plan requires that we should suffer partial ill." Although the fact that this letter was submitted anonymously to the *New York Evening Post* after Hamilton's death for the purpose of proving his piety might otherwise raise some doubt as to its authenticity, the missive's ending (a slightly misremembered quote from Alexander Pope, Hamilton's favorite author) gives the letter the ring of truth, and the sentiments expressed in the epistle jibe with those contained in letters that were unquestionably written by Hamilton, as well as with the memories of his son John. Hamilton did not pen the words "arraign not the dispensations of Providence" lightly. Just a few years earlier he had lost a son to a duel and a daughter to madness.[66]

John Marshall agreed with Hamilton. After his infant son passed away, Marshall wrote a letter to his wife, Mary, in which he assured her of "the wisdom and goodness of Providence." No doubt Marshall was comforted in turn by his wife, for years later he declared in his eulogy for her, "From the hour of our union to that of our separation, I never ceased to thank Heaven for this, its best gift."[67]

James Madison concluded that the rarity of suicide proved that the blessings that God bestowed on life outweighed the hardships. In 1821 he argued, "Afflictions of every kind are the onerous conditions charged on the tenure of life, and [yet] it is a silencing [of criticism of], if not a satisfactory vindication of, the ways of Heaven to Man that there are but few who do not prefer an acquiescence to them to a surrender of the tenure itself."[68]

The founders' supreme confidence in the wisdom and goodness of an omnipotent, interventionist God was crucial to their success. It gave them the fortitude to endure the deaths and disasters so common in their era with a sense of optimism and purpose. Above all, they were convinced that God would ensure the success of the new nation's mission to serve as the world's greatest model of liberty. The resultant assurance that their individual efforts on behalf of the nation would also be blessed gave them the confidence to overcome immense hardships and to succeed in endeavors that most objective observers considered impossible.

5

THE NEW ISRAEL

The founders joined to their belief in divine intervention the widespread American conviction that the United States was destined by God to play an integral role in the spread of freedom by erecting a republican city on a hill, a model of liberty that would serve as a safe haven for the world's oppressed. The founders believed that the United States was the new Israel, a nation chosen by God to accomplish a sacred purpose, a mission that entailed both blessings and responsibilities. This belief in a divine mission gave the founders a sense of identity and purpose and the courage to face the tremendous challenges of their time, most notably the successful conduct of a rebellion against the greatest power on earth and the construction of a durable republic. In an age in which rebellion was considered an act of the darkest villainy and rebels were summarily hanged, the founders could assure themselves that they had the full support of an omnipotent God in securing their independence and in establishing a more perfect union. Nevertheless, even after succeeding in these endeavors, some founders were troubled by the possibility of divine judgment on the United States for slavery, the most serious violation of the nation's covenant with God.

THE DIVINE MISSION

As early as 1765, in "A Dissertation on the Feudal and Canon Law," John Adams declared that the settlement of America was "the opening of a grand scene and design in Providence for the illumination of the ignorant and the emancipation of the slavish part of mankind all over the earth." The same year he claimed, "America was designed by Providence for the Theatre on which Man was to make his true figure, on which science, Virtue, Liberty, Happiness, and Glory were to exist in peace." Thirteen years later, the Massachusetts Board of War wrote to Benjamin Franklin, "The dispensations of Providence thro the whole of this unnatural and cruel War hath been truly astonishing. When we have been brought low, God hath helped us. These young rising States seem designed by Nature as a happy Asylum for the poor and oppressed of every Nation, as their 13 united States are blessed with all the fruitful Climates of our Globe, and here all her various productions, the exoticks, may find a Mother's bed. Many Waste places yet remain, and what compleats the Blessing to the poor and oppressed is a long remove from the land where Tyranny and Oppression reign."[1]

Patrick Henry was convinced that God cared a great deal about what happened to the United States because of its divine mission. In his final speech against the Constitution at the Virginia ratifying convention Henry claimed that he was looking "beyond that horizon which binds mortal eyes" to those celestial beings he claimed were hovering over the scene, waiting with anxiety for a decision that involved happiness or misery to all mankind. At the very moment when Henry invoked these angels, a storm arose that shook the entire building. Astonished delegates fled the scene without waiting for a formal adjournment. Nevertheless, the Federalists regained their nerve and secured a vote for ratification the following day.[2]

Other founders expressed the same belief in a divine national mission. In 1778 Benjamin Rush declared, "I long to see the image of God restored to the human mind. I long to see virtue and religion supported, and vice and irreligion banished, from society by wise and equitable governments. I long to see an asylum prepared for the persecuted and oppressed of all countries and a door opened for the progress of knowledge, literature, the arts, and the gospel of Jesus Christ to the ends of the earth. And these great events are only to be accomplished by establishing and perpetuating liberty in our country." Eleven years later, when George Washington was inaugurated as the first president of the United States, he placed his hand on a Bible that was opened to Genesis 49, which concerns Jacob's prophesy regarding the tribes founded by his twelve sons. In this way Washington designated the United States the new Israel. In a 1790 letter to the Jewish community in Savannah, Washington explicitly connected the American mission to that of Israel, both operating under the same God: "May the same wonder-working Deity who long since delivering the Hebrews from their Egyptian Oppressors, planted them in the promised land—whose providential agency has lately been conspicuous in establishing these United States as an independent nation—continue to water them with the dews of Heaven and to make the inhabitants of every denomination participate in the temporal and spiritual blessings of that people whose God is Jehovah."[3]

In 1794, as war raged throughout Europe, Benjamin Rush noted, "The United States continue to flourish in agriculture, arts, and commerce." He added, "How kind is providence in every deluge, whether of water or blood, to prepare an ark for the preservation of the poor human race." John Jay expressed the same idea of an American mission to serve as a place of refuge for the world's persecuted: "There is something very pleasant in the Reflection that while war, discord, and oppression triumph in so many parts of Europe, their Domination does not extend to our Country. I sometimes flatter myself that Providence, in Compassion to the afflicted in these countries, will continue to leave America in a proper state to be an asylum to them." In 1801 John Dickinson ended a letter to the newly elected president, Thomas Jefferson, as follows:

> Perhaps We are the selected People upon Earth from whom large Portions of Mankind are to learn that Liberty is really a transcendent Blessing, as capable by its enlightened Energies of calmly dissipating its internal Enemies as of triumphantly repelling its foreign Foes. . . . The adorable Creator of the world is infinitely benevolent, tho it is impossible for our finite Capacities to comprehend all his Dispensations. However, We know enough to excite our warmest Gratitude and firmest Confidence. My Belief is unhesitatingly that by his superintending Providence a Period greatly favorable is commencing in the Destinies of the Human Race. That he may be pleased to honour thee as an Instrument for advancing his gracious purposes, and that he may be thy Guide and Protector, is the ardent Wish, the fervent Prayer, of thy truly Affectionate Friend, John Dickinson.

Although the founders considered the United States the most crucial instrument of God in advancing liberty, just as Israel had been the most important implement of the Almighty in advancing ethical monotheism, in both cases the plan itself was universal. The nation in question was merely the chosen means of divine blessing to the entire world.[4]

One of the reasons for the popularity of numerous works, such as Elias Boudinot's *A Star in the West* (1816), that claimed that Native Americans were the descendants of the Ten Lost Tribes of Israel, the tribes that had been taken into captivity by the Assyrians in the eighth century BC, was that these books increased the feeling of kinship between the United States and biblical Israel that so inspired Americans. As the historian Eran Shalev has stated this conception, "Providential history had wonderfully raised America, God's New Israel, in the land in which lost biblical Israelites, a people who had forgotten their own history and lost their unique identity, now resided." The divine torch had been passed from Israel to America, the New Holy Lands. The fact that the nation of Israel had been out of existence for almost two millennia, without any realistic prospect for restoration (or so Americans thought, despite the fact that its resurrection was prophesied in numerous biblical passages, including Ezekiel 37), only enhanced their belief in a "replacement theology" that envisioned Christianity replacing Judaism as the divine religion and the United States replacing Israel as God's favored nation.[5]

DIVINE BLESSINGS

The founders were convinced that the United States' unique mission entailed unique blessings. Indeed, they believed that these divine favors had begun with the earliest European settlers. In 1765 Samuel Adams claimed regarding his Puritan ancestors, "They were prospered in their settlement by Him whose is the Earth & the Fullness thereof beyond all human Expectation." The following year he marveled, "When we look back upon the many dangers from which our country hath, even from the first settlement, been delivered, and the policy and power of those who have to this day sought its ruin, we are sensibly struck with an admiration of Divine goodness and would religiously regard the arm which has so often shielded us." Almost half a century later, John Jay looked back on American history with the same sense of awe as Adams, proceeding from the same belief that God had planned its course from the very first settlements. Jay contended, "A proper history of the United States . . . would develop the great plan of Providence for causing North America to be gradually filled with civilized and Christian people and nations." The history to which Jay referred would be written by George Bancroft a few decades later.[6]

In his resignation message to the state governors immediately following the successful conclusion of the Revolutionary War in 1783, George Washington marveled at "the glorious events which Heaven has been pleased to produce in our favour." He added:

> When we consider the magnitude of the prize we contended for, the doubtful nature of the contest, and the favourable manner in which it has terminated, we shall find the greatest possible reason for rejoicing . . . and we shall have equal occasion to felicitate ourselves on the lot which Providence has assigned us, whether we view it in a natural, a political, or [a] moral point of light. The citizens of America, placed in the most enviable condition, the sole lords and proprietors of a vast tract of continent . . . acknowledged to be possessed of absolute freedom and independency . . . are from this period to be considered as the actors on a most conspicuous theatre which seems to be peculiarly designated by Providence for the display of human greatness and felicity. Here they are not only surrounded with everything that can contribute to the completion of private and domestic enjoyment, but Heaven has crowned all its other blessings by giving a surer opportunity for political happiness than any other nation has ever been favoured with. . . . The free cultivation of letters, the unbounded extension of commerce, the progressive refinement of manners, the growing liberality of sentiment, and above all, the pure and benign light of Revelation, have had a meliorating influence on mankind and increased the blessings of society. At this auspicious period the United States came into existence as a Nation, and if their citizens should not be completely free and happy, the fault will be entirely their own.[7]

In his First Inaugural Address (1801) Thomas Jefferson listed the benefits that a generous God had bestowed on the United States. Among these was the fact that the Almighty had caused Americans to be "enlightened by a benign religion, professed indeed and practiced in various forms, yet all of them inculcating honesty, truth, temperance, gratitude, and the love of man, acknowledging and adoring an overruling providence, which by all its dispensations proves that it delights in the happiness of man here and his greater happiness thereafter." Jefferson's message to Congress the following year listed the divine blessings bestowed on the United States as "peace and friendship abroad; law, order, and religion at home; good affection with our Indian neighbors; our burdens lightened, yet our incomes sufficient, and the produce of the year great." In his Second Inaugural Address (1805) Jefferson declared, "I shall need the favor of that Being in whose hands we are, who led our forefathers, as Israel of old, from their native land and planted them in a land flowing with all the necessaries and comforts of life, who has covered our infancy with His providence and our riper years with His wisdom and power, and to whose goodness I ask you to join me in supplications that He will so enlighten the minds of your servants, guide their councils and prosper their measures that whatsoever they shall do shall result in your good and secure the peace, friendship, and approbation of all nations."[8]

The same year James Monroe declared that Americans had "much cause for grateful acknowledgments to the supreme Author of all things for the manifold blessings which he has been pleased to confer on this highly favored and very happy country." In his First Inaugural Address in 1817 Monroe again referred to the peculiar degree of divine favor the United States habitually received. Monroe ended the speech as follows: "Relying on the aid to be derived from the other departments of the Government, I enter on the trust to which I have been called by the suffrages of my fellow citizens, with my fervent prayers to the Almighty that He will be graciously pleased to continue the protection which He has already so conspicuously displayed in our favor." Three years later, in his annual message to Congress, Monroe claimed, "When, then, we take into view the prosperous and happy condition of our country in all the great circumstances which constitute the felicity of a nation—every individual in the full enjoyment of all his rights, the Union blessed with plenty and rapidly rising to greatness under a National Government which operates with complete effect in every part without being felt in any except by the ample protection which it affords, and under State governments which perform their equal share, according to a wise distribution of power between them, in promoting the public happiness—it is impossible to behold so gratifying, so glorious, a spectacle without being penetrated with the most profound and grateful acknowledgments to the Supreme Author of All Good for such manifold and inestimable blessings." Monroe then referred to "the great perfection of our most excellent system of government" as "the powerful instrument in the hands of our All Merciful Creator in securing to us these blessings."[9]

The founders often attributed the nation's remarkable prosperity to divine Providence. In a 1784 oration to the Virginia House of Burgesses, Patrick Henry called America "a land on which Providence hath emptied the horn of abundance." In the 1790s Alexander Hamilton wrote regarding the refusal of the Whiskey Rebels to pay their taxes, "A scene of unbridled prosperity upbraids the ingratitude and madness of those who are endeavouring to cloud the bright face of our political horizon and to mar the happiest lot that beneficent Heaven ever indulged to undeserving mortals." In George Washington's sixth annual address to Congress in 1794 he declared that the nation should unite "in imploring the Supreme Ruler of nations" to "perpetuate to our country that prosperity which his goodness has already conferred." In 1799, after noting the nation's continued prosperity in spite of the war raging in Europe, John Marshall wrote for the House of Representatives, "We cannot fail to offer up to a benevolent Deity our sincere thanks for these, the merciful dispensations of his protecting providence."[10]

Divine favor also manifested itself in the natural features of the North American continent and in its isolation from the tyranny and turmoil of Europe. In his act to incorporate the American Philosophical Society (1780) Thomas Paine wrote, "This country of North America, which the goodness of Providence hath given us to inherit, from the vastness of its extent, the variety of its climate, the fertility of its soil, the yet unexplored treasures of its bowels, the multitude of its rivers, lakes, bays, inlets, and their conveniences of navigation, offers to these United States one of the richest subjects of cultivation ever presented to any people upon earth." In 1798 John Marshall claimed, "An immense ocean placed by a gracious Providence, which seems to watch over this rising empire, between us and the European world poses such an obstacle to an invading ambition, must so diminish the force which can be brought to bear upon us, that our resources, if duly exerted, must be adequate to our protection, and we shall remain free if we do not deserve to be slaves." Note that Marshall placed more confidence in the God that so positioned the United States than in the positioning itself. Hence his sole fear was that Americans might one day cease to merit divine protection.[11]

Indeed, it was widely understood that the continuance of all of the blessings that God had conferred on the United States depended on the piety and morality of the American people and that these could be rescinded at any time. Thus, in 1776, Governor William Livingston exhorted the New Jersey legislature, "Let us, Gentlemen, both by Precept and Practice, encourage a Spirit of Economy, Industry, and Patriotism, and that public Integrity which cannot fail to exalt a Nation, Setting our Faces at the same Time like a Flint against that Dissoluteness of Manners and political Corruption which will ever be the Reproach of any People [a paraphrase of Proverbs 14:34]. May the Foundation of our Infant State be laid in Virtue and the Fear of God, and the Superstructure will rise glorious and endure for Ages. Then may we humbly expect the Blessings of the Most High, who Divides to the Nations their Inheritance and Separates the Sons of Adam" (a paraphrase of Deuteronomy 32:8). Two years later, according to Benjamin Rush's contemporary notes, "I sat next to Jn. Adams in Congress, and upon my whispering to him and asking if he thought we should succeed in our struggle against G. Britain, he answered me, 'Yes, if we fear God and repent of our sins.'" Upon finding and reading these notes again in 1790, at which time Adams was the nation's first vice president, Rush wrote to him, "This anecdote will I hope teach my boys that it is not necessary to disbelieve Christianity or to renounce morality in order to arrive at the highest political usefulness or fame." Similarly, George Washington wrote in 1789, "The man must be bad indeed who can look upon the events of the American Revolution without feeling the warmest gratitude towards the great Author of the Universe whose divine interposition was so frequently manifested in our behalf. And it is my earnest prayer that we may so conduct ourselves as to merit a continuance of those blessings with which we have hitherto been favoured."[12]

DIVINE ASSISTANCE DURING THE REVOLUTION

One of the most commonly shared beliefs among the founders, and indeed among Americans generally, both during and after the American Revolution, was that the United States' startling triumph over Great Britain, the most powerful nation of the eighteenth century, was the result of divine assistance. Confidence in divine aid began even before the first shots were fired at Lexington. In 1769 George Mason wrote regarding the boycott and the embargo, "These are the Arms with which God and Nature have furnished us for our Defence, a prudent and resolute exertion of which will soon obtain what has been refused to our most ardent Supplications." In his famous "liberty or death" speech of 1775 Patrick Henry declared, "We shall not fight our battles alone. There is a just God who presides over the destinies of nations and who will raise up friends to fight our battles for us." This would later read like a prophecy of the French alliance. The same year, after the British attempted to starve Massachusetts by closing the port of Boston in retribution for the Tea Party but failed because the other colonies came to its aid, Samuel Adams claimed, "We cannot but persuade ourselves that the Supreme Being approves our conduct, by whose all powerful influence the British American continent hath been united and thus far successful in disappointing the enemies of our common liberty in the hopes that, by reducing people to want and hunger, they should force them to yield to their unrighteous demands." In 1776, after the British were compelled to evacuate Boston, he wrote to a member of the Massachusetts Provincial Congress, "I heartily congratulate you upon the sudden and important Change of our Affairs in the Removal of the Barbarians from the Capital. We owe our grateful Acknowledgments to him who is, as he is frequently styled in the sacred Writ, 'the Lord of Hosts,' 'the God of Armies.'"[13]

George Washington, who commanded the army that drove the British from Boston, issued a similar statement to the legislature: "That the metropolis of your Colony is now released from the cruel and oppressive invasion of those who were sent to erect the Standard of lawless domination & to trample on the rights of humanity and is again open &free for its rightful possessors must give pleasure to every virtuous and Sympathetic heart—and, being effected without the blood of our Soldiers and fellow Citizens, must be ascribed to the Interposition of that providence which has manifestly appeared in our behalf thro' the whole of this important struggle." In August, when British General William Howe prepared to attack Washington's ill-trained and ill-equipped amateurs with 32,000 professional soldiers, the largest army ever assembled in America, Washington was unshaken: "We have every reason to expect Heaven will crown with Success so just a cause. . . . We must resolve to conquer or die; with this resolution and the blessing of Heaven, Victory and Success certainly will attend us."[14]

In 1776 John Witherspoon declared in a sermon, "It would be a criminal inattention not to observe the singular interposition of Providence hitherto in behalf of the American colonies. . . . Has not the boasted discipline of regular and veteran [British] soldiers been turned into confusion and dismay before the raw and maiden courage of freemen in defense of their property and right? . . . The signal advantage gained by the evacuation of Boston and the shameful flight of the army and navy of Britain was brought about without the loss of a man." The same year Benjamin Rush wrote to his wife regarding Pennsylvania, "Our cause prospers in every county of the province. The hand of heaven is with us. Did I not think so, I would not have embarked on it. You have everything to hope and nothing to fear from the part which duty to God, to my country, and to my conscience have led me to take in our affairs. The measures which I have proposed have hitherto been so successful that I am constrained to believe I act under the direction of providence. God knows I seek the honor and the best interests of my fellow citizens supremely in all I am doing for my country." In 1778 he wrote regarding congressmen and generals, "Weak minds begin already to ascribe our deliverance to them. Had not heaven defeated their counsels in a thousand instances, we should have been hewers of wood and drawers of water to the subjects of the King of Britain."[15]

William Livingston recognized this divine assistance, even while cautioning the New Jersey assembly against being made complacent by it. In 1776 he told the assemblymen, "I heartily participate with you in the Pleasure of tracing that conspicuous Providential Agency which has hitherto frustrated the sanguinary Purposes of our Enemies and which that it is not more generally and devoutly acknowledged is greatly to be deplored. But while with pious Gratitude we survey the frequent Interpositions of Heaven in our Behalf, we ought to remember that as the Disbelief of an overruling Providence is Atheism, so an absolute Confidence of having our Deliverance wrought out by the Hand of God without our own Exertions is the most culpable Presumption. Let us therefore inflexibly persevere in exerting our most strenuous Efforts in an humble and rational Dependence on the great Governor of the World." The following year, after the British retreated from New Jersey into New York, he declared, "How conspicuous the Finger of Heaven in their Expulsion from this State the most Unobservant may recollect with Wonder, and every serious Man will remember with devout Gratitude." In 1778 he expressed gratitude that "through the blessings of heaven we can now arm thousands with the muskets of the best kind and of one caliber, we have artillery, ammunition, and camp equipage in abundance, and we can feed and pay our troops without difficulty." He opposed the French alliance because he suspected the French of having designs on American territory, declaring, "It is upon God and our right, not upon Lewis the XVI, that we depend for our deliverance." He claimed, "Having entered into the war with the devotion of Christians, as well as the Spirit of Heroes, and being clearly conscious of the purity & rectitude of our intentions, it has accordingly pleased the great Arbiter of Events, 'whose kingdom ruleth over all' [Psalms 10:19] to crown our exertions in the cause of Liberty and of human nature with such a series of Successes & in such a remarkable manner as will astonish Posterity. In his usual direction of the Universe, the Almighty seems to conceal the traces of his providential agency from human sight, and they are rather discoverable by the final result than discerned in their progress towards the Event. But in accomplishing our deliverance, the Footsteps of Providence have in a manner been visible throughout, and the arm of omnipotence, if I may so speak, been bared & rendered conspicuous to Infidelity itself."[16]

George Washington shared both Livingston's reliance on divine Providence and his concern that it might become an excuse for laziness. In 1777, faced with a crisis caused by expiring enlistments, he wrote to his stepson, "How we shall be able to rub along till the new army is raised I know not. Providence has heretofore saved us in a remarkable manner, and on this we must principally rely." But he also wrote three months later, "All agree our claims are righteous and must be supported. Yet all, or at least too great a part among us, withhold the means, as if Providence, who has already done much for us, would continue his gracious interposition and work miracles for our deliverance, without troubling ourselves about the matter." Later that same year, he announced to his soldiers regarding the turning point of the war, the British surrender at Saratoga, "On the 14th instant, General [John] Burgoyne and his whole Army surrendered themselves [as] prisoners of war. Let every face brighten and every heart expand with grateful Joy and praise to the supreme disposer of all events, who has granted us this signal success."[17]

The following year Washington instructed his soldiers, "While we are zealously performing the duties of good Citizens and soldiers, we certainly ought not to be inattentive to the higher duties of Religion. To the distinguished Character of Patriot, it should be our highest Glory to add the more distinguished Character of Christian. The signal instances of providential Goodness which we have experienced and which have now almost crowned our labours with complete Success demand from us in a peculiar manner the warmest returns of Gratitude and Piety to the Supreme Author of all Good." After thanking a friend, he claimed, "Providence has a joint claim to my humble and grateful thanks, for its protection and direction of me through the many difficult and intricate scenes which this contest hath produced and for the constant interposition on our behalf when the clouds were heaviest and seemed ready to burst upon us." He wrote to his brother regarding General Charles Lee's unexpected retreat at the Battle of Monmouth, "The disorder arising from it would have proved fatal to the Army had not that bountiful Providence which has never failed us in the hour of distress enabled me to form a Regiment or two of those that were retreating in the face of the Enemy." He wrote to one of his generals regarding the war, "The hand of Providence has been so conspicuous in all this that he must be worse than an infidel that lacks faith, and more than wicked, that has not gratitude enough to acknowledge his obligations." At the end of 1778, when Washington's army was in a terrible financial state due to Congress's inability to tax (and thus to fund it), and his unpaid officers were "sinking by sure degrees into beggary and want," he concluded a letter to Benjamin Harrison, "I feel more real distress on account of the present appearances of things than I have at any time since the commencement of the dispute; but it is time to bid you once more adieu. Providence has heretofore taken us up when all other means and hope seemed to be departing from us. In this I will confide." A few months later, after deploring the continuing financial distress of the army, he wrote, "And yet, Providence having so often taken us up when bereft of every hope, I trust we shall not fail even in this."[18]

In 1780, after Benedict Arnold's attempt to hand over West Point to the British failed, Washington announced to his soldiers, "Treason of the blackest dye was yesterday discovered! General Arnold, who commanded at West Point, lost to every sentiment of honor, of public and private obligation, was about to deliver up that important Post into the hands of the enemy. Such an event must have given the American cause a deadly wound, if not a fatal stab. Happily, the treason has been timely discovered to prevent the fatal misfortune. The providential train of circumstances which led to it affords the most convincing proof that the Liberties of America are the object of divine Protection." Nor was this a mere cliché presented for public consumption, for a couple of weeks later Washington wrote privately, "In no instance since the commencement of the War has the interposition of Providence appeared more conspicuous than in the rescue of the Post and Garrison of West Point from Arnold's villainous perfidy. . . . An unaccountable deprivation of presence of Mind in a man of the first abilities and the virtuous conduct of three Militia men threw the Adjutant General of the British forces in America (with full proofs of Arnold's treachery) into our hands." Note that Washington attributed to the Almighty both Arnold's uncharacteristic blunders and the quick-mindedness of American militiamen in the timely capture of Major John Andre. Washington was far from alone in this belief. Benjamin Rush claimed, "The discovery of Arnold's treachery and the new Bennington affair in the South [the patriot victory at King's Mountain] have given fresh hopes and spirits to the whigs. We had forgotten the former deliverance under our late losses and mortifications. But we now find that Providence is on our side and that our independence is as secure as the everlasting mountains." Samuel Adams wrote, "Arnold's Conspiracy was to have wrought Wonders, but gracious Heaven defeated it. We have so often seen in the Course of this Conflict the remarkable Interposition of divine Providence in our favor."[19]

Washington continued to attribute patriot success to divine Providence in countless letters throughout the rest of the war. In fact, in one epistle he claimed, "It has at times been my only dependence, for all other resources have failed us." Yet he also continued to warn against a form of complacency that considered human exertion unnecessary. While marching with the French to surround Cornwallis at Yorktown, he wrote to the governors of New Jersey, Delaware, and Virginia pleading for supplies: "A Reflection on the Cause of Failure, should it prove to be the one in which I have my strongest Fears, the Article of Supplies, will not fail to fill us with the most mortifying Regret, when we consider that the bountiful hand of Heaven is holding out to us Plenty of every Article, and the only Cause of Want must be placed to the Account of our Want of Exertion to collect them." Even after the victory at Yorktown, the war continued for over a year, causing Washington to warn, "If the States cannot or will not rouse to more vigorous exertions, they must submit to the consequences.

Providence has done much for us in this contest, but we must do something for ourselves if we expect to go triumphantly through with it."[20]

When the Treaty of Paris that ended the war was finally signed, Washington wrote to the inhabitants of Princeton, "If in the execution of an arduous Office I have been so happy as to discharge my duty to the Public with fidelity and success and to obtain the good opinion of my fellow Soldiers and fellow Citizens, I attribute all glory to that Supreme Being who hath caused the several parts which have been employed in the production of the wonderful Events we now contemplate to harmonize in the most perfect manner and who was able by the humblest instruments as well as by the most powerful means to establish and secure the liberty and happiness of these United States." To the Comte de Rochambeau, his partner in the capture of Cornwallis's army, he wrote privately, "I shall . . . look back on our past toils with a grateful admiration of that beneficent Providence which has raised up so many instruments to accomplish so great a revolution as the one you have had a share in bringing about." In his final statement to his soldiers Washington declared, "A contemplation of the complete attainment (at a period earlier than could have been expected) of the object for which we contended against so formidable a power cannot but inspire us with astonishment and gratitude. The disadvantageous circumstances on our part under which the war was undertaken can never be forgotten. The singular interpositions of Providence in our feeble condition were such as could scarcely escape the attention of the most unobserving, while the unparalleled perseverance of the Armies of the United States through almost every possible suffering and discouragement for the space of eight long years was little short of a standing miracle."[21]

In Washington's resignation message to Congress in 1783, he recalled that he had accepted Congress's commission as commander of the Continental Army with "a diffidence in my abilities to accomplish so arduous a task, which however was superseded by a confidence in the rectitude of our Cause, the support of the Supreme Power of the Union, and the patronage of Heaven." Of these three, Washington clearly considered the last the most important, for he concluded the speech as follows: "I consider it an indispensable duty to close this last solemn act of my Official life by commending the Interests of our dearest Country to the protection of Almighty God and those who have the superintendence of them to his holy keeping." According to James McHenry, at this point Washington's "voice faltered and sunk, and the whole house felt his agitation." Nine years later Washington claimed, "There never was a people who had more reason to acknowledge a divine interposition in their affairs than those of the United States, and I should be pained to believe that they have forgotten that agency which was so often manifested during our Revolution or that they failed to consider the omnipotence of that God who is alone able to protect them." In 1795 Washington contended, "To the Great ruler of events, not to any exertions of mine, is to be ascribed the favorable termination of our late contest for liberty. I never considered the fortunate issue of any measure adopted by me in the progress of the Revolution in any other light than as the ordering of kind Providence."[22]

Other founders shared Washington's belief in divine aid during the Revolutionary War. In 1777 John Jay identified God as the real cause of American success, urging, "Instead of swelling our breasts with arrogant ideas of our prowess and importance, kindle in them a flame of gratitude and piety, which may consume all remains of vice and irreligion." After the capture of the British army at Saratoga the following month, Samuel Adams wrote to General Horatio Gates, "While the Merit of your signal Services remains recorded in the faithful Breasts of your Countrymen, the warmest Gratitude is due to the God of Armies, who has vouchsafed in so distinguished a Manner to favor the Cause of America & Mankind." Similarly, George Mason claimed the following year, "God has been pleased to bless our endeavors in a just cause with remarkable success. To us upon the spot who have seen step by step the process of this great contest, who know the defenseless state of America in the beginning and the numberless difficulties we have had to struggle with, taking a retrospective view of what is passed, we seem to have been treading upon enchanted ground." In 1779, in its proclamation calling for a day of prayer and thanksgiving, Congress declared that Americans should "approach the throne of Almighty God with gratitude and praise" not only for "conducting our forefathers to this western world" and protecting them and their progeny but also because "He hath prospered our arms and those of our ally, been a shield to our troops in the hour of danger, pointed their swords to victory, and led them in triumph over the bulwarks of the foe . . . and, above all, that he hath diffused the glorious light of the gospel whereby, through the merits of our gracious Redeemer, we may become the heirs of eternal glory."[23]

Thomas Paine often proclaimed his confidence in divine assistance during the war, though he emphasized that the aid of Providence came through natural causes, not miracles. In 1775 Paine contended, "He who guides the natural tempest will regulate the political one and bring good out of evil. In our petition to Britain we asked but for peace, but the prayer was rejected. The cause is now before a higher court, the court of providence, before whom the arrogance of kings, the infidelity of ministers, the general corruption of government, and all the cobweb artifice of courts will fall confounded and ashamed." The same year he emphasized that this divine aid would come not through miracles but through the natural means of self-defense. He wrote regarding the pillar of cloud through which God protected the fleeing Israelites in Exodus 13:21, "It protected them in their retreat from Pharaoh while they were destitute of the natural means of defense, for they brought no arms from Egypt, but it neither fought their battles nor shielded them from dangers afterwards." Confidence in divine assistance should not be used to justify inaction in undertaking practical means of defense. In the first of his famous "Crisis" essays (1776) Paine exhorted, "Throw not the burden of the day upon Providence but 'show your faith by your works' [James 2:18] that God may bless you." But Paine was confident that God would bless the patriots' efforts through natural means. In another essay he had the deceased patriot hero Richard Montgomery declare, "God did not excite the attention of all Europe—of the whole world—nay of angels themselves, to the present controversy for nothing. The inhabitants of Heaven long to see the ark finished, in which all the liberty and true religion of the world are to be deposited. The day in which the Colonies declare their independence will be a jubilee." America was the ark of liberty, and the date of its independence would be a day of heavenly rejoicing. After Washington's capture of the Hessian army at Trenton, Paine remarked that "it appeared clear to me, by the late providential turn of affairs, that God Almighty was visibly on our side."[24]

In his 1780 preamble to the bill that abolished slavery in Pennsylvania, Paine claimed, "When we contemplate our abhorrence of that condition to which the arms and tyranny of Great Britain were exerted to reduce us, when we look back on the variety of dangers to which we have been exposed, and how miraculously our wants in many instances have been supplied and our deliverances wrought, when even hope and human fortitude have become unequal to the conflict, we are unavoidably led to a serious and grateful sense of the manifold blessings which we have undeservedly received from the hand of that Being from whom every good and perfect gift cometh" (James 1:17). Paine's ardor uncharacteristically caused him to use the word "miraculously" here. He then presented the abolition of slavery as an act of gratitude to God for His assistance in obtaining American freedom and as an expiation of sin. In an essay soon after Paine claimed, "The hand of providence has cast us into one common lot and accomplished the independence of America."[25]

The conviction that God had given the United States victory in the war soon became an article of faith among all political factions. The same Anti-Federalists who, in 1787–1788, derided the Federalist claim that the new federal constitution was a gift of God had no qualms about crediting the Almighty with the patriot victory over the British. Patrick Henry declared, "Our war was in opposition to the most grievous oppression. We resisted, and our resistance was approved and blessed by Heaven." Not only had God given birth to the new nation, but He had done so at a time when it could avail itself of judicial wisdom based on historical experience. Henry added, "Respecting public justice, it was a nation blessed by Heaven with the experience of past times, not like those nations whose crude systems of jurisprudence originated in the ages of barbarity and ignorance of human rights." Henry later claimed, "The American Revolution was the grand operation which seemed to be assigned by the Deity to the men of this age in our country over and above the common duties of life. I ever prized at a high rate the superior privilege of being one in that chosen age to which providence entrusted its favourite work. With that impression, it was impossible for me to resist the impulse I felt to contribute my mite toward accomplishing that event which in future will give a superior aspect to the men of these times." The Maryland Anti-Federalist Luther Martin wrote to his fellow citizens regarding the Revolutionary War, "Heaven wrought a miracle in your favour, and your efforts were crowned with success."[26]

Other founders besides the Anti-Federalists agreed with this interpretation of recent history. Benjamin Franklin wrote regarding the Revolutionary War, "Our human means were unequal to our undertaking and . . . if it had not been for the Justice of our Cause and the consequent Interposition of Providence, in which we had Faith, we must have been ruined. If I had ever before been an Atheist, I should now have been convinced of the Being and Government of a Deity! It is he who abases the Proud and favours the Humble." In a 1783 sermon delivered on a public day of thanksgiving, John Witherspoon declared, "The separation of this country from Britain has been of God; for every step the British took to prevent it seemed to accelerate it, which has generally been the case when men have undertaken to go in opposition to the course of Providence." Three years later Thomas Jefferson attributed the success of the American Revolution to divine intervention, writing, "We put our existence to hazard, when the hazard seemed against us, and we saved our country, justifying at the same time the ways of Providence, whose precept is to do what is right, and leave the issue to him." In 1790 he wrote in a similar vein, "It is an animating thought that while we are securing the rights of ourselves and our posterity, we are pointing out the way to struggling nations who wish, like us, to emerge from their tyrannies also. Heaven help their struggles and lead them, as it has done us, triumphantly thro' them." In 1811 John Adams contended regarding the American Revolution, "God prospered our labors; and awful, dreadful, and deplorable as the consequences have been [via the French Revolution, which was inspired by the American], I cannot but hope that the ultimate good of the world, of the human race, and of our beloved country is intended and will be accomplished by it." The following year Benjamin Rush wrote that during the Revolution, Congress "appealed to the God of armies and nations for support, and he blessed both their councils and their arms." In his autobiography Rush recalled regarding Charles Thomson, "He was once told in my presence that he ought to write a history of the Revolution. 'No,' said he, 'I ought not, for I should contradict all the histories of the great events of the Revolution and shew by my account of men, motives, and measures that we are wholly indebted to the agency of divine providence for its successful issue. Let the world admire the supposed wisdom and valor of our great men. Perhaps they may adopt the qualities that have been ascribed to them, and thus good may be done. I shall not undeceive future generations.'"[27]

THE CONSTITUTION AS A DIVINE GIFT

It is sometimes suggested that the absence of any mention of God in the U.S. Constitution constitutes evidence of a lack of piety on the part of its framers. Although the framers did indeed omit such a reference—perhaps, in the words of historian Paul Boller, because they were "eager to avoid embroiling the new government in religious controversies" (another manifestation of the risk aversion that led them to omit a bill of rights from the original text)—most of them viewed God as the ultimate force behind the document. Anticipating its ratification, George Washington wrote to the Marquis de Lafayette, "Should every thing proceed with harmony and consent according to our actual wishes and expectations, I will confess to you sincerely, my dear Marquis, it will be so much beyond anything we had a right to imagine or expect eighteen months ago that it will demonstrate as visibly the finger of Providence as any possible event in the course of human affairs can ever designate it. It is impracticable for you or anyone who has not been on the spot to realize the change in men's minds and the progress towards rectitude in thinking and acting which will then have been made." He conveyed to another of his former generals, Benjamin Lincoln, the same belief that the Constitution was a divine gift, calling its ratification "the road to which the finger of Providence has so manifestly pointed." He added regarding the potential failure of ratification, "I cannot believe it will ever come to pass! The Author of all good has not conducted us so far on the Road to happiness and glory to withdraw from us, in the hour of need, his beneficial support."

Washington likewise wrote to Jonathan Trumbull Jr., "We may, with a kind of grateful and pious exultation, trace the finger of Providence through those dark and mysterious events which first induced the States to appoint a general Convention and then led them one after one another (by steps as were best calculated to effect the object) into an adoption of the system recommended by that general Convention—thereby, in all human probability, laying a lasting foundation for tranquility and happiness, when we had but too much reason to fear that confusion and misery were coming rapidly upon us." In another letter he marveled at how God had used the distresses caused by the Articles of Confederation, the nation's original constitution, to bring about a more perfect union: "A multiplication of circumstances, scarcely yet investigated, appears to have cooperated in bringing about that great, and I trust happy, revolution that is on the eve of being accomplished. It will not be uncommon that those things which were considered at the moment as real ills should have been no inconsiderable causes in producing positive and permanent national felicity. For it is thus that Providence works in the mysterious course of events 'from seeming evil still educing good.'" Washington borrowed the latter phrase from James Thomson's "A Hymn" (1730), the underlying concept from the Bible.[28]

In his first year as president Washington often referred to the crucial role of Providence not only in securing American independence but also in leading the nation to a sound constitution. He wrote to the officials of Philadelphia:

> When I contemplate the Interposition of Providence, as it was visibly Manifested in guiding us thro' the Revolution, in preparing us for the Reception of a General Government, and in conciliating the Good will of the People of America towards one another after its Adoption, I feel myself oppressed and almost overwhelmed with a sense of the Divine Munificence. I feel that nothing is due to my personal agency in all these complicated and wonderful Events except what can simply be attributed to the exertions of an honest Zeal for the Good of my Country. . . . If I have distressing apprehensions that I shall not be able to justify the exalted expectations of my countrymen, I am supported under the pressure of such uneasy reflections by a confidence that the most gracious Being who hath hitherto watched over the interests and averted the perils of the United States will never suffer so fair an inheritance to become a prey to anarchy, despotism, or any other species of oppression.[29]

Ten days later Washington returned to this theme in his First Inaugural Address. He declared, "No People can be bound to acknowledge and adore the invisible hand which conducts the Affairs of men more than the people of the United States. Every step by which they have advanced to the character of an independent nation seems to have been distinguished by some token of providential agency. And in the important revolution just accomplished in the system of their United Government the tranquil deliberations and voluntary consent of so many distinct communities from which the event has resulted cannot be compared with the means by which most Governments have been established without some return of pious gratitude, along with an humble anticipation of the future blessings which the past seem to presage. These reflections, arising out of the present crisis, have forced themselves too strongly on my mind to be suppressed." Several months later Washington called for a national day of prayer and thanksgiving to thank God not only for intervening on behalf of the United States in the Revolutionary War, and for the prosperity and freedom since enjoyed, but also "for the peaceable and rational manner in which we have been enabled to establish constitutions of government for our safety and happiness, particularly the national One now lately instituted."[30]

Washington was far from being the only founder who considered the Constitution a divine gift. Two months after Washington's call for a day of thanksgiving, on Christmas Day to be precise, Charles Thomson congratulated the president on North Carolina's ratification of the Constitution, which left eccentric Rhode Island as the only remaining holdout among the original thirteen states. Thomson declared, "I now consider the revolution complete, and now [that] it is accomplished, I cannot but with a mixture of wonder, joy, and gratitude to the Supreme disposer of events reflect on what easy terms compared to what it has cost others in similar circumstances we have obtained a rank among the nations of the earth and with what tranquility a reform has been made in our constitution & government, which bids fair to transmit the blessings of freedom, independence & happiness to future generations."[31]

Despite Benjamin Franklin's disappointment at the failure of the delegates to act on his proposal for daily prayer at the Constitutional Convention, he was confident that the resultant constitution was blessed by God. He wrote to the editor of the *Federal Gazette* on April 8, 1788, "I have so much Faith in the general Government of the World by Providence that I can hardly conceive [that] a Transaction of such momentous Importance to the Welfare of Millions now existing and to exist in the Posterity of a great Nation [as the Constitution] should be suffered to pass without being in some degree influenc'd, guided, and governed by that omnipotent, omnipresent, & beneficent Ruler in whom all inferior Spirits live & move and have their Being" (Acts 17:28).[32]

At the Pennsylvania ratifying convention Benjamin Rush asserted his belief that he and his fellow delegates at the Constitutional Convention had received divine guidance. According to his colleague Thomas Lloyd, Rush declared that the degree of agreement at the former convention and "the general approbation of the Constitution by all classes of people" (an exaggeration) led him "to believe that the adoption of the government was agreeable to the will of Heaven." Lloyd reported, "Here the Doctor added that he believed the same voice that thundered on Mount Sinai, 'thou shalt not steal,' now proclaimed in our ears by a number of plain and intelligible providences, 'thou shalt not reject the new federal government.'" Rush wrote to a friend in the same vein: "The last thing I can believe is that providence has brought us over the red Sea of the late war to perish in the present wilderness of Anarchy & Vice. What has been will be & there is nothing new under the sun [Ecclesiastes 1:9]. We are advancing thro' Suffering (the usual road) to peace & happiness. Night preceded day & Chaos Order in the creation of the world" (Genesis 1:2). After sustaining some criticism from Anti-Federalists for his comments at the Pennsylvania ratifying convention, Rush clarified that he believed that the Constitution was the product of an indirect form of divine intervention rather than direct dictation by the Holy Spirit as with the Ten Commandments: "I do not believe that the Constitution was the offspring of inspiration, but I am as perfectly satisfied that the union of the states, in its form and adoption, is as much the work of a divine providence as any of the miracles recorded in the old and new testaments were the effects of a divine power."[33]

Other Federalists agreed that the Constitution was a divine gift. David Ramsay declared regarding the framers of the Constitution, "Heaven smiled on their deliberations and inspired their councils with a spirit of conciliation; hence arose a system which seems well calculated to make us happy at home and respected abroad." At the New York ratifying convention Alexander Hamilton spoke for many Federalists when he declared that "Heaven patronized us" in the Revolutionary War and "now invites us" to ratify the Constitution. In *Federalist* No. 2 John Jay listed the blessings that God had bestowed on the nation, including fertile soil, navigable rivers, a common language, religion, and political principles, and victory in the Revolutionary War. He concluded, "This country and this people seem to have been made for each other, and it appears as if it was the design of Providence that an inheritance so proper and convenient for a band of brethren, united to each other by the strongest ties, should never be split into a number of unsocial, jealous, and alien sovereignties." Thus, God clearly supported ratification of the Constitution. Nor was this a passing theme for Jay. In his thanksgiving proclamation as governor of New York in 1795, he declared it the duty of citizens to thank God for "his great unmerited mercies and blessings," which included "the civilizing light and influence of his holy gospel," victory in the Revolutionary War, and "the wisdom and opportunity to establish governments and institutions auspicious to order, security, and rational liberty." In *Federalist* No. 37 James Madison wrote regarding the Constitutional

Convention, "The real wonder is that so many difficulties should have been surmounted, and surmounted with an unanimity almost as unprecedented as it must have been unexpected. It is impossible for any man of candour to reflect on this circumstance without partaking of astonishment. It is impossible for the man of pious reflection not to perceive in it a finger of that Almighty Hand which has been so frequently and signally extended to our relief in the critical stages of the revolution."[34]

This was not a judgment that Madison reserved for public consumption. Indeed, perhaps the most startling statement of belief in divine intervention on behalf of the Constitution came in a private letter that the Virginian who was later dubbed "the Father of the Constitution" penned to Thomas Jefferson. Just one month after the close of the Constitutional Convention, Madison wrote to his friend and political ally that balancing all of the interests and concerns presented there "formed a task more difficult than can well be conceived by those who were not concerned in the execution of it." Yet, despite the fact that Madison was generally reticent about expressing his religious beliefs and despite the fact that he was writing to a man he knew did not believe in miracles (however much he believed in Providence), he seemed compelled to add a sentence that must have startled its reader: "Adding to these considerations the natural diversity of human opinions on all new and complicated subjects, it is impossible to consider the degree of concord which ultimately prevailed as less than a miracle." That was as close to a sermon as the one-time divinity student ever preached.[35]

The numerous founders who considered the Constitution a divine gift were well aware that it possessed opponents in every state. But they were genuinely amazed that a collection of diverse and proud men, each a leader in his own state, had managed to set aside their ideological differences, their pride, and their competing interests in order to produce so complex and impressive a document in a few months' time, and even more astounded that every state ratified it, however close the vote and heated the debate in some states.

SLAVERY: THE SUPREME VIOLATION OF THE COVENANT

The founders believed that the nation's unique mission to advance the cause of liberty entailed a unique responsibility and that failure to carry out this duty properly might result in a severe national punishment. John Adams wrote in his preface to *A Defence of the Constitutions of Government of the United States of America* (1787), "The people in America have now the best opportunity and the greatest trust in their hands that Providence ever committed to so small a number since the transgression of the first pair; if they betray their trust, their guilt will merit even greater punishment than other nations have suffered in the indignation of Heaven." While Adams's passing over of biblical Israel as the favorite American precursor to travel all the way back to the Garden of Eden was unusual, his fear of divine judgment was not.[36]

For instance, many of the founders warned that God might punish the United States for its institution of slavery, which they regarded as a direct violation of the covenant of liberty between the Almighty and the New Israel. If it were true, as the founders believed, that God had blessed the United States to a unique degree because of its divine mission to advance freedom, it might also be true that in the future He would judge the nation severely for its gross violation of that very principle—much as God had blessed the former Chosen People because of their divine mission to advance ethical monotheism but sent them into captivity when they fell into forms of immorality and idolatry that violated its defining principles.

As early as 1773, Benjamin Rush wrote an essay called, "On Slave Keeping," in which he warned of the wrath of God against America because of slavery. He advised the nation's clergymen:

> If in the Old Testament, "God swears by his holiness, and by the excellency of Jacob, that the earth shall tremble, and everyone mourn that dwelleth therein for the iniquity of those who oppress the poor and crush the needy," "who buy the poor with silver, and the needy with a pair of shoes" [Amos 4:1–2; 8:6–8], what judgments may you not pronounce upon those who continue to perpetuate these crimes [against Africans] after the more full discovery which God has made of the law of equity in the New Testament? Put them in the mind of the rod which was held over them a few years ago in the Stamp and Revenue Acts. Remember that national crimes require national punish-

> ments, and without declaring what punishment awaits this evil, you may venture to assure them that it cannot pass with impunity, unless God shall cease to be just or merciful.[37]

Two years later the then pious Thomas Paine argued that British tyranny in the American colonies constituted a form of divine judgment on account of slavery. He asked, "How just, how suitable to our crime, is the punishment with which Providence threatens us? We have enslaved multitudes and shed much innocent blood in doing it, and now we are threatened with the same. And while other evils are confessed and bewailed, why not this especially and publicly, than which no other vice, of all others, has brought so much guilt on the land?" Yet seven months later, after the Battles of Lexington and Concord, Paine portrayed Britain as the more proper object of divine wrath because of its central role in the slave trade and its refusal to allow its prohibition in colonies like Virginia and expressed the hope that the Revolution might serve as a mechanism for ending the injustice. He claimed, "I firmly believe that the Almighty, in compassion to mankind, will curtail the power of Britain. . . . I hesitate not for a moment to believe that the Almighty will finally separate America from Britain. Call it Independence or what you will, if it is the cause of God and humanity, it will go on. And when the Almighty shall have blest us, and made us a people dependent only upon Him, then may our first gratitude be shown by an act of continental legislation which shall put a stop to the importation of Negroes for sale, soften the hard fate of those already here, and in time procure their freedom."[38]

In *Notes on the State of Virginia* (1782) Thomas Jefferson expressed anxiety that slavery would bring down God's wrath on the United States. In a famous passage later engraved on a panel at the Jefferson Memorial he wrote, "Can the liberties of a nation be thought secure when we have removed their only firm basis, a conviction in the minds of the people that these liberties are the gift of God? That they are not to be violated but with His wrath? Indeed, I tremble for my country when I reflect that God is just; that His justice cannot sleep forever; that considering numbers, nature, and natural means only, a revolution of the wheel of fortune, an exchange of situation is among possible events; that it may become probable by supernatural interference! The Almighty has no attribute which can take side with us in such a contest." Note that Jefferson's anxiety was not for himself as a slaveholder but for the nation as a whole and that he fully expected divine retribution to come through natural means. Not generally known for dispensing jeremiads, Jefferson did add a hopeful postscript more in line with his optimistic disposition: "The spirit of the master is abating, that of the slave rising from the dust, his condition mollifying, the way I hope preparing, under the auspices of heaven, for a total emancipation, and that this is disposed, in the order of events, to be with the consent of the masters rather than by their extirpation." Jefferson envisioned "total emancipation" as the inevitable result of the divine will. The only question was whether it would come through peaceful means or by slaughter. A few years later he marveled:

> What a stupendous, what an incomprehensible machine is man! Who can endure toil, famine, stripes, imprisonment, and death itself in vindication of his own liberty and the next moment be deaf to all those motives whose power supported him through his trial, and inflict on his fellow men a bondage one hour of which is fraught with more misery than ages of that which he rose in rebellion to oppose. But we must await, with patience, the workings of an overruling Providence and hope that that is preparing the deliverance of these, our suffering brethren. When the measure of their tears shall be full, when their groans shall have involved heaven itself in darkness, doubtless, a God of justice will awaken to their distress, and by suffusing light and liberality among their oppressors, or, at length, by His exterminating thunder, manifest His attention to the things of this world, and they are not left to the guidance of a blind fatality.

Jefferson again presented the possibility that divine intervention might take the form of enlightenment rather than destruction, though the latter was still possible.[39]

Jefferson was far from alone in his fear of divine retribution for slavery. In 1780 John Jay wrote to a member of the New York legislature, "An excellent law might be made out of the Pennsylvania one for the gradual abolition of Slavery. Till America comes into this Measure, her Prayers to Heaven for Liberty will be impious. This is a strong Expression, but it is just. Were I in your Legislature, I would never cease moving it till it became a Law or I ceased to be a member. I believe God governs this World, and I believe it to be a Maxim in his as in our Court that those who ask for Equity ought to do it."[40]

Some Anti-Federalists worried that the Constitution would bring down the wrath of God on the nation because it permitted the slave trade to continue another twenty years. As "A Countryman," the New York Anti-Federalist (and later governor of the state) De Witt Clinton contended, "All good Christians must agree that this [slave] trade is an abomination to the Lord and must, if continued, bring down a heavy judgment upon our land. It does not seem to be justice that one man should take another from his own country and make a slave of him; and yet we are told by this new constitution that one of its great ends is to establish justice; alas, my worthy friend, it is a serious thing to trifle with the great God; his punishments are slow but always sure; and the cunning of men, however deep, cannot escape them." Clinton contrasted God's former blessing of the United States with the divine curse that awaited:

> Even the infidel must confess that God was remarkably generous with us, watched over us in the hour of danger, fought our battles, and subdued our enemies, and finally gave us success. Alas, my good friend, it is a terrible thing to mock the almighty, for how can we expect to merit his favor or escape his vengeance if it should appear that we were not serious in our professions [of the equality of men and of their inalienable rights in the Declaration of Independence] and that they were mere devices to gratify our pride and ambition; we ought to remember, he sees into the secret recesses of our hearts and knows what is passing there. It becomes us then to bear testimony against everything which may be displeasing in his sight and be careful that we incur not the charge mentioned by the prophet Hosea [10:13], "Ye have plowed wickedness, ye have reaped iniquity; ye have eaten the fruit of lies, because thou didst trust in thy way, in the multitude of thy mighty men."[41]

The Virginia Anti-Federalist George Mason agreed with his northern counterparts. At the Constitutional Convention he declared regarding slaves, "They produce the most pernicious effect on manners. Every master of slaves is born a petty tyrant. They bring the judgment of heaven on a Country. As nations cannot be rewarded or punished in the next world, they must be in this. By an inevitable chain of causes & effects, providence punishes national sins by national calamities." Note that Mason envisioned God passing judgment not through miracles but through the natural effects of slavery itself. This view did not contradict the Bible, since God's judgment against nations in the Old Testament, while sometimes accomplished through miracles, often works through natural causes. For instance, God uses Babylonian armies to destroy the Assyrian Empire (Nahum 3) and Persian forces to overwhelm the Babylonian Empire (Daniel 5).[42]

In 1790, during a congressional debate regarding a petition submitted by the Pennsylvania Society for Promoting the Abolition of Slavery and signed by its president, Benjamin Franklin, Elias Boudinot also warned of divine judgment. Boudinot cited the Book of Exodus, in which he claimed that many of "the same arguments as have been used on the present occasion had been urged with great violence by the King of Egypt, whose heart, it is expressly said, had been extremely hardened, to show why he should not consent to let the children of Israel go, who had now become absolutely necessary to him." Boudinot concluded ominously regarding the Hebrew slaves, "Gentlemen cannot forget the consequences that followed: they were delivered by a strong hand and outstretched arm, and it ought to be remembered that the Almighty Power that accomplished their deliverance is the same yesterday, today, and forever" (Hebrews 13:8). Many Americans later considered the Civil War, which remains the bloodiest conflict in the nation's history, the fulfillment of the founders' prophecy of divine punishment of the United States for slavery.[43]

THE BIBLICAL BASIS OF AMERICAN EXCEPTIONALISM

The founders' belief in American exceptionalism, their conviction that the United States was a unique nation with a divine mission, was one of their most strongly held beliefs, uniting them with their fellow Americans and providing them with a powerful sense of identity and purpose. As the historian Eran Shalev has written, "The construction of the United States as a biblical Israel justified, fortified, and perpetuated the self-confidence, dynamism, and assertiveness that characterized much of American culture and history that played out long after that political ideology faded."[44]

The belief that an omniscient, omnipotent God was foursquare behind the American Revolution was essential to the founders' willingness to undergo the enormous hazards of revolution against the greatest power on earth, an effort that nearly every objective observer considered futile. As the historian Robert G. Ferris has written regarding the signers of the Declaration of Independence, "For their dedication to the cause of independence, the signers risked loss of fortune, imprisonment, and death for treason. . . . About one-third of the group served as militia officers, most seeing wartime action. Four of these men . . . were taken captive. The homes of nearly one-third of the signers were destroyed or damaged, and the families of a few were scattered when the British pillaged or confiscated their estates. Nearly all of the group emerged poorer for their years of public service and neglect of personal affairs." Ferris might have added that another signer, John Witherspoon, lost a son in battle and that another patriot leader, James Warren, did not live to see the document signed because he died in battle as well. Regarding the merchant signers, Ferris added, "The businesses of most of them deteriorated as a result of embargoes on trade with Britain and heavy financial losses when their ships were confiscated or destroyed at sea. Several forfeited to the Government precious specie for virtually worthless Continental currency or made donations or loans, usually unrepaid, to their colonies or the [federal] Government. Some even sold their personal property to help finance the war."[45]

No Beardian analysis centered on financial gain can explain why the founders sacrificed so much despite the vast odds against their enterprise. The only plausible explanation is that they trusted in a God who would crown with success their efforts on behalf of liberty. The fact that this trust was so amply vindicated by a victory that shocked the world made it easier for some of them to interpret the new federal Constitution as a further fulfillment of the divine plan. Only the specter of future divine punishment for the nation's violation of the covenant through the institution of slavery clouded the horizon.

6

RELIGION, MORALITY, AND REPUBLICANISM

In addition to the founders' belief in a God who intervened in earthly affairs, especially to advance the cause of liberty through the United States, they also shared beliefs in the superiority of Christian morality over other ethical systems and in the necessity of religion and morality (defined largely in Judeo-Christian terms) to the survival and success of any republic. Not only did they consider piety essential to the nation's retention of God's favor, but they were also convinced that popular virtue, which was vital to the survival and success of all republics, depended on a widespread belief in an omniscient God who rewarded virtue and punished vice.

THE SUPERIORITY OF CHRISTIAN ETHICS

While the founders embraced a combination of classical and Christian ethics, they often asserted the superiority of the latter due to the New Testament's distinctive emphases on humility, benevolence, and forgiveness. Partly as a result of the influence of classical historians and Stoic philosophers, the founders sometimes equated virtue with frugality, simplicity, temperance, fortitude, love of liberty, selflessness, and honor, civic virtues they deemed necessary in a republic. Even George Washington, whose father's untimely death prevented him from receiving a classical education and who was not philosophical by nature, was exposed to

Stoic ethics at an early age. The Fairfaxes, whom Washington considered his second family, read Marcus Aurelius and the other Stoics. At the age of seventeen, Washington read Sir Roger L'Estrange's English translation of Seneca's principal dialogues. As the historian Samuel Eliot Morison noted, "The mere chapter headings are the moral axioms that Washington followed through life."[1]

But the founders' morality was never fully classical. For instance, they placed a high value on the quintessentially Christian but thoroughly unclassical virtue of humility. While classical heroes like Achilles and Odysseus were an exceedingly vain lot, always boasting about their exploits, Christians considered pride the greatest sin, constituting a form of blasphemy. It was the primordial sin, the sin of the devil, who aimed at equality with God (Isaiah 14:13–14), and the sin of Adam and Eve, who believed that by eating the forbidden fruit they would become equal to God (Genesis 3:5). The New Testament taught that God not only had lowered Himself to become a man but also had been born in a stable as a poor carpenter's son. What right to vanity had any mere human then? In the Sermon on the Mount, Jesus declared (Matthew 5:5), "Blessed are the meek, for they will inherit the earth." Paul commanded (Romans 11:20), "Do not become proud but stand in awe."

Steeped in a Christian culture that emphasized humility, the founders' modesty led them to regard the egotism of their own Greek and Roman heroes with embarrassment. Hence John Adams was at pains to defend his hero Cicero against the charge of vanity, a quality that few Romans would have considered a vice. Similarly, Benjamin Franklin audaciously paired Socrates with Jesus as the two greatest models of humility. Socrates's claim that he was "the wisest man in the world" because he was the only one who was aware of his own ignorance—his paradoxical boasting of his own humility—hardly qualified him as a paragon of modesty. Even in his own day, the gleeful arrogance with which the philosopher enticed his opponents into admissions of inconsistency persuaded few Athenians to consider him a humble truth-seeker. However eloquent and frank his final speech to the Athenian jury, its prideful nature contributed substantially to his death sentence. Socrates suggested that, far from punishing him, Athens should honor him with free meals for the rest of his life, like an Olympic victor, for agreeing to serve as its "gadfly" (Plato, *Apology of Socrates*, 36d1–37d1). Even some jurors who had voted to acquit the philosopher were so enraged by this speech that they voted for his execution in the trial's penalty phase. Adams's need to Christianize Cicero and Franklin's need to Christianize Socrates by attributing modesty to them was based on a combination of reverence for these classical figures and Christian discomfort with their vanity. Indeed, out of Franklin's list of the thirteen virtues he wished to acquire—temperance, silence, order, resolution, frugality, industry, sincerity, justice, moderation, cleanliness, tranquility, and humility—only the last could not find substantial support in classical sources.[2]

The founders often urged Christian humility. In *Letters on Education* (1765), which was addressed to a Scottish aristocrat, John Witherspoon wrote, "Humility is the very spirit of the gospel. Therefore, hear your servants with patience. . . . When they are sick, visit them in person, provide remedies for them, sympathize with them. . . . Take care of their interests; assist them with your counsel and influence to obtain what is their right. . . . Suffer me to caution you against that most unjust and illiberal practice of exercising your wit in humorous strokes upon your servants before company while they wait at table. I do not know anything so evidently mean that is at the same time so common. It is, I think, just such a cowardly thing as to beat a man who is bound, because the servant, however happy a repartee might occur to him, is not at liberty to answer."[3]

In a sermon ten years later Witherspoon emphasized humility as one of the distinctive virtues that made Christianity superior to classical, or what he called "worldly," heroism. He declared, "Everyone must acknowledge that ostentation and love of praise, and whatever is contrary to the self-denial of the gospel, tarnish the beauty of the greatest actions. Courage and modesty, merit and humility, majesty and condescension, appear with ten-fold glory when they are united." Witherspoon claimed regarding the effect of Christian humility on its adherents, "It will not suffer them to be ambitious of higher places of honor and trust, but it will make them active and zealous in the duties of that place in which they already are. It will not suffer them to resent injuries and gratify revenge, but it will make them withstand a king upon his throne if he presumes to interfere in the matters of their God. What is there here that is not noble?" Witherspoon added that Christian morality was open to ordinary people in a way that classical virtue, with its emphasis on political and military glory, was not, because the latter required "such talents as do not fall to the lot of many, and such opportunities for its exercise seldom occur." By contrast, Christian virtue, "being indeed the product of a divine grace, is a virtue of the heart and may be obtained by persons of mean talents and narrow possessions in the very lowest stations of human life." Witherspoon concluded the sermon:

> Whoever will visit the solitary walks of life may find in the lowest stations humility, thankfulness, patience under affliction, and submission to Providence such as would do honor to the most approved virtue and the most enlightened mind. To despise riches and restrain the motions of envy and impatience in a needy state is perhaps as truly noble as to improve them wisely in a higher. Thus the honor which is chiefly desirable is equally open to the rich and to the poor, to the learned and to the unlearned, to the wise and to the unwise, as it cometh from God, who is no respecter of persons [Acts 10:34]. One of the greatest and happiest effects of serious reflection is to bring us in a great measure all upon a level; as indeed, in one most important respect, the magistrate with his robes, the scholar with his learning, and the day laborer that stands unnoticed are all upon the same footing—for we must all appear before the judgment seat of Christ [Romans 14:10].[4]

Thomas Jefferson valued Christian humility as well. Although Jefferson approved Epicurus's four cardinal virtues—prudence, temperance, fortitude, and justice (a list Epicurus derived from Plato)—he also contrasted the Christian moral code of "humility, innocence, and simplicity of manners, neglect of riches, [and] absence of worldly ambition and honors" favorably with the more prideful classical code.[5]

Sometimes the founders' humility was the product of another biblical influence, their belief in Providence. Brissot de Warville wrote regarding George Washington, "His modesty is astonishing to a Frenchman. He speaks of the American War and of his victories as of things in which he had no direction." Washington's humility was the product of his self-conception as not merely a Cincinnatus, a republican who surrendered his power after saving the republic, but also as a Moses or a David whose victories were really the work of God.[6]

The founders' preference for Christian morality over classical ethics was also based on a preference for the positive benevolence promoted by the New Testament over the cold duties of Greek philosophy. It was largely on this basis that Thomas Jefferson considered Jesus the greatest ethical philosopher in history. In Jefferson's famous dialogue between his head and heart, the Christian heart informs the Epicurean head that happiness is not "the mere absence of pain" and that the warmth of friendship is a necessary comfort in life. After reminding his head of the numerous times in which the head has chosen safety over aiding those in need, his heart concludes, "In short, my friend, as far as my recollection serves me, I do not know that I ever did a good thing on your suggestion, or a dirty one without it." Here we catch a glimpse of why Jefferson's Christian morality, with its emphasis on loving others, was more necessary to his emotional health than Greek philosophy, which merely taught the avoidance of self-injury and injury to others. Jefferson called Jesus's ethical teachings "the most sublime and benevolent code of morals which has ever been offered to man." In 1801 he wrote, "The Christian religion, when divested of the rags in which they have enveloped it and brought to the original purity & simplicity of its benevolent institutor, is a religion of all others most friendly to liberty, science, & the freest expressions of the human mind." Two years later he claimed regarding Jesus, "His natural endowments [were] great, his life correct and innocent. He was meek, benevolent, patient, firm, disinterested, and of the sublimest eloquence." Jefferson referred to "the peculiar superiority of the system of Jesus above all others," especially "in inculcating universal philanthropy, not only to kindred and friends, to neighbors and countrymen, but to all mankind, gathering all into one family under the bonds of love, charity, peace, common wants, and common aids." He added, "He pushed his scrutinies into the heart of man, erected his tribunal in the region of his thoughts, and purified the waters at the fountainhead." In 1816 Jefferson wrote regarding his own compilation of Jesus's ethical teachings, taken from the Gospels, "A more beautiful or precious morsel of ethics I have never seen; it is a document in proof that I am a real Christian, that is to say, a disciple of the doctrines of Jesus." He approved Jesus's teaching "to love our neighbors as ourselves and to do good to all men." He added, "It is the innocence of His character, the purity and sublimity of His moral precepts, the eloquence of His inculcations, the beauty of the apologues in which He conveys them, that I so much admire."

Jefferson's belief that Christian morality was superior to classical ethics was a reversal of the judgment of Bolingbroke, whose writings Jefferson had copied into his commonplace book in his more impressionable youth. Jefferson's friend and ally James Madison, normally reticent in expressing his religious beliefs, was probably also thinking of ethics when he called Christianity "the best and purest religion" in 1833.[7]

Benjamin Franklin contended that Jesus had given humanity the best system of morals "the World ever saw or is likely to see." For this reason, as a young man, Franklin felt the need to Christianize his hero Cato the Elder just as he later did Socrates, by listing "charity" as one of the Roman statesman's many virtues. Cato was a model of Stoic integrity, but charity was never one of his attributes. The Roman was famous for calling for the destruction of Carthage in every speech long after that city had ceased to be a real threat to Rome, and in his manual on agriculture, he recommended the sale of elderly or sick slaves as superfluous commodities (*On Agriculture*, 2.7). In 1751, as Poor Richard, Franklin both castigated hypocritical Christians and upheld Christian morality as superior to Native American ethics when he wrote,

> To Christians bad, rude Indians we prefer.
> 'Tis better not to know than knowing err.

In 1760 Franklin conflated virtue itself with Christian ethics when he wrote that no knowledge was equal in importance "with that of being a good parent, a good child, a good husband or wife, a good neighbor or friend, a good subject or citizen, that is, in short, a good Christian."[8]

In 1791 Benjamin Rush contended, "There can be no true greatness that is not founded on Christian principles, and the men of this world are great only in proportion as they assume certain Christian virtues." Two years later, in the process of explaining to his absent wife why he felt compelled to shelter two homeless men during the yellow fever epidemic, Rush argued that Christian ethics was superior even to Old Testament morality in requiring charity. He wrote:

> Had I believed that certain death would have been the consequences to myself and the whole family of taking Johnny Stall and Ed Fisher into the house, it would have been my duty to have done it. Neither of them had any other home, for Mr. [John] Stall (where Fisher lodged) had fled into the country, and had I shut my doors upon them, they must have perished in the streets. Remember, my dear creature, the difference between the law [of Moses] and the gospel. The former only commands us "to love our neighbors as ourselves," but the latter bids us to love them better than ourselves. "A new commandment I give unto you, that ye love one another as I have loved you" [John 13:34].

> Had I not believed in the full import of that divine and sublime text of Scripture, I could not have exposed myself with so little concern, nay, with so much pleasure, for five weeks past to the contagion of the prevailing fever. I did not dare to desert my post, and I believed fear even for a moment to be an act of disobedience to the gospel of Jesus Christ.

In 1799 Rush urged, "Let the youth of our country be carefully instructed in reading, writing, arithmetic, and in the doctrines of a religion of some kind. The Christian religion should be preferred to all others, for it belongs to this religion exclusively to teach us not only to cultivate peace with men but to forgive, nay more, to love our enemies." The following year Rush wrote in his autobiography, "The Gospel of Jesus Christ prescribes the wisest rules for just conduct in every situation of life. Happy they who are enabled to obey them in all situations!" In 1809 he scoffed at the idea that deists could be as ethical as Christians, writing, "All that is just in principle or conduct in a Deist is taken from his previous knowledge of the Christian Religion or the influence of Christian company. A man not educated under such circumstances would know nothing of what is good."[9]

Even Thomas Paine, who published an attack on the Bible, possessed a conception of virtue that was profoundly Christian, undoubtedly stemming from his Quaker background. In *The Rights of Man* (1791) Paine wrote regarding an individual's duty, "It is plain and simple and consists of two parts. His duty to God, which every man must feel, and with respect to his neighbour, to do as he would be done by." Paine was clearly reiterating Jesus's summary of the Mosaic Law in Matthew 22:37–39: "You shall love the Lord your God with all your heart, and with all your soul, and with all your mind. This is the first and greatest commandment. And the second is like it: you shall love your neighbor as yourself." Yet it is interesting that Paine refused to cite the obvious biblical source for his conception of morality, perhaps because he was already approaching the anti-biblical stance that would prevail in *The Age of Reason* a few years later. Even so zealous an enemy of the Bible as Paine could not escape its pervasive influence.[10]

As early as 1756, a young John Adams wrote in his diary:

> Suppose a nation in some distant region should take the Bible for their only law-book and every member should regulate his conduct by the precepts there exhibited. Every member would be obliged, in conscience, to temperance and frugality and industry; to justice and kindness and charity towards his fellow men; and to piety, love, and reverence towards Almighty God. In this commonwealth, no man would impair his health by gluttony, drunkenness, or lust; no man would sacrifice his most precious time to cards or any other trifling and mean amusement; no man would steal, or lie, or in any way defraud his neighbor, but would live in peace and good will with all men; no man would blaspheme his Maker or profane his worship; but a rational and manly, a sincere and unaffected, piety and devotion would reign in all hearts. What a Utopia; what a Paradise would this region be!

Adams retained this belief in the superiority of Judeo-Christian ethics to the end of his life, as evidenced by the marginal comments he made in the books he read in his retirement years. To Mary Wollstonecraft's statement in *The French Revolution*, "What moral lesson can be drawn from the story of Oedipus? The gods impel him on, and, led imperiously by blind fate, though perfectly innocent, he is fearfully punished for a crime in which his will had no part," Adams replied, "These were heathen gods, Miss W. Thank Moses and Jesus that you have better notions of divinity." Next to her complaint that improvement in moral philosophy had been slow, Adams remarked, "I know of no improvements in morals since the days of Jesus." To Condorcet's statement in *Outlines of a Historical View of the Progress of Mankind*, "Then alphabetic writing was introduced into Greece . . . among a people which fate had decreed to be the benefactor of all nations and all ages," Adams responded, "As much as I love, esteem, and admire the Greeks, I believe the Hebrews have done more to enlighten and civilize the world. Moses did more than all their legislators and philosophers."[11]

In retirement Adams also wrote, "The Christian Religion as I understand it is the best," teaching the Golden Rule and love of neighbor. He declared, "We must come to the Principles of Jesus. But when will all Men and all nations do as they would be done by? Forgive all injuries and love their Enemies as themselves?" After expressing admiration for *The Golden Verses of Pythagoras*, with its maxims on the sanctity of oaths, the respect due to parents, affection for friends, and connection to mankind, Adams nevertheless added, "How dark, mean, and meagre are these Golden Verses, however celebrated and really curious, in comparison with the Sermon on the Mount and the Psalms of David or the Decalogue!" He agreed with Jefferson that Christianity was "the most sublime and benevolent" system known to man. He concluded, "The Ten Commandments and The Sermon on the Mount contain my Religion."[12]

Adams's reference to forgiveness as one of the cardinal Christian virtues introduces an important point: the founders, like all other adherents to Christian ethics before and since, sometimes failed to follow its extremely demanding tenets. For instance, although Adams was able to forgive his British enemies, writing to Benjamin Franklin during the Revolutionary War, "God forgive them and enable Americans to forget their Ungenerosity," and he was also able to forgive Joseph Priestley for allegedly financing libels against him during his presidency, writing to Thomas Jefferson that he prayed Priestley "may be pardoned for it all above," he was never able to forgive Alexander Hamilton, whom he blamed for destroying his presidency. In a remarkable paragraph of Adams's autobiography that was excised from the first edition of his papers by his grandson, Adams showcased his contempt for Hamilton through a flood of biblical imagery:

> Here again the Honesty of Hamilton appears. The Articles of War and the Institution of the Army during the War were all my Work, and yet he represents me as an Enemy to a regular Army. Although I have long since forgiven this Arch Enemy, yet Vice, Folly, and Villainy are not to be forgotten because the guilty Wretch repented in his dying Moments. Although David repented, We are nowhere commanded to forget the Affair of Uriah; though the Magdalene reformed, We are not obliged to forget her former Vocation; though the Thief on the cross was converted, his Felony is still upon Record. The Prodigal Son repented and was forgiven, yet his Harlots and riotous living, and even the Swine and the husks that brought him to consideration, cannot be forgotten. Nor am I obliged by any Principles of Morality or Religion to suffer my Character to lie under infamous Calumnies because the Author of them, with a Pistol Bullet through his Spinal Marrow, died a Penitent. Charity requires that We should hope and believe that his humiliation [humility] was sincere, and I sincerely hope he was forgiven. But I will not conceal his former Character at the Expence of so much Injustice to my own as this Scottish Creolion Bolingbroke, in the

> days of his disappointed Ambition and unbridled Malice and revenge, was pleased falsely to attempt against it. Born on a Speck more obscure than Corsica, from an Original not only contemptible but infamous, with infinitely less courage and Capacity than Bonaparte, he would in my Opinion, if I had not controuled the fury of his Vanity, instead of relieving this Country from Confusion as Bonaparte did France, have involved it in all the Bloodshed and distractions of foreign and civil War at once.

While Adams's distinction between forgiving and forgetting is biblical, the tone of deep bitterness that pervades the passage and the denigrating references to Hamilton's parentage and place of birth reveal clearly that Adams never forgave Hamilton at all. By contrast, according to the Episcopalian bishop Benjamin Moore, Hamilton forgave his (literal) mortal enemy, Aaron Burr, on his deathbed. Whether Adams, when staring his own mortality in the face twenty-two years later, finally forgave Hamilton is unknown.[13]

Like all adherents to Christian ethics, Benjamin Franklin struggled with forgiveness, a trait he considered crucial. Franklin expressed a preference for the New Testament doctrine of forgiveness over what he regarded as the greater harshness of the Old Testament. He complained that some psalms "imprecate, in the most bitter terms, the vengeance of God on our adversaries, contrary to the spirit of Christianity, which commands us to love our enemies and to pray for those that hate us and despitefully use us" (Matthew 5:44). On the one hand, Franklin forgave Pennsylvania Governor William Keith for leaving him stranded and penniless in England at the age of eighteen after giving him false promises of aid in establishing a business there. Franklin wrote in his autobiography, "But what shall we think of the Governor's playing such pitiful Tricks and imposing so grossly on a poor ignorant boy! It was a Habit he had acquired. He wished to please everybody; and having little to give, he gave Expectations. He was otherwise an ingenious, sensible Man, a pretty good Writer, and a good Governor for the people." Yet, as Gordon Wood has noted regarding Franklin, "He never forgave his son William for remaining loyal to the British Crown and went out of his way to disown and wound him." Franklin could not overcome the deep-seated feelings of anger and resentment that resulted from his belief that his son had chosen a tyrannical king over his own father. He saw William only once after the Revolution, and it was an icy meeting. Franklin bequeathed almost nothing to his son, writing in his will, "The part he acted against me in the late war, which is of public notoriety, will account for my leaving him no more of an estate he endeavored to deprive me of." It appears that, in this instance, the classical republican conception of a patriotism that transcended all other human ties—fueled by such stories as Junius Brutus's execution of his own sons for treason or the even more extreme tale of Manlius killing his own son for violating a military order—prevailed over Franklin's Christian ethics, however much he might extol the latter over the former.[14]

Benjamin Rush struggled with the necessity of forgiveness throughout the last two decades of his life, with varying degrees of success. In 1790 he confessed that he found himself more willing to forgive personal enemies than treacherous, erstwhile friends: "I feel no difficulty in exercising the Christian virtue of forgiveness towards my enemies. They are open and sincere in their enmity against me. . . . But my friends were unkind, ungrateful, and even treacherous. . . . I wish I could love them as I ought." Two days later, he wrote regarding Charles Nisbet, a clergyman whom he had recruited to serve as president of Dickinson College but whose contentious spirit had plagued both Rush and the college, "No one in our city believes him when he accuses me of the want of friendship to him or to the College. It would be happy for his character as a moral and religious man if he stopped with this charge against me. But he has made others against me which are equally false and malicious. Poor man! I pity him and wish him—as the best means of promoting his own happiness and the honor of the College—a more Christian spirit." In 1807 Rush claimed, "In reviewing my medical life I can find nothing in it that gives me pain except too much ardor in propagating my principles and too little forbearance of the ignorance, dullness, and malice that opposed them. Would to God that I had always said of my enemies, 'Father, forgive them, they know not what they do.'" (Luke 23:34). The following year Rush noted regarding his fellow Philadelphia physician William Shippen, "He was my enemy from the time of my settlement in Philadelphia in 1769 to the last year of his life. He sent for me to attend him notwithstanding, in his last illness, which I did with a sincere desire to prolong his life. Peace and joy to his soul forever and forever."[15]

Near the end of his own life Rush worked assiduously to persuade John Adams and Thomas Jefferson, once close friends before becoming political enemies, to forgive one another and reestablish their old friendship. Rush pleaded with Adams in 1811, "Fellow laborers in erecting the great fabric of American independence!—fellow sufferers in the calumnies and falsehoods of party rage!—fellow heirs of the gratitude and affection of posterity!—and fellow passengers in a stage that must shortly convey you both into the presence of a Judge with whom forgiveness and love of enemies is the condition of acceptance!—embrace—embrace one another." At Rush's instigation, Adams and Jefferson reconciled, and their restored friendship produced a priceless correspondence. No doubt the pious Rush recalled Jesus's words in Matthew 5:9: "Blessed are the peacemakers, for they will be called the children of God."[16]

For his part, Jefferson preached both forgiveness and benevolence, two of the Christian traits he valued highest, to his daughter Mary. In 1790 he wrote to her, "Never be angry with anybody nor speak harm of them; try to let everybody's faults be forgotten, as you would wish yours to be; take more pleasure in giving what is best to another than in having it for yourself, and then all the world will love you, and I more than all the world."[17]

Although Patrick Henry was willing to forgive loyalists, even proposing bills to readmit them into Virginia, he was unwilling to forgive the British. Henry once justified his unwillingness by making a distinction between forgiveness for private and public injuries. When defending Virginia debtors against British creditors in court following the Revolutionary War, Henry declared, "I know, sir, how well it becomes a liberal man and a Christian to forget and to forgive. As individuals professing a holy religion, it is our bounden duty to forgive injuries done to us as individuals. But when to the character of a Christian you add the character of a patriot, you are in a different situation. Our mild and holy system of religion inculcates an admirable maxim of forbearance. If your enemy smites one cheek, turn the other to him [Matthew 5:39]. But you must stop there. You cannot apply this to your country. As members of a social community, this maxim does not apply to you. When you consider injuries done to your country, your political duty tells you of vengeance. Forgive as a private man, but never forgive public injuries. Observations of this nature are exceedingly unpleasant, but it is my duty to use them." Henry's argument might have been stronger had he used the word "justice" rather than "vengeance," but it would have been difficult for him to do so since he was defending a group of men who had used the war as a pretext for the refusal to pay their debts, an act that was neither just nor

Christian. The idea that past oppression by the British government justified the nonpayment of debts lawfully incurred by American citizens to private British lenders was nonsensical. Therefore, the only logical argument left to Henry was one of "vengeance" against an entire nation. Such "patriotism" was more classical than Christian; one can imagine Cato the Elder adopting such a course of action against the Carthaginians while denouncing it if adopted by a Roman against a fellow citizen. The U.S. Supreme Court later ruled on behalf of the British creditors.[18]

William Livingston made a distinction between personal forgiveness, which was the duty of every Christian, and the obligation of government officials to punish criminals as a matter of public safety. While governor of New Jersey during the Revolutionary War, Livingston was especially interested in punishing loyalists who aided the enemy. In 1778 he claimed, "We have suffered so much from Tories & there is in some of our Counties so rooted an Aversion against that sort of Gentry that the more sanguine Whigs would think it extremely hard to proffer them all the immunities of that happy constitution which they, at the risk of their lives & fortunes, have battled out of the Jaws of Tyranny—while the others have meditated our destruction, spilt our blood & in all protracted the War at least a year longer than it would otherwise have lasted. And as to our heartily forgiving them, I think that will require a double portion of the grace of God." Livingston's recognition of personal forgiveness as a Christian duty did not deter him from advocating the expulsion of loyalists, whom he considered treasonous and untrustworthy. He asked, "Should we not be much happier, together with the Abolition of regal misrule, to purge the Continent also of this political Pollution, which must necessarily tarnish the Lustre, and may gradually infect some of the still uncorrupted Sons of America? Will it not be better Policy to insist upon a perpetual Separation from those whose Intercourse with us must constantly revive the most painful Ideas and whose very Presence among the genuine Sons of Freedom would seem as unnatural as that of Satan among the Sons of God?"[19]

When the Quaker Samuel Allinson rebuked Livingston for such rhetoric and argued that loyalists should be pardoned, citing the Bible in the process, Livingston disputed the meaning of Allinson's scriptures and presented others of his own. Livingston replied to Allinson, "'The Rain undoubtedly falls & the Sun shines on the just & on the unjust' [Matthew 5:45], by which I suppose Scripture means that Providential goodness extends to the greatest sinners as well as to the most eminent Saints. But if you infer from thence that the civil magistrate is to make no distinction between offenders against & observers of the law (for the purpose of which it seems to be quoted [in your letter]), you will pardon me if I do not apprehend the logicalness of the conclusion, nor has the personal forgiveness of injuries any relation to civil punishments because the first is universally the duty of all men, but is society to pardon all offenders? I never yet heard of the Man who avowed the principle." Livingston then took issue with what he regarded as Allinson's misuse of another scripture: "You are, in my opinion, equally mistaken in concluding from the text that 'vengeance belongeth to the Lord' [Deuteronomy 32:35] that civil Rulers are not to punish offenders, for, whatever be the meaning of that passage of holy writ, certain I am that the best definition that ever was given of a good magistrate is given by infinite Wisdom in other passages impossible to be misunderstood, as that he is a 'a terror to evildoers & a praise to them that do well' [1 Peter 2:14] & that 'he beareth the sword not in vain' [Romans 13:4]. And how is it possible for a man to become a terror to all evil doers by indiscriminate clemency & forgiveness—or, in other words, by doing nothing that is terrible to any? Or where is the significance of a Sword never to be used?"[20]

Thomas Paine appeared to confuse forgiveness with reconciliation in *Common Sense*. In arguing for American independence he wrote regarding Britain, "There are injuries which nature cannot forgive; she would cease to be nature if she did. As well can the lover forgive the ravisher of his mistress as the Continent forgive the murders of Britain. The Almighty hath implanted in us these inextinguishable feelings for good and wise purposes. They are the Guardians of his Image in our hearts. They distinguish us from the herd of common animals. The social compact would dissolve, and justice be extirpated from the earth, or have only a casual existence, were we callous to the touches of affection. The robber and the murderer would often escape unpunished did not the injuries which our tempers sustain provoke us into justice." Paine's appeal to justice and to distrust of the British constituted a valid argument against reconciliation but not against forgiveness, which, for various reasons, cannot and does not always lead to reconciliation.[21]

Richard Henry Lee found it impossible to forgive French radicals for executing King Louis XVI, whose alliance with the United States had proved crucial to patriot victory in the Revolutionary War. After calling the execution "cruel, unnecessary, and highly impolitic," Lee wrote, "I have a deep rooted affection for this good King because he so effectually aided us in the day of our distress. And I will say with Queen Elizabeth, 'God may forgive his Murderers, but I never can.'"[22]

Like Alexander Hamilton's marital infidelity and the founders' other ethical lapses, their failure to forgive on occasion, as commanded by Jesus in the Lord's Prayer (Matthew 6:12–15), might lead one to the false conclusion that their espousal of Christian ethics constituted mere lip service. But if this is true, then all human references to ethical ideals constitute mere lip service, since ideals are, by their very nature, unattainable by imperfect humanity. It makes more sense to conclude that a failure to achieve one's ideals perfectly is evidence of human fallibility, not duplicity, and that ideals, however unattainable they may be, given the realities of human nature, perform the vital service of making human behavior better than it would otherwise be. Indeed, this is precisely what Benjamin Franklin concluded about the failure of his own rigorous program to achieve moral perfection: "On the whole, though I never arrived at the perfection I had been so ambitious of obtaining but fell far short of it, yet I was by that endeavour a better and happier man than I otherwise should have been if I had not attempted it."[23]

Thomas Paine was alone among the founders, as in so much else, in renouncing Christian morality—though, as we have seen, his statement of ethical principles parroted Jesus, and even he did not criticize Christian ethics until late in life. Paine actually began *The Age of Reason* in a conciliatory tone, writing, "Nothing that is said here can apply, even with the most distant disrespect, to the real character of Jesus Christ. He was a virtuous and an amiable man. The morality that he preached and practiced was of the most benevolent kind." But as the work advanced, Paine's criticism of nearly every aspect of the Bible became increasingly caustic, until he finally declared, "As to the fragments of morality that are irregularly and thinly scattered in those books [of the Bible], they make no part of this pretended thing, revealed religion. They are the dictates of conscience, and the bonds by which society is held together, and without which it cannot exist, and are nearly the same in all religions." Paine then claimed that Jesus's admonition to turn the other cheek turned "man into a spaniel" and that His commandment to love one's enemies was absurd: "To say that we can love voluntarily, and without virtue, is morally and physically impossible. . . . It is not incumbent on man to reward a bad action with a good one."[24]

RELIGION AND MORALITY: PILLARS OF REPUBLICAN GOVERNMENT

The founders derived from the Bible and from their own experience a fervent belief that religion and morality were crucial to the survival and success of republican government. They believed that in any system of government in which the majority held most of the power, it was vital that most citizens be ethical, and they considered religious belief essential to morality. By "religion," some of the founders meant orthodox Christianity, while others meant only the belief in an omniscient, omnipotent God who rewarded virtue and punished vice either in this life or in the next. While the latter definition did not entail an adherence to all biblical doctrines, it did involve, at a minimum, belief in a God who was very similar to the deity presented in the Bible. In short, the founders contended that religious belief was essential in two ways: supernaturally, by securing for the nation the favor of an omniscient, interventionist God, and naturally, by inclining individuals toward virtues necessary to society and against vices that endangered it.

George Washington expressed a belief in the importance of religion to republican government at the beginning and end of his administration. Upon assuming the presidency in 1789, Washington called "true religion" "the best security of temporal peace and the sure means of attaining universal felicity." He added the promise, "It will be my endeavor (as far as human frailty can resolve) to inculcate the belief and practice of opinions which lead to the consummation of those desirable objects." He professed agreement with the statement, "While just government protects all in their religious rights, true religion affords to government its surest support." In his Farewell Address (1796) Washington was famously emphatic concerning the need for religious belief in a republic:

> Of all the dispositions and habits which lead to political prosperity, religion and morality are indispensable supports. In vain would that man claim the tribute of patriotism who should labor to subvert these great pillars of human happiness, these firmest props of the duties of men and citizens. The mere politician, equally with the pious man,

> ought to respect and to cherish them. A volume could not trace all their connections with private and public felicity. Let it simply be asked: Where is the security for property, for reputation, for life, if the sense of religious obligation desert the oaths which are the instruments of investigation in courts of justice? And let us with caution indulge the supposition that morality can be maintained without religion. Whatever may be conceded to the influence of refined education on minds of peculiar structure, reason and experience both forbid us to expect that national morality can prevail in exclusion of religious principle.

Far from being a conventional nod to piety that one might expect from a politician of Washington's era, this was a full-throated assault on contemporary European irreligion, especially the famous claim of French revolutionaries that religious belief was unnecessary to virtue. Washington's final address to the American people constituted a heartfelt warning by an American who had witnessed the French Revolution unravel and who, like many Federalists, attributed the disastrous result to a barbarism that proceeded inevitably from atheism.[25]

Washington was far from alone in the conviction that religious belief was essential to morality and, thus, to republican government. In a 1774 lecture John Witherspoon told his students, "To promote true religion is the most effectual way of making a virtuous and regular people. Love to God and love to man is the substance of religion; when these prevail, civil laws will have little to do. . . . The magistrate (or ruling part of society) ought to encourage piety by his own example and by endeavoring to make it an object of public esteem." In a sermon the following year Witherspoon declared, "Nothing is more certain than that a general profligacy and corruption of manners makes a people ripe for destruction. A good form of government may hold the rotten materials together for some time, but beyond a certain pitch, even the best constitution will be ineffectual, and slavery must ensue. On the other hand, when the manners of a nation are pure, when true religion and internal principles maintain their vigour, the attempts of the most powerful enemies to oppress them are commonly baffled and disappointed. . . . What follows from this? That he is the best friend to American liberty who is most sincere and active in promoting true and undefiled religion and who sets himself with the greatest firmness to bear down profanity and immorality of every kind. Whoever is an avowed enemy of God, I scruple not to call him an enemy of his country." He added quickly, "Do not suppose, my brethren, that I mean to recommend a furious and angry zeal for the circumstantials of religion or the contentions of one sect with another about their peculiar distinctions. I do not wish you to oppose anybody's religion, but everybody's wickedness. Perhaps there are few surer marks of the reality of religion than when a man feels himself more joined in spirit to a true holy person of a different denomination than to an irregular liver of his own. It is therefore your duty in this important and critical season to exert yourselves, everyone in his proper sphere, to stem the tide of prevailing vice, to promote the knowledge of God, the reverence of his name and worship, and obedience to his laws." In 1782 John Dickinson replied to a letter congratulating him on a gubernatorial "proclamation against vice and immorality" that he was convinced "that the happiness of men in this life as well as in the next depends on the prevalence of piety and virtue among them." Fourteen years later he wrote a tract called, *A Fragment*, that defended Christianity. Regarding this pamphlet he wrote, "My ardent desire, my fervent prayer, is that my fellow creatures may be happy, and I am certain they cannot be so without religion." Similarly, Richard Henry Lee claimed, "The experience of all times shews Religion to be the guardian of morals."[26]

Benjamin Franklin frequently emphasized both the social destructiveness of sin and the social utility of faith. As early as 1739, in the guise of Poor Richard, he asserted, "Sin is not hurtful because it is forbidden, but it is forbidden because it is hurtful." In 1751 he contended, "The Christian Doctrine hath had a real Effect on the Conduct of Mankind which the mere Knowledge of Duty without the Sanctions Revelation affords never produced among the Heathens." Six years later the normally affable Franklin replied to the author of a manuscript that denied that virtue was dependent on religious belief with uncharacteristic fury:

> Think how great a proportion of Mankind consists of weak and ignorant Men and Women, and of inexperienc'd Youth of both Sexes, who have need of the Motives of Religion to restrain them from Vice, to support their Virtue, and retain them in the Practice of it till it becomes habitual, which is the great Point for its Security. And perhaps you are indebted to her originally, that is, to your Religious Education, for the Habits of Virtue upon which you now justly value yourself. You might easily display your excellent Talents of reasoning on a less hazardous Subject, and thereby obtain Rank with our most distinguished Authors. For among us, it is not necessary, as among the Hottentots, that a

> Youth, to be received into the Company of Men, should prove his Manhood by beating his Mother. I would advise you, therefore, not to attempt unchaining the Tyger, but to burn this Piece before it is seen by any other Person, whereby you will save yourself a great deal of Mortification from the Enemies it may raise against you, and perhaps a good deal of Regret and Repentance. If Men are so wicked as we now see them *with Religion* [emphasis in original], what would they be without it?

Franklin's analogy between writing against religion and beating one's mother illustrates the primacy that the New England native assigned to religious belief as an incubator of morality. His reference to "unchaining the Tyger" harkened back to his own statement as Poor Richard: "Talking against Religion is unchaining a Tyger. The Beast let loose may worry his Deliverer." While Franklin believed that a select few might be virtuous without faith—and Franklin doubted even those cases, sometimes attributing their virtue, as he does here, to an earlier religious education—he was fairly certain that most people could not achieve this distinction. He was convinced that a widespread experiment to test the hypothesis would be calamitous, hence his unusually passionate reply and uncharacteristic advice to burn a manuscript.[27]

In his autobiography Franklin again demonstrated a distaste for public assaults on scripture when he recalled that an innkeeper named Dr. Brown once "wickedly undertook . . . to travesty the Bible in doggerel Verse as Cotton had done Virgil." Franklin added, "By this means he set many of the Facts in a very ridiculous Light and might have hurt weak minds if his Work had been published."[28]

John Adams possessed a similar view. In 1776 he wrote to his cousin, a Congregationalist minister, "Statesmen, my dear Sir, may plan and speculate for liberty, but it is religion and morality alone which can establish the principles on which freedom can securely stand." He urged his cousin to pull "down the strong-holds of Satan," adding, "This is not cant, but the real sentiment of my heart." As the principal drafter of the Massachusetts Constitution of 1780, Adams approved the assertion that "the happiness of a people, and good order and preservation of civil government, essentially depend upon piety, religion, and morality." While president, Adams wrote in his diary, "One great advantage of the Christian religion is that it brings the great principles of the law of nature and nations—Love your neighbor as yourself and do to others as you would the others should do to you—to the knowledge, belief, and veneration of the whole people. . . . No other institution for education, no kind of political discipline, could defuse this necessary information so universally among all ranks and descriptions of citizens. The duties and rights of the man and the citizen are thus taught from early infancy to every creature." In his copy of the *Letter to Dr. Waterland*, he wrote next to Conyers Middleton's assertion that Matthew Tindal wanted to abolish Christianity and set up reason as a national religion of Britain, "Abolish Christianity! Set up reason! The authority of reason is not stern enough to keep rebellious appetites and passions in subjection." Next to a reference to Tindal's contention that Christianity was unnecessary to good government, Adams retorted, "Deistical cant. Atheists are the most cruel persecutors."[29]

In 1784 another of Adams's cousins, his second cousin Samuel Adams, expressed the same belief in the importance of religion and morality. He wrote to Richard Henry Lee, "If, my honored Friend, the leading Men in the United States would by Precept & Example disseminate thro' the lower Classes of People the Principles of Piety to God, Love to our Country & universal Benevolence, should we not secure the Favor of Heaven & the Honor & Esteem of the wise and virtuous Part of the World?"[30]

Benjamin Rush concurred. In "A Plan for the Establishment of Public Schools and the Diffusion of Knowledge in Pennsylvania" (1786) he argued, "The only foundation for a useful education in a republic is to be laid in Religion. Without this, there can be no virtue, and without virtue there can be no liberty, and liberty is the object and life of all republican governments." Rush added that although even Confucianism and Islam were better than no religion at all, "The religion I mean to recommend in this place is the religion of Jesus Christ." He contended, "All its doctrines and precepts are calculated to promote the happiness of society, and the safety and well-being of civil government. A Christian cannot fail of being a republican. The history of the creation of man and the relation of our species to each other by birth which is recorded in the Old Testament is the best refutation that can be given to the divine right of kings and the strongest argument that can be used in favor of the origin and natural equality of mankind. A Christian, I say again, cannot fail of being a republican for every precept of the Gospel inculcates those degrees of humility, self-denial, and brotherly kindness which are directly opposed to the pride of monarchy and the pageantry of a court. A Christian cannot fail of being wholly inoffensive, for his religion teacheth him in all things to do to others what he would wish, in like circumstances, they should do to him."[31]

The following year Rush asserted, "The melioration of our world is to be brought about not so much by the improvement of human reason as by a faithful imitation of the examples of our Saviour and a general obedience to the plain and humble precepts of the Gospel. But why do I prefer these to the improvement of reason? Reason accords with them all, and its brightest improvement consists of obeying the doctrines and obeying the precepts of the Christian religion." In 1788 he called upon ministers of different denominations to form an association, adding, "Its objects will be morals, not principles, and the design of it will be not to make men zealous members of any one church but to make them good neighbors, good husbands, good fathers, good masters, good servants, and of course good rulers and good citizens."[32]

In 1789 Rush wrote to farmers who planned to settle the frontier, "The last advice I shall give is for families of the same religion to settle in a country together. By those means they will be able sooner to erect a place of worship and to support ministers and schoolmasters. Without the restraints of religion and social worship, men become savages much sooner than savages become civilized by means of religion and civil government." Two years later, in supporting the continued use of the Bible as a school book, he wrote, "In contemplating the political institutions of the United States I lament that we waste so much time and money in punishing crimes and take so little pains to prevent them. We profess to be republicans, and yet we neglect the only means of establishing and perpetuating our republican forms of government, that is, the universal education of our youth in the principles of Christianity by means of the Bible; for this divine book, above all others, favours that equality among mankind, that respect for just laws, and all those sober and frugal virtues which constitute the soul of republicanism." In 1793 Rush claimed concerning the Reign of Terror in France, "The conduct of the French Convention seems intended to prove that human reason alone in its most cultivated state will not make men free or happy without the aid of divine revelation and the influences of the Spirit of the Gospel upon the hearts of men." Five years later he wrote to Noah Webster, "Alas, my friend, I fear all our attempts to produce political happiness by the solitary influence of human reason will be as fruitless as the search for the philosopher's stone. It seems to be reserved to Christianity alone to produce universal, moral, political, and physical happiness. Reason produces, it is true, great and popular truths, but it affords motives too feeble to induce mankind to act agreeably to them. Christianity unfolds the same truths and accompanies them with motives agreeable, powerful, and irresistible. I anticipate nothing but suffering to the human race while the present systems of paganism, deism, and atheism prevail in the world. New England may escape the storm which impends our globe, but if she does, it will only be by adhering to the religious principles and moral habits of the first settlers of that country."[33]

In his autobiography (1800) Rush contrasted the pious and virtuous Edinburgh he knew as a medical student with more recent reports, writing, "I have heard that a great change for the worse has taken place in the morals and manners of the inhabitants of that once happy city. Nor was I surprised at it when I heard that the works of several of the most popular writers against Christianity were to be met with in the hands of journeymen mechanics of all descriptions." In 1802 he contended, "Everything good in man, and all his knowledge of God and a future state, are derived wholly from scattered and traditional rays of the successive revelations in the Bible. Without them, men should have been elevated above beasts of prey only in wickedness and misery." In 1807 he wrote in his commonplace book, "Reject natural religion. We should have become not Pagans, but Brutes, without Revelation." In 1809, after reviewing the wrongdoings of political parties, he asked, "What has become of the tribunal of Reason? It would seem as if the history of our country would furnish new proofs that men are to be governed only by the Bible or the bayonet." The following year he wrote that religion "is no less necessary to 'peace with all men' than it is to our present and future happiness."[34]

Rush consistently held that there was a symbiotic relationship between Christianity and republicanism; each strengthened the other. In 1789 he claimed, "Republican forms of government are more calculated to promote Christianity than monarchies. The precepts of the Gospel and the maxims of republicanism in many instances agree with each other." Two years later he contended, "Republican forms of government are the best repositories of the Gospel. I therefore suppose they are intended as preludes to a glorious manifestation of its power and influence in the hearts of men. The language of these free and equal governments seems to be like that of John the Baptist of old, 'Prepare ye the way of the Lord; make his paths straight'" (Matthew 3:3). In 1792 he wrote, "I am and have been several years before the memorable 1776 a republican in principle not only because I conceive republican governments are more conformable to reason but to revelation likewise. The pride of monarchy and the servility of that state which it induces in all its subjects are alike contrary to the humility and dignity of the Christian character. It is the Spirit of the Gospel (though unacknowledged) which is rooting monarchy out of the world." In 1800 he declared, "I have always considered Christianity as the strong ground of Republicanism. Its Spirit is opposed not only to the Splendor but even to the very forms of monarchy, and many of its precepts have for their Objects religious liberty & equality, as well as simplicity, integrity, and Economy in government. It is only necessary for Republicanism to ally itself to the Christian Religion to overturn all the corrupted political & religious institutions in the World."[35]

In 1811 Rush urged John Adams to bequeath a testament to the nation. He wrote, "In such a performance you may lay the foundation of national happiness *only* in religion, not leaving it doubtful whether morals can exist without it [emphasis in original]. . . . Under this head may be included public worship and the observance of the Sabbath, with which national prosperity has always been intimately connected. . . . Next to the duties nations owe the Supreme Being may be inculcated the influence of early marriage and fidelity to the marriage bed upon public happiness." Rush also recommended that Adams condemn drunkenness and advocate the education of women and the poor in this final statement to his fellow citizens.[36]

While Adams declined the task because he doubted it would have a positive effect, he replied, "I agree with you in sentiment that religion and virtue are the only foundations not only of republicanism and of all free government but of social felicity under all governments and in all the combinations of human society." In 1817 Adams confessed that the contemplation of past crimes committed in the name of religion sometimes made him wonder whether the world would be better off without it. But he added quickly that the truth was otherwise: "Without Religion this World would be Something not fit to be mentioned in polite Company, I mean Hell."[37]

In his law lectures James Wilson declared that religion was essential to the attainment of virtue. He explained, "Reason and conscience can do much, but still they stand in need of support and assistance. They are useful and excellent monitors, but, at some times, their admonitions are not sufficiently clear; at other times, they are not sufficiently powerful; at all times, their influence is not sufficiently extensive." He added that the scriptures "present the warmest recommendations and the strongest inducements in favour of virtue; they exhibit the most powerful dissuasions from vice."[38]

While unwilling to assert that religious belief was essential to the attainment of virtue, Jefferson viewed the former as a strong encouragement to the latter. In 1787 he wrote to his nephew Peter Carr regarding religious inquiry, "Do not be frightened from this enquiry by any fear of the consequences. If it ends in a belief that there is no god, you will find incitements to virtue in the comfort and pleasantness you feel in its exercise and the love of others which it will procure you." This was similar to what Jefferson wrote in 1814 regarding French atheists: "Diderot, d'Alembert, d'Holbach, Condorcet are known to have been among the most virtuous of men. Their virtue, then, must have had some other foundation than the love of God." Jefferson believed that this foundation was the moral sense, or conscience, which was itself a gift of God to every human being and which gave every person pleasure in doing good. Yet, in the letter to his nephew, Jefferson also espoused the view that while religious belief might not be essential to virtue, it was a valuable aid to it: "If you find reason to believe there is a god, a consciousness that you are acting under his eye, and that he approves you, it will be a *vast* additional incitement [emphasis added]. If that there be a future state, the hope of a happy existence in that increases the appetite to deserve it; if that Jesus was also a god, you will be comforted by a belief in his aid and love." Similarly, in 1814, Jefferson listed belief in an afterlife characterized by rewards and punishments as among the most powerful factors that motivated individuals to lead lives that were beneficial to society. Thus, as we have seen, Jefferson donated the then large sum of $50 to the American Bible Society and supported other missionary efforts in the United States based not only on a desire to spread Christian ethics but also on the belief that some of the Bible's accompanying doctrines, including even the doctrine of Jesus's divinity that he himself rejected, led many people to virtue.[39]

Alexander Hamilton was more emphatic about the necessity of Christian morality to the success of the republic. In 1794 he began an attack on French radicals with the statement:

> Facts, numerous and unequivocal, demonstrate that the present Era is among the most extraordinary which have occurred in the history of human affairs. Opinions, for a long time, have been gradually gaining ground which threaten the foundations of Religion, Morality, and Society. An attack was first made upon the Christian Revelation, for which natural Religion was offered as the substitute. The Gospel was to be discarded as a gross imposture, but the being and attributes of God, the obligation of piety, even the doctrine of a future state of rewards and punishments, were to be retained and cherished. In proportion as success has appeared to attend the plan, a bolder project has been unfolded. The very existence of a Deity has been questioned, and in some instances denied. The duty of piety has been ridiculed, the perishable nature of man asserted, and his hopes bounded to the short span of his earthly state.

Hamilton continued, "As a corollary from these premises, it is a favourite tenet of the sect that religious opinion of any sort is unnecessary to Society, that the maxims of a genuine morality and the authority of the Magistracy and the laws are a sufficient, and ought to be the only, security for civil rights and private happiness." Hamilton considered such a view not only fallacious but also devastating to republican government. Four years later he accused French radicals of conspiring to subvert republican government in their nation by replacing Christianity with atheism. He added, "Equal pains have been taken to deprave the morals as to extinguish the religion of the country, if indeed morality can be separated from religion." Hamilton cited as his principal examples laws making divorce as easy "as to discard a worn out habit" and encouraging children to inform on their parents, laws that struck at the very heart of the family, the institution that formed the basis "of domestic and ultimately of social attachment." He concluded, "Morality overthrown (and morality *must* fall with religion), the terrors of despotism can alone curb the impetuous passions of man and confine him within the bounds of social duty [emphasis in original]." Hamilton connected the survival of the American republic so closely with religious belief that by 1802 he was urging his fellow Federalists to establish an organization called "The Christian Constitutional Society, its objects to be: 1. The support of the Christian Religion. 2. The support of the Constitution of the United States."[40]

In 1799, the year of Patrick Henry's death, he echoed Hamilton's alarm at the threat of French "infidelity." Henry claimed regarding France:

> Whilst I see the dangers that threaten us from her intrigues and her arms, I am not so much alarmed [by these] as at the apprehension of her destroying the great pillars of all government and of social life: I mean virtue, morality, and religion. This is the armor, my friend, and this alone, that renders us invincible. These are the tactics we should study. If we lose these, we are conquered, fallen indeed. In vain may France show and vaunt her diplomatic skill and brave troops; so long as our manners and principles remain sound, there is no danger. But believing as I do that these are in danger, that infidelity in its broadest sense, under the name of philosophy, is fast spreading, and that under the patronage of French manners and principles, everything that ought to be dear to man is covertly but successfully assailed, I feel the value of those men amongst us who hold out to the world the idea that our continent is to exhibit an originality of character.[41]

Note that Henry, like most of the other founders, connected his concept of American exceptionalism paradoxically to Americans' greater fidelity to their chief inheritance from the Old World—the Bible. Indeed, his reference to biblical religion as the "armor" that Americans must fasten tightly around themselves was taken directly from Ephesians 6:11: "Put on the whole armor of God, that you may be able to withstand the wiles of the devil." While in Europe the Enlightenment produced a decline in the number of appeals to biblical authority, principles, and exemplars in political discourse from the high-water mark of the Reformation and post-Reformation eras, it had no such effect in America. The historian Eric Nelson writes regarding Europe, "Whereas so many seventeenth-century readers had found toleration, republican liberty, and a care for equality [in the Bible], the *gens de lettres* of the eighteenth century tended to detect only barbarity, despotic legalism, and a chauvinistic particularity." Just as the founders continued to read and admire the works of seventeenth-century British Whigs that were no longer popular in the mother country by the late eighteenth century, so they continued to study their Bibles and find models of toleration, liberty, and equality there. In short, their brand of exceptionalism revolved around the insistence that Americans should depart from the practice of European radicals by continuing to focus on earlier texts. As we shall see in the next chapter, far from producing a reactionary politics, this loyalty to old texts led to the overthrow of ancient institutions, such as hereditary monarchy, titled aristocracy, and, at least in the northern part of the United States, slavery, when these institutions were deemed incompatible with the spirit of the revered texts.[42]

When Henry died later in 1799, he left behind, in addition to his will, a copy of his May 29, 1765, resolutions against the Stamp Act and a message to his countrymen. The message declared regarding the independence that he had helped the nation establish, "Whether this will prove a blessing will depend upon the use our people make of the blessings which a gracious God hath bestowed on us. If they are wise, they will be great and happy. If they are of a contrary character, they will be miserable. Righteousness alone can exalt them as a nation. Reader! Whoever thou art, remember this, and in thy sphere practice virtue thyself and encourage it in others." Henry's decision to quote a famous biblical verse (Proverbs 14:34: "Righteousness exalts a nation, but sin is a reproach to any people") in his final testament to the nation, at a time in his life when he was studying the Bible daily, was pregnant with meaning. In declaring that the success of the American republican experiment depended on the people's display of "righteousness," a word closely associated in the popular mind with biblical exemplars whose actions were deeply rooted in faith, he was denying the reliability of virtue rooted in less fertile ground, such as the virtue touted by classical authors and French radicals, based on reason or intuition alone.[43]

On the rare occasions when the founders decried the influence of religion on morality, excepting Thomas Paine they always referred to "religion" in its post-biblical historical trappings. In other words, far from assaulting biblical principles, they lamented historic Christianity's distortions and violations of those very principles. For instance, in 1787, James Madison wrote regarding Christianity from the days of Constantine (fourth century) to modern times, "It has been much oftener a motive to oppression than a restraint from it." Yet Madison had no such qualms about the social effects of belief in the biblical concept of an omniscient, omnipotent deity who judged humanity. On the contrary, in 1825, he claimed, "The belief in a God All Powerful, wise, and good is so essential to the moral order of the world and to the happiness of man that arguments which enforce it cannot be drawn from too many sources nor adapted with too much solicitude to the different characters and capacities to be impressed with it."[44]

Even Thomas Paine, who lambasted "revealed religion," considered his own "natural religion"—which, it must always be emphasized, was deeply rooted in the biblical concept of an omniscient, omnipotent deity—vital to society. In *The Age of Reason* he contended, "The most detestable wickedness, the most horrid cruelties, and the greatest miseries that have afflicted the human race have had their origin in this thing they call revelation, or revealed religion. It has been the most dishonourable belief against the character of the divinity, the most destructive to morality and the peace and happiness of man that ever was propagated since man began to exist." Yet in the same work Paine also contended, "Were a man impressed fully and strongly as he ought to be with the belief in a God, his moral life would be regulated by the force of belief; he would stand in awe of God and of himself and would not do the thing that could not be concealed from either." In fact, Paine's expressed purpose in writing *The Age of Reason* while imprisoned by Maximilien de Robespierre in France was to defeat the atheism then growing among French radicals, atheism Paine believed stemmed from the inadequacies of the Bible, inadequacies he feared might lead people to reject theism altogether.[45]

Even Thomas Paine, by far the most outspoken critic of the Bible among the founders, drew a strong connection between religious belief and the popular virtue essential to the survival and success of a republic. Even he was unable to escape the power of the Bible's central concept, the existence of an omniscient, omnipotent, intervening God, and the firm conviction that the regulation of human life by belief in such a deity was essential to the endurance of republics and thus to human happiness.

7

OTHER SHARED BELIEFS

In addition to their belief in the superiority of Christian ethics and the importance of religion and morality to the survival and success of republican government, the founders also shared crucial beliefs in spiritual equality, free will, and an afterlife characterized by divine rewards and punishments, each of which they clearly derived from the Bible. By convincing them that they possessed equal rights with the inhabitants of Great Britain, their belief in spiritual equality spurred them to rebel against the mother country. By assuring many of them that African American slaves also possessed equal rights, the belief also led them to abolish slavery throughout the North and to end the foreign slave trade, actions that eventually led to civil war and the abolition of slavery throughout the entire nation. Their belief in free will and in an afterlife filled with rewards and punishments helped motivate their efforts and sacrifices on behalf of the nation during the Revolutionary, constitutional, and early republican eras.

SPIRITUAL EQUALITY

The concept of spiritual equality, the principle that all people are equal in God's eyes, whatever their intellectual and physical capacities, is suggested in the first book of the Bible, where all of humanity is traced to a common pair of ancestors. The Old Testament is filled with prophets of low birth who admonish the Jews to care for widows and orphans, the poorest and most powerless people in ancient society. Jesus comes into the world as a poor carpenter's son, born in a stable (Luke 2:7). Shepherds are the first to hear the news of His birth (Luke 2:8–11), and women of His resurrection (Matthew 28:5–6), from an angel. His brother James admonishes Christians to treat the poor the same as the rich at church gatherings (James 2:1–4). The apostle Paul declares (Galatians 3:28), "There is neither Jew nor Greek, there is neither slave nor free, there is neither male nor female, for you are all one in Christ Jesus." Peter is quoted in Acts 10:34–35: "God is no respecter of persons. But in every nation he that fears Him and works righteousness is acceptable to Him."

The Christian emphasis on spiritual equality increased the religion's appeal to women of the Roman Empire, who constituted a solid majority of early church members. They gladly introduced the religion to their husbands since it taught the revolutionary doctrines that husbands should love their wives "as Christ loved the Church and gave Himself for it" (Ephesians 5:25) and that adultery was as serious a sin in a husband as in a wife (Matthew 5:27–28). In sharp contrast to classical biographers, who focused almost exclusively on political and military affairs, areas of life from which women were excluded, Christian authors included numerous female saints in their hagiography.[1]

The treasuries of Christian churches were often used to finance the manumission of slaves. Several freedmen became bishops. The church contradicted Roman law in recognizing marriages between free people and slaves. While Paul instructed slaves to obey their masters, he also commanded masters to treat their slaves well, "remembering that you have a Master in heaven" (Ephesians 6:5–9). Although Aelius Aristides's accusation that Christians "show their impiety as you would expect them to, by having no respect for their betters" was more than slightly exaggerated, it expressed the outrage of aristocratic pagans at the much greater degree of egalitarianism among early Christians than in pagan society. Although the biblical concept of spiritual equality did not bring an end to slavery in the United States until the nineteenth century, as the result of a civil war caused by the agitation of an abolitionist movement led by evangelical Christians, and did not lead to the enfranchisement of women on a large scale until the twentieth century, as the result of a suffrage movement also led by Christians, it did represent a huge advancement for the powerless even in Roman times, one pregnant with potential for the future.[2]

Far from being a uniquely American phenomenon, slavery was an ancient and ubiquitous institution. Near Eastern Muslims began the sub-Saharan African slave trade in the seventh century, a full millennium before Europeans became involved in it, and imported as many as fourteen million African slaves over the next thirteen centuries, a number roughly equal to those removed by the Europeans. Both Near Eastern and European slave traders were actively assisted by African tribal leaders eager to profit from the trade. These tribal leaders undertook nearly all of the actual capturing of slaves, generally through wars against opposing tribes. Only 6 percent of the African slaves whom Europeans carried to the New World were brought to what is now the United States. What was remarkable about eighteenth- and nineteenth-century American Christians was not that they participated in an ancient, global institution but that they began a movement that restricted and eventually abolished that institution in their nation, just as British evangelicals led by William Wilberforce ended it in British possessions in 1833. At the heart of that movement was the biblical concept of spiritual equality.[3]

The American colonists' belief in spiritual equality, when combined with the fact that very few European aristocrats had any reason to settle in America, resulted in the colonies beginning their existence as radically egalitarian societies by the standards of the age. A European-style aristocracy of birth never developed in America. Although an aristocracy of wealth did arise, and a considerable amount of property was passed from one generation to the next, wealth in the relatively free market economy of colonial America was certainly much more fluid than birth, so that the absence of formal hereditary distinctions provided far greater opportunity for the industrious and ingenious poor (e.g., Benjamin Franklin) than the European caste system. As James Monroe noted in 1801, "The principles on which our ancestors colonized here, by precluding hereditary distinctions, placed man on the elevated ground he was destined to hold by his Creator." Indeed, the founders based the American Revolution largely on the belief that their own equality with the citizens of Britain entitled them to the same right to be taxed only with their consent. The Revolution also brought an end to American submission to the British monarch, thereby abolishing what had long been the sole element of hereditary government in America.[4]

Yet the founders were also acutely aware that the institution of slavery stood as the most glaring contradiction to their self-image as the world's leading advocates of both human equality and natural rights. The unprecedented degree of equality among whites in the United States only served to highlight the aberration. As the historian John Miller put it, "The United States, the first nation to make the doctrine of human equality an integral part of its official ideology, had in some respects attained a closer approximation to this ideal than had any other nation, but where racial distinctions were involved, few nations had farther to go."[5]

The biblical concept of spiritual equality undergirded the founders' abolitionist efforts. In 1774 John Witherspoon told his students, "It is very doubtful whether any original cause of servitude can be defended but legal punishment for the commission of crimes. . . . The practice of ancient nations of making their prisoners of war slaves was altogether unjust and barbarous." Witherspoon's implication was clear: If converting prisoners of war into slaves was morally wrong, how much more the enslaving of African tribesmen with whom Americans were not at war? As president of the College of New Jersey, Witherspoon admitted and personally tutored two free blacks. In 1790 he proposed a gradual emancipation bill in New Jersey that accorded with the long-held wishes of the state's former governor, William Livingston, who passed away the same year. As early as 1778 Livingston had written regarding the abolition of slavery in his state, "I am determined, as far as my influence extends, to push the matter till it is affected, being convinced that the practice is utterly inconsistent both with the principles of Christianity & Humanity & in Americans, who have almost idolized liberty, peculiarly odious & disgraceful." In the preamble to the act that abolished slavery in Pennsylvania (1780) Thomas Paine wrote, "It is not for us to inquire why, in the creation of mankind, the inhabitants of several parts of the earth were distinguished by a difference in feature or complexion. It is sufficient to know that all are the work of the Almighty Hand. . . . We may reasonably as well as religiously infer that He who placed them in their various situations extended equally His care and protection to all and that it becometh not us to counteract his mercies." Writing in the wake of American independence, Paine added, "We find our hearts enlarged with kindness and benevolence towards men of all conditions and nations, and we conceive ourselves at this particular period particularly called upon by the blessings which we have received to manifest the sincerity of our profession and to give a substantial proof of our gratitude." In 1788 Benjamin Rush wrote to a fellow opponent of slavery regarding African

Americans, "Let us continue to love and serve them, for they are our brethren not only by creation but by redemption." Shortly before his death in 1790, Benjamin Franklin, as president of the Pennsylvania Society for Promoting the Abolition of Slavery, helped draft a petition to Congress that declared, "Mankind are all formed by the same Almighty Being, alike objects of his care and equally designed for the enjoyment of happiness." Therefore, it was Congress's duty to secure "the blessings of liberty to the People of the United States without distinction of color" by granting "liberty to those unhappy men who alone in this land of freedom are degraded into perpetual bondage." In 1799, based on the same biblical principle of spiritual equality, John Jay was finally able to sign into law the emancipation bill he had sought for years as governor of New York. His three sons all became active in both the Episcopalian Church and the antislavery movement.[6]

Even in his later, biblically unorthodox years, Thomas Paine continued to trace the doctrine of equality back to an understanding of the Creation that he clearly derived from the Bible. In *The Rights of Man* (1791) Thomas Paine contended that the problem with traditionalists like Edmund Burke, who distinguished kings, aristocrats, and clergymen from ordinary folk and recognized the former's inherited privileges and prerogatives, was that they failed to go back far enough in their reverence for tradition. They should go back to the Creation itself, when God had established equality. Paine contended, "Every child born into the world must be considered as deriving its existence from God. The world is as new to him as it was to the first man that existed, and his natural right in it is of the same kind." Paine added that such a conception of natural rights, by removing false intermediaries between God and man, fostered a sense of duty as well as right: "By considering man in this light, and by instructing him to consider himself in this light, it places him in a close connection with all his duties, whether to his Creator or to the creation." The fact that Paine refused to cite the Book of Genesis was irrelevant; every reader knew that "the first man" to whom he referred was Adam, and that the Bible was Paine's source for his understanding of the Creation.[7]

In the founders' day, belief in spiritual equality led not only to the abolition of slavery throughout the northern United States by 1804, and of the foreign slave trade by 1808, but also to the manumission of large numbers of slaves throughout the South (in the years after the Revolution, more slaves were freed voluntarily in the South than by law in the North) and to some real soul-searching among even those who were unwilling to support immediate emancipation in the South. As early as 1769, in an unsuccessful bid to pass a bill facilitating manumissions in Virginia, Thomas Jefferson declared, "Under the law of nature, all men are born free, and everyone comes into the world with a right to his own person." In "A Summary View of the Rights of British America" (1774), the essay that first won Jefferson notoriety outside Virginia, one of his complaints against George III was that the king would not allow the colonies to prohibit the African slave trade, a prohibition that Jefferson viewed as a prerequisite to abolishing slavery itself. Jefferson characterized the king as "preferring the immediate advantages of a few British corsairs to the lasting interests of the American states and to the rights of human nature deeply wounded by this infamous practice." Jefferson later included a similar statement in the Declaration of Independence, though it was excised to placate delegates from South Carolina and Georgia, which depended on the foreign slave trade.[8]

Although Jefferson denigrated the intellectual capacities of African Americans in *Notes on the State of Virginia* (1782), he never doubted their spiritual equality and thus their natural right to freedom. Indeed, he went out of his way to affirm their possession of the moral sense, writing, "The disposition to theft with which they have been branded must be ascribed to their situation and not to any depravity of the moral sense. The man in whose favour no laws of property exist probably feels himself less bound to respect those made in favour of others." On the other hand, slavery degraded the morality of whites: "There must doubtless be an unhappy influence on the manners of our people produced by the existence of slaves among us. The whole commerce between master and slave is a perpetual exercise of the most boisterous passions, the most unrelenting despotism on the one part, and degrading submission on the other. Our children see this and learn to imitate it." Jefferson went out of his way to embrace the biblical concept of a single creation, and the spiritual equality among all of the descendants of Adam and Eve that it entailed, against the racist and unbiblical doctrine, espoused by some European intellectuals, of separate creations of different species of humanity on different continents. Jefferson called God "the common Creator of man" and "the Father of all the members of the human family."[9]

Although he wavered on the question of the intellectual inferiority of African Americans, Jefferson always insisted on the issue's irrelevance to the slavery issue. When presented with evidence of black intellectual achievement in 1809, he replied, "Be assured that no person living wishes more sincerely than I do to see a complete refutation of the doubts I have myself entertained and expressed on the grade of understanding allotted to them by nature and to find that in this respect they are on a par with ourselves. My doubts were the result of personal observation in the limited sphere of my State, where the opportunities for the development of their genius were not favorable and those of exercising it still less so. I expressed them therefore with great hesitation; but whatever be their degree of talent, it is no measure of their rights. Because Sir Isaac Newton was superior to others in understanding, he was not therefore lord of the person or property of others." For this reason, Jefferson successfully pushed for the exclusion of slavery in the Ohio River valley under the Northwest Ordinance of 1787 and, while president, helped influence Congress to abolish the foreign slave trade.[10]

During the Revolutionary War, George Washington supported the emancipation of thousands of slaves and their enlistment in the Continental Army. He stopped buying slaves of his own in 1786, thirteen years before his death, and not only freed those previously purchased in his will but also bequeathed funds for those too young or old to care for themselves.[11]

The very questioning by numerous American leaders of an institution that had been a ubiquitous and unquestioned way of life throughout most of the world for millennia is far more remarkable than their inability to abolish it in the section of the nation where it was most socially and economically entrenched. There can be little doubt that the biblical concept of spiritual equality, with which their habits of studying scripture and hearing biblically inspired sermons made them intimately familiar, played a crucial role in their willingness to overturn centuries of contradictory practice. The end result, the abolition of slavery throughout the North, established a balance of power between free and slave states that ultimately led to a civil war that eradicated slavery throughout the United States.

Many of the founders also extended the principle of spiritual equality to Native Americans. In *Notes on the State of Virginia*, Jefferson discerned in Native Americans the "moral sense of right and wrong, which, like the sense of tasting and feeling in every man, makes a part of his nature." In 1784 Patrick Henry and John Marshall sponsored a bill in the Virginia legislature to promote marriages between Native Americans and whites that included financial inducements.[12]

All of the founders extended the principle of equality to frontiersmen, and a few proposed economic and constitutional measures they hoped would make it a reality for future generations. The Northwest Ordinance was a revolutionary document not only because it prohibited slavery in the Northwest Territory but also because, in establishing a process through which territories would eventually become equal states, the founders rejected the colonialism from which they themselves had suffered: settlers of the new western territories would not surrender their equality and become second-class citizens subservient to those who remained in the eastern states, as American colonists had been forced into a subservient status when they crossed the Atlantic Ocean. Thomas Paine applied the same principle to future generations. In *The Rights of Man* he declared, "The illuminating and divine principle of the equal rights of man (for it has its origin from the Maker of man) relates not only to the living individuals but to generations of men succeeding each other. Every generation is equal in rights to generations which preceded it by the same rule that every individual is born equal in rights with his contemporaries." Paine's belief in the equality of generations led him to assert the existence of a universal right to access to land. In other words, he insisted that the failure of a person's ancestors to acquire land did not negate his own right to a plot of it. Thus, Paine proposed land redistribution. In *Agrarian Justice* (1797) Paine claimed, "It is wrong to say [like the Bishop of Llandaff that] God made rich and poor; he made only male and female, and he gave them the earth for their inheritance." Paine's reference to "male and female" was clearly taken from Genesis 1:27 ("God created man in his own image; male and female He created them"), constituting one of several instances in which Paine continued to cite the Bible even after he had publicly repudiated its authority. Jefferson famously referred to the same principle of the equality of generations in an 1824 letter: "Can one generation bind another and all others in succession forever? I think not. The Creator has made the earth for the living, not the dead." Thus, Jefferson argued that each generation should have its own constitution. James Madison retorted that generations were unequal in the sense that each was indebted to its predecessors, that constant change in the nation's fundamental law would be destabilizing, and that Jefferson's reasoning led inevitably to a principle of unanimous consent, which was hardly practical.[13]

In addition to drawing on the biblical concept of spiritual equality to further their abolitionist measures, some of the founders also countered efforts to use the Bible to justify the mistreatment of Native Americans and Africans with their own scriptural arguments. For instance, beginning in the early colonial period, some Americans had been justifying the mistreatment of Native Americans by likening Christian settlers to the Israelites and Native Americans to the pagan Canaanites whom God had ordered the Israelites to expel from the Promised Land and even to slaughter. Benjamin Franklin could not tolerate such a view. Incensed by the "Paxton boys'" attempt to use the Bible to justify their massacre of innocent natives in 1763, Franklin responded in an essay, "It seems that these People think they have a better Justification [than revenge], nothing less than the Word of God. With the Scriptures in their Hands and Mouths, they can set at naught that express Command, 'Thou shalt do no Murder' [Exodus 20:13], and justify their Wickedness by the Command given to Joshua to destroy the Heathen [Joshua 6 and 8]. Horrid Perversion of Scripture and of Religion! To father the worst of Crimes on the God of Peace and Love! Even the Jews, to whom that particular Commission was directed, spared the Gibeonites on Account of their Faith, once given. The Faith of this Government has been frequently given to those Indians, but that did not avail them with People who despise Government." The Gibeonites (Joshua 9) secured a peace treaty with the Israelites by lying about their identity; yet the Israelites honored the treaty even after discovering the deception. Similarly, the Native Americans who had been massacred were under the protection of the government of Pennsylvania at the time. But, unlike the Israelites, the Paxton boys had violated a sacred agreement of their own government. Franklin concluded, "O ye unhappy Perpetrators of this horrid Wickedness! Reflect a Moment on the Mischief ye have done, the Disgrace ye have brought on your Country, on your Religion and your Bible, on your Families and Children."[14]

Some of the founders also expressed contempt for efforts to use the Bible to support slavery. As early as 1773 Benjamin Rush wrote an essay "On Slave Keeping" in which he declared regarding Africans, "Nor let it be said in the present age that their black color (as it is commonly called) either subjects them to or qualifies them for slavery. The vulgar notion of their being descended from Cain, who was supposed to have been marked with this color [Genesis 4:15 states only that God marked Cain], is too absurd to need a refutation. Without inquiring into the Cause of this blackness, I shall only add upon this subject that so far from being a curse, it subjects the Negroes to no inconveniences, but on the contrary qualifies them for that part of the Globe on which providence has placed them." Rush then cited the Song of Solomon 1:5, "I am black, but I am comely." He also quoted Montesquieu's condemnation of the slave trade, a business based on a hypocritical and unbiblical view of Africans: "It is impossible for us to suppose these creatures to be men, because allowing them to be men, a suspicion would follow that we ourselves are not Christians."[15]

Rush also rejected the attempt of slave owners to use the Hebrew practice of slavery as a biblical argument in its favor. He claimed, "The design of providence in permitting this evil was probably to prevent Jews from marrying among strangers, to which their intercourse with them upon any other footing than that of slavery would naturally have inclined them. Had this taken place, their Natural Religion would have been corrupted, they would have contracted all their vices, and the intention of providence in keeping them a distinct people in order to accomplish the promise made to Abraham that 'in his Seed all the Nations of the earth shall be blessed' [Genesis 22:18] would have been defeated, so that the descent of the Messiah from Abraham could not have been traced, and the divine commission of the Son of God would have wanted one of its most powerful arguments to support it." Rush added, "But with regard to their own countrymen, it is plain, perpetual slavery was not tolerated. Hence, at the end of seven years or in the year of the jubilee, all the Hebrew slaves were set at liberty, and it was unlawful to detain them in servitude longer than that time except by their own consent." Rush's reference to the seven-year limit of servitude is taken from Deuteronomy 15:12–15, which adds regarding the freedman, "And when you send him free, you shall not let him go away empty-handed. You shall furnish him liberally out of your own flock, granary, and winepress—of that with which the Lord has blessed you. And you shall remember that you were a slave in the land of Egypt, and the Lord your God redeemed you. Therefore, I command this thing today."[16]

Rush included references to the New Testament as well. He noted:

> Christ commands us to look upon all mankind, even our enemies, as our neighbours and brethren, and "in all things to do unto them whatever we would wish that they should do to us" [Matthew 7:12]. He tells us further that his "Kingdom is not of this World" [John 18:36], and therefore constantly avoids saying anything that might interfere directly with the Roman and Jewish governments, so that altho' he does not call upon masters to emancipate their slaves, or upon slaves to assert that liberty wherewith God and nature had made them free, yet there is scarcely a parable or a sermon in the whole history of his life but what contains the strongest arguments against slavery. Every prohibition of covetousness, intemperance, pride, uncleanness, theft, and murder which he delivered—every lesson of meekness, humility, forbearance, charity, self-denial, and brotherly love which he taught—are leveled against this evil, for slavery, while it includes all the former vices, necessarily excludes the practice of all the latter virtues, both from the master and the slave. Let such, therefore, who vindicate the traffic of buying and selling souls seek some modern systems of religion to support it and not presume to sanctify their crimes by attempting to reconcile them to the sublime and perfect Religion of the Great Author of Christianity.[17]

Rush also rejected the oft-expressed view that slavery was justified because it promoted evangelism. He noted, "There are those amongst us who cannot help allowing the force of our last argument, but plead as a motive for supporting and keeping slaves that they become acquainted with the principles of the religion of our country. This is like justifying a highway robbery because part of the money acquired in this manner was appropriated to some religious use. Christianity will never be propagated by any other methods than those employed by Christ and his apostles. Slavery is an engine as little fitted for that purpose as fire or the sword." Rush explained that the example presented by the ostensibly Christian slaveholder—his anger, luxury, and lust—would never inspire a slave to become a Christian. Rush informed the slaveholder, "All the money you save or acquire by their labor is stolen from them, and however plausible the excuse may be that you form to reconcile it to your consciences, yet be assured that your crime stands registered in the court of Heaven as a breach of the eighth commandment."[18]

Rush's belief that the Bible condemned slavery led him to help establish the first antislavery society in America, the Pennsylvania Society for Promoting the Abolition of Slavery and the Relief of Free Negroes Unlawfully Held in Bondage, in 1774. In 1787, after the society was reorganized, Benjamin Franklin served as its president, Rush as its secretary. Rush became president of the organization in 1803, retaining this post until he died a decade later. He addressed the meetings and attended the funerals of African Americans, expressing the hope for a union "as brethren and members of one great family." He also collected funds from British abolitionists for the first black church in Philadelphia (1793).[19]

In one of his earliest essays in 1775, when he was still biblically orthodox, Thomas Paine also assaulted all efforts to use scripture to support slavery. He contended, "So much innocent blood have the Managers and Supporters of this inhuman Trade to answer for to the common Lord of all! . . . Most shocking of all is alleging the Sacred Scriptures to favour this wicked practice." To the argument that the Jews had owned slaves, Paine retorted, "They were suffered to use polygamy and divorces and other things utterly unlawful to us under clearer light. . . . They had no permission to catch and enslave people who never injured them. . . . Such arguments ill become us since the time of reformation came, under Gospel light. All distinctions of nations and privileges of one above others are ceased. Christians are taught to account all men their neighbours and love their neighbours as themselves and do to all men as they would be done by, to do good to all men, and Man-stealing is ranked with enormous crimes. Is the barbarous enslaving of our inoffensive neighbours and treating them like beasts subdued by force reconcilable with all these Divine precepts? Is this doing to them as we would desire they should do to us?" Paine added that the slave trade worked against the spreading of the Gospel:

> The past treatment of Africans must naturally fill them with abhorrence of Christians—lead them to think our religion would make them more inhuman savages if they embraced it; thus the gain of that trade has been pursued in opposition to the Redeemer's cause and the happiness of men. Are we not, therefore, bound in duty to him and to them to repair these injuries, as far as possible, by taking some proper measures to instruct not only the slaves here but the Africans in their own countries? Primitive Christians laboured always to spread their Divine

> Religion, and this is equally our duty while there is an Heathen nation. But what singular obligations are we under to these injured people![20]

Not long before his death in 1790, Benjamin Franklin published an essay satirizing efforts to use scripture to support slavery. The essay purported to be an address by Sidi Mehemet Ibrihim of Algiers in 1687. Ibrihim not only foreshadows southern American advocates of slavery by declaring that Muslims need Christian slaves because of the "hot climate" of the Near East but also adds, "And is there not more compassion and more favor due to us as Mussulmen than to these Christian dogs? . . . Here they are brought into a land where the sun of Islamism gives forth its light and shines in full splendor, and they have an opportunity of making themselves acquainted with the true doctrine, and thereby saving their immortal souls. Those who remain at home have not that happiness. Sending the slaves home then would be sending them out of light and into darkness." Ibrihim claims that slavery does not violate the Qur'an, "nor can the plundering of infidels in that sacred book be forbidden, since it is well known from it that God has given the world and all that it contains to his faithful Mussulmen, who are to enjoy it of right as fast as they conquer it."[21]

FREE WILL

The Bible has long provided fodder for advocates of both predestination (the belief that before time began God determined who would be saved and who would be damned) and free will (the belief that the individual determines his own eternal destiny). For instance, while Paul appears to affirm predestination when he writes regarding God in Romans 8:29, "For those whom He foreknew, He also predestined to be conformed to the image of His Son, that He might be the firstborn among many children," he appears to contradict it when referring to "God our Savior, who would have everyone saved and come to knowledge of the truth" in 1 Timothy 2:3–4. Likewise, 2 Peter 3:9 declares that the Almighty does not wish any soul to be damned: "The Lord is not negligent concerning His promise [to return], as some men count negligence, but is long-suffering toward us, not willing that any should perish, but that all should come to repentance." In the two latter scriptures the implication is that souls are damned by their own free will in rejecting the gospel.

Although most Christian denominations in America today proclaim a belief in free will, in the seventeenth and eighteenth centuries many Americans belonged to Calvinist denominations, such as the Congregational and Presbyterian churches, that preached predestination. Yet the founders embraced a doctrine of free will. In his Bill for Establishing Religious Freedom (1779) Thomas Jefferson emphasized the doctrine, writing, "Almighty God hath created the mind free . . . [and] being lord of both body and mind, yet chose not to propagate it by coercions on either, as was in his Almighty power to do, *but to extend it by its influence on reason alone*." (The Virginia Senate deleted the italicized words.) In 1823 Jefferson wrote to John Adams regarding the most famous modern advocate of predestination, "I can never join Calvin in addressing his god. . . . If ever man worshipped a false god, he did. The being described in his 5 points is not the God whom you and I acknowledge and adore, the Creator and benevolent governor of the world, but a daemon of malignant spirit. It would be more pardonable to believe in no god at all than to blaspheme him by the atrocious attributes of Calvin." The previous year Jefferson identified the following as one of the five points of Calvin: "That God, from the beginning, elected certain individuals to be saved, and certain others to be damned; and that no crimes of the former can damn them, no virtues of the latter save." The latter statement constituted a gross distortion of Calvinist theology, which merely held that God's decision to save a person caused him to possess faith, which, in turn, produced good deeds, rather than his faith (and good deeds, in some denominations) causing his salvation.[22]

John Adams attended Congregationalist services for most of his life but rejected the doctrine of predestination to which his denomination held. Indeed, Adams's belief in free will probably played a large role in his fateful decision to pursue a career in law rather than in the ministry. On August 22, 1756, the day after making the decision, Adams wrote in his diary, "Necessity drove me to this Determination, but my Inclination I think was to preach. However, that would not do. . . . Although the Reason of my quitting Divinity was my opinion concerning some disputed Points, I hope I shall not give Reason of offense to any in that Profession by imprudent Warmth." Although Adams did not identify the opinion or collection of opinions that precluded his service in the clergy at the time, years later, in his autobiography, he connected the decision to the fact that, as a Harvard student, he had been appalled by ecclesiastical councils held in the house of his father, who was a deacon, to investigate the Reverend Lemuel Briant's alleged espousal of a belief in free will. Adams recalled the "Spirit of Dogmatism and Bigotry" exhibited at those gatherings, which had caused him to worry that "the study of Theology and the pursuit of it as a Profession would involve me in endless Altercations and make my Life miserable without any prospect of doing any good to my fellow Men." Adams's connection of his decision not to enter the ministry with the case of the Reverend Briant suggests the likelihood that Adams's belief in free will was the principal opinion that precluded his service as a clergyman in a Calvinist church.[23]

In any case, Adams made it clear in the private correspondence of his later years that he was a believer in free will. In 1813 he castigated Calvin, writing that it was absurd for God to create 90 percent of the human race solely to make these hapless souls eternally miserable for His own glory. (The source from which Adams obtained the 90 percent figure is uncertain, but it did not come from the writings of Calvin.) In 1819 Adams asked, "Is liberty a word devoid of sense? If it is, there [is] no merit or guilt, and there can be neither reward nor punishment in the universe." The same year he declared, "Fatalism . . . appears to me to render all prayer futile and absurd."[24]

Also raised in the Congregational Church, Benjamin Franklin wrote an essay in support of predestination in 1725 but soon regretted it so much that he attempted to retrieve and burn every copy. Seven years later he wrote an essay ridiculing the doctrine. In the latter essay he contended that it was "highly absurd" to believe that God "has decreed the greatest Part of Mankind shall in all Ages put up their earnest Prayers to him, both in private and publicly in great Assemblies, when all the while he had so determined their Fate that he could not possibly grant them any Benefits on that Account, nor could such Prayers be any way available. Why then should he ordain them to make such Prayers?" Franklin also deduced the free agency of humans from the same quality in God since the former were made in the image of the latter (Genesis 1:27). He claimed, "God is infinitely Powerful, Wise, and Good, and also a free Agent; and you will not deny that he has communicated to us a part of his Wisdom, Power, and Goodness (i.e., he has made us in some Degree Wise, potent, and good); and is it then impossible for him to communicate any Part of his

Freedom and make us also in some Degree Free? Is not even his infinite Power sufficient for this?" Franklin concluded, "Men are in some Degree free Agents and accountable for their Actions."[25]

Although he was a Presbyterian for many years, Benjamin Rush rejected predestination because he believed that it made God the author of evil. In his commonplace book in 1791 Rush insisted, "Free will was necessary to happiness. It was abused." God had not predestined the rebellion of the devil or the sin of Adam and Eve and thus was not responsible for them. All He had done was to give His creatures free will; they were responsible for their own poor decisions and their tragic consequences.[26]

In one of his last essays Thomas Paine argued that predestination "hath a tendency to demoralize mankind." He asked, "Can a bad man be reformed by telling him that if he is one of those who was decreed damned before he was born his reformation will do him no good and if he was decreed to be saved, he will be saved whether he believes or not?" Like Jefferson's formulation, this was a misunderstanding of the doctrine of predestination, which held that since faith was an inevitable effect of grace (God's decision to save a person) and good works an inevitable effect of genuine faith, it was impossible for a wicked person to be among the saved.[27]

William Livingston claimed that Calvinists erred in their insistence that "mankind are purely passive in their reformation from vice to virtue." He added that people were not entirely dependent on "a supernatural and irresistible agency" that reduced them to "mere machines, void of intelligence and free volition." This too was a distortion of Calvinist theology, which did not claim that people were devoid of intelligence or volition, only that their choices were based on many factors that they did not choose.[28]

Despite having been born and raised as a strict Presbyterian in Scotland, James Wilson departed from predestination. As a young man, he often debated his friend Billy White, who was studying to become an Anglican clergyman, on the subject. As a result of these debates, Wilson was gradually converted to a free will position.[29]

Even the founder one would most expect to have espoused the doctrine of predestination did not do so. John Witherspoon was a clergyman of the Presbyterian Church, a church that had espoused the doctrine of predestination from the time of its founder, John Knox. Yet Witherspoon carried with him the precepts of Scottish Realism, the dominant philosophical position in eighteenth-century Scottish universities, which emphasized man's status as a free agent.[30]

The founders' thorough reading of both the Bible and the Greco-Roman classics, often in the original languages, made them fairly independent judges of the foundational texts of the Christian and classical traditions that dominated their intellectual world. They were no more dependent on the Protestant reformers for their comprehension of the Bible than they were on their favorite British Whigs for their understanding of the classics. Thus, unlike Luther and Calvin, they came to the conclusion that both the Bible and their own reason accorded with the doctrine of free will rather than with predestination.

The founders' belief in free will undoubtedly gave them a strong sense of responsibility for the outcome of events. While they trusted in divine Providence to provide crucial aid in their endeavors, they also believed that such aid would not be forthcoming unless, by free acts of the will, they selected endeavors that were worthy of success and fully exerted their own intellects and energy on behalf of those endeavors. The Revolution and the Constitution were two such enterprises.

AN AFTERLIFE OF REWARDS AND PUNISHMENTS

The founders also derived from the Bible a shared belief in an afterlife characterized by rewards and punishments. There are some intimations of an afterlife in the Old Testament, though the doctrine is not emphasized there. The Book of Job, the oldest book in the Bible, suggests a resurrection (19:25–26): "For I know that my redeemer lives, and that he shall stand at the latter day upon the earth. And though worms destroy this body, yet in my flesh shall I see God." The Book of Daniel contains a similar reference to some sort of resurrection. Daniel 12:2 states, "And many of them that sleep in the dust of the earth shall awaken, some to everlasting life, and some to shame and everlasting contempt." The famous twenty-third psalm that begins, "The Lord is my shepherd," concludes, "and I will dwell in the house of the Lord forever," suggesting an eternal afterlife. The death of Old Testament figures is often accompanied by the statement that they were "gathered to their ancestors" (e.g., Genesis 49:29; Judges 2:10; 2 Kings 22:20; 2 Chronicles 34:28), which makes no sense if they are thought to be moldering individually in widely separated graves. But it was the New Testament that emphasized the existence of an eternal heaven and hell that awaited the deceased since the chief importance of Jesus's death and resurrection was to enable believers to go to the former place and avoid the latter.

The Christian doctrine of the afterlife was one of the principal reasons that it overcame Roman persecution and defeated its pagan rivals. It was a great consolation during the late imperial period, when barbarian invasions, bloody civil wars, despotism, and recurrent epidemics severely limited life expectancy. Homer had portrayed Hades, the Greek afterlife, as a dismal, shadowy realm of reduced consciousness for most and painful punishment for a few. Achilles, by then a resident of the place, informs the visiting Odysseus that it is better to be a slave on earth than the king of Hades (*Odyssey* 11.489–91). As a result, the Greek poets and playwrights often brooded over death. In Euripides's *Iphigenia in Aulis* (1218–1219, 1251–1252), Iphigenia pleads with her father, Agamemnon, who is about to sacrifice her to appease the gods: "Oh, my father, do not kill me. Life is so sweet, the grave is so black. . . . Death is nothingness. The most wretched life is better than the most glorious death." The Roman Catullus called Hades "a sad place from which no one returns," adding, "My hatred rises against your power, you that devours all things beautiful" (3.12–14). Even Virgil, who was not a brooder, referred to "Death's unpitying harness," which carried all away without exception. His Eurydice tells her husband Orpheus, "Goodbye, forever. I am borne away, wrapped in endless night, stretching to you, no longer yours, these hands, these helpless hands" (*Georgics* 4.497–98). While the pagan Hades was not regarded as a place of extreme torture for most of its inhabitants, it was dismal enough that the New Testament writers felt comfortable employing it as their Greek name for hell.[31]

Thus deprived of the prospect of a pleasant existence in the afterlife, the Greek and Roman aristocratic classes sought immortality through fame. But fame as the ultimate reward for virtue possessed severe deficiencies. As the Roman emperor and Stoic philosopher Marcus Aurelius noted (*Meditations* 4.19), sounding much like Solomon in the Book of Ecclesiastes, "Those who pursue posthumous fame do not take into account that posterity will be the same kind of men as those whom they now dislike. Posterity too will be mortal. What is it to you, anyway, what words they will utter about you or how they may think of you?" Even in the unlikely event that one attained posthumous fame, one would not be around to enjoy it. Many Romans of the Christian era decided that, like Woody Allen, they wanted immortality not through their work but through not dying.

Although the Stoics and Neoplatonists did possess the concept of an afterlife, it centered on the soul's reintegration into a highly abstract World Soul, which involved the loss of individuality. The deficiencies of this bland afterlife led their philosophers to a fatal emphasis on earthly happiness as the ultimate good—fatal because human life is prone to hardship. It was far easier for Christians to justify suffering by claiming that earthly existence was but a fleeting condition easily trumped by an eternal afterlife than for classical philosophers to justify it while locating the ultimate good in this life.[32]

Belief in an afterlife was so universal among the founders that even Thomas Paine hypothesized the likelihood of one. In *The Age of Reason* he wrote, "I content myself with believing, even to positive conviction, that the power that gave me existence is able to continue it in any form and manner he pleases, either with or without this body, and it appears more probable to me that I shall continue to exist hereafter than that I should have had existence, as I now have, before that existence began." Paine added, "The belief in a future state is a rational belief, founded upon facts visible in the creation, for it is not more difficult to believe that we shall exist hereafter in a better state and form than at present than that a worm should become a butterfly and quit the dung hill for the atmosphere, if we did not know it as a fact." In one of his last essays he stated that although "I hold it to be presumptuous in man to make an article of faith as to what the creator will do with us hereafter," he hypothesized that "those whose lives have been spent in doing good and endeavouring to make their fellow mortals happy will be happy hereafter, and that the very wicked will meet with some punishment. But those who are neither good nor bad, or are too insignificant for notice, will be dropt entirely." Paine did not identify his criteria for being "too insignificant for notice," but this rather callous and high-handed aside does not square well with his frequent assertions of human equality. Nevertheless, Paine clearly derived his belief in the afterlife, like his conviction that moral obligations consisted in duty to God and man, from the Bible. Although he insisted that he based all of his beliefs on reason alone, the fact that so many of them happened to accord with the Bible leads one to the conclusion that his Christian upbringing and lifelong habitation in Christian societies were far more influential to his thought than he was willing to acknowledge.[33]

Thomas Jefferson espoused a belief in the afterlife throughout his life. As an adolescent he copied into his literary commonplace book a few lines from Nicholas Row's popular play *Lady Jane Gray*:

> Those who with Honest Hearts pursue the Right,
> And follow faithfully Truth's sacred Light,
> Tho' suffering here shall from their Sorrows cease,
> Rest with the Saints & dwell in endless Peace.

In one of his earliest extant letters (1762), after decrying the fact that rain dripping through a leaky roof had destroyed the portrait of Rebecca Burwell in his pocket watch, Jefferson expressed confidence in the existence of an afterlife: "However, whatever misfortunes may attend the picture or lover, my hearty prayers shall be that all the health and happiness which heaven can send may be the portion of the original, and that so much goodness may ever meet with what may be most agreeable in this world, as *I am sure* it must in the next" (emphasis added). The following year he wrote to his close friend John Page that the two of them should "proceed with a pious and unshaken resignation till we arrive at our journey's end, where we may deliver up our trust into the hands of him who gave it, and receive such reward as to him shall seem proportioned to our merit."[34]

Over three decades later Jefferson referred to the resurrection and divine judgment in a letter to Francis Willis. Jefferson claimed, "It is too soon for us as yet to despair of a rendezvous but in the valley of Jehoshaphat. I had rather flatter myself with seeing you here [at Monticello] or visiting you in Gloucester." The valley of Jehoshaphat in Israel is identified as the place of divine judgment in Joel 3:12. In 1804 Jefferson again wrote to Page, this time to commiserate over the deaths of so many of their common friends over the years. Jefferson claimed, "We have, however, the traveler's consolation. Every step shortens the distance we have to go; the end of our journey is in sight, the bed wherein we are to rest, and to rise in the midst of the friends we have lost. 'We sorrow not as others who have no hope.'" This last statement was a quotation from 1 Thessalonians 4:13–14, in which the apostle Paul discusses the resurrection. Jefferson's quoting of Paul regarding the afterlife is striking considering his strong disagreement with some of the apostle's other doctrines, as we shall see later. Indeed, the same famous Jefferson Bible that excluded Paul's epistles and so much of the remainder of the actual Bible included Jesus's parables concerning divine judgment and the coming of the Kingdom of God.[35]

In his later years Jefferson often alluded to the afterlife in letters to Abigail and John Adams. In 1817 Jefferson wrote to Abigail regarding their deceased friends, "Our next meeting must then be in the country to which they have flown—a country for us not now very distant. For this journey we shall need neither gold nor silver in our purse, nor scrip, nor coats, nor staves" (Matthew 10:9–10). He added, "Perhaps, however, one of the elements of the future felicity is to be a constant and unimpassioned view of what is happening here." When Abigail died the following year, Jefferson wrote to John, "Nor, although mingling sincerely my tears with yours, will I say a word more where words are vain, but that it is of some comfort to us both that the term is not very distant at which we are to deposit in the same cerement our sorrows and suffering bodies and to ascend in essence to an ecstatic meeting with the friends we have loved and lost, and whom we shall still love and never lose again. God bless you and support you under your heavy affliction." The same year he also wrote to John, "We shall be lookers on, from the clouds above, as now we look down on the labors, hurry, and bustle of the ants and bees." He added that "we may be amused with seeing the fallacy of our own guesses" about the future. In 1823 Jefferson wrote to John regarding heaven, "May we meet there again, in Congress, with our antient Colleagues, and receive with them the seal of approbation, 'Well done, good and faithful servants.'" This, of course, was a reference to the master's greeting of the good servant in Jesus's parable concerning Judgment Day (Matthew 25:23).[36]

In 1825, a year before his death, Jefferson wrote to a baby boy named Thomas Jefferson Smith, "This letter will, to you, be as one from the dead. The writer will be in the grave before you can weigh its counsels. Your affectionate and excellent father has requested that I would address to you something which might possibly have a favorable influence on the course of life you have to run, and I too, as a namesake, feel an interest in that course. Few words will be necessary, with good dispositions on your part. Adore God. Reverence and cherish your parents. Love your neighbor as yourself, and your country more than yourself. Be just. Be true. Murmur not at the ways of Providence." Just as Jefferson began with biblical advice, so he ended with a reference to the biblical reward for following that advice: "So shall the life into which you have entered be the portal to one of eternal and ineffable bliss. And if to the dead it be permitted to care for the things of this world, every action of your life will be under my regard. Farewell." Jefferson added his beloved fifteenth psalm as a postscript. Two days before his death, Jefferson penned a farewell poem for his daughter Martha that referred, in Old Testament style, to "going to my fathers" and to "welcoming the shore" at the end of life's voyage where "two seraphs [Jefferson's deceased wife and another daughter] await me."[37]

Jefferson derived considerable comfort from his belief in an afterlife. Upon his wife Martha's death in 1782, he was plunged into an overwhelming, paralyzing grief that eventually subsided but never fully departed. After his own death, his family discovered small envelopes containing locks of hair from his wife and each of his deceased children, along with words of endearment about each written in his own hand, in a secret drawer of a private cabinet. The envelopes showed signs of frequent handling. Unlike Jefferson's other religious beliefs, each of which he attempted to justify rationally, he knew that it was impossible to "prove" the existence of an afterlife; yet he chose to believe in it unwaveringly throughout his life based on faith alone—the very trait he often decried in more orthodox Christians regarding other issues.[38]

Benjamin Franklin also believed in an afterlife characterized by rewards and punishments. While still a young man in 1728, he composed his own epitaph:

The Body of
B. Franklin,
Printer;
Like the Cover of an old Book,
Its Contents torn out,
And stript of its Lettering and Gilding,
Lies here, Food for Worms.
But the Work shall not be wholly lost:
For it will, as he believed, appear once more,
In a new & more perfect Edition,
Corrected and amended
By the Author.

In 1731 Franklin contended, "Men's Minds do not die with their Bodies, but are made more happy or miserable after this Life according to their Actions."[39]

Although more inclined to focus on heaven, Franklin did not refrain from writing about hell. As Poor Richard, in 1756, he quoted a poem by Charles Palmer about the depravations of the latter place:

> How will the sensual Mind its Loss sustain,
> When its gross Objects shall be sought in vain?
> Incapable to act its darling Lust,
> Yet spurred and prompted by a sharper Gust;
> Pained for its Choice, would still its Choice resume,
> Which (by sure Want) but more augments the Doom,
> Made by Heaven at one Conjunctive Time,
> Its Wish and Grief, its Punishment and Crime.
> Naught there the destined Wretch e'er shall find
> To please the Senses, or relieve the Mind;
> No luscious Banquet or delicious Bowl
> To drown in lewd Excess th' intemperate Soul;
> Nor gay Amusements more, nor jovial Throng
> That to their thoughtless Hours did once belong![40]

Franklin retained a strong belief in the afterlife throughout his life. In 1756, following the death of his brother John, he wrote to his niece:

> I condole with you; we have lost a most dear and valuable relation, but it is the will of God and Nature that these mortal bodies be laid aside, when the soul is to enter into real life; 'tis rather an embryo state, a preparation for living; a man is not completely born until he be dead. Why then should we grieve that a new child is born among the immortals? A new member added to this happy society? We are spirits. That bodies should be lent us, while they can afford us pleasure, assist us in acquiring knowledge, or doing good to our fellow creatures, is a kind and benevolent act of God. When they become unfit for these purposes and afford us pain instead of pleasure, instead of an aid become an encumbrance and answer none of the intentions for which they were given, it is equally kind and benevolent that a way is provided by which we may get rid of them. Death is that way. . . . Our friend and we are invited abroad to a party of pleasure that is to last forever. His chair was first ready and he is gone before us. We could not all conveniently start together, and why should you and I be grieved at this since we are soon to follow and we know where to find him?

The following year this lifelong advocate of education wrote that the existence of an afterlife rendered piety and virtue even more important than learning: "Learning is a valuable Thing in the Affairs of this Life, but of infinitely more Importance is Godliness, as it tends not only to make us happy here but hereafter. At the Day of Judgment, we shall not be asked what proficiency we have made in Languages or Philosophy, but whether we have lived virtuously and piously as Men endued with Reason, guided by the Dictates of Religion." Replying to George Whitefield, who prayed for Franklin's soul, Franklin wrote in 1764, "Your frequently repeated Wishes and Prayers for my Eternal, as well as temporal, Happiness are very obliging. I can only thank you for them and offer you mine in return. I have myself no Doubts that I shall enjoy as much of both as is proper for me. That Being who gave me Existence and thro' almost three score Years has been continually showering Favours upon me, whose very Chastisements have been Blessings to me, can I doubt that he loves me? And if he loves me, can I doubt that he will go on to take care of me not only here but hereafter? This to some may seem Presumption; to me it appears the best grounded Hope, Hope of the Future, built on Experience of the Past." In his 1781 letter to Madame Brillon, Franklin concluded with a discussion of his religious beliefs: "4. The human soul is immortal. 5. In a future life, as in the present, vice is punished & Virtue is rewarded."[41]

In an emotional letter to James Hutton during the Revolutionary War, Franklin connected his belief in the afterlife to a belief in divine justice. Having learned of the unprovoked slaughter of ninety-five Moravian Indians by American frontiersmen, he despaired of justice in this life for either the murderers or the wicked man he saw behind this and so many other miseries, King George III. Franklin wrote:

> The Dispensations of Providence in this World puzzle my weak Reason. I cannot comprehend why cruel Men should have been permitted thus to destroy their Fellow Creatures. Some of the Indians may be supposed to have committed Sins, but one cannot think the little Children have committed any worthy of Death. Why has a single Man in England, who happens to love Blood and to hate Americans, been permitted to gratify that bad Temper by hiring German Murderers [Hessians] and, joining them with his own, to destroy in a continual Course of bloody Years, near 100,000 human Creatures, many of them possessed of useful Talents, Virtues, and Abilities to which he has no

> Pretension!? It is he who has furnished the Savages with Hatchets and Scalping Knives and engages them to fall upon our defenceless Farmers and murder them with their Wives and Children, paying them for their Scalps, of which the Account kept already amounts, as I have heard, to near two Thousand. Perhaps the People of the Frontier, exasperated by the cruelties of the Indians, have in their [rage] been induced to kill all Indians that fall in their Hands, without Distinction, so that even these horrid Murders of our poor Moravians may be laid to his Charge. And yet this Man lives, enjoys all the good Things this World can afford, and is surrounded by Flatterers, who keep even his Conscience quiet by telling him he is the best of Princes! I wonder at this, but I cannot therefore part with the comfortable Belief of a divine Providence, and the more I see the Impossibility, from the number & Extent of his Crimes, of giving equivalent Punishment to a wicked Man in this Life, the more I am convinced of a future State, in which all that here appears to be wrong shall be set right, all that is crooked made straight. In this Faith let you & I, my dear Friend, comfort ourselves. It is the only Comfort in the present dark Scene of things that is allowed us.

Seven years later Franklin wrote to his sister, "With respect of the Happiness hereafter which you mention, I have no Doubts about it, confiding as I do in the goodness of that Being who, thro' so long a Life, has conducted me with so many Instances of it." A month before his death in 1790, Franklin listed the following as one of his beliefs: "That the Soul of Man is immortal and will be treated with Justice in another Life respect[ing] its Conduct in this."[42]

When Franklin's daughter told him on his deathbed that she hoped he would recover and live for many more years, he replied, "I hope not." Franklin died with a portrait depicting the Day of Judgment by his bedside. Louis Otto, the French consul in New York, reported to Paris that Franklin's last words were that "a man is perfectly born only after his death." Unlike some deathbed reports, this one has the ring of truth about it because it is almost precisely what Franklin wrote after his brother's death thirty-four years earlier.[43]

Contemplating the trial of the British soldiers involved in the Boston Massacre, Samuel Adams claimed, "It is solemn, as it brings to our minds the tribunal of God himself, before whose judgment seat the scriptures assure us all must appear." Although disappointed by the acquittal of most of the soldiers, Adams declared, "I am not about to arraign the late jurors before the bar of the publick. They are accountable to God and their own consciences, and in their day of trial, may God send them good deliverance." He claimed that his newly departed brother-in-law's sister Kitty was "still more happy, however, in another Life, as we [have] abundant Reason to be assured, for the Christian Temper and Behavior she constantly exhibited." He contended, "The Man who is conscientiously doing his Duty will ever be protected by that Righteous and all powerful Being, and when he has finished his Work, he will receive an ample Reward."[44]

As a law student in the 1750s, John Adams argued on behalf of a "future State of Rewards and Punishments" against his mentor. In 1770 or 1771 John Adams wrote in his diary, "Virtue, by the constitution of nature, carries in general its own reward, and vice its own punishment, even in this world. But, as many exceptions to this rule take place upon earth, the joys of heaven are prepared, and the horrors of hell in a future state, to render the moral government of the universe perfect and complete." In 1796 he wrote to Thomas Jefferson regarding the French Revolution, "A Century must roll away before any permanent and quiet System will be established. An Amelioration of human affairs I hope and believe will be the result, but You and I must look down from the Battlements of Heaven if We ever have the Pleasure of Seeing it." In 1815 he noted, "I believe too in a future state of rewards and punishments, but not eternal." The following year Adams contended, "All Nations, known in History, or in Travels, have hoped, believed, and expected a future and better State. The Maker of the Universe, the Cause of all Things, whether we call it Fate or Chance or God, has inspired this Hope." In 1818 he declared, "I believe in God and in his Wisdom and Benevolence, and I cannot conceive that such a Being could make such a Species as the human merely to live and die on this Earth. If I did not believe [in] a future State, I should believe in no God. . . . And if there be a future State, why should the Almighty dissolve forever all the tender Ties which Unite Us so delightfully in this World and forbid Us to see each other in the next?" Less than six months before his death, he wrote, "I am certainly very near the end of my life. I am far from trifling with the idea of Death, which is a great and solemn event. But I contemplate it without terror or dismay, 'aut transit, aut finit' ['either it is a transformation or it is the end']; if finit, which I cannot believe, and do not believe, there is then an end of all but I shall never know it, and why should I dread it, which I do not; if transit, I shall ever be under the same constitution and administration of Government in the Universe, and I am not afraid to trust and confide in it."[45]

James Wilson also expressed a belief in the afterlife. In his law lectures he paraphrased 1 Corinthians 13:12 regarding the complete knowledge acquired there: "We see, at present, but darkly and as through a glass, but hereafter we shall see even as we are seen, and shall know even as we are known."[46]

George Washington shared the same belief. In 1784 he wrote to John Trumbull Jr. regarding his father, the governor of Connecticut, "[Tell your father] that it is my wish [that] the natural friendship and esteem which have been planted and fostered in the tumult of public life may not wither and die in the serenity of retirement; tell him that we should rather amuse our evening hours of Life in cultivating the tender plants and bringing them to perfection before they are translated to a happier clime." Four years later he expressed the hope that a namesake "will have long enough to enjoy it [the name], long after I have taken my departure for the world of Spirits." In his Farewell Address (1796) Washington stated that he hoped his mistakes would be "consigned to oblivion, as myself must soon be to the mansions of rest." This was a reference to Jesus's statement in John 14:2: "In my Father's house are many mansions. If it were not so, I would have told you. I go to prepare a place for you." Three years later, only nine months before his death, Washington wrote regarding the affairs of his estate, "My greatest anxiety is to leave all these concerns in such a clear and distinct form as that no reproach may attach itself to me when I have taken my departure for the land of Spirits." Washington's belief in the afterlife was perhaps responsible for the deathbed statement, reported by his secretary Tobias Lear, "Doctor, I die hard, but I am not afraid to go." Washington's fellow Americans had no doubt about his place in "the mansions of rest," for after his death the nation was flooded with various paintings titled "The Apotheosis of Washington" that depicted him ascending into heaven flanked by angels.[47]

When writing to Judge Bartholomew Dandridge about the death of a mutual friend in 1785, Patrick Henry questioned the rationality of lamenting "the exchange of a bad world for one where sorrow never enters." The following year, in seeking to console his sister over the death of her husband, Henry wrote, "I turn my eyes to heaven, where he is gone I trust, and adore with humility the unsearchable ways of that Providence which calls us off this stage of action at such time and in such manner as its wisdom and goodness directs. We cannot see the reason of these dispensations now, but we may be assured they are directed by wisdom and mercy. This is one of the occasions that calls your and my attention back to the many precious lessons of piety given us by our honored parents, whose lives were indeed a constant lesson and worthy of imitation. This is one of the trying scenes in which the Christian is eminently superior to all others and finds a refuge that no misfortunes can take away. To this refuge let my dearest sister fly with humble resignation."[48]

John Jay drew tremendous comfort from his belief in the afterlife. In 1776, after Robert Livingston lost a parent, Jay wrote to him, "It gives me Consolation to reflect that the human Race are immortal, that my Parents and Friends will be divided from me only by a Curtain which will soon be drawn up, and that our great and benevolent Creator will (if I please) be my Guide thro this Vale of Tears to our eternal and blessed Habitation." Four years later, after he lost an infant daughter named Susan, he wrote to congratulate Livingston on the birth of his own daughter Elizabeth: "I most cordially congratulate you on this Event and sincerely join in all the good wishes you may find applicable to it in the Book of Psalms. Not many Weeks ago we had also a fine, hearty Girl, but a violent Fever has since carried her to Heaven where I expect one Day or other to see her much more charming and accomplished than if she had been educated either in Europe or America. You see, I have not left my Philosophy, or rather my Christianity, behind me." (Jay's scriptural reference was probably to Psalms 127:3–5: "Children are a heritage of the Lord, and the fruit of the womb is His reward. As arrows are in the hand of a mighty man, so are children of the youth. Happy is the man who has his quiver full of them.") A few weeks later Jay declared, "I believe that a wise and good Being governs this World, that he has ordered us to travel through it to a better, and that We have nothing but our Duty to do on the Journey, which will not be a long one. Let us therefore travel on with Spirit and Cheerfulness, without grumbling much at the Bad Roads, bad Inns, or bad Company we will be obliged to put up with on the Way. Let us enjoy Prosperity when We have it, and in adversity endeavour to be patient and resigned, without being lazy or insensitive."[49]

In 1783, while in France helping to negotiate the Treaty of Paris, Jay contemplated the possibility that the deceased might be able to observe him from heaven. He reported, "Our little one is doing well, and will have a Brother or Sister next month. If people in Heaven see what is going on here below, my [Huguenot] ancestors must derive Pleasure from comparing the Circumstances attending the Expulsion of some of them from this Country with those under which my Family will be increased in it."[50]

Eighteen years later, when Jay's wife died, he took his family into the next room, read 1 Corinthians 15 regarding Jesus's resurrection, and led them in prayer. In 1818, after another daughter died, Jay declared, "The removal of my excellent daughter from the house of her earthly to the house of her Heavenly Father leaves me nothing to regret or lament on *her* account [emphasis in original]. . . . This temporary separation will terminate in a perpetual reunion."[51]

A sickly youth, James Madison kept one eye on eternity. In 1772 he wrote to a close friend that it was acceptable to have earthly ambition "if we do not allow it to intercept our views towards a future State." He added, "A watchful eye must be kept on ourselves lest while we are building ideal monuments of Renown and Bliss here we neglect to have our names enrolled in the Annals of Heaven. . . . As to myself, I am too dull and infirm now to look out for any extraordinary things in this world, for I think my sensations for many months past have intimated to me not to expect a long or healthy life." He lived to be eighty-five, having played pivotal roles in the drafting and ratification of the U.S. Constitution and the Bill of Rights, in addition to serving as the fourth president.[52]

James Monroe appears to have possessed the same belief in an afterlife. In 1778 he wrote to Baron von Steuben's military secretary, Peter Duponceau, who was seriously ill, "The summit of the Christian fortitude [is] to prevail over the views of this transitory life and turn the mind on the more lasting happiness of that to come." He went on to say, "Beware of heresy: danger, ruin, and perpetual misery await it," though he failed to define it.[53]

Grief stricken over the death of his wife Mary, who was a devout Christian, John Marshall was certain of her continued existence in heaven. In his eulogy for her he recited part of a poem, ironically written by America's Revolutionary War enemy, British General John Burgyone:

> Encompassed in an angel's frame
> An Angel's virtues lay.
> How soon did Heaven assert its claim,
> And take its own away![54]

After Benjamin Rush nearly died of pleurisy in 1788, he wrote regarding the planning of his own funeral, "It pleased God to enable me to do this with an uncommon degree of composure, for the promises of the Gospel bore up my soul above the fear of death and the horrors of the grave. O! My friend, the religion of Jesus Christ is indeed a reality. It is comfortable in life, but in a near view of the last enemy its value cannot be measured or estimated by the pen or tongue of a mortal." In his autobiography Rush (1800) vividly recalled hearing George Whitefield deliver a funeral sermon in London many years earlier. Whitefield had declared, "Be not discouraged by the frowns and persecutions of the world. Your heavenly Father is not unmindful of your sufferings. When St. Stephen was stoned, all heaven was in an uproar. The Son of God himself is moved at the sight. He cannot sit still. He rises from his throne and stands ready to receive the holy proto-martyr into his arms." This was a reference to Acts 7:55, the only instance in the New Testament in which Jesus is referred to as standing, rather than sitting, at the right hand of God, apparently in preparation to embrace Stephen, the first Christian martyr. The following year Rush wrote regarding his fellow physicians, "Our business leads us daily into the abodes of pain and misery. It obliges us likewise frequently to witness the fears with which our friends leave the world and the anguish which follows in their surviving relatives. Here the common resources of our art fail us, but the comfortable views of the divine government and of a future state which are laid open by Christianity more than supply their place. A pious word dropped from the lips of a physician in such circumstances of his patients often does more good than a long and perhaps an ingenious discourse from another person, inasmuch as it falls upon the heart in the moment of its deepest depression from grief." Rush added, "Criminal is the practice among some physicians of encouraging patients to expect a recovery in diseases which have arrived at their incurable stage. The mischief done by falsehood in this case is the more to be deplored as it often prevents the dying from settling their worldly affairs and employing their last hours in preparing for their future state." In 1810 Rush composed a poem on the death of the nine-year-old son of his former apprentice:

> Oh! Spare our son, his weeping parents cry.
> Oh! Spare our boy, his weeping aunts reply.
> Think of his distant sire with grief oppresst,
> And let his woes the deadly stroke arrest.

I am not death, the fell disease replies,
I bring a Cherub message from the skies.
I come to bear the object of your love
From earth's low follies to the World above.
Nor will he die when he resigns his breath.
Future Unhappiness alone is death.[55]

Despite the numerous New Testament scriptures that refer to both heaven and hell as "everlasting" or "eternal," the otherwise orthodox Rush (like John Adams, as we have seen) believed that the experience of hell was limited in duration. In the 1780s Rush became a leading Universalist. Universalism is the belief that every soul eventually arrives in heaven, even those condemned to spend some time in hell. In his autobiography Rush wrote regarding the 1780s, "From that time I have never doubted upon the subject of the salvation of all men." Rush added that he did believe in "future punishment [of the wicked] and of long, long duration" but not for eternity. In 1785 Rush helped draft the articles and plan of government of the Universalist Church at its first convention. In 1792 he wrote in his commonplace book, "Endless punishment cannot be true, for it is disproportioned to the force of the mind to conceive of it in the present state." That this was equally true of an eternal heaven appears to have escaped Rush's notice. In 1810 he claimed, "The ministers complain that it is impossible to make their hearers feel the truth of eternal punishment. Why? Nothing in the nature of man accords with it. Not so with other truths, as existence of a God & c." Rush's response to the numerous biblical references to "everlasting punishment" was to allegorize them: "If time is tedious in proportion to suffering, then the pains of hell may well [be] said to be eternal, though only temporal."[56]

In the essay concerning a devastating hurricane that won Alexander Hamilton his first notoriety, written at the age of eighteen, he writhes in the anguish of uncertainty between the "eternal bliss" or "eternal misery" that seems to await him. When saved from death, he breathes a sigh of relief but, in the aftermath of devastation, advises the rich man, "Succor the miserable and lay up a treasure in Heaven," a reference to Jesus's admonition concerning the afterlife in the Sermon on the Mount (Matthew 6:20). A month later Hamilton published "The Soul Ascending into Bliss, in Humble Imitation of Pope's 'Dying Christian to His Soul,'" in which he wrote:

> Hark! hark! A voice from yonder sky,
> Methinks I hear my Saviour cry,
> Come, gentle spirit, come away,
> Come to thy Lord without delay;
> For thee the gates of bliss unbar'd
> Thy constant virtue to reward. . . .
> O Lamb of God! thrice gracious Lord
> Now, now I feel how true thy word;
> Translated to this happy place,
> This blessed vision of thy face;
> My soul shall thy steps attend
> In songs of triumph without end.

In 1801 Hamilton informed his wife Elizabeth, "On Saturday, My Dear Eliza, your sister took leave of her sufferings and friends, I trust, to find repose and happiness in a better country. . . . Remember the duty of Christian Resignation."[57]

At the end of his life Hamilton displayed a strong belief in an afterlife under dramatic circumstances. Although he felt that honor bound him to accept Aaron Burr's challenge to a duel, he was equally insistent, against the pleas of his closest friends, that Christian duty prohibited him from actually firing at Burr, hoping that Burr would show the same forbearance. (It was not uncommon for duelists to fire above each other's heads and return home unscathed, honor satisfied.) In two final letters Hamilton wrote to his wife:

> This letter, my dear Eliza, will not be delivered to you unless I shall have first terminated my earthly career, to begin, as I humbly hope, from redeeming grace and divine mercy, a happy immorality. . . . The consolations of Religion, my beloved, can alone support you, and these you have a right to enjoy. Fly to the bosom of your God and be comforted. With my last Idea I shall cherish the sweet hope of meeting you in a better world. . . . The Scruples of a Christian have determined me to expose my own life to an extent rather than subject myself to the guilt of taking the life of another. This must increase my hazards & redouble my pangs for you. But you had rather I should die innocent than live guilty. Heaven can preserve me, and I humbly hope will, but in the contrary event, I charge you to remember that you are a Christian. God's Will be done. The will of a merciful God must be good.

After he was mortally wounded, Hamilton called for and received the Lord's Supper from an Episcopalian bishop. On his deathbed, Hamilton often told his wife whenever she gave way to tears, "Remember, my Eliza, you are a Christian."[58]

Hamilton's death appears to have been the result of a peculiar combination of aristocratic and Christian values. A low-born West Indian continually attempting to prove his worthiness to be counted a member of the American aristocracy, he did not believe that he could refuse a challenge to duel without violating its code of honor and thus forfeiting his hard-earned membership. Yet, as a sincere Christian, he was also certain that he could not fire a weapon at another man without sufficient cause. In addition to being immoral, such an act might endanger his immortal soul.

Whether Burr possessed the same belief in an afterlife based on divine judgment is difficult to say, but the State of New Jersey appears to have doubted it, if the wording of its indictment of the vice president of the United States for murder is any indication. The indictment referred to Burr as "not having the fear of God before his eyes but being moved and seduced by the instigation of the Devil."[59]

The biblical doctrine of the afterlife provided the founders with priceless comfort. While they emulated their classical heroes in placing a high valuation on fame, which they defined as the favorable "judgment of History," a valuation that inspired them to perform great deeds (just as it continues to motivate modern presidents to establish a "legacy"), they were also aware of fame's severe limitations. True immortality rested on the judgment of an omniscient God and manifested itself in eternal bliss; it did not rest on the often conflicting judgments of subjective historians or manifest itself in the fleeting praise of fellow mortals, a glory that could not even be enjoyed by the deceased. While the founders' Protestant denominations interpreted the Bible to assert that salvation came through faith alone, not good deeds, they also taught that good deeds were the inevitable product of a genuine faith and earned their doers greater rewards in heaven than those received by the slothful. This belief was probably more responsible for the staggering sacrifices in time and money the founders made, and the tremendous risks they took to secure American independence and to establish the new republic on solid ground, than their ambition for fame.

8

DIFFERENCES

Although the founders possessed numerous significant areas of agreement on religious issues, they also differed in some important respects. While most of the founders believed in the divine origin and authority of the Bible, a few did not. While nearly all revered Jesus as the greatest ethical philosopher in history, a few doubted or denied His divinity. While most embraced the New Testament doctrine that faith in Jesus was essential to salvation, a few rejected it.

THE DIVINE ORIGIN AND AUTHORITY OF SCRIPTURE

The biblical authors themselves frequently refer to the divine origin and authority of scripture. In Psalms 119:11 David declares to God regarding the Torah, the first five books of the Bible, "Your Word have I hidden in my heart that I might not sin against you." In 2 Timothy 3:16 the apostle Paul states, "All scripture is given by inspiration of God, and is profitable for doctrine, for reproof, for correction, and for instruction in righteousness." 2 Peter 1:20–21 claims, "No prophecy of the Scripture is of any private interpretation. For the prophecy came in old time not by the will of man; but holy men of God spoke as they were moved by the Holy Spirit."

A few founders were clergymen, whose very choice of vocation in the eighteenth century almost always indicated a belief that the Bible was the Word of God, and many other founders were close relatives of clerics.

Four signers of the Declaration of Independence were trained as ministers, seven were the sons of clergymen, another (Benjamin Rush) was the nephew and student of a cleric, and yet another (John Adams) was both the cousin of a minister and the son of a deacon. The most important ordained clergyman among the founders was John Witherspoon, who received a masters degree in divinity from the University of Edinburgh after writing a thesis arguing that the human soul was immortal and destined for eternal bliss "on condition that in this life it pursues correctly the path assigned to it by God." Recruited to the presidency of the College of New Jersey by Rush, another founder with fairly orthodox views, Witherspoon led the institution for a quarter of a century. His graduates included James Madison (who was himself a cousin of the first Episcopalian bishop in Virginia), ten cabinet officers, and sixty members of Congress. In 1774 Witherspoon told his students, "There is nothing certain or valuable in moral philosophy but what is perfectly coincident with the scripture."[1]

The presence of clergymen and their relatives among the founders is not surprising, considering the fact that ministers were among the most highly educated members of American society, comprising nearly half of all college graduates. Seventeen clergymen were elected to the Massachusetts ratifying convention, which met at one church and then moved to another. Fourteen of these ministers supported the Constitution. In response to this turn of events, as well as to the large number of pastors preaching ratification from the pulpit (a phenomenon common throughout the states), a group of Massachusetts Anti-Federalists proposed taxing the churches, a measure that went nowhere.[2]

Most of the founders considered the Bible the Word of God. In 1765 Benjamin Rush exulted, "How full of comfort are the Holy Scriptures to those who are reconciled to God! And how much should it enhance to us the value of divine Revelation!" In 1788 he declared:

> I consider the Bible as I do the works of nature. The truths contained in it, like discoveries in [natural] philosophy, are of a progressive nature. We see the mysteries of both but in part. As in the works of nature discoveries have often been made by accident and by men of plain understanding without education, so truths have often been brought to light from the Bible by accident or by persons of little or no education. As a familiarity with the works of nature leads to discoveries in philosophy, so a constant and an attentive perusal of the Scriptures leads to a

> discovery of the truths of the Gospel. . . . How many things in the works of creation once thought useless have lately had the most sublime uses ascribed to them! And how many parts of the globe once thought to be deserts in the creation have lately been proved to be necessary to the health or convenience of mankind! In like manner how many passages and texts of Scripture once thought to be unmeaning or contrary to its general tenor have been found to have a reference to some sublime truth of the Gospel and to be in perfect consistency with the whole tenor of revelation! . . . I never read a chapter of the Bible without seeing something in it I never saw before.

In 1807 he contended, "By renouncing the Bible, philosophers swing from their moorings upon all subjects. Our Saviour in speaking of it calls it 'Truth' in the abstract. It is the only correct map of the human heart that has ever been published. It contains a faithful representation of all its follies, vices, and crimes. All systems of religion, morals, and government not founded upon it must perish, and how consoling the thought—it will not only survive the wreck of these systems but the world itself. 'The Gates of Hell shall not prevail against it'" (Matthew 16:18). In 1811 Rush declared, "In rejecting history and biography, I wish always to except the events and characters recorded in the Old and New Testaments. They are true because they are natural, for they ascribe the former to a divine hand and they never fail to mention the weaknesses and vices of the latter." The Bible differed from most other histories in presenting its heroes not as perfect individuals but as flawed people whose heroism involved rising above those flaws to accomplish great deeds. Scripture eschewed hero worship, the sole exception being its glorification of Jesus, whose sinless nature and status as "the Saviour of the World" merited this distinctive treatment.[3]

Rush found a kindred spirit in Charles Thomson. In 1810 Rush wrote regarding Thomson, "When he is asked what sect he is of, he answers, 'Of none; I am a Christian. I believe only in the Scriptures and in Jesus Christ, my Saviour.'"[4]

James Wilson held to the New Testament teaching that conscience, reason, and study of the Bible were all essential to the acquisition of virtue. In one of his famous law lectures he declared regarding "the will of God":

> We discover it by our conscience, by our reason, and by the Holy Scriptures. The law of nature and the law of revelation are both divine; they flow, though in different channels, from the same adorable source. It is indeed preposterous to separate them from each other. . . . In compassion to the imperfection of our internal powers, the Creator, Preserver, and Ruler has been pleased to discover and enforce his laws by a revelation given to us immediately and directly from himself. This revelation is contained in the holy scriptures. The moral precepts delivered in the sacred oracles form a part of the law of nature, are of the same origin, and of the same obligation, operating universally and perpetually. On some subjects, those in particular which relate to the Deity, to Providence, and to a future state, our natural knowledge is greatly improved, refined, and exalted by that which is revealed. On these subjects one who has had the advantage of a common education in a Christian country knows more, and with more certainty, than was known by the wisest of the ancient philosophers.[5]

John Jay agreed. In 1784 he claimed, "The Bible is the best of all Books, for it is the word of God, and teaches us the way to be happy in this world and in the next." Twelve years later he asserted, "I have long been of the opinion that the evidence of the truth of Christianity requires only to be carefully examined to produce conviction in candid minds."[6]

In 1790 Roger Sherman called the Bible "the only rule of faith in matters of religion." Although he agreed with the seventeenth-century English Puritan Richard Baxter's views on the Lord's Supper, he added, "I do not think that his or any other man's opinion is of any authority in the case unless supported by the word of God," and then presented scriptures supporting his and Baxter's positions.[7]

In his final years Alexander Hamilton reasserted his youthful belief in the authenticity of the Bible as God's Word. According to his son John, Hamilton told a boyhood friend, "I have examined carefully the evidence of the Christian religion, and if I was sitting as a juror upon its authenticity, I should unhesitatingly give my verdict in its favor." To another person he said of the Bible, "I have studied it, and I can prove its truth as clearly as any proposition ever submitted to the mind of man."[8]

At the opposite end of the spectrum from these orthodox founders was Thomas Paine, the author of *The Age of Reason*, a full-scale assault on the Bible. Paine denied that any written work could be the Word of God, since human languages were imprecise vehicles that changed constantly.

Instead, "the Word of God is the Creation we behold, and it is in this word which no human invention can counterfeit or alter that God speaketh universally to man." (Note Paine's use of the linguistic style of the King James Version of the Bible to add gravitas to his religious expressions. He appeared unaware of the irony involved in his frequent employment of a biblical rhetorical style to attack the Bible.) The Creation taught that God was powerful, wise, generous, and merciful, since he blessed even the unthankful. Paine added, "I totally disbelieve that the Almighty ever did communicate anything to man by any mode of speech, in any language, or by any kind of vision or appearance or by any means which our senses are capable of receiving, otherwise than by the universal display of himself in the works of creation and by the repugnance we feel in ourselves to bad actions and dispositions to good ones." Paradoxically, Paine quoted Joseph Addison's translation of Psalms 19 concerning the glory of creation to advance the argument that scripture was unnecessary. Even the Bible's chief critic among the founders could not escape his many years of scriptural training.[9]

Paine assaulted nearly everything in the Bible. Regarding the Old Testament he contended, "It is a book of lies, wickedness, and blasphemy, for what can be greater blasphemy than to ascribe the wickedness of man to the orders of the Almighty?" This was a reference to God's order to the Israelites to slaughter the Canaanites. Paine also claimed, "Whenever we read the obscene stories, the voluptuous debaucheries, the cruel and torturous executions, the unrelenting vindictiveness, with which more than half the Bible is filled, it would be more consistent that we called it the word of a demon than the Word of God. It is a history of wickedness that has served to corrupt and brutalize mankind and, for my own part, I sincerely detest it, as I detest everything that is cruel." Concerning the story of the fall of Adam he contended, "It is impossible to conceive a story more derogatory to the Almighty, more inconsistent with his wisdom, more contradictory to his power, than this story is."[10]

Paine subjected the New Testament to the same scorn. Concerning Jesus's atonement for human sin he contended, "God was too good to do such an action and also too almighty to be under necessity of doing it." Paine also denied that "one person could stand in the place of another." He wrote regarding his namesake, "Thomas did not believe in the resurrection and, as they say, would not believe without having oracular and manual demonstration himself. So neither will I, and the reason is equally as good for me and for every other person as for Thomas. . . . The story, so far as relates to the supernatural part, has every mark of fraud and imposition stamped on the face of it. . . . [It is a] fable, which for absurdity and extravagance is not exceeded by anything that is to be found in the mythology of the ancients."[11]

The first part of *The Age of Reason* was riddled with errors because Paine, who was then under arrest in France and facing the threat of execution by the order of Robespierre, lacked access to a Bible. That Paine's inability to consult the work he was assaulting did not deter him from doing so is a powerful testimony to his missionary zeal. He was determined that he would not die before issuing what he hoped would be a lethal blow to what he regarded as a work whose absurdities were the true source of the atheism that was then sweeping France and likely to prevail everywhere else in the future. Ironically, Paine's chief motivation in writing *The Age of Reason*, that of combating French atheism, was precisely the same as that of the biblically orthodox Federalists whom he abhorred.[12]

After Paine was finally released from prison, partly at the behest of the United States government, he continued writing on religious matters. In one of his last essays he claimed, "In Cicero we see that vast superiority of the mind, that sublimity of right reasoning and justness of ideas, which man acquires, not by studying bibles and testaments, and the theology of schools built thereon, but by studying the creator in the immensity and unchangeable order of his creation, and the immutability of his law." He quoted the Roman (*Republic* 3.33): "There cannot be one law now, and another hereafter; but the same eternal immutable law comprehends all nations, at all times, under one common master and governor of all—God." Paine then used this doctrine of divine immutability to assault the belief that God had propounded two very different sets of laws, one vested in the Old Testament, the other in the New. He rejected the New Testament doctrine that the death of Jesus for humanity's sin had allowed a reconciliation, a new relationship, between God and humanity—in other words, the belief that God had not changed between the testaments, but His relationship to humanity had been altered dramatically.[13]

It is important to understand that although Paine unquestionably deserves the title of "founder"—no one was more responsible for persuading the American people to declare their independence from Britain and for maintaining their morale throughout the long, arduous Revolutionary

War—he was also the least American of the founders. Whatever some of the other founders might say while in a cosmopolitan mood, he was the only one who genuinely considered himself a citizen of the world rather than of the United States. An international revolutionary, he spent only twenty of his seventy-two years in America and testified regarding his American Revolutionary experience, "It was neither the place nor the people but the Cause itself that irresistibly engaged me in its support, for I should have acted the same part in any other country could the same circumstances have arisen there which have happened here." Having arrived in America in 1774, just a year before the Revolutionary War began, Paine left the United States for Europe only four years after its conclusion, alternating between England and France before finally settling in the latter nation in order to participate in the French Revolution. He never held elective office in America and wrote with a rage that befuddled the other founders. But what most distinguished him from the others was his public assault on the Bible, an attack that no other founder, even those few who shared some of his opinions privately, would ever have undertaken, not merely because it constituted political and social suicide in a pious nation but also because they shared the public's respect for the Bible and its crucial roles in uniting, stabilizing, and reforming American society. Indeed, each of the other founders called himself "a Christian" and praised Christianity, although, as we shall see, a few of them used these terms primarily in reference to ethics.[14]

The Age of Reason was almost universally vilified in America, and far from heeding Paine's call for "natural religion," many Americans began flocking to a variety of evangelical churches that transformed American society through the Second Great Awakening. Paine's name was so closely associated with that of Beelzebub by the time he returned to the United States in 1802 that curiosity seekers came to his Washington hotel to watch him dine, "as at an orangutan" in a zoo, and in Boston a young poet of the same name begged permission from the Massachusetts General Court to change it to "a Christian name." Having invited Paine to stay at the President's House, Thomas Jefferson eventually grew tired of his drinking and boorish behavior and evicted him. While Jefferson shared some of Paine's views, he could not understand Paine's zealotry on behalf of them. As the historian Merrill Peterson noted, "Jefferson was tolerant of religious differences, only wishing that they might not foul the republican nest." Paine then moved to New Rochelle, New York, where local authorities questioned his citizenship and right to vote. As Gordon Wood has written regarding Paine's fall from grace (no pun intended) following the publication of his broadside, "Most who had known him were embarrassed by the connection and wanted only to forget him." None of his fellow founders publicly eulogized him after his death in 1809. In fact, only six people attended his funeral, a number barely sufficient to serve as pall bearers. The Quakers denied his request for burial in one of their cemeteries, so he was laid to rest on his own farm. Ten years later, a British supporter encountered no American opposition to his plan to exhume Paine's bones and carry them back to England, but the remains were lost before they could be reinterred. It was a sad but strangely fitting end to the sole founder without a country.[15]

Even some founders who did not consider the Bible inerrant revered it and reacted passionately when it was criticized. In his autobiography (1802–1807) John Adams recalled that, in a private conversation in 1776, Thomas Paine had "expressed a Contempt of the Old Testament, and indeed of the Bible at large, which surprised me." Adams added, "He saw that I did not relish this, and soon check'd himself." Since Adams's recollection of the alleged incident came thirty years after the fact, in the wake of the public furor over *The Age of Reason*, and since it conflicts with Paine's appeals to biblical authority throughout the 1770s, the recollection may tell us more about Adams's views in the 1800s than Paine's in the 1770s. Similarly, in 1812, Benjamin Rush recalled that during a session of the Continental Congress, Adams took issue with some of Thomas Jefferson's comments about Christianity. Rush reminded Adams, "You said you were sorry to hear such sentiments from a gentleman whom you so highly respected and with whom you agreed upon so many subjects, and that it was the only instance you had ever known of a man of sound mind and real genius that was an enemy to Christianity." Jefferson allegedly apologized. Again, the recollection came decades after the fact, in this case in the wake of public accusations of deism and atheism launched by Jefferson's political opponents. It was not even Adams's own remembrance, and its accuracy is made suspect by the fact that Jefferson was so shy and so poor a public speaker that he rarely spoke in Congress on any subject, much less concerning sensitive religious issues. Thus, like Adams's recollection regarding Paine, its real value lies in demonstrating Adams's own long-standing reputation for disliking criticism of the Bible. This was a trait that did not decline with age. In 1808

Adams lambasted Voltaire for his attacks on the ancient Hebrews and his "ribaldry against the Bible." By contrast, Adams called the Hebrews "the most glorious nation that ever inhabited this earth" and "the most essential instrument for civilized nations."[16]

Adams often expressed great respect for the Bible. In 1805 he exempted it from his agreement with Sir Robert Walpole that all historical writing was pure fiction or "romance." Two years later Adams claimed, "The Bible contains the most profound philosophy, the most perfect morality, and the most refined policy that ever was conceived upon the earth. It is the most republican book in the world." In 1810 he declared confidently that Paine's attacks "will never discredit Christianity, which will hold its ground in some degree as long as human nature shall have anything moral or intellectual left in it." He added, "The Christian religion, as I understand it, is the brightness of the glory and express portrait of the character of the eternal, self-existent, independent, benevolent, all powerful and all merciful creator, preserver, and father of the universe, the first good, first perfect, and first fair. It will last as long as the world. Neither savage nor civilized man, without a revelation, could ever have discovered or invented it. Ask me not, then, whether I am a Catholic or Protestant, Calvinist or Arminian. As far as they are Christians, I wish to be a fellow-disciple with them all." Three years later he wrote, "The general principles of Christianity are as eternal and immutable as the Existence and Attributes of God." On Christmas Day he added, "I have examined all [religions], as well as my narrow sphere, my straitened means, and my busy life would allow me; and the result is that the Bible is the best book in the world. It contains more of my little philosophy than all the libraries I have seen." In 1815 Adams summarized his religious views. The first statement, "My religion is founded on the love of God and my neighbor," was a clear reference to Jesus's statement in Matthew 22:37–40: "You shall love the Lord your God with all your heart, and with all your soul, and with all your mind. This is the first and greatest commandment. The second is like it. You shall love your neighbor as yourself. On these two commandments hang all the Law and the prophets." The other foundations for his religion that Adams listed were equally consistent with the Bible: "My religion is founded . . . on the hope of pardon for my offences; upon contrition; upon the duty as well as necessity of supporting with patience the inevitable evils of life; on the duty of doing no wrong but all the good I can to the creation of which I am but an infinitesimal part."[17]

Yet Adams's passionate defense of the Bible did not mean that he considered it inerrant. On the contrary, in 1813, he wondered whether the Ten Commandments had been altered between the time of their promulgation and their recording in the Book of Exodus, and, as we shall see, Adams rejected at least one fundamental doctrine of the New Testament.[18]

John was not the only Adams who was angered by Thomas Paine's attack on the Bible. Samuel Adams complained directly to Paine about *The Age of Reason*. As a result of Paine's *Common Sense* and his *Crisis* essays, Adams wrote, "I therefore esteemed you as a warm friend to the liberty and lasting welfare of the human race." He then added, "But when I heard that you had turned your mind to a defence of infidelity, I felt myself much astonished and more grieved that you had attempted a measure so injurious to the feelings, and so repugnant to the true intent, of so great a part of the citizens of the United States." Adams concluded defiantly, "The people of New England, if you will allow me to use a Scripture phrase, are fast returning to their first love." This was a reference to Revelation 2:4, in which Jesus tells the members of the church at Ephesus, "I have something against you, that you have left your first love," namely, the initial ardor of their Christian faith.[19]

Elias Boudinot devoted countless hours of his spare time, while learning his duties as the first director of the U.S. Mint, to the preparation of a rebuttal to *The Age of Reason*, which he called, *The Age of Revelation* (1801). In the preface Boudinot wrote regarding Paine, "I have endeavored to detect his falsehoods and misrepresentations and to show his extreme ignorance of the divine scriptures, which he makes the subject of his animadversions—not knowing that 'they are the power of God unto salvation to everyone who believeth'" (Romans 1:16).[20]

While Paine attacked the whole Bible publicly, Thomas Jefferson assaulted portions of it privately. Jefferson combined Christianity with elements of Epicureanism, a combination that could be sustained only by rejecting much of the Old Testament and by insisting that the New Testament was a corrupted record of Jesus's teachings.

When Jefferson was a young man in the 1760s, the largest single collection of passages that he copied into his literary commonplace book, comprising almost 40 percent of it, consisted of excerpts from Bolingbroke's *Philosophical Works*, which attacked the Bible. Bolingbroke summarized his position on the matter as follows: "There are gross defects and palpable falsehoods in almost every page of the scriptures, and the whole tenor of them is such as no man who acknowledges a supreme all-perfect being can believe [them] to be his word."[21]

Jefferson adopted Bolingbroke's skepticism regarding the integrity of the scriptures. In 1814 Jefferson wrote concerning the Old Testament, "The whole history of these books is so defective and doubtful that it seems vain to attempt minute inquiry into it, and such tricks have been played with their text, and with the texts of other books relating to them, that we have a right, from that cause, to entertain much doubt what parts of them are genuine."[22]

Jefferson rejected Old Testament miracles. In 1786 he dismissed the Great Flood as the explanation for the discovery of seashells on mountain tops. He gave the biblical flood credence only as "a partial deluge in the country lying around the Mediterranean." The following year Jefferson wrote to his nephew that he should read the Bible "as you would read Livy or Tacitus." He added, "For example, in the book of Joshua [10:12–14] we are told the sun stood still several hours. Were we to read that fact in Livy or Tacitus we should class it with their showers of blood, speaking of statues, beasts & c., but it is said that the writer of the book was inspired. The pretension is entitled to your inquiry because millions believe it. On the other hand, you are Astronomer enough to know how contrary it is to the law of nature that a body revolving on its axis, as the earth does, should have stopped, shall not by that sudden stoppage have prostrated animals, trees, buildings, and should after a certain time have resumed its revolution, and that without a second general prostration. Is this arrest of the earth's motion, or the evidence which affirms it, most within the law of probabilities?" Jefferson's own answer was clear.[23]

As the historian Daniel Boorstin has noted, Jefferson borrowed from the Bible (as even the deists did) the belief in an omniscient, omnipotent Creator but departed from it in denying that the Creator ever violated his own "natural laws" through miracles. While Jefferson never doubted the capacity of an omnipotent Creator to suspend His own laws and to circumvent the consequences that would otherwise result from such a suspension, he denied the rationality of His doing so. To Jefferson, God was the quintessential rationalist who could never act in any way that Jefferson deemed irrational. Jefferson never questioned whether humans, as limited beings, possessed the unlimited knowledge, experience, and wisdom that would logically be necessary to judge what was rational for an omniscient being to do. Part of Jefferson's abhorrence of the concept of a God who would violate His own "laws" derived from the traditional use of that term in reference to the causal sequences of the material world. It is one thing to state that God cannot violate His own moral laws without being both immoral and hypocritical, and quite another to state that He cannot suspend causal sequences of His own creation on rare occasions in order to advance a good or to draw human attention to something important (indeed, the Greek New Testament word for miracle, *semeion*, means "sign," suggesting that its authors interpreted miracles as divine attempts to draw attention to something) without similar imputations to His character. The former would constitute an ethical violation, the latter a mere suspension of entirely amoral processes. For instance, to call the causal sequences associated with gravity "a law" is to endow them with a moral dimension they do not logically possess. Once the inherently ethical word "law" was attached to mere causal sequences, as it had been for a century by Jefferson's day, the crucial distinction between the moral and the amoral was fatally blurred.[24]

Furthermore, while Jefferson loved the psalms and often referred to ethical models in the Old Testament, he was extremely critical of the Mosaic Law and other aspects of Old Testament morality. In 1803, after congratulating the Jews of the Old Testament for their belief in a single God, he added, "But their ideas of him and of his attributes were degrading and injurious. Their Ethics were not only imperfect but often irreconcilable with the sound dictates of reason and morality as they respect intercourse with those around us, and repulsive and anti-social as respecting other nations." In 1819 he declared, "I am not a Jew, and therefore do not adopt their theology, which supposes the God of infinite justice to punish the sins of the fathers upon their children unto the third and fourth generation" (Exodus 20:5).[25]

Jefferson identified Jesus as the great reformer of this corrupt ethical system. Jefferson wrote regarding the Old Testament Jews, "That sect had presented for the object of their worship a Being of terrific character, cruel, vindictive, capricious, and unjust. Jesus, taking for his type the best qualities of the human head and heart, wisdom, justice, [and] goodness, and adding to them power, ascribed all of these, but in infinite perfection, to the Supreme Being and formed Him really worthy of their adoration." Here Jefferson inverts the biblical narrative: instead of a God who creates humans in His own image, Jefferson presents a God fashioned by Jesus in humanity's image. Jefferson continued, "Moses had bound the Jews to many idle ceremonies, mummeries, and observances of no effect towards producing the social utilities which constitute the essence of virtue; Jesus exposed their futility and insignificance. The one instilled into his people the most anti-social spirit towards other nations; the other preached philanthropy and universal charity and benevolence."[26]

Though an ardent champion of Christian ethics, Jefferson was as skeptical regarding the integrity of New Testament accounts as he was of the Old. In 1814 he contended, "In the New Testament there is internal evidence that parts of it have proceeded from an extraordinary man and that other parts are of the fabric of very inferior minds. It is as easy to separate those parts as to pick out diamonds from dunghills. The matter of the first was such as would be preserved in the memory of the hearers, and handed on by tradition for a long time; the latter such stuff as might be gathered up for embedding it anywhere at any time." He considered Jesus the victim of biographers who were "unlettered and ignorant men, who wrote too from memory, and not till long after the transactions had passed." Jefferson rejected the New Testament claim (John 14:26) that the Holy Spirit guided the memories of the Gospel writers. Rather, Jefferson contended regarding Jesus that "fragments only of what he did deliver have come to us mutilated, misstated, and often unintelligible." Jefferson complained of "the follies, the falsehoods, and the charlatanisms" that Jesus's biographers foisted on him. This corruption was tragic, Jefferson lamented, because, "Had the doctrines of Jesus been preached always as pure as they came from his lips, the whole civilized world would now have been Christian." Jefferson trusted, however, that "the dawn of reason and freedom of thought in the United States" would tear down "the artificial scaffolding" set up by these biographers. He concluded, "And the day will come when the mystical generation of Jesus by the supreme being as his father in the womb of a virgin will be classed with the fable of the generation of Minerva in the brain of Jupiter."[27]

By 1820 Jefferson was so displeased with the Bible that he literally cut and pasted passages from it to form his own. Shorn of the Old Testament, all miracles, all references to Jesus's divinity, and all apocalyptic prophecies, Jefferson's tiny volume, which he titled "The Life and Morals of Jesus," emphasized the ethical teachings of the Sermon on the Mount. The Jefferson Bible ended, "There laid they Jesus, and rolled a great stone to the door of the sepulcher, and departed." While Jefferson believed in a general resurrection on Judgment Day, he did not believe that Jesus Himself had risen from the dead.[28]

How was Jefferson able to extract the true meaning of the doctrines of Jesus from their corrupt texts—to separate the diamonds from the dunghill, as he so colorfully put it? In 1813 Jefferson explained how one might compose an accurate account of the teachings of Jesus: "We must reduce our volume to the simple evangelists, select, even from them, the very words of Jesus, paring off the Amphibologisms into which they had been led by forgetting often, or not understanding, what had fallen from him, by giving their own misconceptions as his dicta, and expressing unintelligibly for others what they had not understood themselves. There will be found remaining the most sublime and benevolent code of morals which has ever been offered to man." In 1816 he claimed that a true biographer of Jesus should note only those incidents of His life "as are within the physical laws of nature, and offending none by a denial or even a mention of what is not." In 1820 Jefferson wrote concerning Jesus, "Among the sayings and discourses imputed to him by his biographers I find many passages of fine imagination, correct morality, and the most lovely benevolence; and others again, of so much ignorance, so much absurdity, so much untruth, charlatanism, and imposture, as to pronounce it impossible that such contradictions should have proceeded from the same being. I separate, therefore, the gold from the dross, restore him the former, and leave the latter to the stupidity of some and roguery of others of his disciples. Of this band of dupes and imposters, Paul was the great Coryphaeus [leader of the chorus] and first corruptor of the doctrines of Jesus. These palpable interpolations and falsifications of his doctrines led me to try to sift them apart. I found the work obvious and easy." Thus, Jefferson excluded Paul's epistles from his Bible, though they constitute almost half of the New Testament. Jefferson declared regarding Jesus that he was trying to "rescue his character." He wrote regarding Jesus's perfect morals, "These could not be the invention of the groveling authors who relate them. They are far beyond the powers of their feeble minds." True, even after completing the distillation process, Jefferson was left with some objectionable passages, but he dismissed these as products of Jesus's need to escape the clutches of bloodthirsty priests.[29]

Despite Jefferson's repeated claim of rationality, his enterprise of cutting and pasting passages from the New Testament in order to create a Jesus whose opinions mirrored his own was far from rational. In fact, they represented a giant leap of faith from one of the leading figures of the "Age of Reason."

Though less critical of the Bible, Benjamin Franklin doubted the divine origin and authority of at least some portions of it. In 1784 he claimed, "There are several Things in the Old Testament impossible to be given by divine Inspiration." For instance, Franklin balked at "the Approbation ascribed to the Angel of the Lord of that abominably wicked and detestable Action of Jael, the wife of Heber the Kenite." This was a reference to Judges 4:17–21 in which God throws Sisera's Canaanite army into disarray, causing Sisera to hide in Jael's tent. After giving Sisera false assurances of protection, Jael impales him with a tent stake while he sleeps. In the next chapter (5:24) the angel declares, "Blessed above women shall be Jael, the wife of Heber the Kenite." Franklin concluded, "If the rest of the Book were like that, I should rather suppose it given Inspiration from another Quarter and renounce the whole."[30]

George Washington's opinion concerning the origin and authority of scripture is a mystery. In his 1783 resignation message to the state governors he did allude to "the pure and benign light of Revelation," a clear reference to the Bible. In notes for a public address he also referred to "the blessed religion revealed in the word of God," though he did not include the statement in the actual speech. But these are the only such references in his voluminous papers.[31]

THE DIVINITY OF JESUS

The New Testament repeatedly proclaims the divinity of Jesus. This is clearest in the Gospel of John, whose first verse declares that Jesus is the *Logos* (Word) that is God Himself and whose third verse proclaims that "all things were made through Him." In the same Gospel, Jesus declares, "I and my Father are one" (10:30) and "He who has seen me has seen the Father" (14:9). In John 8:58 Jesus calls Himself "I am," which was the Hebrew name for God (*Yahweh*; Exodus 3:13–14), a declaration that leads scandalized Jews to pick up stones with which to kill a man they regard as a blasphemer (8:59). He also calls Himself "the light of the world" (8:12) and "the truth" (14:6), and declares, "Apart from me you can do nothing" (15:5).

But John is far from being the only New Testament author who claims divinity for Jesus. Matthew 9:2–3 presents Him forgiving people's sins against the murmurs of the outraged scribes. In Matthew 22:41–45 Jesus presents a riddle to the Pharisees: How is it, He asks, that David calls the Messiah, his own descendant, "my Lord" in Psalms 110, when everyone knows that an ancestor is greater than his descendant? The implicit answer is that the Messiah, Jesus, is more than just a man. In Titus 2:13 Paul calls Jesus "the great God." In Colossians 1:15–16 he describes Jesus as "the image of the invisible God, the firstborn of every creature, for by Him were all things created that are in heaven and that are on earth, visible and invisible." To prove Jesus's divinity, Christians even referred to the Old Testament, where they noted that Isaiah (9:6) calls the Messiah "mighty God" and "everlasting Father" and that Daniel (7:13–14), who refers to the Messiah as "the Son of Man," has Him descend from heaven to judge the nations and rule an "everlasting dominion."

Most of the founders believed in the divinity of Jesus. While a student at Princeton who was considering a career in ministry in the early 1770s, James Madison noted in his commonplace book, "Christ's divinity appears by St. John, ch. XX, v. 28." John 20:28 states regarding Jesus, "And Thomas answered and said unto Him, 'My Lord and my God.'" It was Jesus to whom Alexander Hamilton prayed when frightened by a hurricane at the age of eighteen and whom he called his "deliverer." When French atheists challenged John Jay's belief in Christ in 1783, while he was in Paris to conclude the treaty that ended the Revolutionary War, Jay replied "that I did [believe], and that I thanked God for it." In his later years Jay compiled a list of verses in the Book of Revelation that indicated the divinity of Jesus. In his law lectures James Wilson referred to Jesus as "him by whom our nature was both made and assumed." In 1809 Benjamin Rush wrote in his commonplace book regarding Jesus's declaration (Matthew 24:36) that only God knew the day and hour of Jesus's own return: "He disrobed himself not only of the glory which he had with his Father before the world was, not only of his riches and power, but of a part of his Omniscience in order to complete the great work of man's redemption." Elias Boudinot argued on behalf of the divinity of Jesus in *The Age of Revelation*.[32]

John Adams, on the other hand, denied Jesus's divinity. In 1813 he rejected the related doctrine of the Holy Trinity, writing to Thomas Jefferson, "One is not three nor can three be one." Four years later he told his son, John Quincy, that the biblical doctrine that the creator of the universe had been crucified was blasphemous, thereby eliciting a spirited rebuttal from his more orthodox son. In 1825 he ridiculed the idea that the God who "has produced this boundless Universe, Newton's Universe and Hershell's Universe, came down to this little Ball to be spit upon by Jews." The fact that Adams often contended that God aided the United States, which constituted only a small fraction of that "little Ball," demonstrates that his problem was not with the concept of divine intervention but with the doctrine of the incarnation. By the time Adams died in 1826, he was a member of a Unitarian church in Quincy. Yet it is important to note that Adams had referred to Jesus in his presidential thanksgiving proclamations as "Redeemer of the World" and "the Great Mediator and Advocate." Rather than indicating either insincerity or a change in belief on Adams's part, this apparent contradiction was probably no contradiction at all but simply an indication that Adams, like his wife Abigail, adopted an Arian position on the Trinity, one that recognized Jesus as the Son of God and the Redeemer of humankind but not as God Himself. This was different from Jefferson's Socinian position that Jesus had been a mere man, albeit a great one.[33]

Benjamin Franklin doubted the divinity of Jesus. In 1773 he coauthored the preface to his friend the Baron Le Despencer's *An Abridgment of the Book of Common Prayer*, a work that included a revision of the Apostle's Creed that removed all reference to the crucifixion and resurrection of Jesus. A month before Franklin's death in 1790, he wrote to Ezra Stiles, the president of Yale, "As to Jesus of Nazareth . . . I have, with most of the present Dissenters in England, some Doubts as to his Divinity, tho' it is a question I do not dogmatize upon, having never studied it, and I think it needless to busy myself with it now, when I expect soon an Opportunity of knowing the Truth with less Trouble. I see no harm, however, in its being believed if that Belief has the good Consequence, as probably it has, of making his [moral] Doctrines more respected and better observed."[34]

Thomas Jefferson was more forceful in rejecting the divinity of Jesus. As early as 1788 Jefferson claimed that his longtime doubts about the Trinity precluded his service as an Episcopalian godfather. He explained, "The person who becomes sponsor for a child, according to the ritual of the church in which I was educated, makes a solemn profession before god and the world of faith in articles which I had never sense enough to comprehend, and it has always appeared to me that comprehension must precede assent. The difficulty of reconciling the ideas of Unity and Trinity have, from a very early part of my life, excluded me from the office of sponsorship, often proposed to me by my friends, who would have trusted, for the faithful discharge of it, to morality alone, instead of which the church requires faith."[35]

Jefferson's rejection of the doctrine of the Trinity, when combined with his judgment that Jesus was the greatest ethical philosopher in history, led him to either dismiss or reinterpret each of the various New Testament accounts of Jesus's claims to divinity. Surely the greatest ethical philosopher in history would not lie; therefore, the New Testament authors must be, wittingly or unwittingly, the real sources of the popular misconception regarding Jesus. In 1803 Jefferson declared, "I am a Christian in the only sense in which he wished any one to be: sincerely attached to his doctrines, in preference to all others; ascribing to himself every human excellence; and believing he never claimed any other." In some instances, rather than accuse the Gospel writers of deception, Jefferson attempted improbable interpretations of their statements. Thus, according to Jefferson, the *Logos* that had been with God from the beginning, as related in the first verse of the Gospel of John, did not refer to the Trinity but to reason. To draw such an inference Jefferson had to ignore verse 14 of the same chapter, "And the Word became flesh and dwelt among us," which is followed by a narrative of the life of Jesus. Jefferson used very little material from John's gospel, the one that most emphasized Jesus's divinity, when compiling his Bible. In 1820 Jefferson contended, "That Jesus did not mean to impose himself on mankind as the Son of God, physically speaking, I have been convinced by the writings of men more learned than myself in that lore. But that he might conscientiously believe himself inspired from above is very possible."[36]

Jefferson contended that the doctrine of the Trinity had been foisted on the Western world by Platonists, who, intent on establishing and maintaining power for a dissolute class of priests, had engrafted onto Christianity the "sophisms" of that pernicious philosopher. In 1814 Jefferson claimed, "The Christian priesthood, finding the doctrines of Jesus leveled to every understanding, and too plain to need explanation, saw in the mysticisms of Plato materials with which they might build an artificial system which might, from its indistinctiveness, admit everlasting controversy, give employment for their order, and introduce it to profit, power, and pre-eminence. The doctrines which flowed from the lips of Jesus himself are within the comprehension of a child; but thousands of volumes have not yet explained the Platonisms engrafted on them; and for the obvious reason that nonsense can never be explained." Influenced by the clergyman and chemist Joseph Priestley, Jefferson believed that conniving theologians like Augustine had converted John's simple reference to reason into the *Logos* of the Platonists, a divinity begotten by the supreme deity ("the Good," in Plato's terminology, "the One" in Plotinus's) and through which the supreme deity created the universe. Jefferson's and Priestley's conspiracy theory ignored the many other references to Jesus's divinity contained in John's gospel and in the other books of the New Testament in order to make the Trinity an invention of fourth-century priests.[37]

Jefferson maintained that this clerical conspiracy continued in his own day. American clergymen continued to appeal to mystical and absurd doctrines like that of the Trinity, and to slander those like Jefferson and Priestley who rejected them, as part of an effort to establish their individual sects as the state churches of the United States and Great Britain. Jefferson argued, "The mild and simple principles of the Christian religion would produce too much calm, too much regularity of good, to extract from its disciples a support for a numerous priesthood were they not to sophisticate it, ramify it, split it into hairs, and twist its texts till they cover the divine morality of its author with mysteries and require a priesthood to explain them." In 1820 he referred to "the metaphysical insanities of Athanasius," the leading advocate of the doctrine of the Trinity in ancient times, which he termed "mere relapses into polytheism, differing from paganism only in being more unintelligible." He added, "The religion of Jesus is founded in the Unity of God, and this principle chiefly gave it triumph over the rabble of heathen gods then acknowledged. Thinking men of all nations rallied readily to the doctrine of only one God and embraced it with the pure morals which Jesus inculcated." In 1822 Jefferson claimed, "Nor was the unity of the Supreme Being ousted from the Christian creed by the force of reason, but by the sword of the civil government, wielded at the will of the fanatic Athanasius. The hocus-pocus phantasm of a God like another Cerberus, with one body and three heads, had its birth and growth in the blood of thousands and thousands of martyrs." But Jefferson hoped that Christians would not, in the end, "give up morals for mysteries, and Jesus for Plato."[38]

What Jefferson stated privately Thomas Paine declared publicly. In *The Age of Reason*, Paine claimed that Jesus "was the son of God in like manner that every person is, for the Creator is the Father of All." He ridiculed the "Christian system of arithmetic that three are one and one is three." He complained, "The notion of a Trinity of Gods has enfeebled the belief in one God. . . . A man is preached instead of a God."[39]

George Washington again presents a puzzle. In his resignation message to the state governors following the Revolutionary War, Washington referred to Jesus as "the Divine Author of our blessed Religion." But this is the only such reference to the divinity of Jesus in Washington's papers. It is true that this message, like many of the public statements Washington issued during the Revolutionary War, was probably written by a member of his staff, but it is also true that Washington read and edited such documents, especially addresses of this significance, carefully. Thus, at the very least, Washington declined to strike this reference from the document.[40]

Washington's reticence in referring to his beliefs concerning Jesus, even in letters to close friends, may simply reflect the man's intensely private nature, a quality so often noted (and admired) by his contemporaries, as well as the conviction that his religious beliefs were no one else's business. Washington's granddaughter, Nelly Custis, recalled, "He communed with his God in secret. . . . He was a silent, thoughtful man." By contrast, Thomas Jefferson often declared passionately that his own beliefs were no one else's business but then proceeded to detail them to intimate friends or, for that matter, to anyone he considered like-minded. Jefferson's reputation for reticence is actually a sham, which is precisely why we know so much about his religious views. Washington's similar reputation is far more genuine, which is why we know so little about his opinions. On the other hand, Washington never displayed any reticence in conveying publicly his strong beliefs in divine Providence and in the vital importance of religious belief to the survival and success of the republic, nor was he shy about alluding to his belief in an afterlife. Perhaps he considered his beliefs regarding Jesus more personal, or perhaps his views on the subject were less orthodox and thus less likely to be popular than his other beliefs. We simply do not know. Too often both Christians and secularists have sought to fill the vacuum of documentary evidence regarding Washington's religious beliefs with a depressing combination of dubious hearsay evidence and vast speculative leaps that reveal more about these authors' beliefs than their subject's.[41]

The later James Madison and James Monroe present similar puzzles. While at Princeton studying to be a clergyman and for some time thereafter, Madison appears to have been a biblically orthodox Christian who led family worship in his father's house. There is no reason to question the sincerity of his expressions of belief in the divinity of Jesus and of zeal for "the cause of Christ" at that time. But soon after he became engaged in law and politics, he grew silent about his religious opinions. He treated religion with respect, attended worship services, and invited ministers to his house to administer the Lord's Supper to his devout mother. There was some gossip about biblically unorthodox beliefs, and there were claims that he became orthodox again in later life, but no direct statements from the man himself. Monroe's beliefs, except for his oft-expressed confidence in divine Providence, are an even greater mystery. The fact that Washington, Madison, and Monroe were all Virginia Episcopalians may suggest that reticence in expressing religious opinions was a cultural tendency of this group, though by no means one shared by all members.[42]

SALVATION BY FAITH

The New Testament states repeatedly that salvation comes solely through faith in Jesus. The most famous such verse is John 3:16: "For God so loved the world that He gave His only-begotten Son, so that whoever believes in Him should not perish but have everlasting life." Two verses later, the doctrine is made even clearer: "Whoever believes in Him is not condemned, but whoever does not believe in Him is already condemned, because he has not believed in the name of the only begotten Son of God." In John 6:47 Jesus declares, "Very truly, I say to you, whoever believes in me has everlasting life." Although the thief on the cross beside Jesus has performed no good deeds—on the contrary, the Gospels of Matthew and Mark call him and his unrepentant colleague "plunderers" (the same Greek word Homer uses for "pirates"), the Gospel of Luke "evildoers"—his simple expression of faith, "Lord, remember me when you come into your kingdom," prompts Jesus to tell him, "Today you will be with me in paradise" (Luke 23:42–43). In Romans 10:9 Paul declares,

"If you confess with your mouth that Jesus is Lord and believe in your heart that God raised Him from the dead, you shall be saved." In Ephesians 2:8–9 Paul states, "For you are saved by grace through faith—and that not of yourselves, it is the gift of God—not of works, lest anyone should boast." While some Christian denominations have added works (good deeds) as a requirement for salvation, others, following the path of Martin Luther, have argued that such works are merely the by-products of a saving faith. But all biblically orthodox Christians have accepted the necessity of faith in Jesus for salvation since it is one of the clearest and most reiterated teachings of the New Testament. This belief in the efficacy of faith for salvation is grounded in the view, also repeatedly expressed in the New Testament, that Jesus's death on the cross constituted an atonement for the sins of humanity, a benefit received only by those who believe in and follow Him. In John 1:29 John the Baptist declares concerning Jesus, "Behold, the Lamb of God who takes away the sins of the world," a reference to both the Passover lamb, an unblemished lamb whose smeared blood on the doorpost protected Israelites from the angel of death (Exodus 12), and the spotless lamb whose blood was sprinkled on the Ark of the Covenant once a year on Yom Kippur to cover the sins of the people. Similarly, in 2 Corinthians 5:19, Paul states, "God was in Christ, reconciling the world to Himself, not imputing their trespasses to them."

Most of the founders believed in salvation by faith. George Mason alluded to its corollary, Jesus's substitutionary atonement for the sins of believers, in his will in 1773: "My soul I resign into the hands of my Almighty Creator, whose tender mercies are all over his works, who hateth nothing that he hath made, and to the Justice and Wisdom of whose Dispensations I willingly and cheerfully submit, humbly hoping, from his unbounded mercy and benevolence thro the Merits of my blessed Savior, for a remission of my sins." In a 1776 sermon John Witherspoon declared, "There can be no true religion till there be a discovery of your lost state by nature and practice and an unfeigned acceptance of Christ Jesus as he is offered in the gospel." Witherspoon then quoted Acts 4:12 regarding Jesus: "There is no other name under heaven given among men by which we must be saved." He emphasized to an audience preoccupied by the Revolution, "Unless you are united to him by a lively faith, not the resentment of a haughty monarch but the sword of divine justice hangs over you, and the fullness of divine vengeance shall speedily overtake you." He then quoted Jesus in John 3:3: "Unless a man is born again, he cannot see the kingdom of God." This rebirth experience was widely understood to refer to an indwelling of the Holy Spirit that followed belief in Jesus. In 1780 Samuel Adams wrote to his daughter, "You know you cannot gratify me as much as by seeking most earnestly the Favor of Him who made & supports you, who will supply you with whatever his infinite Wisdom sees best for you in this World, and above all, who has given us his Son to purchase for us the Reward of Eternal Life." In his will Adams declared his reliance "on the merits of Jesus Christ for the pardon of all my sins." In 1786, when Patrick Henry wrote to his sister Anne regarding the death of her husband, he declared, "May we meet in that heaven to which the merits of Jesus will carry those who love and serve him." In 1789 Roger Sherman referred to Jesus as "our Lord and master" and "an infinitely suitable Saviour" and expressed "a cheerful confidence in his power and grace for salvation." He added that the only hope for salvation was "faith in Jesus," which meant that "we receive it for an undoubted truth that Jesus Christ was made an atoning sacrifice for sin." In 1804 Christopher Gadsden wrote in his will, "My Soul, with humble submission and confidence in the merits of my blessed Savior Jesus Christ, I hope to resign with cheerfulness to that Almighty and Merciful being who gave it."[43]

In assaulting Thomas Paine's *Age of Reason* in his own book, *The Age of Revelation*, Elias Boudinot emphasized the centrality of faith in human life. Regarding skeptics like Paine, Boudinot noted, "They will mount the horse recommended by its owner or enter a public carriage provided for passengers without doubting of their safety. . . . Does any person refuse to swallow his victuals before he fully understands the method of digestion? . . . In short, innumerable important facts, the causes of which, with their modes of operation, we cannot comprehend . . . are yet firmly believed and, in the course of life, acted upon by us." When Boudinot's nephew Samuel Bayard tried to comfort him on his deathbed in 1821 by reminding him of the many good deeds he had performed during his lifetime, Boudinot would have none of it. Bayard recorded, "His hopes rested on Jesus Christ alone."[44]

Returning to the piety of his youth in his last years, Alexander Hamilton expressed a firm belief in salvation by faith. In one of Hamilton's final letters to his wife he expressed the confidence that, should he be killed in the duel with Aaron Burr, he would experience "a happy immortality" not through his own merit but "from redeeming grace and divine mercy." Benjamin Moore, the Episcopal bishop who administered the Lord's Supper to Hamilton on his deathbed, claimed that he "expressed a strong confidence in the mercy of God through the intercession of the Redeemer." A short while earlier, when Reverend John Mason of the Dutch Reformed Church explained that the sacrament was not a cause, but merely a symbol, of salvation, since salvation could be secured only through faith, Hamilton replied, "I perceive it to be so. I am a sinner; I look to his mercy."[45]

Benjamin Rush consistently held to a belief in salvation by faith. In 1764 he wrote to Ebenezer Hazard regarding Hazard's deceased father, "Think, my dear Ebenezer, with what peculiar pleasure he will look down from the Abodes of Happiness above and see you struggling against the corruptions and temptations of a wicked world and nobly striving to imitate his example, who through Faith now inherits the promises." The following year Rush referred to the death of a member of his congregation and "the triumphant manner in which he went to Heaven," adding significantly, "for he was a Christian." Rush declared in his autobiography, "Of all the poor services I have rendered to any of my fellow creatures I shall say nothing. They were full of imperfections and have no merit in the sight of God. I pray to have the sin that was mixed with them forgiven. My only hope of salvation is in the infinite transcendent love of God manifested to the world by the death of his Son upon the Cross. Nothing but his blood will wash away my sins. I rely exclusively upon it. Come, Lord Jesus! Come quickly! And take home thy lost but redeemed Creature! I will believe, and I will hope in thy salvation! Amen, and amen!" Of course, a saving faith led inevitably to the performance of good deeds in gratitude for divine grace. But Rush always emphasized the centrality of faith even while in the process of performing good deeds. In 1797 he sent this note to a local jail, one of the many prisons in which he provided free medical care: "Peter Brown, Robert Wharton, Mrs. Susanna Bradford, and Dr. Rush request the prisoners in the new Jail under confinement and labor to accept a dinner of turkeys as a proof that they are still remembered in their present suffering condition by some of their fellow creatures. They hope that they will be led by this small present on the anniversary day of the Birth of their Saviour to consider the infinite love of God to their Souls in sending his Son into the world to redeem them from all evil and introduce them when penitent into a state of everlasting rest and happiness." In 1804 Rush responded to Thomas Jefferson's offer to send him "The Philosophy of Jesus" (a precursor to the Jefferson Bible) by declaring that Jefferson was welcome to send this work "upon the character of the Messiah," but "unless it advances it to divinity and renders his death as well as his life necessary for the restoration of mankind, I shall not accord with its author." Jefferson did not send the manuscript. In 1810 Rush jotted these notes in his commonplace book: "Unbelief the radical sin of all sins. No condemnation but for not believing in the Gospel."[46]

But the other Pennsylvania Benjamin among the founders rejected the doctrine of salvation by faith. In fact, Franklin stopped attending Presbyterian services in Philadelphia when he became disgruntled with what he considered the Reverend Jedidiah Andrews's overemphasis on a Calvinist theology that conflicted with Franklin's belief that faith was unnecessary to salvation except insofar as it bolstered virtue, the true path to both earthly and heavenly rewards. Franklin claimed that Andrews's sermons "were all to me very dry, uninteresting, and unedifying, since not a single moral Principle was inculcated or enforced, their Aim seeming to be rather to make us Presbyterians than good Citizens." Franklin then composed a fairly elaborate liturgy for his own personal worship at home. He started attending services again when a junior pastor named Samuel Hemphill arrived, but critics soon attacked Hemphill, alleging that he promoted an unbiblical, works-based theology. Franklin defended Hemphill in writing, but in the process he went beyond Hemphill's teaching of salvation by both faith and works to espouse a completely unbiblical doctrine of salvation by works alone. Franklin's statements that "Faith would be a Means of producing Morality, and Morality of Salvation," and "Morality or Virtue is the End, Faith only a Means to obtain that End" clearly contradicted scripture, however desperately he attempted to reconcile them. The same year, in another pamphlet defending Hemphill, Franklin went so far as to declare "imputed righteousness," the doctrine that God attributed to believers the perfection of Christ, thereby allowing their salvation through faith in Him, which was one of the central concepts of the New Testament, "ridiculous." Franklin later appeared to withdraw from a works-based theology, reassuring his worried sister that he did not believe that "Good Works would merit heaven," adding, "I imagine there are few, if any, in the World so weak as to imagine that the little Good we can do here can merit so vast a Reward hereafter."[47]

But Franklin's amplification on this view, in 1753, revealed that he still possessed an unscriptural view of salvation. He wrote to Joseph Huey:

> You will see in this, my Notion of Good Works, that I am far from expecting (as you suppose) that I shall merit Heaven by them. By Heaven, we understand a State of Happiness infinite in Degree and eternal in Duration. I can do nothing to deserve such a Reward. He that for giving a Draught of Water to a thirsty Person should expect to be paid with a good Plantation would be modest in his Demands compared with those who think they deserve Heaven for the little Good they do on Earth. Even the mixed, imperfect Pleasures we enjoy in this World are rather from God's Goodness than our Merit; how much more such [the] Happiness of Heaven. For my own part, I have not the Vanity to think I deserve it, the Folly to expect it, nor the Ambition to desire it, but content myself in submitting to the Will and Disposal of that God who made me, who has hitherto preserved and blessed me, and in whose fatherly Goodness I may well confide, that he will never make me miserable, and that even the Afflictions I may at any time suffer shall tend to my benefit.
>
> The Faith you mention has doubtless its uses in the World; I do not desire to see it diminished, nor would I endeavour to lessen it in any Man. But I wish it were more productive of Good Works than I have generally seen it.

From this interesting passage, as well as from Franklin's discussion of Matthew 25 that follows in the same letter, in which he has Jesus saving those who have performed good deeds and damning those who have not on Judgment Day, one concludes that while Franklin considered works alone insufficient for salvation in a direct sense, he believed that good deeds were not only necessary for salvation but also the chief factor that caused God to overlook sin and allow sinners into heaven. Absent here are the New Testament teachings that since a holy God could not overlook sin, perfection alone merited heaven, and that sinful humans could achieve this aura of perfection in God's eyes solely through the attribution of Jesus's perfection via faith. To Franklin, good works prompted God's grace (his "Goodness," in Franklin's terminology). Faith played no role in salvation except to encourage good deeds, which it sometimes failed to do. There is no mention of the redemptive work of Jesus's death on the cross, the central theme of the New Testament, which is not surprising when one considers Franklin's earlier rejection of the doctrine of imputed righteousness. Franklin even adopted an idiosyncratic interpretation of Matthew 25:38–39, in which he took the statement of the saved to Jesus, "When did we take you in, or clothe you when you were naked, or visit you when you were sick or in prison?" to mean that this group included people who "never heard of his name," thus severing completely the link between salvation and faith in Christ. In so doing Franklin went well beyond the apostle James's famous statement that "faith without works is dead" (James 2:17) to embrace a thoroughly unbiblical theory of salvation.[48]

Seven years later Franklin reiterated his view that faith in Christ could be helpful in implanting virtue, the true goal, insofar as faith led to good habits, which was the true path to virtue and salvation, but habit was the key method. In reference to the system of self-training in virtue through habit formation that Franklin had begun a few decades earlier, and would discuss more fully in his autobiography a few decades later, Franklin claimed:

> Christians are directed to have Faith in Christ as the effectual Means of obtaining the Change [in behavior] they desire. It may, when sufficiently strong, be effectual with many. A full Opinion that a Teacher is infinitely wise, good, and powerful, and that he will certainly reward and punish the Obedient and Disobedient, must give great Weight to his Precepts and make them much more attended to by his Disciples. But all Men cannot have Faith in Christ, and many have it in so weak a Degree that it does not produce the Effect. Our Art of Virtue may therefore be of great Service to those who have not Faith and come in Aid of the weak Faith of others. Such as are naturally well-disposed and have been carefully educated, so that good Habits have been early established, and bad ones prevented, have less Need of this Art, but all may be more or less benefited by it. It is, in short, to be adapted for universal Use.

In portraying habit as the sole connection between Christian faith and virtue, Franklin here ignored the New Testament teaching of the spiritual rebirth Christians experienced upon their salvation by faith, an infusion of the Holy Spirit that allowed the believer to follow the demanding ethical teachings of Jesus more completely, though still imperfectly due to original sin (John 7:39).[49]

Yet there may have been a veiled reference to the Holy Spirit in Franklin's revised version of the Lord's Prayer (probably 1768). Franklin's version declared, "Heavenly Father, May all revere thee, and become dutiful children and faithful Subjects. May thy Laws be obeyed on Earth as perfectly as they are in Heaven. Provide for us this Day as thou has hitherto daily done. Forgive us our Trespasses, and enable us likewise to forgive those that offend us. Keep us out of Temptation, and deliver us from Evil." While Franklin's changes to the original wording of the prayer were largely cosmetic, the alteration of "Forgive us our trespasses, as we forgive those who trespass against us" to "Forgive us our Trespasses and enable us likewise to forgive those that offend us" was significant. Franklin explained, "This, instead of assuming that we have already in and of ourselves the Grace of Forgiveness, acknowledges our Dependence on God, the Fountain of Mercy, for any Share we may have of it, praying that he would communicate it to us." Franklin did not make clear how God would communicate this grace, but the conduit identified repeatedly in the New Testament is the Holy Spirit. In any case, habit is nowhere to be found in this rather orthodox view. Franklin's other major alteration was converting "thy kingdom come," a clear reference to Jesus's millennial rule, to "[may all] become dutiful Children and faithful Subjects."[50]

But Franklin's rare reference to the need for divine aid in achieving virtue had no impact on his continuing disbelief in the need for faith in Jesus as a requirement for salvation. In the same 1790 letter in which he wrote that he doubted the divinity of Jesus, he added that faith in Jesus or even God was irrelevant to salvation: "I do not perceive that the Supreme takes it amiss, by distinguishing the Unbelievers in his Government of the World with any peculiar Marks of his Displeasure. I shall only add, respecting myself, that, having experienced the Goodness of that Being in conducting me prosperously thro' a long life, I have no doubt of its Continuance in the next, though without the smallest Conceit of meriting such Goodness." Despite Franklin's denial of any belief that he merited salvation because of his good deeds, a less scriptural view of salvation was hardly possible, given his complete disconnection of salvation from faith. It contradicted numerous scriptures, including Hebrews 11:6: "Without faith, it is impossible to please God, for he who comes to God must believe that He exists and that He rewards those who seek Him diligently."[51]

Like Franklin, Thomas Jefferson rejected the doctrine of salvation by faith. Jefferson rejected it because it conflicted with his conviction that beliefs were solely the products of reason operating on facts and, therefore, not subject to the will. His Bill for Establishing Religious Freedom (1779) began with a significant clause that was, just as significantly, deleted by the Virginia Senate: "Well aware that the opinions and belief of men depend not on their own will, but follow involuntarily the evidence proposed to their minds." Jefferson's complete severance of belief from the will stood in direct contradiction to the New Testament conception of faith as fundamentally an act of the will, a conception that made faith a legitimate criterion for salvation. Jefferson did not explain how the same facts could lead people of equal reasoning ability to different conclusions.[52]

In a 1783 letter to his daughter Martha, Jefferson suggested that salvation was the result of the avoidance of wrongdoing. He wrote:

> I hope you will have good sense enough to disregard those foolish predictions that the world is to be at an end soon. The almighty has never made known to anybody at what time he created it, nor will he tell anybody when he means to put an end to it, if ever he means to do it. As to preparations for that event, the best way is for you to be always prepared for it. The only way to be so is never to do nor say a bad thing. If ever you are about to say anything amiss or to do anything wrong, consider beforehand. You will feel something within you which will tell you it is wrong and ought not to be said or done: this is your conscience, and be sure to obey it. Our maker has given us all this faithful internal Monitor, and if you always obey it, you will always be prepared for the end of the world, or for a much more certain event, which is death. This must happen to all; it puts an end to the world as to us, and the way to be ready for it is never to do a wrong act.

The complete avoidance of wrongdoing was a very high, most would say impossible, standard.[53]

Four years later Jefferson wrote to his nephew Peter Carr regarding religious inquiry, "Your own reason is the only oracle given you by heaven, and you are answerable not for the rightness but uprightness of the decision." In 1801 Jefferson referred to his effort to merit salvation, which was the terminology of salvation by works rather than faith. He wrote that rather than concerning himself with the afterlife, "I have thought it better, by nourishing the good passions and controlling the bad, to merit an inheritance in a state of being of which I can know so little and to trust for the future to him who has been so good for the past." While Jefferson's reference to trusting in the deity for his salvation without regard to faith in Jesus was similar to that of Franklin, his reference to the attempt to merit it was not; neither was biblical. In 1813 Jefferson claimed, "Of all the systems of morality, ancient or modern, which have come under my observation, none appear to me as pure as that of Jesus." He added, "He who follows this steadfastly [regardless of faith] need not, I think, be uneasy" about his salvation. Jefferson could not imagine that a person could be damned for coming to a wrong conclusion about Jesus any more than for coming to a wrong conclusion about a scientific question. This conception of belief as the mere product of reason operating on facts was a very different conception from that of the apostle Paul, who maintained that unbelievers rejected the truth by an act of the will because its acceptance would force them to give up a life of sin they relished (Romans 1:20–25; Thessalonians 2:11–12). In 1819 Jefferson declared, "My fundamental principle would be the reverse of Calvin's, that we are to be saved by our good works, which are within our power, and not by faith, which is not within our power."[54]

Thomas Paine also rejected the concept of salvation by faith. In *The Age of Reason* he contended, "The fall of man, the account of Jesus Christ being the Son of God, and of his dying to appease the wrath of God, and of salvation by that strange means, are all fabulous inventions, dishonourable to the wisdom and power of the Almighty." He complained, "Morality is banished to make room for an imaginary thing called faith." In one of his last essays he alleged that believers in salvation by faith "become as careless in morals as a spendthrift would be of money were he told that his father had engaged to pay all of his scores." He added, "It is a doctrine not only dangerous to morals in this world but to our happiness in the next world because it holds out such a cheap, easy, and lazy way of getting to heaven as has a tendency to induce men to hug the delusion of it to their own injury."[55]

Four founders—Thomas Paine, Thomas Jefferson, Benjamin Franklin, and John Adams—differed from all of the others who left documentary evidence concerning their religious opinions in possessing beliefs concerning the origin and authority of the Bible, the divinity of Jesus, and the means of salvation that were fundamentally at odds with the New Testament. While each of these differences between the more and the less biblically orthodox founders possessed tremendous spiritual importance, their much larger areas of agreement were far more significant to the nation's formation. The founders' shared beliefs in divine Providence, the nation's divine mission, God-given individual rights, the superiority of Christian ethics, the necessity of religion and morality to the survival and success of republican government, spiritual equality, free will, and the existence of an afterlife provided their principal motivations to create and shape a new republic.

9

HUMAN NATURE AND BALANCED GOVERNMENT

In addition to their differences of opinion concerning the origin and authority of the Bible, the divinity of Jesus, and the means of salvation, the founders also differed regarding human nature. While most of the founders possessed a pessimistic view of human nature that accorded with the biblical doctrine of original sin, a few possessed a more optimistic outlook. The pessimistic conception of human nature that prevailed had crucial consequences. It encouraged the founders to resist British claims to unchecked power and led them to establish numerous checks and balances in their national and state constitutions.

THE BIBLICAL VIEW

Contrary to the thesis of some historians, the doctrine of original sin was not the creation of Augustine four centuries after Christ but is clearly present in both testaments of the Bible. It is no accident that, in the Book of Genesis, the fall of Adam and Eve (chapter 3) is followed immediately by the first murder (chapter 4), committed by their son Cain. The narrative clearly suggests that the propensity to sin was transmitted from one generation to the next. 1 Kings 8:46 states, "There is no one who does not sin." The psalmist declares (Psalms 51:5), "I was born guilty, a sinner when my mother conceived me." Proverbs 20:9 asks, "Who can say, 'I have kept my heart pure; I am clean and without sin?'" Ecclesiastes 7:20

reiterates, "There is not a righteous man on earth who does what is right and never sins." Isaiah 64:6 proclaims, "We are all unclean, and all our righteous deeds are like filthy rags." Jeremiah 17:9 claims, "The heart is deceitful above all things and desperately wicked."[1]

The New Testament is even clearer in this regard. 1 John 1:8 declares, "If we claim to be without sin, we deceive ourselves and the truth is not in us." Paul explains (Romans 5:12, 19), "By one man sin entered into the world, and death through sin, and so death spread to all because all have sinned. . . . For just as by one man's disobedience many were made sinners, so by one man's obedience many will be made righteous." Just as sin and death came into world through Adam, redemption and life came into the world through Christ. Paul clearly ties the doctrine of original sin, humankind's inherited propensity to sin, to the doctrine of imputed righteousness, human salvation through faith in Jesus.

ORIGINAL SIN AND BRITISH RULE

One of the most fundamental differences in belief among the founders concerned human nature. While most of them possessed a pessimistic view of human nature largely derived from the Bible, a few held a more optimistic outlook that was derived either from the blank slate theory of Epicurus and John Locke or from the even more optimistic, Platonic conception of humans as creatures who tended toward the good.

During the Revolutionary era, nothing was more common among patriots than the assertion that the depravity of human nature rendered it unsafe to accede to British claims of unlimited power over the colonies. In 1775 Alexander Hamilton argued, "A fondness for power is implanted in most men, and it is natural to abuse it when acquired. This maxim, drawn from the experience of all ages, makes it the height of folly to entrust any set of men with power which is not under every possible controul. . . . We ought not, therefore, to concede any greater authority to the British parliament than is absolutely necessary." The following year John Witherspoon declared in a sermon that a realistic understanding of human nature was essential to a comprehension of both religious and political truth. He contended, "Nothing can be more absolutely necessary to true religion than a clear and full conviction of the sinfulness of our nature and state. Without this all that is said in scripture of the wisdom and mercy of God in providing a Saviour is without force and without meaning. Justly does our Saviour say, 'The whole have no need of a physician but those that are sick. I came not to call the righteous but sinners to repentance' [Mark 2:17]. Those who are not sensible that they are sinners will treat every exhortation to repentance and every offer of mercy with disdain or defiance." Witherspoon continued, "Others may, if they please, treat the corruption of our nature as a chimera; for my part, I see it everywhere and feel it every day. All the disorders in human society, and the greatest part of the unhappiness we are exposed to, arise from the envy, malice, covetousness, and other lusts of man. If we and all about us were just what we ought to be in all respects, we should not need to go any further for heaven, for it would be upon earth. But war and violence present a spectacle still more awful. How affecting it is to think that the lust of dominion should rarely be satisfied with their own possessions and acquisitions, or even with the benefit that would arise from mutual service, but should look upon the happiness and tranquility of others as an obstruction to their own?" Thus, Witherspoon concluded regarding members of the British Parliament, "I do not refuse submission to their unjust claims because they are corrupt or profligate, although probably many of them are so, but because they are men, and therefore liable to all the selfish bias inseparable from human nature."[2]

CHECKS AND BALANCES

While none of the various governmental checks and balances contained in the U.S. Constitution was biblical in origin, their inclusion in the document was, to a large extent, predicated on a pessimistic conception of human nature that was rooted in scripture, emphasized in Calvinist sermons, reiterated in political speeches, and transmitted from one generation to the next. It was Plato who, despite his optimistic conception of human nature, first suggested the theory of mixed government, the belief that governmental power should be balanced between the one, the few, and the many (the one leader, the few well-born or wealthy, and the masses of ordinary folk). It was the French Enlightenment author Montesquieu who popularized the separation of powers theory, the theory that the legislative, executive, and judicial functions of government—the power to make, execute, and interpret law—should be separated into different branches. Federalism, the belief that power should be balanced between national and state governments, was equally modern in formulation (though the Greeks had possessed some confederacies). But the popularity of all of these systems of checks and balances in the modern world was based on the belief that innate human selfishness necessitated the dispersion of power, a conviction that was based largely on the Bible, which was by far the most widely read work in the Western world, and the weekly diet of sermons based on it. While a person may derive a pessimistic view of human nature from a number of different sources—from the study of history, from reading newspapers, from observing toddlers (whose first spoken word is usually "mine!"), or from honest introspection, for instance—the most prevalent source for such a view in the founders' day was the Bible.

John Adams, the most forceful advocate of mixed government in America, endorsed it on the basis of a conception of human nature that was thoroughly biblical. As early as 1763 he claimed in "An Essay on Man's Lust for Power," "No simple form of Government can possibly secure Men against the Violences of Power. Simple Monarchy will soon mould itself into Despotism, Aristocracy will commence on Oligarchy, and Democracy will soon degenerate into Anarchy, such an Anarchy that every Man will do what is right in his own Eyes, and no Man's life or Property or Reputation or Liberty will be safe." Thus, a mixed government that balanced the power of the three orders of society was absolutely essential. Adams's "every Man will do what is right in his own Eyes" was a paraphrase of Judges 17:6. In a 1772 diary entry he referred to the "Mass of Corruption human Nature has been in general since the Fall of Adam." While far from deeming a nation's educational system irrelevant, Adams argued, in *A Defence of the Constitutions of Government of the United States of America* (1787–1788), his longest and most influential treatise on mixed government, "Millions must be brought up, whom no principles, no sentiments derived from education, can restrain from trampling on the laws. Orders of men, watching and balancing each other, are the only security; power must be opposed to power, and interest to interest. . . . Religion, superstition, oaths, education, laws, all give way before passions, interest, and power. . . . Although reason ought always to govern individuals, it certainly never did since the Fall, and never will till the Millennium." Adams's embrace of a theory of human nature very similar to that of original sin and his references "to the Fall" are all the more remarkable given his rejection of the literal truth of the Book of Genesis. In 1814 he wrote regarding Joseph Priestley and "the history of the Fall of Man in the book of Genesis," "I believe with him, and have maintained in all my writings, that this history is either an allegory or founded on uncertain tradition, that it is an hypothesis to account for the origin of evil adopted by Moses, which by no means accounts for the facts." What mattered to Adams was not the literal truth of the Genesis account, but rather its accurate portrayal of human nature, a regrettable reality that necessitated a balance of governmental power between the three orders of society.[3]

Alexander Hamilton and John Witherspoon based their support for mixed government on the same conception of human nature. Hamilton's outline for a speech delivered at the Constitutional Convention on behalf of mixed government on June 18, 1787, included this statement: "If a government [is] in the hands of the few, they will tyrannize over the many. If [it is in] the hands of the many, they will tyrannize over the few. It ought to be in the hands of both, and they should be separated." Thus, Hamilton endorsed the Constitution because it established a balance between the one (the president), the representatives of the few (the Senate), and the representatives of the many (the House). As a delegate to the New Jersey ratifying convention, Witherspoon supported the Constitution on the same basis. He claimed that the Bible alone "gives a clear and consistent account of human depravity." Since Adam was "the federal head of the human race," his fall led to "the corruption of human nature." Witherspoon asked, "What is the history of the world but the history of human guilt?" He added, "Those who have been the most conversant in public life and have obtained most of what is called a knowledge of the world have always the worst opinion of human nature. . . . It seems plainly to be the point of view in every human law to bridle the fury of human inclination and hinder one man from making a prey of another." Mixed government was necessary so that one power might check another.[4]

A delegate to the Constitutional Convention from Connecticut, Roger Sherman was the chief architect of "the Great Compromise" that assigned states equal representation in the Senate while granting more populous states greater representation in the House, thereby balancing the power of large and small states. Two years later he gave some insight into the theory of human nature that undergirded his support for such a balance when he wrote that humans were "in a state of depravity, guilt, and misery . . . dead in trespass and sin—by nature prone to evil and adverse to the good." In 1790 he wrote approvingly regarding Jonathan Edwards Jr.'s iteration of the biblical doctrine of original sin: "He supposes original righteousness in man was a supernatural principle which was withdrawn on his first transgression, and his natural principles of agency remaining were exercised wrong[ly], and his affections set on wrong objects in consequence of such withdrawal."[5]

Supporters of the separation of powers based their endorsement on the same pessimistic theory of human nature. At the Constitutional Convention, James Madison declared, "All men having power ought to be distrusted to a certain degree." In a letter that year he wrote that, as a consequence of human nature, "Divide et impera [divide and rule], the reprobated maxim of tyranny, is, under certain qualifications, the only policy by which a republic can be administered on just principles." In *Federalist* No. 51 he contended, "The great security against a gradual concentration of the several powers in the same department consists of giving to those who administer each department the necessary constitutional means and personal motives to resist encroachments of the others. . . . Ambition must be made to counteract ambition. . . . It may be a reflection on human nature that such devices should be necessary to controul the abuses of government. But what is government itself but the greatest of all reflections on human nature? If men were angels, no government would be necessary." In No. 55 he claimed, "There is a degree of depravity in mankind which requires a certain degree of circumspection and distrust." Madison's selection of the word "depravity," the favored term of Calvinist preachers, is significant. The same year Madison declared, "Wherever there is an interest and power to do wrong, wrong will generally be done, and not less readily by a powerful and interested party than by a powerful and interested prince." Similarly, despite Alexander Hamilton's support for an energetic executive, in *Federalist* No. 75 he cautioned that it was absolutely necessary that the Senate possess the power to reject treaties negotiated by the president: "The history of human conduct does not warrant that exalted opinion of human nature which would make it wise in a nation to commit interests of so delicate and momentous a kind as those which concern its intercourse with the rest of the world to the sole disposal of a magistrate created and circumstanced as would be a president of the United States." Thus, the

Constitution established a balance between the legislative, executive, and judicial branches.[6]

The Federalist argument for a balance between national and state power was based on the same conception of human nature. In 1781 Alexander Hamilton advocated greater power for the federal Congress, which was extremely weak under the Articles of Confederation. Without a balance between national and state power, Hamilton argued, states would go to war against one another: "Political societies in close neighborhood must be strongly united under one government or there will infallibly exist emulations and quarrels. This is in human nature, and we have no reason to think ourselves wiser or better than other men." In *Federalist* No. 6 he claimed, "A man must be far gone in Utopian speculations who can seriously doubt that if these States should either be wholly disunited or only united in partial confederacies, the subdivisions into which they might be thrown would have frequent and violent contests with each other. To presume a want of motives for such contests as an argument against their existence would be to forget that men are ambitious, vindictive, and rapacious. . . . Have republics in practice been less addicted to war than monarchies? Are not the former administered by men as well as the latter? Are there not aversions, predilections, rivalships, and desires of unjust acquisitions that affect nations as well as kings?" In No. 15 Hamilton expressed a concern that without a stronger union, the states would infringe on federal authority: "Why has government been instituted at all? Because the passions of men will not conform to the dictates of reason and justice, without constraint. Has it been found that bodies of men act with more rectitude or greater disinterestedness than individuals? The contrary of this has been inferred by all accurate observers of mankind." In No. 34 he contended that a stronger federal government was necessary because the same human nature that ruled Americans held sway over foreigners. In other words, Congress must have the power to tax in order to pay for wars thrust upon the nation by hostile powers acting according to their own depravity: "To judge from the history of mankind, we shall be compelled to conclude that the fiery and destructive passions of war reign in the human breast with much more powerful sway than the mild and beneficent sentiments of peace and that to model our political systems upon speculations of lasting tranquility is to calculate on the weaker springs of the human character."[7]

George Washington agreed with Hamilton's view that human nature required a much closer balance between state and federal power than existed under the Articles of Confederation. In 1786, the year before the new constitution was drafted, Washington wrote to John Jay, "Your sentiments that our affairs are drawing rapidly to a crisis accord with my own. . . . We have probably had too good an opinion of human nature in forming our confederation. Experience has taught us that men will not adopt & carry into execution measures the best calculated for their own good without the intervention of a coercive power. I do not conceive we can exist long as a nation without having lodged somewhere a power which will pervade the whole Union in as energetic a manner as the authority of the different state governments extends over the several States. . . . We must take human nature as we find it. Perfection falls not to the share of mortals."[8]

Although many Anti-Federalists possessed the same pessimistic view of human nature as the Federalists, they considered state sovereignty essential to thwarting it. They opposed the stronger federal government created by the new constitution, however balanced against one another its branches might be, precisely on the grounds that human nature, as accurately portrayed in the Bible, made it dangerous to grant excessive power to flawed individuals. They believed that the Constitution created too powerful a federal government, one that would eventually become tyrannical.

After listening to the Reverend Samuel West endorse the Constitution at the Massachusetts ratifying convention, the Anti-Federalist Samuel Thompson declared in amazement, "One thing surprises me. It is to hear the worthy gentleman insinuate that our federal rulers will undoubtedly be good men and that therefore we have little to fear from their being entrusted with all power. This, sir, is quite contrary to the common language of the clergy, who are continually representing mankind as reprobate and deceitful and that we really grow worse and worse day after day. I really believe we do, sir, and I make no doubt to prove it before I sit down, from the Old Testament. When I consider the man that slew the lion and the bear, and that he was a man after God's own heart [1 Samuel 17:34–36]; when I consider his son, blest with all wisdom [1 Kings 4:29–31]—and the errors they fell into, I extremely doubt the infallibility of human nature. Sir, I suspect my own heart, and I shall suspect our rulers." Thompson's biblical references were to David, who had murdered Uriah (2 Samuel 11:14–17), and to David's son Solomon, whose foreign wives seduced him into the worship of false gods (1 Kings 11:3). Thompson assumed that he did not have to explain such references to a contemporary audience.[9]

Patrick Henry and George Mason invoked the same specter of a wicked human nature against the Constitution at the Virginia ratification convention. Henry's speech centered on the prediction that Article 1, Section 8 of the Constitution, a clause that granted Congress the power to "make all laws which shall be necessary and proper" to carrying out its listed functions and that later became known as "the elastic clause" because it became the principal tool used to expand federal power, would inevitably be abused by federal officials because of humans' innate lust for power. Henry declared, "I dread the depravity of human nature. . . . I will never depend on so slender a protection as the possibility of being represented by virtuous men." His colleague Mason also used "the natural lust of power so inherent in man" as an argument against a stronger federal government.[10]

Although James Madison stood on the opposite side of the ratification debate from the Anti-Federalists, he shared their concerns about human nature. He supported the Constitution because he considered the federal government under the Articles of Confederation too weak to balance the power of the states. But soon after the Constitution was enacted, Madison became alarmed by what he regarded as a rapid growth in federal power, a development he attempted to counter through claims of state authority. Later in life, frightened by South Carolina's attempt to nullify a federal law, he reverted to supporting federal power. However inconsistent his actions seemed to some contemporaries, and still appear to some historians, they were based on a consistent desire for balance that was, in turn, rooted in an equally consistent belief in a fundamentally selfish human nature.[11]

Indeed, the essay for which Madison is most famous reflected this conception of human nature. In *Federalist* No. 10 Madison claimed, "The latent causes of faction . . . are sown into the nature of man." Madison contended that human nature invariably produced differences in belief and in attachment to particular leaders, which, in turn, inevitably "divided mankind into parties, inflamed them with mutual animosity, and rendered them much more disposed to vex and oppress each other than to cooperate for their common good." Madison then famously argued that a stronger federal government was acceptable because there were so many different interests in a large commercial republic like the United States that majorities must be weak coalitions incapable of prolonged tyranny. But perhaps what is most intriguing about this essay is that Madison went beyond the commonplace assertion that humans were selfish to the biblical proposition that they were wicked—specifically, that they were creatures whose innate love of strife made them eager to fight about almost anything. Madison claimed, "So strong is this propensity of mankind to fall into mutual animosities that where no substantial occasion presents itself, the most frivolous and fanciful distinctions have been sufficient to kindle their unfriendly passions and excite their most violent conflicts."[12]

CONTINUING PESSIMISM IN THE EARLY REPUBLICAN ERA

Nothing that the pessimistic founders experienced in the years after the ratification of the Constitution altered their opinion of human nature. In 1794 Alexander Hamilton ascribed the rise of a despotic government in France to French radicals' denial of the dark realities of human nature and their resultant utopianism. He claimed that some revolutionaries went beyond the advocacy of a limited government to embrace anarchy, based on the foolish belief "that as human nature shall refine and ameliorate by the operation of a more enlightened plan, government itself will become useless, and Society will subsist and flourish free from its shackles." Hamilton decried "the mischiefs which are inherent in so wild and fatal a scheme, every modification of which aims a mortal blow at the vitals of human happiness." Hamilton continued regarding utopianism, "The practical development of this pernicious system has been seen in France. It has served as an engine to subvert all her antient institutions, civil and religious, with all the checks that served to mitigate the rigour of authority; it has hurried her headlong through a rapid succession of dreadful revolutions, which have laid waste property, made havoc among the arts, overthrown cities, desolated provinces, unpeopled regions, crimsoned her soil with blood, and deluged it in crime, poverty, and wretchedness, and all this as yet for no better purpose than to erect on the ruins of former things a despotism unlimited and uncontrouled, leaving to a deluded, an abused, a plundered, a scourged, and an oppressed people not even the shadow of liberty to console them for a long train of substantial misfortunes, of bitter sufferings." Ironically, by producing an anarchy that ended inevitably in despotism, the same utopians who sought to create an earthly paradise had produced a hellish society. Hamilton feared the same result in the United States as in France since some Americans were attempting "to induce our government to sanction and promote her odious principles and views with the blood and treasure of our citizens."[13]

Ten years later Hamilton attributed the Federalist Party's electoral failures to a naïve view of human nature. He claimed that too many Federalists assumed that man was a rational animal, whereas Democratic-Republican politicians, however much they might preach that very conception publicly, understood privately that men were "for the most part governed by the impulse of passion." While it was true that the Federalists might change their style and start appealing to the good passions of the public, "Unfortunately, however, for us in the competition for the passions of the people, our opponents have great advantages over us, for the plain reason that the vicious are far more active than the good passions."[14]

In 1795 George Washington wrote that if men were honest and just, "Wars would cease and our swords would soon be converted into reaping-hooks." Instead, the earth was "moistened with human gore." Washington added, "The restless mind of man can not be at peace; and when there is disorder within, it will appear without, and sooner or later will shew itself in acts. So it is with Nations, whose mind is only the aggregate of those of the individuals where the Government is Representative and the voice of a Despot where it is not."[15]

John Adams also remained pessimistic regarding human nature in his later years. In 1812 he wrote that politics had not improved because human nature had not changed. He claimed regarding politics, "This is still the sport of passions and prejudices, of ambition, avarice, intrigue, faction, caprice, and gallantry as much as ever. Jealousy, envy, and revenge govern with as absolute a sway as ever." The following year he preached his favorite theme: "Checks and balances, Jefferson, are our only Security for the progress of Mind, as well as the Security of Body. Every Species of these Christians would persecute Deists as [much as] either Sect would persecute another, if it had unchecked and unbalanced Power. Nay, the Deists would persecute Christians, and Atheists would persecute Deists, with as unrelenting Cruelty as any Christian would persecute them or one another. Know thyself, Human nature!" Although Adams considered piety and virtue vital to the survival of the republic, the sacred text of the very religion on which he relied, combined with his reading of history and his own experiences, taught him the folly of relying exclusively on these twin pillars. Human nature necessitated the erection of a third pillar, balanced government.[16]

James Madison retained a similar view. In 1825 he claimed, "All power in human hands is liable to be abused. . . . The superior recommendation of the federo-Republican system is that, whilst it provides more effectually against external danger, it involves a greater security to the minority against the hasty formation of oppressive minorities." At the Virginia Constitutional Convention of 1829, Madison took direct aim at the Scottish "common sense" theory of human nature, a theory based on the writings of Plato and the Stoics that emphasized the goodness of human nature by focusing on the moral sense or conscience as the origin of humans' social nature. After observing that there were those who "would find a security [against tyranny] in our social feelings, in a respect for character, in the dictates of the monitor within," Madison declared, "But man is known to be a selfish as well as social being. . . . We all know that conscience is not a sufficient safeguard, and besides that, conscience itself may be deluded, may be misled . . . into acts which an enlightened conscience would forbid."[17]

CONFIDENCE IN CHECKS AND BALANCES: ORTHODOX AND UNORTHODOX

Although the popularity of various theories of checks and balances owed much to the pervasiveness of the biblical doctrine of original sin in American society, the supreme confidence in the ability of balanced political structures to overcome the depravity of human nature that their advocates sometimes expressed was not biblical at all. For instance, John Adams sometimes rested unbiblical, utopian hopes on his favorite form of balanced government. By contrast, James Madison had more limited, and thus more biblical, expectations.

Having reviewed the horrors of the Peloponnesian War, the bloody conflict between Athens and Sparta that laid waste to all of Greece in the fifth century BC, in the *Defence* (1787), John Adams concluded, "Such things ever will be, says Thucydides, so long as human nature remains the same. But if this nervous historian had known a balance of three powers, he would not have pronounced the distemper so incurable, but would have added—so long as parties in cities remain unbalanced." It is a testament to the powerful hold of Enlightenment optimism that Adams could write the latter sentence despite his knowledge of the fact that the most revered classical models of mixed government, Sparta and the Roman republic, had fallen in spite of their vaunted balance, and despite the fact that he himself had argued during the Revolution that the most revered modern model, Great Britain, had become corrupted. Enlightenment philosophers emphasized the power of human reason to solve every sort of problem, and theories of checks and balances were products of human reason intended to solve problems caused by the less attractive attributes of human nature. Adams was simultaneously a man of the Bible who believed deeply in the darkness of human nature and a man of the Enlightenment who believed deeply in the power of human reason to solve problems. The result was a fervent, almost obsessive, regard for mixed government as the answer to the problem posed by human nature. Thus, Adams even suggested that it was possible for a constitution to last forever, regardless of the qualities of the republic's citizens, if only it possessed a proper balance among the orders. Adding one piece of hyperbole to another, Adams added, "Perhaps it would be impossible to prove that a republic cannot exist even among highwaymen, by setting one rogue to watch another; and the knaves themselves may, in time, be made honest men by the struggle." Adams's euphoria over the power of mixed government to circumvent human nature resembled that of the more zealous advocates of laissez-faire economics, who also began with the premise of a selfish human nature, yet still somehow managed to sound utopian when expressing supreme confidence in the checks imposed by a free marketplace.[18]

To be certain, Adams's giddy flight of optimism ended with a crash. By 1806 he was writing, "I once thought our Constitution was quasi or mixed government, but they have now made it, to all intents and purposes, in virtue, in spirit, and effect, a democracy. We are left without resources but in our prayers and tears, and having nothing that we can do or say, but the Lord have mercy upon us." But it is crucial to note that Adams's renewed pessimism involved no loss of faith in the ability of mixed government to counter human nature—only the conviction that the

American system had been democratized to a dangerous degree by such innovations as the rise of political parties and the elimination of property qualifications for voting. It does not appear to have occurred to Adams that part of the problem of human nature might lie in its propensity to destroy carefully constructed balances. Adams's unwillingness to face this truth is all the more startling given the long list of once balanced republics that had fallen from a loss of balance that he himself presented in the *Defence*.[19]

Both Madison's more nuanced understanding of human nature and his greater circumspection concerning the ability of checks and balances to thwart that nature were biblical. While conceding the general selfishness of human nature to Patrick Henry and George Mason at the Virginia ratifying convention, he noted that republican government was based on the assumption that some degree of popular virtue was not only possible but also essential. Why were republican orators constantly calling for greater piety and virtue if people were really incapable of it? Madison declared, "Is there no virtue among us? If there be not, we are in a wretched situation. No theoretical checks, no form of government, can render us secure. To suppose that any form of government will secure liberty or happiness without any virtue in the people is a chimerical idea." Madison was cautiously optimistic that a modicum of popular virtue, combined with checks and balances, could preserve a republic for a long time, though by no means create a utopia. In this he reflected the teaching of his mentor, John Witherspoon, who claimed that although "man now comes into the world in a state of impurity or moral defilement," it was a mistake to conclude regarding human nature that "every act in every part of it is evil," and warned against going "to an extreme on the one hand or on the other in speaking of human nature." Witherspoon explained, "It is of consequence to have as much virtue among the particular members of a community as possible, but it is folly to expect that a state should be supported in integrity in all who have a share in managing it. They must be so balanced that when everyone draws to his own interest or inclination, there may be an even poise upon the whole."[20]

POSTMILLENNIALIST CONTRADICTIONS

Like the Hebrew prophets, most of the founders combined a deep confidence in their society's status as the chosen people of God with an equally profound belief in the universality of human selfishness. Thus, like the prophets, these founders viewed their nation's selection by God for a divine mission as an act of grace rather than as a reward for possessing a nature superior to the rest of humanity. Just as the prophets made a nuisance of themselves by repeatedly reminding their own people that God had not chosen them because of their superior morality but, rather, in spite of their stubborn tendency to immorality, so some of the founders issued their own jeremiads warning that violations of the covenant risked provoking divine judgment.

Yet it was almost inevitable that just as some Jews, such as the Pharisees, had become arrogant because of their special status as God's chosen people, so some of even the most biblically orthodox founders sometimes became so enthralled by signs of divine favor that they forgot biblical teachings regarding the universality of sin and began to believe that the perfection of the Millennium lay just around the corner. The success of the American Revolution and the Constitution occasionally led some founders to believe that God's plan was to use the United States as a spearhead to bring about liberty throughout the world as a means of generating an increasing perfection that would culminate in the Millennium. That this form of postmillennialism—the belief that Jesus would return only after humans created the Millennium through their own progressive efforts—contradicted biblical teachings regarding the universal depravity of humanity, the apocalyptic nature of the end times, and the necessity of the Messiah's global rule to humanity's survival and regeneration went largely unnoticed. In addition to the Book of Revelation's famous account of unprecedented natural disasters and the wickedness of the Antichrist's global regime, for instance, there is also Paul's statement in 2 Timothy 3:1–5: "Know this also, that in the last days perilous times shall come. For men shall be lovers of themselves, covetous, boasters, proud, blasphemers, disobedient to their parents, unthankful, unholy, inhuman, implacable, slanderers, lacking self-control, haters of good, traitors, reckless, arrogant, lovers of pleasure rather than lovers of God, having a form of spirituality but denying the power thereof." Biblical accounts clearly taught that human affairs were going to get much worse, necessitating the coming of the Messiah.

Countervailing beliefs of equal power in original sin and in the inevitable success of the American mission to advance liberty around the world led men like Samuel Adams into contradictory statements. On the one hand, there was often a biblical tenor to his observations about human nature. In 1776 he claimed, "All men are fond of power. . . . Even public Bodies of men legally constituted are too prone to covet more power than the Public hath judged it safe to entrust them with. It is happy when their Power is not only subject to Controul while it is exercised, but frequently reverts into the hands of the People from whom it is derived and to whom Men in Power ought forever to be accountable." In 1784 he declared, "There is a Degree of Watchfulness over all Men possessed of Power or Influence upon which the Liberties of Mankind much depend. It is necessary to guard against the Infirmities of the best, as well as the Weakness of the worst, of men. Such is the Weakness of human Nature that Tyranny has oftener sprung from that than any other Source. It is this that unravels the Mystery of Millions being enslaved by a few." In 1790 he wrote to his second cousin John regarding Adam, the progenitor of their family surname as well as of humanity, "Even the heart of our first father was grievously wounded at the sight of the murder of one of his Sons by the hand of the other. . . . The same Tragedies have been acted on the Theatre of the World; the same Arts of tormenting have been studied and practiced to this day. . . . The best formed constitutions that have yet been contrived by the wit of Man have and will come to an End—because the Kingdoms of the Earth have not been governed by Reason."[21]

Yet, in the very same letter, Adams went on to present education as the means not merely to a limited progress but to the utopia of the Millennium itself. This peculiar view was partly a product of Adams's failure to study scriptures related to the end times. Adams wrote, "Is the Millennium commencing? I have not studied the Prophecies and cannot even conjecture." Having pleaded ignorance of end time prophecy, he proceeded to prove it, writing that education could bring about "that Golden Age beautifully described in figurative language, when the Wolf shall dwell with the Lamb, and the Leopard lie down with the Kid—the Cow and the bear shall feed; their young ones shall lie down together, and the Lyon shall eat straw like the Ox—none shall then hurt or destroy, for the Earth shall be full of the Knowledge of the Lord. When this Millennium shall commence, if there shall be any need of Civil Government, indulge me in the fancy that it will be in the republican form or something better." Despite Adams's accurate quoting of Isaiah 11:6–9 regarding the utopian conditions of the Millennium, the idea that it would be brought about by education contradicted all of the prophetic scriptures, which depicted the world in a terrible state upon the arrival of the Messiah and attributed the utopian conditions to His subsequent rule. Adams's strain of postmillennialism, which had captivated some of the figures of the Great Awakening and would soon reach its height of popularity in the Second Great Awakening, was completely unscriptural. Furthermore, Adams's fanciful hope that the millennial form of government would be republican contradicted numerous scriptures related to the Messiah's rule. Adams was apparently so ardent a republican that he could not accept monarchical rule even under the Messiah. Adams's postmillennialism was even more evident the following month when he claimed that an increase in knowledge and virtue "is one of the most essential means of further and still further improvements in Society, and of correcting and amending moral sentiments and habits and political institutions till by human means directed by divine influence, Men shall be prepared for that happy and holy State when the Messiah is to reign." This flatly contradicted the biblical narrative, which is not one of increasing moral progress brought about "by human means," no matter how directed.[22]

Like Adams, Benjamin Rush possessed a divided mind on the subject of human nature, one that wavered between postmillennialist optimism and dark references to original sin. In 1786 he claimed regarding man that through "science, religion, liberty, and good government," "it is possible to produce such a change in his moral character as shall raise him to a resemblance of angels—nay more, to the likeness of God himself." Yet four years later he wrote, "Man is indeed fallen! He discovers it every day in domestic, in social, and in political life. Science, civilization, and government have in vain been employed to cure the defects of his nature." Two years after that, he was again referring to the coming utopia: "I anticipate the end of war and such a superlative tenderness for human life as will exterminate capital punishments from all our systems of legislation. In the meantime let us not be idle with such prospects before our eyes. Heaven works by instruments and even supernatural prophecies are fulfilled by natural means. It is possible we may not live to witness the approaching regeneration of our world, but the more active we are in bringing it about the more fitted we shall be for that world where justice and benevolence eternally prevail." Like Adams, Rush referred to humans "bringing about" the Millennium.[23]

In his later years Rush appears to have returned to a more consistent pessimism about human nature that resulted partly from a closer study of biblical prophecy regarding the end times. In 1801 he wrote regarding Jesus's Second Coming, "Much yet remains to be done before that great event can take place. Infidelity must increase and prevail much more than it now does, so that when he comes, 'shall he find faith on the earth' [Luke 18:8]? Knowledge likewise must become universal [Daniel 12:4]. The effects of this knowledge will be to produce revolutions, liberty, a general intercourse of all nations by means of commerce and—be not surprised when I add—universal misery. The more nations and individuals know, till they know God, the more unhappy will they be. The effects of this unhappiness in nations and individuals will appear in a general dissatisfaction with their governments (though the work of their own hands), with each other, and with themselves. Injustice, vice, and tyranny will prevail everywhere. Then and not till then will all nations, worn down by their sufferings, unite in wishing for a Deliverer, and then and not till then will 'the Desire of all nations come'" (Haggai 2:7). Five years later, as the Napoleonic wars raged in Europe, Rush noted, "It was predicted of the Messiah that he would be 'the desire of all nations.'" He added, "Should the present system of violence and subjugation of the nations continue, that prophecy must soon be fulfilled, for I believe that there is at this time scarcely a nation upon the face of the earth that is satisfied with its government or its rulers and that would not exchange both for others, though probably, in their present state of ignorance, not for the government of the future King of Saints and Nations. A few more years of suffering will probably bring about the fulfillment of the prophecy and render him indeed 'the desire of all nations.'" Rush added, "Were I to turn clergyman, I think I could preach a whole year on two short texts. They are, 'Put not your faith in man' [Psalms 146:3 actually states, 'Put not your faith in princes'] and 'Beware of men'" (Matthew 10:17). In 1809 Rush rejected the idea that "human depravity" arose from economic conditions, lack of education, or any of the other environmental sources often blamed for it. Instead, Rush endorsed the biblical view that depravity was innate. Regarding the former theories, he contended, "Legislation founded upon any of these opinions must necessarily be erroneous and productive of misery. In the Bible alone man is described as he is. He can be governed of course only by accommodating law to his nature, as depicted in that sacred book." Three years later Rush noted, "It is somewhat remarkable that in none of the works of the primitive fathers or reformers do we find plans for perpetual and universal peace. They knew too well what was in man to believe it possible in his present weak and depraved state. Such plans have been suggested chiefly by infidels and atheists, who ascribe all that is evil in man to religion and bad governments."[24]

James Wilson was yet another biblically orthodox founder whose occasional professions of optimism regarding human progress sounded postmillennialist. In one of his law lectures he declared, "In the order of Providence, as has been observed on another occasion, the progress of societies towards perfection resembles that of an individual. This progress has hitherto been slow; by many unpropitious events, it has often been interrupted. But may we not indulge the pleasing expectation that, in future, it will be accelerated and will meet with fewer and less considerable interruptions? . . . The principles and the practice of liberty are gaining ground in more than one section of the world. Where liberty prevails, the arts and sciences flourish. Where the arts and sciences flourish, political and moral improvements will likewise be made. All will receive from each, and each will receive from all, mutual support and assistance. Mutually supported and assisted, all may be carried to a degree of perfection hitherto unknown, perhaps, hitherto not believed."[25]

THE CONSISTENT OPTIMISTS

Only three of the founders were fairly consistent in rejecting the biblical doctrine of original sin for a more optimistic conception of human nature. Not surprisingly, one of these founders was Thomas Paine. This was true even in his early, more orthodox days. In *Common Sense* (1776) Paine disparaged the concept of original sin by likening it to the theory that undergirded the hereditary succession of monarchs. In both cases the current generation was allegedly doomed by the bad decisions of its ancestors: in the former case, humans were condemned to sin by the error of Adam; in the latter case, they were doomed to suffer under the oppression of the original king's descendant by the ancestors who selected his progenitor. Paine rejected both forms of fatalism, claiming, "We have it in our power to begin the world over again. A situation similar to the present hath not happened since the days of Noah until now." This sense of a new start, so powerful for so long in a nation made up not only of immigrants from another hemisphere but also of settlers continually relocating westward, was unbiblical, ignoring the possibility that innate selfishness might doom such a start as surely as it had all other beginnings. Indeed, Paine's reference to Noah is interesting because it makes no mention of the fact that immediately after the Flood one of Noah's sons was cursed for a sexual impropriety (Genesis 9:22–27) or the fact that the next major account of Noah's descendants concerns their wickedness and construction of the Tower of Babel (Genesis 11). Writing under the pseudonym "Forester" the same year, Paine used Lockean language to express his conception of human nature and thus the limitless possibilities of America's new start. He declared that Americans, free from European corruption, had "a blank sheet to write upon," just as John Locke had referred to the infant's mind as a "white paper, void of all characters" in his influential *Essay Concerning Human Understanding* (1690). (Contrary to the popular misconception, the term *tabula rasa* [blank slate] was not used by Locke but by the Epicurean Pierre Gassendi, who influenced Locke, in 1655.) While it is true that, in *Common Sense*, Paine made a conventional reference to the existence of government as "a necessary evil" resulting from human lapses in obedience to conscience, he soon decided that the reverse was true—that government was the cause, and not the result, of human corruption—writing, "Man, were he not corrupted by governments, is naturally the friend of man, and human nature is not of itself vicious." This conclusion did not cause Paine to become an anarchist, but it did lead him to endorse simple democracies, such as the unicameral government created by the Pennsylvania Constitution of 1776, rather than mixed governments because, unlike most of the other founders, he had no fear that majority rule would become majority tyranny.[26]

Thomas Jefferson's rejection of the doctrine of original sin also led him to endorse a simpler and more democratic form of government than that favored by most of the other founders. After a brief flirtation with mixed government theory during the Revolution, Jefferson became an advocate of a simple representative democracy based on the conviction that the agricultural lifestyle of the vast majority of American voters rendered the majority capable of wielding supreme power. Influenced by classical poets and historians, Jefferson praised this lifestyle partly for the practical reason that it left the small farmer free from an overlord and therefore capable of thinking and acting independently. But Jefferson also suggested that it was the favored lifestyle of the Almighty: "Those who labour in the earth are the chosen people of God, if ever he had a chosen people, whose breasts He has made His peculiar deposit for genuine and substantial virtue. He keeps alive that sacred fire which otherwise might escape from the face of the earth. Corruption of morals in the mass of cultivators is a phenomenon of which no age or nation has furnished an example. It is the mark set on those who, not looking up to heaven and to their own soil and industry as does the husbandman, for their subsistence, depend for it on the casualties and caprices of customers." When touring southern France in 1787, Jefferson noted disapprovingly, "No farm-houses, all the people being gathered in villages. Are they thus collected by that dogma of their religion which makes them believe that to keep the Creator in good humor with His own works, they must mumble a mass every day? Certain it is that they are less happy and less virtuous in the villages than they would be insulated with their families on the grounds they cultivate." He later claimed, "Cultivators of the earth are the most valuable citizens. They are the most vigorous, the most independent, the most virtuous, and they are tied to their country, and wedded to its liberty and interests by the most lasting bonds." Hence Jefferson predicted, "I think our governments will remain virtuous for many centuries; as long as they remain chiefly agricultural; and this will be as long as there will be vacant lands in any part of America." Jefferson rested his hopes of a bright future for the new nation not on checks and balances intended to thwart a corrupt human nature but on the positive effects of a rural, agricultural lifestyle on a slate that was at worst blank, at best already inclined to goodness by the moral sense. For this reason, as president, Jefferson was willing to sacrifice one of his most cherished political principles, strict construction of the Constitution, in order to purchase Louisiana from France. When the absence of a constitutional provision allowing Jefferson to buy foreign territory threatened the republic's future agricultural base, and thus its virtue and longevity, he reluctantly sacrificed constitutional scruples in order to extend the life of the republic.[27]

In addition to the agricultural lifestyle, Jefferson rested his hopes on the power of education. Even the most pessimistic letter he ever wrote ended with a hint of the confidence he placed in education. In 1814 Jefferson wrote regarding "self-love," "It is the sole antagonist of virtue, leading us constantly by our propensities to self-gratification in violation of our moral duties to others. Accordingly, it is against this enemy that are erected the batteries of the moralists and religionists, as the only obstacle to the practice of morality. Take from man his selfish propensities, and he can have nothing to seduce him from the practice of virtue. Or subdue those propensities by education, instruction, or restraint, and virtue remains without a competitor." This passage begins in a seemingly Calvinist tone, though a peculiar one since it asserts that "the sole antagonist of virtue" and "the only obstacle to the practice of morality" is human nature itself, but then reveals that this trait of self-love is actually so lightly rooted that it can be displaced by education, leaving virtue "without a competitor."

Even this rather weak reference to the existence of an innate self-love in humanity is absent from most of Jefferson's other writings, which focus on the power of education to bring about progress. In 1816 he contended, "Enlighten the people generally, and tyranny and oppressions of body and mind will vanish like evil spirits at the dawn of day. Although I do not, with some enthusiasts, believe that the human condition will ever advance to such a state of perfection as that there shall no longer be pain or vice in the world, yet I believe it susceptible of much improvement, and most of all, in matters of government and religion; and that the diffusion of knowledge among the people is to be the instrument by which it is to be effected." Two years later he helped draft a report concerning his beloved University of Virginia. The report declared that education "engrafts a new man on the native stock and improves what in his nature was vicious and perverse into qualities of virtue and social worth." The report continued, "And it cannot but be that each generation succeeding to the knowledge acquired by all those who preceded it, adding it to their own acquisitions and discoveries, and handing the mass down for successive and constant accumulation, must advance the knowledge and well-being of mankind not infinitely, as some have said, but indefinitely, and to a term no one can fix and foresee." The references to virtue and vice in this report make it clear that Jefferson and his coauthors were referring not merely to the certainty of scientific, technological, or even economic progress, about which none of the founders expressed any significant doubt, but also to that of social and moral progress, about which there was considerable debate, with most coming down on the side of biblical pessimism.[28]

Benjamin Franklin rejected the doctrine of original sin for the view that human behavior was almost solely the product of habit. Franklin labeled the imputation to humankind "of old Father Adam's first Guilt . . . every whit as ridiculous as that of Imputed Righteousness." Franklin added, "'Tis a notion invented, a Bugbear set up by Priests (whether Popish or Presbyterian I know not) to fright and scare an unthinking Populace out of their Senses. 'Tis absurd in itself, and therefore cannot be fathered upon the Christian Religion as delivered in the Gospel. Moral Guilt is so personal a Thing that it cannot possibly in the Nature of Things be transferred from one Man to Myriads of others that were no way accessory to it. And to suppose a Man liable to Punishment upon account of the Guilt of another is unreasonable and actually to punish him for it is unjust and cruel." While Franklin's understanding of the doctrine of original sin was a bit flawed—it does not hold that the guilt of Adam was directly transferred to his progeny, only that his propensity to sin was transmitted to them, thus producing personal sins for which each was individually liable—more significant were his admission that his opponents in this argument were able to present some scriptures that appeared to support their view and his response to this predicament. Franklin declared, "These Passages are intricate and obscure. And granting that I could not explain them after a Manner more agreeable to the Nature of God than the Maintainers of this Monstrous System do, yet I could not help thinking that they must be understood in a Sense consistent with it, tho' I could not find it out." Franklin then claimed that even if there existed a scripture that more clearly espoused the doctrine of original sin, "For my own Part, I should not in the least hesitate to say that it could not be genuine, being so evidently contrary to Reason and the Nature of Things." Like Jefferson, Franklin was quite willing to delete from the Bible passages that were objectionable to his conception of reason, though more comfortable with Jefferson's other method of contorting them to make them fit his unorthodox views.[29]

In accord with his rejection of original sin Franklin engaged in a quest for moral perfection, a struggle recounted in his autobiography. Franklin recalled, "It was about this time I conceived the bold and arduous project of arriving at moral perfection. I wished to live without committing any fault at any time." Franklin began by drafting a list of the thirteen virtues he considered worthy of acquisition. Each week he attempted to master a different virtue by striving to get through the period without committing any infraction against it. Franklin believed that such training would eventually render the virtues a matter of habit and allow him to achieve moral perfection, a confidence clearly based on a blank slate theory of human nature. When Franklin abandoned the plan, it was not because he arrived at the conclusion that moral perfection was impossible but because he decided that it might not be all that it was cracked up to be: if he became morally perfect, people might envy him. Because of Franklin's customary ironic ending to the story, some historians have refused to take this passage seriously, but Franklin was quite sincere about the project, as part of a treatise he intended to write called, "The Art of Virtue," and referred to it in letters that spanned several decades. All of his writings make it abundantly clear that he considered habit the key to moral progress and, thus, to the happiness of individuals and societies, a view consistent with a Lockean theory of human nature.[30]

Nevertheless, while Franklin's belief in human moral perfectibility was unbiblical, there were two Christian elements to his methodology. First, the intense introspection involved in his weekly moral self-examination was clearly a product of his Puritan upbringing. Second, Franklin added divine aid to habit as essential to success in his enterprise: "Conceiving God to be the fountainhead of wisdom, I thought it right and necessary to solicit his assistance for obtaining it." So Franklin composed a prayer: "O powerful Goodness, bountiful Father, merciful Guide! Increase in me that wisdom which discerns my truest interests; strengthen my resolutions to perform what that wisdom dictates. Accept my kind offices to thy other children as the only return in my power for thy continual favours to me."[31]

Even the sole religious difference among the founders that possessed significant political import, their conflicting conceptions of human nature, was less influential than might have been expected because those who rejected the biblical doctrine of a selfish human nature were so greatly outnumbered that they fell in line. Although Benjamin Franklin had supported a simple form of government dominated by a unicameral legislature as president of the Pennsylvania Constitutional Convention (1776), he expressed no objection to the bicameral legislature and complex system of checks and balances established by the U.S. Constitution. On the contrary, for nationalist reasons, he became one of the document's leading supporters. Thomas Jefferson was in Paris, serving as U.S. minister to France, at the time of the constitutional debates and did not participate in them. Although his conception of human nature was even more optimistic than that of Franklin, he soon joined his friend and ally James Madison in endorsing a type of federalism in which the states acted as a check on the national government. Thomas Paine left for Europe and did not return for another decade and a half, by which point his published attack on the Bible had left him a pariah devoid of political influence. The victory of balanced government based on a biblical conception of human nature was complete.

10

CHURCH AND STATE

Just as the founders differed in some of their religious beliefs while sharing broad and significant areas of agreement, they also differed in their precise definition of religious freedom while sharing a powerful belief in its importance to any republic worth the name and an equally strong conviction that it included, at a minimum, the right to worship freely, a right that was routinely infringed in most of the rest of the world. Not surprisingly, given the enormous influence of the Bible in American society, the founders' most frequent argument for a separation of church and state was thoroughly biblical: the contention that no government had the authority to interpose itself between the individual and an omniscient Creator who cared deeply about the inner beliefs of His creatures. Thus, the individual possessed both the right and the duty to define his own relationship with God in the manner of his own choosing, free from all compulsion. The founders called this "the right of conscience" and held it to be the most sacred of all God-given rights. To bolster the biblical basis of their argument, the founders often noted that Jesus Himself and His early disciples never compelled anyone to express any belief but relied solely on the power of the Holy Spirit to attract souls to the faith.

THE ANCIENT, MEDIEVAL, AND EARLY MODERN BACKGROUNDS

Although God instructs the Hebrews of the Old Testament to kill or drive out the Canaanite tribes that have occupied Israel during the four centuries in which the Hebrews have been held captive in Egypt, in order to protect themselves from corruption by Canaanite idolatry (Joshua 6 and 8), there is never any instruction to convert Gentiles by force. On the contrary, beginning with the story of Adam and Eve, there is a sense that each individual must make a free choice regarding whether to follow God and must live with the consequences. While God judges and punishes Israel collectively when large numbers of its people become idolatrous and unethical, He also judges individuals. The New Testament accentuates this individualism by emphasizing the concept of the afterlife: not only is each soul judged individually, but the stakes, everlasting life versus eternal damnation, are the highest imaginable. Though Jesus possesses supernatural powers, He never coerces anyone, either mentally or physically, to follow Him. His early disciples continued this policy of non-coercion. Far from being the persecutors of members of other faiths, early Christians were the victims of both Jewish and Roman persecution.

The biblical conception of individual religious obligation and accountability contrasted sharply with the social focus of Greco-Roman religion, whose gods were not omniscient and therefore cared only about outward displays of devotion carried out by the entire community, not the inner faith of individual believers. Roman priesthood was a political office, and all citizens were expected to participate in collective forms of devotion in order to prevent the gods from lashing out at the whole society.[1]

The biblical paradigm of individual choice was overturned in the fourth century AD when the emperor Constantine's conversion or, rather, partial conversion, transformed the Christian Church from a victim of the Roman establishment into an integral part of it. As in a classical polity, church and state were firmly united. Augustine supported Christian emperors' suppression of heresy. In the Middle Ages, Thomas Aquinas defended the execution of heretics, arguing that they were worse than pagans since they corrupted the faith. The medieval church sometimes joined with the state in launching inquisitions against heretics and pogroms against Jews. Nor were the heretics themselves libertarians; nearly all sought merely to substitute their own dogmas for their opponents' as the recipients of state support. Protestants were no more tolerant than Catholics. In his early years Martin Luther supported the expulsion of heretics from his principality and, in his later years, Jews from all of Europe. John Calvin endorsed the execution of the famous heretic Michael Servetus. He contended that rulers must "execute vengeance on . . . [those] who adulterate true doctrine with their own errors and so dissipate the unity of the faith and disturb the peace of the church."[2]

The classical concern for social stability that had undergirded the unity of church and state remained in the medieval and early modern West, but to it was now added the Christian concern for the salvation of eternal souls, while the biblical principle that salvation must be based on the free choice of the individual was ignored. Late Roman, medieval, and early modern Christians were deeply preoccupied with thoughts of the eternal fate that awaited them at the end of their short lives. They did not consider it a friendly act for political leaders to allow heretics to continue espousing errors that leaders believed threatened both the heretics' own immortal souls and those of their listeners. Hence even as late as the seventeenth century, every government in Europe expelled or executed heretics.[3]

THE COLONIAL AMERICAN BACKGROUND

Although many colonists came to America to escape religious persecution, these dissenters were hardly modern libertarians; their desire for freedom to practice their own religions did not always signify a willingness to allow others to do the same, much less a belief in the separation of church and state. Even so, the American colonies, with the notable exception of the early Puritan colonies of New England, possessed a greater degree of religious freedom than nearly all other contemporary societies. While Americans often had to pay taxes to support their colony's established church (generally the majority church), and had to obey Christian blue laws (instituted more for social order than for the salvation of souls), they were generally free to worship as they wished.

Even in the New England colonies religious toleration increased fairly rapidly. This growth in toleration was the result of a variety of factors: the failure of the "city on a hill," the Puritan mission to reform the Church of England by example; the death of the first generation of Puritans; and an explosion in commerce that distracted the Puritans from their religious mission. By the 1670s the Puritans were tolerating small Anglican, Baptist, and Quaker congregations. Thus, when the English monarchs William and Mary imposed toleration on them in 1691, three years after deposing James II in the Glorious Revolution, the effect was more symbolic than real.[4]

The Middle Colonies practiced a high degree of religious toleration from the beginning. The Dutch enacted a policy of toleration in the New Netherlands, which the English continued after seizing the colony and renaming it New York in 1664. This policy attracted Huguenots, Mennonites, Lutherans, Presbyterians, Quakers, and Sephardic Jews to the colony. The English even allowed Dutch settlements to assign their church taxes to the Dutch Reformed Church, a reform of the usual religious establishment, in which the official church of each colony (usually the Church of England) received all of the funds set aside for that purpose.[5]

The Quakers who established Pennsylvania were even more tolerant. There was no tax-supported church there, though the English government forced the colony's proprietor, William Penn, to prohibit Catholics and Jews from voting or holding office. Pennsylvania's policy of toleration stemmed from the Quaker advocacy of the separation of church and state. Like Roger Williams, the founder of Rhode Island, Quakers believed that governmental power corrupted churches.[6]

Toleration attracted immigrants from a great variety of denominations, a variety that encouraged further tolerance. By 1776 there were twelve denominations in Pennsylvania, including thousands of Catholic and Jewish colonists.[7]

But even in Quaker Pennsylvania the legislature took it upon itself to pass traditional blue laws that prohibited cursing, plays, cards, dice, lotteries, "or such like enticing, vain, and evil Sports and Games." Such laws, though clearly rooted in Christian morality, were considered secular, not religious, since they were thought vital to civic order. To Quakers, the separation of church and state meant the strict separation of institutions, not the intellectual separation of religious belief from governance, a separation they would have considered neither possible nor desirable.[8]

Despite the economic motives that played a larger role in the settlement of the southern colonies, most southerners were no less devoted to Protestant religion than their counterparts in New England and the Middle Colonies. The first permanent English colony in America, Jamestown, was established by the Company of Virginia in 1607. Sir Edwin Sandys, a major figure in the company, had studied in Calvinist Geneva after graduating from Puritan-dominated Cambridge University. Jamestown's settlers began the construction of a church the first day they landed. Though Anglican, most southerners were theologically closer to the Calvinism of the Puritans than to the near Catholicism that had by this time prevailed in the Church of England. Their blue laws were similar to those of the other colonies. These laws mandated church attendance; imposed stiff fines for gambling, blasphemy, and drunkenness; prescribed whipping for disrespect to clergy and tongue-boring for blasphemy (death for the third offense); and confiscated the property of citizens excommunicated for consorting with prostitutes. It is indicative of the general piety of the era, and of the near universal desire for social order, that Virginia used this strict code as an advertisement for settlers in London. The chief leader of the colony, Captain John Smith, was himself a Puritan who had a favorable opinion of Puritan Massachusetts.[9]

But toleration spread even more quickly in the South than in New England. Since no Anglican bishopric was ever created in America, the church hierarchy exerted little control over American congregations, which generally appointed their own pastors. The task of regulating the church fell first to apathetic royal governors, and then to the bishop of London, who was equally neglectful. Not only did the lack of a strong authority largely free the Anglican Church in America from external control, but it also made it more difficult for the church to infringe the freedom of other denominations. With the encouragement of Maryland's Catholic proprietor, Lord Baltimore, the colony's legislature passed the first toleration act in the New World in 1649. The act granted religious freedom to all Trinitarian Christians. Religious toleration in South Carolina was more complete than in any other colony except Rhode Island and Pennsylvania. North Carolina was similarly tolerant, though the initial requirement of oaths prevented the Quaker population, who were opposed to all oaths based on Matthew 5:34–37, from seeking office. In Georgia, the last of the thirteen colonies, all Christians except Catholics were tolerated. While dissenters had to join Anglicans in paying fairly low taxes to support Anglican churches throughout the South, most of the funds that sustained these churches came from the Society for the Propagation of the Gospel in Foreign Parts, a charitable organization founded by Thomas Bray in England in 1701.[10]

The Great Awakening increased religious toleration further. As both the supporters and the opponents of revivalism within each denomination struggled against each other, they reached out to their counterparts in other denominations for support. In the process they realized that they had more in common with similarly inclined elements of other denominations than they had with the opposing elements within their own. As a result, an ecumenical spirit grew. Though George Whitefield never criticized the theory of apostolic succession popular among the hierarchy of his own Anglican Church, he placed no emphasis on it, considering the ordinations of other denominations as legitimate as those of his own. A profound ecumenicist, he angered the dogmatists of his church by declaring, "Oh, that the partition-wall were broken down and we all with one heart and mind could glorify our common Lord and Saviour Jesus Christ!" He recalled, "I bless God, the partition-wall of bigotry and sect-religion was soon broken down in my heart; for as soon as the love of God was shed abroad in my soul, I loved all of whatsoever denomination who loved the Lord Jesus in sincerity of heart." Once, when Whitefield was preaching from the balcony of the courthouse on Market Street in Philadelphia, he cried out, "'Father Abraham, who have you in heaven? Any Episcopalians?' 'No.' 'Any Presbyterians?' 'No.' 'Any Baptists?' 'No.' 'Have you any Methodists, Seceders, or Independents there?' 'No, no, no.' "Why, who have you there?' 'We don't know those names here. All who are here are Christians, believers in Christ—men who have overcome by the blood of the Lamb and the word of his testimony' [Revelation 12:11]. 'Oh, is that the case? Then God help me, God help us all, to forget party names and to become Christians in deed and in truth.'" (Decades later this account convinced John Adams that there was "no Philosopher, no Theologian or Moralist, ancient or modern, more profound" than Whitefield.) Similarly, the Presbyterian revivalist Samuel Davies declared, "I care but little whether Men go to Heaven from the Church of England or Presbyterian, if they do but go there."[11]

THE REVOLUTIONARY AND CONFEDERATION ERAS

The toleration promoted by the Great Awakening bore fruit in the Revolutionary and Confederation eras. By 1760, although the New England colonies still harbored tax-supported churches, each congregation could assign its taxes to support its own ministers. Similar multidenominational establishments were begun in Maryland (1776), Georgia (1777), and South Carolina (1778). In 1787 Congress passed the Northwest Ordinance, whose first article stated, "No person demeaning himself in a peaceable and orderly manner shall be molested on account of his mode of worship or religious sentiments in said territory."[12]

The founders were united in advocating religious freedom, however differently they might sometimes define it. In 1774 John Witherspoon told his students, "The magistrate ought to defend the rights of conscience and tolerate all in their religious sentiments that are not injurious to their neighbors." Over a decade later, when Witherspoon took the lead in uniting various Presbyterian synods into a national church and in writing a constitution for it, he used the Westminster Confession of Faith (1647) as his model. But whereas the Westminster Confession declared that it was a civil magistrate's duty to see to it "that the truth of God be kept pure and entire, that all blasphemies and heresies be suppressed, all corruptions and abuses in worship and discipline prevented or reformed, and all the ordinances of God duly settled, administered, and observed," Witherspoon declared that magistrates could not "in the least interfere in matters of faith," giving "no preference to any denomination of Christians above the rest." In *Common Sense* (1776) Thomas Paine urged religious toleration as a means of exhibiting the Christian virtue of kindness. He claimed, "I fully and conscientiously believe that it is the will of the Almighty that there should be a diversity of religious opinions among us. It affords a larger field for our Christian kindness: were we all of one way of thinking, our religious dispositions would want matter for probation; and on this liberal principle I look on the various denominations among us to be like children of the same family differing only in what is called their Christian names." George Mason also based his support for religious tolerance on Christian principles. He contended in the Virginia Declaration of Rights, "Religion, or the duty which we owe our Creator and the manner of discharging it, can be directed only by reason and conviction, not by force or violence; therefore, all men are equally entitled to the free exercise of religion according to the dictates of conscience, and it is the mutual duty of all to practice Christian forbearance, love, and charity towards each other."[13]

The same year Thomas Jefferson used the example of Jesus in support of the separation of church and state. In the outline for his argument on behalf of the disestablishment of the Church of England in Virginia, Jefferson wrote, "Obj. Religion will decline if not supported [by taxpayer money]. Ans. Gates of Hell shall not prevail." This was a reference to Jesus's statement in Matthew 16:18: "You are Peter, and upon this rock I will build my church, and the gates of hell shall not prevail against it." Jefferson's implication was that God would uphold the church without state support of the clergy. Jefferson's notes also cited John Locke's comments: "Our Saviour chose not to propagate his religion by temporal punmts. or civil incapacitation; if he had, it was in his almighty power. But he chose to extend it by its influence on reason, thereby shewing to others how [they] should proceed." Jesus, the greatest of all authorities in a predominantly Christian nation, had disdained the use of force, such as that entailed by the collection and redistribution of the taxes of unbelievers, to propagate the gospel. Three years later, in his Bill for Establishing Religious Freedom, Jefferson wrote regarding the human mind, "All attempts to influence it by temporal punishments or burthens or temporal incapacitation . . . are a departure from the plan of the holy author of our religion, who being lord both of body and mind, yet chose not to propagate it by coercion on either, as was in his Almighty power to do." Jefferson then used the terminology and concerns of Christianity itself to condemn religious coercion: "To compel a man to furnish contributions of money for the propagation of opinions which he disbelieves and abhors is sinful and tyrannical. . . . [Such a policy] tends also to corrupt the principles of that very religion it is meant to encourage by bribing, with a monopoly of worldly honours and emoluments, those who will externally praise and conform to it."[14]

In his autobiography Benjamin Franklin recalled the persecution of his own great-great grandfather in England and remembered that his grandfather, Peter Folger, had written about freedom of conscience, even going so far as to attribute "Indian Wars and other calamities" to his own Puritan community's persecution of Quakers and Anabaptists. In 1780 Franklin argued, "When a Religion is good, I conceive that it will support itself, and when it cannot support itself, and God does not take care to support [it], so that its Professors are obliged to call for the help of the Civil Power, 'tis a Sign, I apprehend, of its being a bad one." Franklin was instrumental in persuading King Louis XVI to issue a decree increasing religious toleration in France in 1788, a measure Franklin called "a good step towards general toleration and to the abolishing in time of all party spirit among Christians and the mischiefs that have so long attended it." Franklin also persuaded Ruiz de Padron to deliver a sermon attacking the Spanish Inquisition, the first sermon delivered in the Spanish language in the United States, and then to carry the cause to his homeland, where Padron and his allies finally achieved the abolition of the Inquisition in 1813.[15]

In 1776 Benjamin Rush denounced the proposed requirement that delegates at the Pennsylvania Constitutional Convention take an oath affirming a belief in the divinity of Jesus and in the divine inspiration of the Bible. Despite his own orthodox positions on these subjects, Rush noted that there were "good men" who did not believe as he did. Nine years later he claimed that he looked forward to the day "when the different religious sects, like the different strings in a musical instrument, shall compose a harmony delightful in the ears of Heaven itself!"[16]

After considering a career in ministry, James Madison became involved in Revolutionary politics principally because of his hatred of the Church of England's establishment in Virginia and the resultant mistreatment of dissenters. In 1774 he declared, "That diabolical, Hell-conceived principle of persecution rages among some, and to their eternal Infamy the Clergy can furnish their Quota of Imps for such business. This vexes me the most of anything whatever." Madison was especially upset about the imprisonment of a group of Baptists "for publishing their religious Sentiments." He wrote regarding religious freedom, "I have squabbled and scolded, abused and ridiculed, so long about it to so little purpose that I am without common patience." Madison succeeded in having the phrase "the equal right to the free exercise of religion" substituted for the word "toleration" in the Virginia Declaration of Rights. While the latter term implied a favor dispensed by the legislature, a favor that might be withdrawn at any time, the former phrase made it clear that the freedom of worship was an inalienable right.[17]

Like Jefferson, Madison often stated his arguments for religious liberty in quintessentially Christian terms. In his "Memorial and Remonstrance Against Religious Assessments" (1785), which played a crucial role in securing the abolition of taxpayer funding of churches in Virginia the following year, Madison called religious freedom not only a natural right but also "a duty towards the Creator," explaining, "It is the duty of every man to render to the Creator such homage and such only as he believes acceptable to him. This duty is precedent both in order of time and in degree of obligation to the claims of Civil Society. Before any man can be considered a member of Civil Society, he must be considered as a subject of the Governor of the Universe." Thus, Madison reasoned, "Whilst we assert for ourselves a freedom to embrace, to profess, and to observe the Religion which we believe to be of divine origin, we cannot deny an equal freedom to those whose minds have not yet yielded to the evidence which has convinced us. If this freedom be abused, it is an offense against God, not against man. To God, therefore, not to man, must an account be rendered."

Madison denied that Christianity required the support of taxpayer funds, a claim that stood as "a contradiction to the Christian Religion itself, for every page of it disavows a dependence on the powers of this world; it is a contradiction to fact, for it is known that this Religion both existed and flourished not only without the support of human laws but in spite of every opposition from them, and not only during the period of miraculous aid but long after it had been left to its own evidence and the ordinary care of Providence." Madison went further, claiming that forcing non-Christians to fund Christian churches actually hindered "the diffusion of the light of Christianity," which he considered a work of the greatest importance, writing, "The first wish of those who enjoy this precious gift ought to be that it may be imparted to the whole race of mankind." Madison explained that forcing inhabitants to pay taxes to support Christian churches "discourages those who are strangers to the light of revelation from coming into the Region of it and countenances by example the nations who continue in darkness in shutting out those who might convey it to them." Madison ended by declaring that opponents of a religious establishment such as himself were "earnestly praying, as we are in duty bound, that the Supreme Lawgiver of the Universe, by illuminating those to whom it is addressed, may on the one hand, turn their Councils from every act which would affront his holy prerogative or violate the trust committed to them and, on the other, guide them in every measure which may be worthy of his [blessing, may] redound to their own praise, and may establish more firmly the liberties, the prosperity, and the happiness of the Commonwealth."[18]

Unlike Madison, George Washington was not frightened by the concept of a multidenominational religious establishment. After reading Madison's "Memorial and Remonstrance," Washington confided to George Mason, a supporter of disestablishment, "Altho' no man's Sentiments are more opposed to any kind of restraint upon religious principles than mine are, yet I must confess that I am not amongst the number of those who are so much alarmed at the thought of making People pay towards the support of that which they profess, if of the denominations of Christians, or declare themselves Jews, Mahomitans or otherwise & thereby obtain proper relief." Washington saw nothing tyrannical in requiring Christians to support their own denominations while allowing exemptions for non-Christians. On the other hand, he did not explain the utility of requiring people to do that which they already allegedly wished to do. Nevertheless, Washington added that, because he was concerned by the "disquiet of a respectable minority," which he feared might "rankle and perhaps convulse the State," he hoped that the multidenominational establishment bill would "die an easy death." Thus, in the end, Washington quietly sided with Jefferson and Madison for complete disestablishment.[19]

Washington's opinion regarding the harmlessness of a multidenominational establishment accorded with that of other prominent Virginians, including Patrick Henry, John Marshall, Richard Henry Lee, and thousands of the state's other inhabitants, not to mention the numerous supporters of multidenominational establishments in other states. Far from being an enemy of religious freedom, Henry had been the leader of that cause in Virginia during the Revolution. Although officially a member of the Church of England, he had attended Presbyterian services with his mother for years, had personally paid the fines of at least one Baptist preacher, had defended others in court as an attorney, had supported a bill to exempt Quakers from military service due to their pacifist convictions, had been an influential force behind the religious freedom provisions of the Virginia Declaration of Rights, and would soon demand a similar guarantee in a federal bill of rights. But he and the other supporters of a multidenominational establishment believed that piety was as crucial to virtue as virtue was to the survival and success of any republic, and they could not imagine that religion could thrive without government support.

For nearly a millennium and a half, since the time of Constantine, Christianity had possessed state support, and it appeared to these Virginians that it was a dangerous experiment—dangerous not merely to Christianity but also to the republic itself—to depart from this tradition, especially since they believed that American piety and virtue were already in decline following the Revolution. For instance, Henry noted that a decrease in church tithes had resulted in a diminishment of aid to the poor. It seemed eminently reasonable that public money should continue to help churches foster the virtue that was vital to the republic's success, as it had in Christendom for over a millennium, only now in a nondiscriminatory manner, while to withdraw such aid appeared radical and dangerous. Significantly, Henry's multidenominational establishment bill referred to ministers as "teachers of the Christian religion," signifying his own understanding of their crucial role in teaching the biblically based moral values he considered essential to a republic. The act began, "Whereas the general diffusion of Christian knowledge hath a tendency to correct the morals of men, restrain their vices, and preserve the peace of society, which cannot be effected without a competent provision for learned teachers."[20]

But Madison, who believed as strongly as his opponents in the necessity of piety and virtue in a republic, could point to the early church, which had thrived not only without government support but also in spite of state persecution, as well as to a few contemporary societies that possessed strong religious communities despite the absence of any establishment. The most famous such example was Pennsylvania, whose founding by Quakers and whose plethora of denominations had long prevented the formation of any establishment. In his notes for a speech against the multidenominational establishment bill Madison wrote that "the true question" was not whether religion was necessary to society and good government but "are Religs. Estabts. necessary for Religion? no." More important, the rising tide of religious dissenters in Virginia, who during the long years of the Anglican/Episcopalian establishment had arrived at a principled rejection of all religious establishments, even ones in which they themselves might be invited to participate, helped Madison squelch the multidenominational establishment bill and pass Jefferson's Virginia Statute of Religious Freedom in its place.[21]

Meanwhile, the actions of the Continental Congress during the Revolutionary and Confederation periods often violated strict separationist principles. Congress declined to meet on the Sabbath except on rare occasions, attended the funerals of members as a body, and often worshipped collectively at various churches. The body also employed chaplains and designated public days of prayer. Its presidents often used religious language in diplomatic letters. Congress even considered the purchase of 20,000 Bibles to alleviate a wartime shortage, explaining, "The use of the Bible is so universal, and its importance [is] so great." When unable to procure sufficient Bibles overseas, Congress then formally endorsed the first American edition of the Bible, produced by that legislature's own printer, Robert Aitken.[22]

Likewise, as commander of the Continental Army during the Revolutionary War, George Washington enforced rules on his soldiers that were founded in Judeo-Christian ethics and that would certainly be opposed by modern libertarians. At the outset of his command in 1775 he approved articles of war based on those of the Massachusetts militia that included a prohibition on cursing and a requirement of church attendance "to implore the blessings of heaven upon the means used for our safety and defence." Nor was this a mere formality to be announced and then forgotten. Washington repeatedly reminded his brigade commanders to enforce church attendance, especially but not exclusively on congressionally designated days of prayer. Having been a champion of the use of army chaplains since the French and Indian War, he sought to employ clergymen of numerous denominations and insisted that these chaplains conduct services weekly; if military operations prevented them from doing so on a particular Sunday, chaplains were to schedule them for a different day. No more than one-third of chaplains were allowed leave at the same time, and, when not preaching, they must visit the wounded in hospitals. Washington added to this rule a firm offer of support: "While they are thus publicly and privately engaged in performing the sacred duties of their office, they may depend upon his [Washington's] utmost encouragement and support on all occasions and that they will be considered in a very respectable point of light by the whole Army." This was no empty promise. Washington succeeded in persuading Congress to increase the chaplains' pay to $33 per month, at a time when captains earned only $20. Later in the war he wrote, "In justice to the zeal and ability of the Chaplains, as well as to his own feelings, the Commander-in-Chief thinks it a duty to declare [that] the regularity and decorum with which divine service is now performed every Sunday will reflect great credit on the army in general, tend to improve the morals and the same time to increase the happiness of the soldiery, and must afford the most pure and rational entertainment for every serious and well disposed mind." On three occasions—after the patriot victory at Saratoga, following the announcement of the Treaties of Alliance with France, and after the patriot triumph at Yorktown—Washington designated a day of prayer and thanksgiving for the army rather than waiting for Congress to act.[23]

Washington often repeated his initial orders against blasphemy as well. To prevent the Almighty from being dissuaded from assisting the patriots due to the bad behavior of some soldiers, Washington issued this order: "The General is sorry to hear that the foolish and wicked practice of profane cursing and swearing (a Vice heretofore little known in the American Army) is growing into fashion; he hopes the officers will, by example as well as by influence, endeavour to check it and that both they and the men will reflect that we can have little hopes of the blessing of Heaven on our Arms if we insult it by our impiety and folly. Added to this, it is a vice so mean and low, without any temptation, that every man of sense and character detests and despises it." The following year he reminded his officers regarding "profane Swearing," "Officers of every rank are bound to discourage it, first by their examples, and then by punishing offenders." In 1779 he again complained, "The Name of That Being from whose bountiful goodness we are permitted to exist and enjoy the comforts of life is incessantly imprecated and profaned in a manner as wanton as it is shocking. For the sake therefore of religion, decency, and order, the General hopes and trusts that officers of every rank will use their influence and authority to check a vice which is as unprofitable as it is wicked and shameful."[24]

Washington also forbade insults to Catholicism on both moral and practical grounds. As Benedict Arnold prepared to lead a patriot invasion of British-held Quebec, which was heavily populated by French Catholics, Washington instructed him, "As the Contempt of the Religion of a Country by ridiculing any of its Ceremonies or affronting its Ministers or Votaries has ever been deeply resented, you are to be particular careful to restrain every Officer & Soldier from such Imprudence & Folly & to punish every Instance of it. On the other Hand, as far as lays in your Power, you are to protect & support the Free Exercise of the Religion of the Country & the undisturbed Enjoyment of the Rights of Conscience in religious Matters with your utmost Influence & Authority." In a letter accompanying these instructions, Washington added, "While we are contending for our own Liberty, we should be very cautious of violating the Rights of Conscience in others, ever considering that God alone is the Judge of the Hearts of Men, and to him only in this Case they are answerable." Two months later Washington again addressed the issue in reference to Pope's Day (November 5), the colonial equivalent of Britain's anti-Catholic Guy Fawkes' Day:

> As the Commander in Chief has been apprized of a design formed for the observance of that ridiculous and childish Custom of burning the Effigy of the pope, he cannot help expressing his surprise that there should be Officers and Soldiers in this army so void of common sense as not to see the impropriety of such a step at this Juncture, at a time when we are soliciting and have really obtained the friendship & alliance of the people of Canada, whom we ought to consider as brethren embarked in the same Cause, the defence of the general Liberty of America. At such a juncture, and in such Circumstances, to be insulting their Religion is so monstrous as not to be suffered or excused. Indeed, instead of offering the most remote insult, it is our duty to address public thanks to these, our Brethren, as to them we are so much indebted for every late, happy Success over the common Enemy in Canada.

Washington's rebuke may have played a significant role in ending Pope's Day. There is no record of such a celebration in the United States thereafter. Granted, that holiday had by then largely become little more than an excuse for partying and mayhem. For instance, the members of rival gangs in Boston commemorated the occasion by beating one another senseless with cudgels with the goal of capturing and destroying the other side's papal effigy—until 1765, that is, when Samuel Adams brokered a peace between the gangs so that he could use them both for revolutionary purposes.[25]

THE U.S. CONSTITUTION

The delegates at the Constitutional Convention unanimously adopted a prohibition on any religious test for federal office holding. At the North Carolina ratifying convention James Iredell cited no less an authority than

Jesus for this prohibition: "It would be happy for mankind if religion was permitted to take its own course and maintain itself by the excellence of its own doctrines. The divine Author of our religion never wished for its support by worldly authority. Has he not said that the gates of hell shall not prevail against it?" Iredell responded to a Protestant's complaint that the absence of a religious test might lead to the presidency of even the pope himself, "A native American must have very singular good fortune who, after residing fourteen years in this country, should come to Europe, enter Romish orders, obtain the promotion of cardinal, afterward that of Pope, and at length be so much in the confidence of his country as to be elected President." Considering the vast difference between the power of the papacy in the 1780s and that of the presidency of a new and fairly weak nation, Iredell added, "It would be still more extraordinary if he should give up his popedom for our presidency."[26]

Most Anti-Federalists were alarmed by the absence of a bill of rights in the Constitution, and the first right whose guarantee they generally demanded was "the right of conscience." Richard Henry Lee was emphatic on that score. These Anti-Federalists were joined by Thomas Jefferson, who wrote to James Madison that, although he approved of the Constitution in general, "I will now add what I do not like: first, the omission of a bill of rights providing clearly & without the aid of sophisms for freedom of religion." The Federalists responded to this complaint by promising to incorporate a bill of rights into the Constitution through a series of amendments.[27]

The First Amendment to the Constitution declares, "Congress shall make no law respecting an establishment of religion, or prohibiting the free exercise thereof." The first clause of the amendment has been a subject of great controversy, with some claiming that it prohibits the federal government only from giving preferential treatment to any particular denomination or religion, while others have contended that it prohibits all federal financial aid to religious institutions in general. The best case for the latter view has been advanced by Leonard Levy, who writes, "After the American Revolution seven of the fourteen states that comprised the Union in 1791 authorized establishments of religion by law. Not one state maintained a single or preferential establishment of religion. An establishment of religion meant to those who framed and ratified the First Amendment what it meant in those states, and in all seven it meant public support of religion on a nonpreferential basis. It was specifically this public support on a nonpreferential basis that the establishment clause of the First Amendment sought to forbid." According to this theory, the establishment clause prohibited not only the establishment of a single national religion but also federal financial support for religious groups even on an impartial basis. If this were not so, Levy claims, the establishment clause of the First Amendment would have to be construed, in contradiction to the rest of the Bill of Rights, as an expansion of federal power since the Constitution itself granted no power to Congress to pass laws respecting religion. Indeed, many supporters of the Constitution, including Alexander Hamilton, James Madison, James Wilson, and Edmund Randolph, claimed that there was no need for the establishment clause because the Constitution granted Congress no such power.[28]

But even Levy concedes that some of the congressmen who passed and the state representatives who ratified the First Amendment, not to mention the many thousands of Americans who voted for these representatives, probably interpreted the establishment clause in a much narrower fashion than these Federalists, with no intention of prohibiting all federal support for religion. This view is supported by Congress's passage of the Northwest Ordinance the year before it passed the First Amendment. The ordinance began, "Religion, morality, and knowledge being necessary to good government and the happiness of mankind, schools and the means of education shall forever be encouraged." The ordinance set aside a plot of land in each township for a public school that the congressmen must have assumed would include the usual component of nonsectarian Bible reading, a practice common in New England public schools for the previous century and a half as well as in private schools throughout the nation. Not only did the act include no prohibition of this common practice, but its statement of the religious and moral purpose of the act's educational provisions strongly suggests congressional approval of the practice. As the historians Lorraine Smith Pangle and Thomas Pangle have written, "The fact that the ordinance was re-approved without alteration by the same Congress that drew up, under Madison's floor management, the Bill of Rights would seem to suggest that no one at the time thought that state-sponsored education aimed at cultivating religious faith was contrary in spirit or letter to freedom of conscience or the First Amendment." Indeed, nonsectarian Bible reading remained common in American public schools throughout the nineteenth and much of the twentieth century, endorsed even by reformers like Horace Mann.[29]

Furthermore, one must add that the establishment clause presented no barrier to the seven states that continued to possess multidenominational establishments, nor did it restrict in any way the right of federal officials to express their own religious views publicly, to apply those views to policy matters within the limits of the law, or to promote piety verbally. Indeed, nearly all of the founders engaged in these activities, considering it neither possible nor desirable that the religious convictions of citizens and officials should have no effect on public policy. Even the strict separationist Madison wrote regarding public officials' right to freedom of religious expression, "In their individual capacities, as distinct from their official statements, they might unite in recommendations of any sort whatever, in the manner that other individuals might do. But then their recommendations ought to express the true character from which they emanate." As Levy and others have noted, the chief political impetus for the establishment clause was not the nation's small number of deists but its multitudes of religious dissenters, including Baptists, Quakers, and others, who opposed federal financial support for churches due to their own religious convictions. These pious Americans certainly did not seek the banishment of religious expression from public life.[30]

Finally, it is crucial to note that even the stricter separationists, such as Jefferson and Madison, located church-state separation squarely within the framework of a federal government whose functions they both demanded and expected would be strictly limited. They did not envision a Leviathan, a government of colossal power that would intrude into the most personal areas of life, and thus whose actions must continually trample on the consciences of one segment or another of a diverse population. In other words, the end result for which Jefferson and Madison struggled was state neutrality respecting religion, a neutrality that was approachable only under a strictly limited government. An intrusive government acting in every area of human life could not, by its very nature, be neutral since its actions must constantly touch on issues of conscience and must do so in reflection of values of some kind. The combination of an ever more intrusive government and a broad interpretation of the prohibitions of the First Amendment leads inevitably not to the state neutrality regarding religion that Jefferson and Madison sought, but to the governmental privileging of nontheistic philosophies, something none of the founders ever envisioned, much less intended.

THE EARLY REPUBLICAN PERIOD

During the early republican era there remained disputes over the precise degree of separation between church and state. Stricter separationists like Thomas Jefferson and James Madison sought a greater degree of governmental impartiality concerning religion than others did. While serving as the United States minister to France in 1790, Jefferson discontinued his predecessor Benjamin Franklin's practice of contributing American funds to a Paris chapel used by diplomats, considering it an improper use of public money, though he readily donated his own money to various denominations even while president. In 1801 he wrote to the Delaware Baptist Association, "I join you, fellow-citizens, in rendering the tribute of thankfulness to the Almighty ruler who, in the order of his providence, hath willed that the human mind shall be free in this portion of the globe; that society shall here know that the limit of its rightful power is the enforcement of social conduct, while the right to question the religious principles producing that conduct is beyond their cognizance." Although Jefferson had helped draft a 1774 proclamation by the House of Burgesses calling on Virginians to observe a day of prayer and fasting (in fact, Edmund Randolph claimed that it was Jefferson's idea, intended "to electrify the people from the pulpit"), and, in 1779, as governor of Virginia, Jefferson had urged Virginia's ministers to lead their congregations in observing the day of prayer and thanksgiving proclaimed by the Congress, he refused to issue such proclamations while president, citing the lack of any such authority under the Constitution, though conceding that state governments had the power to do so. In 1802, in a now famous letter to the Danbury Baptists, he wrote, "Believing with you that religion is a matter which lies solely between man and his God, that he owes no account to none other for his faith or his worship, that the legislative powers of government reach actions only, and not opinions, I contemplate with sovereign reverence that act of the whole American people which declared that their legislature should 'make no law respecting an establishment of religion, or prohibiting the free exercise thereof,' thus building a wall of separation between Church and State."[31]

Jefferson opposed a professorship of divinity at the University of Virginia on the ground of avoiding giving preference to one denomination over another, though he did support a proposal to allow each denomination to have a place of its own on campus for voluntary religious instruction. After the proposal was approved, in 1822, Jefferson denied any intention of slighting theology: "It was not, however, to be understood that instruction in religious opinion and duties was meant to be precluded by the public authorities as indifferent to the interests of society. On the contrary, the relations which exist between man and his Maker, and the duties resulting from those relations, are the most interesting and important to every human being, and the most incumbent on his study and investigation. The want of instruction in the various creeds of religious faith existing among our citizens presents, therefore, a chasm in a general institution of the useful sciences. But it was thought that this want, and the entrustment to each society of instruction in its own doctrine, were evils of less danger than a permission to the authorities to dictate modes or principles of religious instruction, or than opportunities furnished them by giving countenance or ascendancy to any one sect over another." In his later years he counted the Virginia Statute for Religious Freedom as one of his three greatest achievements, along with the Declaration of Independence and the establishment of the University of Virginia, directing that references to these accomplishments be placed on his tombstone.[32]

But while Jefferson opposed nearly all attempts to use public funds for religious purposes, he never opposed religious groups' use of public facilities, as long as such use was awarded on a non-preferential basis. While president, he not only attended multidenominational services in the Hall of the House of Representatives but also allowed the U.S. Marine band to provide the music, permitted the Treasury and War Offices to be used for services, and made no complaint when the building in which the Supreme Court met was used for the same purpose. Jefferson was accustomed to the use of public buildings for worship services, a common practice in the South (just as it was common in New England for public business, such as the Massachusetts ratifying convention, to be conducted in churches). Indeed, denominations continued to hold services in the Hall of the Virginia House of Delegates for years after that legislature passed Jefferson's Statute of Religious Freedom, with no complaint from the law's author himself. After Jefferson retired from politics, he himself regularly attended multidenominational services in the Albemarle County Courthouse.[33]

On rare occasions, whenever Jefferson believed that an overriding public interest was at stake, he was even willing to make exceptions to his otherwise steadfast opposition to the use of public funds for religious purposes. Despite concerns expressed by his secretary of state, James Madison, Jefferson allowed the War Department to provide funds for a Presbyterian school among the Cherokees. Jefferson also supported a treaty that furnished federal money to build a church and maintain a Catholic priest for the Kaskaskia tribe. He evidently believed that the benefit to the United States' relations with Native Americans provided by these religious institutions outweighed his own separationist concerns.[34]

Although Jefferson refused to issue official proclamations calling for national days of prayer while president, he often called for individual expressions of gratitude to the Almighty, thus demonstrating that he had no objection to religious expression by public officials. In his first address to Congress (1801), after reporting the end of the first Napoleonic War, Jefferson declared regarding the Almighty, "We are bound with peculiar gratitude to be thankful to Him that our own peace has been preserved." A year later he called for "thankfulness" to God for "peace and friendship abroad, law, order, and religion at home." In 1803, when the British and French resumed their war, he wrote to Congress, "Let us bow with gratitude to that kind Providence" for keeping the United States out of the conflict. Despite his disagreements with orthodox Christianity, Jefferson never feared it. What he feared was ecclesiastical power, which he sought to separate from political authority. His goal was religious freedom, not freedom from religion.[35]

James Madison opposed the appointment of chaplains for Congress and the army, believing they violated the religious establishment clause of the First Amendment since they involved the payment of taxpayer dollars to the clergy of particular denominations. In 1789 Madison proposed a constitutional amendment that would have abolished all religious establishments in the states. The following year he even expressed a desire to omit ministers from the list of occupations included in the census, saying, "As to those who are employed in teaching and inculcating the duties of religion, there may be some indelicacy in singling them out, as the general government is proscribed from the interfering, in any manner whatsoever, in matters respecting religion, and it may be thought to do this in ascertaining who and who are not ministers of the gospel." He opposed tax exemptions for religious institutions on the same basis. As president, he vetoed a bill to give federal land to a church that had already built on it due to a surveying error. After leaving office, Madison continued to support a strict separation of church and state on New Testament grounds, writing, "Ye States of America which retain in your Constitutions or Codes any aberration from the sacred principle of religious liberty by giving to Caesar what belongs to God, or joining together what God has put asunder, hasten to revise and purify your systems and make the example of your Country as pure and complete in what relates to the freedom of the mind and its allegiance to its maker as in what belongs to the legitimate objects of political and civil institutions." Madison then referred to religious freedom as a "truly Christian principle." Here Madison followed a common use of Jesus's command to "render unto Caesar what is Caesar's and unto God what is God's" (Matthew 22:21) to advocate the separation of church and state but added a surprising inversion of His admonition regarding marriage ("what God has joined, let no man put asunder"; Matthew 19:6) to claim that one should not join together (church and state) what God has put asunder.[36]

Much like Jefferson, John Adams believed that Christianity had been corrupted from its early, purer form and that the only way to distinguish the pure from the corrupt elements was by a rational examination and discourse that blasphemy laws, such as those still on the books (though rarely enforced) in the New England states, prevented. Adams argued, "I think such laws a great embarrassment, great obstructions to the improvement of the human mind. Books that cannot bear examination certainly ought not to be established as [the products of] divine inspiration by penal laws. . . . The substance and essence of Christianity, as I understand it, is eternal and unchangeable and will bear examination forever, but it has been mixed with extraneous ingredients, which I think shall not bear examination, and they ought to be separated."[37]

Benjamin Rush was another promoter of religious freedom. In 1788 when reporting on a parade in honor of the ratification of the Constitution, he wrote proudly of Jacob Raphael Cohen, rabbi of the Micveh Israel congregation of Philadelphia, "The Rabbi of the Jews locked in the arms of the ministers of the gospel was a most delightful sight. There could not have been a more happy emblem contrived of that section of the new Constitution which opens all its power and offices alike not only to every sect of Christianity but to worthy men of every religion." Two years later, when writing to Europeans who were considering immigration to the United States, Rush listed as one of the reasons for doing so, "the equal share of power it holds forth to men of every religious sect. As the first fruits of this perfection in our government, we already see three gentlemen of the Roman Catholic Church [serving as] members of the legislature of the United States." In 1800 Rush wrote to Jefferson:

> I agree with you likewise in our wishes to keep religion and government independent of each Other. Were it possible for St. Paul to rise from his grave at the present juncture, he would say to the Clergy who are now so active in settling the political Affairs of the World: "Cease from your political labors; your kingdom is not of this World. Read my Epistles. In no part of them will you perceive me aiming to depose a pagan Emperor or to place a Christian upon a throne. Christianity disdains to receive support from human Governments. From this it derives its preeminence over all religions that ever have or ever Shall exist in the World. Human Governments may receive Support from Christianity but it must be only from the love of justice and peace which it is calculated to produce in the minds of men. By promoting these and all the Other Christian Virtues by your precepts and example you will much sooner overthrow errors of all kinds and establish our pure and holy religion in the World than by aiming to produce by your preaching or pamphlets any change in the political state of mankind."

Rush regarded the multiplicity of Christian denominations as the will of God. In 1810 he claimed, "It would seem as if one of the designs of Providence in permitting the existence of so many Sects of Christianity was that each Sect might be a depository of one great truth of the Gospel, and that it might by that means be better preserved. . . . Let the different Sects of Christians not only bear with each other, but love each other for this kind display of God's goodness whereby all the truths of their Religion are so protected that none of them can ever become feeble or be lost. When united they make a great whole, and that whole is the salvation of all men."[38]

George Washington shared Rush's belief that religious tolerance was pleasing in the sight of God. During his first year as president, he wrote to his fellow Episcopalians, "On this occasion it would ill become me to conceal the joy I have felt in perceiving the fraternal affection which appears to increase every day among the friends of genuine religion. It affords edifying prospects indeed to see Christians of different denominations dwell together in more charity, and conduct themselves in respect to each other with a more Christian-like spirit, than ever they have done in any former age or in any other nation." He wrote to the Quakers, "The liberty enjoyed by the People of the States of worshipping Almighty God agreeable to their Consciences is not only among the choicest of their Blessings but also of their Rights. While men perform their social Duties faithfully, they do all that Society or the State can with propriety demand or expect, and remain responsible only to their Maker for the Religion or modes of faith which they may prefer or profess." He wrote regarding disputes between Protestants and Catholics in Ireland, "Of all the animosities which have existed among mankind, those which are caused by a difference of sentiments in religion appear to me the most inveterate and distressing, and ought most to be deprecated. I was in hopes that the enlightened and liberal policy which has marked the present age would at least have reconciled *Christians* of every denomination so far that we should never again see their religious disputes carried to such a pitch as to endanger the peace of Society" (emphasis in original).[39]

Thomas Paine also used religious arguments in support of the separation of church and state. Like Madison and others, Paine disliked the word "toleration" because it implied that governments had the right to interpose themselves between God and man and determine what to tolerate. In *The Rights of Man*, Paine lapsed into King James English, as he frequently did when making a religious argument: "Who then art thou, vain dust and ashes [Genesis 18:27], by whatever name thou art called, whether a King, a Bishop, a Church or a State, a Parliament, or anything else that obtrudest thy insignificance between the soul of man and its Maker? Mind thine own concerns. If he believes not as thou believest, it is a proof that thou believest not as he believes, and there is no earthly power that can determine between you." Paine portrayed God as a father with many children who relished the great variety of tokens of love and gratitude given by these diverse children and who was grieved to find them quarreling about which gift was best. Paine asked, "Why may we not suppose that the great Father of all is pleased with a variety of devotion and that the greatest offense we can act is that by which we seek to torment and render each other miserable?"[40]

Some states went to such extremes to ensure the separation of church and state that they infringed the civil rights of clergymen. The Kentucky Bill of Rights of 1792 excluded ministers from public office, as had the earlier constitutions of New York, Delaware, and Virginia. Georgia and the Carolinas excluded the clergy from some but not all offices. Thomas Jefferson's own draft of a new state constitution for Virginia (1783) contained such an exclusion, which James Madison opposed on the grounds of religious freedom. Madison may have been influenced on this issue by his mentor, the clergyman-politician John Witherspoon. Witherspoon lampooned Georgia's constitution, writing, "No clergyman of any denomination shall be capable of being elected a member of the Senate or House of Representatives because (here insert grounds of offensive disqualification, which I have not been able to discover)—provided always, and it is the true intent and meaning of this part of the constitution, that if at any time he shall be completely deprived of the clerical character by those by whom he was invested with it, as by deposition for cursing and swearing, drunkenness or uncleanness, he shall then be restored to all the privileges of a free citizen; his offence shall no more be remembered against him; but he may be chosen either to the Senate or the House of Representatives, and shall be treated with all the respect due to his brethren, the other members of the Assembly." Madison must have converted Jefferson to his and Witherspoon's position because, in 1800, Jefferson wrote that while he understood the historical reasons for the exclusion of clergy from public office, he now disapproved of it: "The clergy [in Europe], by getting themselves established by the law & engrafted into the machine of government, have been a very formidable engine against the civil & religious rights of man. . . . [But] the clergy here seem to have relinquished all pretensions to privilege & to stand on a footing with lawyers, physicians & c. They ought therefore to possess the same rights." Yet Jefferson's anticlerical views still led him to propose the exclusion of clergymen from serving as "visitors" (supervisors) at Virginia public schools in his "Act for Establishing Elementary Schools" in 1817.[41]

Other state constitutions went in the opposite direction. Massachusetts retained its establishment clause until 1833, four other states nearly as long. Furthermore, numerous states possessed religious tests for state office holding. Delaware and Maryland required that officeholders express a belief in Christianity, Pennsylvania and Tennessee that they express a belief in God, the afterlife, and the divine inspiration of scripture, including the New Testament, which prevented Jews from holding office there. New Jersey, Georgia, South Carolina, Massachusetts, and New Hampshire allowed only Protestants to hold office. States continued to penalize blasphemy and violations of Sunday closing laws, laws that continued to be viewed as guarantors of social order rather than religious restrictions, despite their indisputably Christian character.[42]

As noted earlier, most of the founders continued to support government calls for days of public prayer. As the historian Thomas Curry has aptly noted:

> Customs like days of prayer and thanksgiving appeared not so much as matters of religion as part of the common coin of civilized living. Sabbath laws enjoyed widespread support and were so little the subject of dissent that citizens never even felt challenged to think how those laws might impose a particular religious viewpoint. . . . The vast majority of Americans assumed that theirs was a Christian, Protestant country, and they automatically expected that government would uphold the commonly agreed on Protestant ethos and morality. In many instances, they had not come to grips with the implications their belief in the powerlessness of government in religious matters held for a society in which the values, customs, and forms of Protestant Christianity thoroughly permeated civil and political life. The contradiction between their theory and practice became evident to Americans only later, with the advent of a more religiously pluralistic society, when it became the subject of a disputation that continues into the present.

In other words, most of the founders, like most eighteenth- and nineteenth-century Americans in general, could support both "religious liberty" and a host of traditional Christian governmental practices without any cognitive dissonance because they lived in a society that was almost entirely Christian. Only later, when it ceased to be so, did this disparity between libertarian and Christian principles become a matter of confict.[43]

When the state religious establishments finally ended, many Americans who had predicted disaster were shocked to discover that their opponents had been correct in asserting that Christianity did not need them. Indeed, disestablishment coincided with the Second Great Awakening. Several decades after disestablishment in Virginia, the Episcopalian bishop William Meade claimed, "Nothing could have been more injurious to the cause of true religion in the Episcopal Church, or to its growth in any way, than the continuance of either stipend or glebes," adding that revival of the church commenced when "she was thrown upon her own resources." Likewise, having fought to save the establishment of the Congregational Church in Connecticut, the revivalist preacher Lyman Beecher soon found that disestablishment was "the best thing that ever happened to the State of Connecticut." Using language similar to

Meade's, he explained, "It cut the churches loose from dependence on state support. It threw them wholly on their own resources and on God." When the clergy and laity could no longer sit back and expect the government to promote Christianity, they were forced to do so themselves, and the mission imparted a new vitality to their churches. Furthermore, once the church was separated from the state, the inevitable periodic surges of popular anger against the latter no longer spilled over onto the former. Garry Wills has argued persuasively that the separation of church and state is one of the principal reasons why Christianity continued to thrive in America after it waned in western Europe, where religious establishments remained the order of the day long after they were abolished in the United States. The state-supported church of each western European nation became a corrupt and apathetic political institution devoid of inspiration—in other words, just another despised government bureaucracy, a spiritual DMV.[44]

EPILOGUE

The Americans who followed the founders' generation were also a people of the book. Parents, grammar school masters, college professors, and preachers continued to teach the Bible. Political rhetoric remained suffused with biblical references. Americans still proclaimed the existence of a providential God who aided the United States in its mission to spread liberty throughout the world by becoming a model republic that offered a haven for the oppressed. They continued to assert the superiority of Christian morality to classical ethics, even while studying and valuing the classics as much as their forebears, and they continued to declare that the success of the American republican experiment rested on the degree of piety and virtue exhibited by its citizens.[1]

Before the founders even left the political stage, the country was rocked by a Second Great Awakening that transformed American society. Beginning in 1795 and reaching a climax in 1800–1801, James McGready and four Presbyterian colleagues, joined by a Methodist preacher, spearheaded a series of summer revivals in central Kentucky. McGready's revival soon spread throughout the South and into Ohio, western Pennsylvania, and New York. Meanwhile, Timothy Dwight, the new president of Yale, stirred the college to a religious fervor that produced six revivals in twenty-five years. Within a few decades the entire nation had felt the reverberations of the Second Great Awakening.[2]

The Second Great Awakening transformed American religion. First, it led to the rise of new denominations, such as the Church of Jesus Christ of Latter-day Saints (Mormons) and the Seventh-day Adventists, and popularized certain older denominations, such as the Methodist Episcopal Church and various Baptist sects. Second, it spurred the growth of even greater toleration. As Americans participated in an increasing number of interdenominational revivals and reform societies, all of which emphasized moral concerns over sectarian dogma, their ecumenism grew. Third, it increased the popularity of the doctrine of free will, yet another development foreshadowed by the founders. Methodists, who had inherited the free will position from the Anglican Church, disseminated it throughout the United States. Even within Calvinist denominations, "New School" theologians like Nathaniel Taylor revised the doctrine of predestination, bringing it much closer to a free will position, a development supported by many prominent Calvinist ministers. By the mid-nineteenth century most Americans had abandoned predestination. Fourth, it spread postmillennialism, a development foreshadowed by Samuel Adams, Benjamin Rush, and James Wilson. Revivalist preachers like Lyman Beecher and Charles Finney suggested that the triumph of American-style democracy and freedom of thought and expression around the world would bring on the Millennium, a utopian vision that was destroyed by the bloodshed of the Civil War. Finally, the Second Great Awakening launched a plethora of social reform movements, including efforts on behalf of public education, temperance, aid for the poor and the mentally ill, prison reform, and women's rights.[3]

One of the most consequential reform efforts produced by the Second Great Awakening was the abolitionist movement. As late as 1830, most American emancipation societies were conservative, gradualist institutions located in the slave states of the South. But in the 1830s the movement shifted to the North and became much more evangelical (and therefore much more radical). On January 1, 1831, twenty-six-year-old William Lloyd Garrison established the first antislavery newspaper in America, the *Liberator*. Like many of the founders, Garrison declared that the Bible was opposed to slavery. In advocating northern secession from the corrupt South, he revealed his religious lineage: his fears were similar to Puritan fears of contamination by the Church of England and American Revolutionary fears of corruption by Britain. Furthermore, he angered northern racists by demanding the recognition of equal rights for free blacks in the North, where African Americans were disfranchised and legally segregated. In 1833 he joined with New York merchants Arthur and Lewis Tappan to form the American Antislavery Society, which called for the immediate emancipation of slaves without compensation to slaveholders. With the financial backing of the Tappans, the society filled the mails with 750,000 samples of abolitionist literature within five years. By that time the organization possessed 250,000 members. Garrison's passionately moralistic rhetorical style and his themes of sin, damnation, and salvation were as evangelical as those of the revivalists. In 1839 he wrote, "Genuine abolitionism . . . is of heaven, not of men."[4]

Most of the other abolitionists were also evangelical Christians. The western part of New York, which had become known as the "Burned-Over District" because of its fiery revivalists, became one of the strongholds of antislavery agitation. Abolitionists there were led by Theodore Weld, whose father and older brother were ministers and who had himself attended Lane Theological Seminary. Often beaten and pelted with rocks, eggs, and vegetables by angry mobs, Weld toured New England, New York, Pennsylvania, and Ohio on behalf of abolitionism. His wife and fellow abolitionist Angelina Grimké trusted that slavery, "a crime against God and man," would soon end. Her sister Sarah declared, "No abolitionism is of any value which is not accompanied with deep, heartfelt repentance." The Tappan brothers, sizable contributors to every major reform organization in the nation, were equally devout, requiring their employees to pray every morning and evening and to abstain from smoking, drinking, attending plays, and staying out after 10 p.m. Harriet Beecher Stowe was the daughter of one of the most famous preachers of the period. Gradually, the antislavery movement absorbed most of the reformers and the zeal of the other movements.[5]

Persevering amid persecution, the antebellum abolitionists gradually secured enough sympathy for their cause in the North that Abraham Lincoln, though fighting the Civil War primarily to save the Union, was able to envision the Emancipation Proclamation as a measure that would bring support, rather than dissension, to the Union war effort. Thus did the abolitionists bring to a successful conclusion the effort begun by the founders in their abolition of slavery throughout the North to apply the biblical principle of spiritual equality to the issue of servitude.

Of course, the abolition of slavery in the United States, although a tremendous accomplishment, did not lead to social equality for African Americans. Slavery was replaced by the lesser but still appalling evils of segregation and disfranchisement. It would take another century before a Christian clergyman would successfully combine an appeal to the biblical principle of spiritual equality with the New Testament technique of nonviolent resistance to secure yet another "birth of freedom." When he arose, he would cite the Book of Exodus and be called the Moses of his people.

NOTES

INTRODUCTION

1. The historian Matthew Stewart adds Ethan Allen and Thomas Young (one of the leaders of the Boston Sons of Liberty) to the extremely short list of founders who can be proven by their own words (as opposed to hearsay evidence and wild speculation) to have been biblically unorthodox. See Stewart's *Nature's God: The Heretical Origins of the American Republic* (New York: W. W. Norton, 2014), 11–14, 18, 21. But the extent of Allen's sole contribution to the Revolution, his role in the capture of Fort Ticonderoga, is disputed, and Young died only a year after independence. If these men qualify as founders, justice will require the expansion of the list to include many others, including numerous prominent state legislators (at a time when state governments were very powerful), whose contributions were far greater than those of these two men. In such a case, I suspect that the ratio of orthodox to unorthodox founders will be even greater than under my accounting here.

2. For reference to the accusation that Jefferson planned to confiscate Bibles, see Ron Chernow, *Alexander Hamilton* (New York: Penguin, 2004), 633.

3. For a misguided attempt to identify deists among the founders based on the mere use of such terms as "Nature's God," "the Grand Architect," and even the thoroughly traditional "Providence," see David L. Holmes, *The Faiths of the Founding Fathers* (Oxford: Oxford University Press, 2006), 65, 139–40. By contrast, Jeffry H. Morrison notes that even the most biblically orthodox founders, such as the Reverend John Witherspoon, referred to God by such appellations as "the Author of nature." See Jeffry H. Morrison, *John Witherspoon and the Founding of the American Republic* (South Bend, IN: University of Notre Dame Press, 2005), 90.

1. A PEOPLE OF THE BOOK

1. William G. McLoughlin, *Revivals, Awakening, and Reform: An Essay on Religion and Social Change in America, 1607–1977* (Chicago: University of Chicago Press, 1978), 45; Emery Battis, *Saints and Sectaries: Anne Hutchinson and the Antinomian Controversy in the Massachusetts Bay Colony* (Chapel Hill: University of North Carolina Press, 1962), 9; Jon Butler, *Becoming America: The Revolution Before 1776* (Cambridge, MA: Harvard University Press, 2000), 111; Sheldon S. Cohen, *A History of Colonial Education, 1607–1776* (New York: Wiley, 1974), 17.

2. Edmund S. Morgan, *The Puritan Dilemma: The Story of John Winthrop* (Boston: Little, Brown, 1958); Lawrence Cremin, *American Education: The Colonial Experience, 1607–1783* (New York: Harper and Row, 1970), 207; Cohen, *History of Colonial Education*, 37, 43–49, 67; Robert Middlekauff, *Ancients and Axioms: Secondary Education in Eighteenth-Century New England* (New Haven, CT: Yale University Press, 1963), 168.

3. Cremin, *American Education*, 129–30, 362.

4. Cohen, *History of Colonial Education*, 61–63, 97; James Axtell, *The School upon a Hill: Education and Society in Colonial New England* (New Haven, CT: Yale University Press, 1974), 143–44; Adrienne Koch and William Peden, eds., *The Selected Writings of John and John Quincy Adams* (New York: Alfred A. Knopf, 1946), *Diary of John Adams*, 1756, 6.

5. Cohen, *History of Colonial Education*, 103, 114, 121, 130, 141, 143, 145, 165, 172, 180–81, 184, 192; Cremin, *American Education*, 343; Bernard Bailyn, *Education in the Formation of American Society: Needs and Opportunities for Study* (Chapel Hill: University of North Carolina Press, 1960), 40.

6. Cohen, *History of Colonial Education*, 47, 60; Axtell, *School upon a Hill*, 34–35, 174, 187–88; Middlekauff, *Ancients and Axioms*, 14; John E. Rexine, "The Boston Latin School Curriculum in the Seventeenth and Eighteenth Centuries," *Classical Journal* (March 1977): 263–66; Jean S. Straub, "Teaching in the Friends' Latin School in Philadelphia in the Eighteenth Century," *Pennsylvania Magazine of History and Biography* 91 (October 1967), 447.

7. Middlekauff, *Ancients and Axioms*, 76; Merrill D. Peterson, *James Madison: A Biography in His Own Words* (New York: Harper and Row, 1974), 18; Cremin, *American Education*, 506–8; Theodore Sizer, ed., *The Autobiography of Colonel John Trumbull, Patriot Artist, 1756–1843* (New Haven, CT: Yale University Press, 1953), 5, 9–10.

8. George W. Corner, ed., *The Autobiography of Benjamin Rush: His "Travels Through Life" Together with His Commonplace Book for 1789–1813* (Princeton, NJ: Princeton University Press, 1948), 31–34, 37; Nathan G. Good-

man, *Benjamin Rush: Physician and Citizen, 1746–1813* (Philadelphia: University of Pennsylvania Press, 1934), 6.

9. Perry Miller, *The New England Mind* (New York: Macmillan, 1939), 1:88, 448; Emory Elliott, *Power and the Pulpit in Puritan New England* (Princeton, NJ: Princeton University Press, 1975), 47; Cremin, *American Education*, 175, 321; Cohen, *History of Colonial Education*, 64, 98–99, 136–37.

10. Cohen, *History of Colonial Education*, 167, 173–75; Paul K. Conkin, *The Uneasy Center: Reformed Christianity in Antebellum America* (Chapel Hill: University of North Carolina Press, 1995), 57; E. Digby Baltzell, *Puritan Boston and Quaker Philadelphia: Two Protestant Ethics and the Spirit of Class Authority and Leadership* (New York: Free Press, 1979), 163; Leonard W. Labaree et al., eds., *The Papers of Benjamin Franklin* (New Haven, CT: Yale University Press, 1959–), Franklin to Samuel Johnson, December 24, 1751, 4:222; Gottfried Achenwall, "Observations on America from Oral Information Provided by Dr. Franklin," 1766, 13:363.

11. Gilbert Chinard, *Honest John Adams* (Boston: Little, Brown, 1933), 11–12; Forrest McDonald, *Alexander Hamilton: A Biography* (New York: W. W. Norton, 1979), 11–12; Richard M. Gummere, *The American Colonial Mind and the Classical Tradition: Essays in Comparative Culture* (Cambridge, MA: Harvard University Press, 1963), 56–57.

12. Cremin, *American Education*, 213–15; Cohen, *History of Colonial Education*, 66; Chinard, *Honest John Adams*, 14; Labaree et al., *Papers of Benjamin Franklin*, Franklin to Samuel Johnson, December 24, 1751, 4:222; Richard B. Morris, ed., *John Jay: The Making of a Revolutionary, Unpublished Papers, 1745–1780* (New York: Harper and Row, 1975), "Statutes of King's College," March 23, 1763, 1:56; "King's College Commencement," May 22, 1764, 1:62–63; May 19, 1767, 1:85.

13. Robert A. Rutland et al., eds., *The Papers of James Madison* (Chicago: University of Chicago Press, 1962–1977; Charlottesville: University Press of Virginia, 1977–), Editor's Note, 1:46–47n4; "Notes on Commentary on the Bible, 1770–1773," 1:51–56; Madison to William Bradford, September 25, 1773, 1:96–97n2; David L. Holmes, *The Faiths of the Founding Fathers* (Oxford: Oxford University Press, 2006), 80, 92–93; William Lee Miller, *The First Liberty: Religion and the American Republic* (New York: Alfred A. Knopf, 1986), 89.

14. Broadus Mitchell, *Alexander Hamilton: Youth to Maturity, 1755–1788* (New York: Macmillan, 1957), 57–58; Douglass Adair, *Fame and the Founding Fathers*, ed. H. Trevor Colbourn (New York: W. W. Norton, 1974), 145–46; McDonald, *Alexander Hamilton*, 10–11; Gregg L. Frazer, "Alexander Hamilton, Theistic Rationalist," in Daniel L. Dreisbach et al., eds., *The Forgotten Founders*

on Religion and Public Life (South Bend, IN: University of Notre Dame Press, 2009), 108.

15. C. Dewitt Hardy and Richard Hofstadter, *The Development and Scope of Higher Education in the United States* (New York: Columbia University Press, 1952), 5–6.

16. L. Jesse Lemisch, ed., *Benjamin Franklin: The Autobiography and Other Writings* (New York: Penguin, 1961), *Autobiography*, 20–22, 24–25; Labaree et al., *Papers of Benjamin Franklin*, Acrostic from Benjamin Franklin the Elder, July 15, 1710, 1:4–5; Alfred Owen Aldridge, *Benjamin Franklin and Nature's God* (Durham, NC: Duke University Press, 1967), 12; Thomas J. Woody, ed., *Educational Views of Benjamin Franklin* (New York: McGraw-Hill, 1931), 3–4.

17. Woody, *Educational Views of Benjamin Franklin*, 5–7; Walter Isaacson, *Benjamin Franklin: An American Life* (New York: Simon and Schuster, 2003), 26; Aldridge, *Benjamin Franklin and Nature's God*, 62–63.

18. William Wirt Henry, ed., *Patrick Henry: Life, Correspondence, and Speeches* (New York: Charles Scribner's Sons, 1891; reprint, New York: Burt Franklin, 1969), 1:4; David A. McCants, *Patrick Henry, The Orator* (Westport, CT: Greenwood, 1990), 8, 12; Gary Scott Smith, "Samuel Adams: America's Puritan Revolutionary," in Dreisbach et al., *Forgotten Founders on Religion and Public Life*, 45; Holmes, *Faiths of the Founding Fathers*, 144.

19. Corner, *Autobiography of Benjamin Rush*, 27, 166.

20. Marvin R. Zahniser, *Charles Cotesworth Pinckney: Founding Father* (Chapel Hill: University of North Carolina Press, 1967), 270–71.

21. Kate M. Rowland, ed., *The Life and Correspondence of George Mason* (New York: Russell and Russell, 1964), 1:162–63.

22. L. H. Butterfield, ed., *The Letters of Benjamin Rush* (Princeton, NJ: Princeton University Press, 1951), Rush to Elias Boudinot, October 2, 1793, 2:692; Rush to Rachel Rush Montgomery, October 29, 1793, 2:730.

23. Charles B. Sanford, *The Religious Life of Thomas Jefferson* (Charlottesville: University Press of Virginia, 1984), 3, 7.

24. Holmes, *Faiths of the Founding Fathers*, 145–46.

25. Ibid., 114.

26. Frazer, "Alexander Hamilton," 115; Ron Chernow, *Alexander Hamilton* (New York: Penguin, 2004), 205.

27. Kevin R. Hardwick, "Anglican Moderation: Religion and the Political Thought of Edmund Randolph," in Dreisbach et al., *Forgotten Founders on Religion and Public Life*, 202–3.

28. John Edward Oster, ed., *The Political and Economic Doctrines of John Marshall: Letters and Speeches* (New York: Burt Franklin, 1967), "Autobiography," 197; Eulogy for His Wife, December 25, 1832, 204.

29. Edith B. Gelles, "The Way of Duty: Abigail Adams on Religion," in Dreisbach et al., *Forgotten Founders on Religion and Public Life*, 26, 31–36; Holmes, *Faiths of the Founding Fathers*, 118–20.

30. Rowland, *Life and Correspondence of George Mason*, 1:48, 56, 159, 162.

31. Labaree et al., *Papers of Benjamin Franklin*, Franklin to Richard Jackson, April 11, 1763, 10:248.

32. Axtell, *School upon a Hill*, 49; Cremin, *American Education*, 451; Irving Brant, *James Madison: The Virginia Revolutionist, 1751–1780* (New York: Bobbs-Merrill, 1941), 52.

33. Koch and Peden, *Selected Writings of John and John Quincy Adams*, John Adams to Benjamin Rush, August 28, 1811, 161; L. H. Butterfield, ed., *The Adams Family Correspondence* (Cambridge, MA: Harvard University Press, 1963), John to Abigail Adams, October 9, 1774, 1:167; March 30, 1777, 2:189; Peter Shaw, *The Character of John Adams* (Chapel Hill: University of North Carolina Press, 1976), 308.

34. Robert A. Rutland, ed., *The Papers of George Mason* (Chapel Hill: University of North Carolina Press, 1970), Mason to George Mason Jr., May 20, 1787, 3:881.

35. Donald Jackson and Dorothy Twohig, eds., *The Diaries of George Washington* (Charlottesville: University Press of Virginia, 1976–1979), September 25, 1774, 3:280; October 9, 1774, 3:285; May 27, 1787, 5:163; Editor's Note, 5:452; November 1, 1789, 5:488; July 3, 1791, 6:168.

36. Marie Kimball, *Thomas Jefferson: The Road to Glory, 1743–1776* (New York: Coward-McGann, 1943), 123; James H. Hutson, "Thomas Jefferson's Letter to the Danbury Baptists: A Controversy Rejoined," *William and Mary Quarterly* 56 (October 1999): 785–86, 788.

37. Corner, *Autobiography of Benjamin Rush*, 115–16.

38. Dagobert D. Runes, ed., *The Selected Writings of Benjamin Rush* (New York: The Philosophical Library, 1947; reprint, Omaha: The Classics of Liberty Library, 2012), "On Manners," 377.

39. Ralph Ketcham, *From Colony to Country: The Revolution in American Thought, 1750–1820* (New York: Macmillan, 1974), 46–47.

40. Labaree et al., *Papers of Benjamin Franklin*, "Poor Richard," 1747, 3:103; Franklin to Samuel Johnson, July 11, 1751, 4:41–42; Franklin to Sarah Franklin, November 8, 1764, 11:449–50; Franklin to Thomas Coombe Jr., July 22, 1774, 21:246.

41. Holmes, *Faiths of the Founding Fathers*, 56; Aldridge, *Benjamin Franklin and Nature's God*, 188–89, 241–42.

42. Butterfield, *Letters of Benjamin Rush*, Rush to Enoch Green, 1761, 1:3.

43. Eran Shalev, *American Zion: The Old Testament as a Political Text from the Revolution to the Civil War* (New Haven, CT: Yale University Press, 2013),

11; Carl Bridenbaugh and Jessica Bridenbaugh, *Rebels and Gentlemen: Philadelphia in the Age of Franklin* (New York: Reynal and Hitchcock, 1942; reprint, Westport, CT: Greenwood, 1978), 73; Joseph Towne Wheeler, "Reading Interests of the Professional Classes in Colonial Maryland, 1700–1776," *Maryland Historical Magazine* 36 (June 1941): 184.

44. Moshe Davis, *America and the Holy Land* (Westport, CT: Praeger, 1995), 13–14, 137–41.

45. George William Pilcher, *Samuel Davies: Apostle of Dissent in Colonial Virginia* (Knoxville: University of Tennessee Press, 1971), 20–21; Conkin, *Uneasy Center*, 54, 58; Patricia J. Tracy, *Jonathan Edwards, Pastor: Religion and Society in Eighteenth-Century Northampton* (New York: Hill & Wang, 1979), 79–80, 113; Paul K. Conkin, *Puritans and Pragmatists: Eight Eminent American Thinkers* (Bloomington: Indiana University Press, 1968), 53, 55.

46. John Frederick Woolverton, *Colonial Anglicanism in North America* (Detroit: Wayne State University Press, 1984), 191, 198.

47. Labaree et al., *Papers of Benjamin Franklin*, Extracts from the *Gazette*, 1739, 2:242, 244; Lemisch, *Benjamin Franklin, Autobiography*, 118, 338.

48. Labaree et al., *Papers of Benjamin Franklin*, Extracts from the *Gazette*, 1734, 1736, 1740, 1742, and 1746, 1:377, 379; 2:161, 287–88, 358, 361; 3:98; Ledger D, 1739–1747, 2:232; Franklin to George Whitefield, July 2, 1756, 6:468; Franklin to Noah Wimberly Jones, March 5, 1771, 18:53; Lemisch, *Benjamin Franklin, Autobiography*, 93, 317; Aldridge, *Benjamin Franklin and Nature's God*, 113.

49. Woolverton, *Colonial Anglicanism in North America*, 191, 194–96, 200; Randall Balmer, *A Perfect Babel of Confusion: Dutch Religion and English Culture in the Middle Colonies* (Oxford: Oxford University Press, 1989), 123; Axtell, *School upon a Hill*, 42, 46.

50. Bridenbaugh and Bridenbaugh, *Rebels and Gentlemen*, 19; Butterfield, *Letters of Benjamin Rush*, Rush to Ebenezer Hazard, March 21, 1765, 1:14; John C. Miller, *Sam Adams: Pioneer in Propaganda* (Stanford, CA: Stanford University Press, 1936), 6.

51. Harry Alonzo Cushing, ed., *The Writings of Samuel Adams* (New York: Octagon Books, 1968), Valerius Poplicola, October 5, 1772, 2:336; Labaree et al., *Papers of Benjamin Franklin*, "Rules by which a Great Empire May Be Reduced to a Small One," *The Public Advertiser*, September 11, 1773, 20:395; Thomas Miller, ed., *The Selected Writings of John Witherspoon* (Carbondale: Southern Illinois University Press, 1990), "The Dominion of Providence over the Passions of Men," May 17, 1776, 140–41.

52. Henry F. May, *The Enlightenment in America* (Oxford: Oxford University Press, 1976), 91–93; Jon Butler, *Awash in a Sea of Faith: Christianizing the American People* (Cambridge, MA: Harvard University Press, 1990), 201–4;

Butler, *Becoming America*, 243; Pilcher, *Samuel Davies*, 98; Cremin, *American Education*, 459; Butterfield, *Adams Family Correspondence*, John to Abigail Adams, July 23, 1775, 1:254; Henry, *Patrick Henry*, 1:189; Rhys Isaac, *The Transformation of Virginia, 1740–1790* (Chapel Hill: University of North Carolina Press, 1982), 170, 261; Mark A. Noll, *Christians in the American Revolution* (Washington, DC: Christian University Press, 1977), 65; Jeffry H. Morrison, *John Witherspoon and the Founding of the American Republic* (South Bend, IN: University of Notre Dame Press, 2005), 71.

53. Miller, *Sam Adams*, 85, 129; Isaac, *Transformation of Virginia*, 246.

54. Charles Royster, *A Revolutionary People at War: The Continental Army and American Character, 1775–1783* (New York: W. W. Norton, 1979), 158; Noll, *Christians in the American Revolution*, 59–61.

55. For fuller discussions of the classical influence on the founders, see Carl J. Richard, *The Founders and the Classics: Greece, Rome, and the American Enlightenment* (Cambridge, MA: Harvard University Press, 1994); Carl J. Richard, *Greeks and Romans Bearing Gifts: How the Ancients Inspired the Founding Fathers* (Lanham, MD: Rowman & Littlefield, 2008).

56. Noll, *Christians in the American Revolution*, 37; Miller, *Sam Adams*, 6, 85, 228–29; Cushing, *Writings of Samuel Adams*, Adams to John Scollay, December 30, 1780, 4:238.

57. Henry, *Patrick Henry*, 1:4, 8, 15, 212, 220, 264–65; 2:501; Pilcher, *Samuel Davies*, 83; McCants, *Patrick Henry*, 22, 26, 30, 110; Robert Douthat Meade, *Patrick Henry: Patriot in the Making* (Philadelphia: J. P. Lippincott, 1957), 31, 56–57, 71, 173–78; Miller, *First Liberty*, 25; Gummere, *American Colonial Mind*, 62.

58. Sacvan Bercovitch, *The American Jeremiad* (Madison: University of Wisconsin Press, 1978), 125; Noll, *Christians in the American Revolution*, 52; Nathan O. Hatch, *The Sacred Cause of Liberty: Republican Thought and the Millennium in Revolutionary New England* (New Haven, CT: Yale University Press, 1977), 63, 95.

59. Ruth Bloch, *Visionary Republic: Millennial Themes in American Thought, 1756–1800* (Cambridge: Cambridge University Press, 1988), 4; Morrison, *John Witherspoon and the Founding of the American Republic*, 82.

60. Donald S. Lutz, *The Origins of American Constitutionalism* (Baton Rouge: Louisiana State University Press, 1988), 140.

61. Charles Francis Adams, ed., *The Life and Works of John Adams* (Boston: Little, Brown, 1850–1856), John Adams to H. Niles, January 14, 1818, 10:275.

2. A LIFELONG PASSION

1. L. H. Butterfield, ed., *The Diary and Autobiography of John Adams* (Cambridge, MA: Harvard University Press, 1962), Diary, July 21, 1756, 1:35; August 1, 1761, 1:220; Albert Ellery Bergh and Andrew A. Lipscomb, eds., *The Writings of Thomas Jefferson* (Washington, DC: Thomas Jefferson Memorial Association, 1904), John Adams to Jefferson, December 25, 1813, 1:40; Edwin S. Gaustad, *Faith of Our Fathers: Religion and the New Nation* (San Francisco: Harper and Row, 1987), 88; Peter Shaw, *The Character of John Adams* (Chapel Hill: University of North Carolina Press, 1976), 308.

2. Julian P. Boyd, ed., *The Papers of Thomas Jefferson* (Princeton, NJ: Princeton University Press, 1950–), Jefferson to John Stockdale, July 1, 1787, 11:523; Jefferson to Van Damme, March 23, 1788, 12:688–89; January 25, 1789, 14:490; Caleb Alexander to Jefferson, February 20, 1793, 25:235n; Nicholas Gouin Dufief to Jefferson, December 23, 1800, 32:345n; Jefferson to Henry Remsen, December 31, 1800, 32:376; Charles B. Sanford, *The Religious Life of Thomas Jefferson* (Charlottesville: University Press of Virginia, 1984), 102; Lester J. Cappon, ed., *The Adams-Jefferson Letters: The Complete Correspondence between Thomas Jefferson and Abigail and John Adams* (Chapel Hill: University of North Carolina Press, 1959), Jefferson to John Adams, October 12, 1813, 2:385–86; John Adams to Jefferson, November 14, 1813, 2:394.

3. W. W. Abbot, ed., *The Papers of George Washington: Colonial Series* (Charlottesville: University Press of Virginia, 1983–1995), Washington to Robert Cary & Co., July 20, 1771, 8:509.

4. Leonard W. Labaree et al., eds., *The Papers of Benjamin Franklin* (New Haven, CT: Yale University Press, 1959–), "A Parable against Persecution," July 1755, 6:123–24; "A Parable on Brotherly Love," July 1755, 6:127–28; Alfred Owen Aldridge, *Benjamin Franklin and Nature's God* (Durham, NC: Duke University Press, 1967), 196–97.

5. Labaree et al., *Papers of Benjamin Franklin*, Franklin to Samuel Cooper, May 15, 1781, 35:70.

6. William Wirt Henry, ed., *Patrick Henry: Life, Correspondence, and Speeches* (New York: Burt Franklin, 1969), 2:519, 575.

7. Douglass Adair, *Fame and the Founding Fathers*, ed. H. Trevor Colbourn (New York: W. W. Norton, 1974), 154–56, 159; Forrest McDonald, *Alexander Hamilton: A Biography* (New York: W. W. Norton, 1979), 356.

8. George W. Corner, ed., *The Autobiography of Benjamin Rush: His "Travels Through Life" Together with His Commonplace Book for 1789–1813* (Princeton, NJ: Princeton University Press, 1948), *Commonplace Book*, 1791, 192–93; L. H. Butterfield, ed., *The Letters of Benjamin Rush* (Princeton, NJ:

Princeton University Press, 1951), Rush to Jeremy Belknap, April 5, 1791, 1:579; Rush to Elizabeth Graene Ferguson, January 18, 1793, 1:628.

9. Butterfield, *Letters of Benjamin Rush*, Rush to Julia Rush, October 30, 1793, 2:732, 734; November 11, 1793, 2:745; Rush to John Dickinson, February 16, 1796, 2:770; J. Jefferson Looney, ed., *The Papers of Thomas Jefferson: Retirement Series* (Princeton, NJ: Princeton University Press, 2004–), Benjamin Rush to Jefferson, February 1, 1811, 3:357.

10. Milton E. Flower, *John Dickinson: Conservative Revolutionary* (Charlottesville: University Press of Virginia, 1983), 287.

11. Edmund S. Morgan, "The Puritan Ethic and the American Revolution," *William and Mary Quarterly* 24 (January 1967): 29.

12. Dickinson W. Adams, ed., *Jefferson's Extracts from the Gospels* (Princeton, NJ: Princeton University Press, 1983), 32; Mark David Hall, "Roger Sherman: An Old Puritan in a New Nation," in Daniel L. Dreisbach et al., eds., *The Forgotten Founders on Religion and Public Life* (South Bend, IN: University of Notre Dame Press, 2009), 254, 256, 259–61; William R. Casto, "Oliver Ellsworth's Calvinist Vision of Church and State in the Early Republic," in Dreisbach et al., *Forgotten Founders on Religion and Public Life*, 66.

13. For an in-depth discussion of the critics of the classical languages requirement in the schools, a group that included Franklin, Rush, and Paine, see Carl J. Richard, *The Founders and the Classics: Greece, Rome, and the American Enlightenment* (Cambridge, MA: Harvard University Press, 1994), 196–231.

14. Wilson Smith, ed., *Theories of Education in Early America, 1655–1819* (New York: Bobbs-Merrill, 1973), John Witherspoon, *Letters on Education*, 1765, 213–14.

15. Thomas Miller, ed., *The Selected Writings of John Witherspoon* (Carbondale: Southern Illinois University Press, 1990), Lectures on Eloquence, 1782, 297; Michael Novak, "The Jewish and Christian Principles of the Founders," in Daniel N. Robinson and Richard N. Williams, eds., *The American Founding: Its Intellectual and Moral Framework* (London: Continuum, 2012), 20; Jeffry H. Morrison, *John Witherspoon and the Founding of the American Republic* (South Bend, IN: University of Notre Dame Press, 2005), 12, 77.

16. John C. Miller, *Sam Adams: Pioneer in Propaganda* (Stanford, CA: Stanford University Press, 1936), 84; Harry Alonzo Cushing, ed., *The Writings of Samuel Adams* (New York: Octagon Books, 1968), Adams to Hannah Adams, August 17, 1780, 4:201.

17. Cushing, *Writings of Samuel Adams*, Adams to James Warren, February 12, 1779, 4:124–25; Adams to John Adams, October 4, 1790, 4:343; To the Legislature of Massachusetts, January 20, 1794, 4:359; January 30, 1797, 4:401.

18. Labaree et al., *Papers of Benjamin Franklin*, Franklin to Catherine Ray, October 16, 1755, 6:225; "Final Report on the Franklin and Hall Account," 1766, 13:90; "Franklin's Proposed New Version of the Bible," 1782, 38:520–22.

19. Henry, *Patrick Henry*, 2:198–99, 308, 570–71; Thomas E. Buckley, "Patrick Henry, Religious Liberty, and the Search for Civic Virtue," in Dreisbach et al., *Forgotten Founders on Religion and Public Life*, 139.

20. George Adams Boyd, *Elias Boudinot: Patriot and Statesman, 1740–1821* (Princeton, NJ: Princeton University Press, 1952), 8, 254–60, 291; David L. Holmes, *The Faiths of the Founding Fathers* (Oxford: Oxford University Press, 2006), 150–51.

21. Richard B. Morris, ed., *John Jay: The Making of a Revolutionary, Unpublished Papers, 1745–1780* (New York: Harper and Row, 1975), Jay to Peter Augustus Jay, April 8, 1784, 2:709; Jonathan Den Hartog, "John Jay and the 'Great Plan of Providence,'" in Dreisbach et al., *Forgotten Founders on Religion and Public Life*, 149–52, 164; Holmes, *Faiths of the Founding Fathers*, 160.

22. Marvin R. Zahniser, *Charles Cotesworth Pinckney: Founding Father* (Chapel Hill: University of North Carolina Press, 1967), 272–74.

23. John Edward Oster, ed., *The Political and Economic Doctrines of John Marshall: Letters and Speeches* (New York: Burt Franklin, 1967), Marshall to John Marshall, November 7, 1834, 57.

24. Butterfield, *Letters of Benjamin Rush*, Rush to Julia Rush, July 31, 1791, 1:601–2; Rush to John Rush, May 18, 1796, 2:776.

25. Frederick Rudolph, ed., *Essays on Education in the Early Republic* (Cambridge, MA: Harvard University Press, 1965), Benjamin Rush, "A Plan for the Establishment of Public Schools and the Diffusion of Knowledge in Pennsylvania," 1786, 12–13.

26. Ibid., "Thoughts upon Female Education," 1787, 31–32; Butterfield, *Letters of Benjamin Rush*, "To the Citizens of Philadelphia: A Plan for Free Schools," March 28, 1787, 1:414–15; "To American Farmers about to Settle in the New Parts of the United States," March 1789, 1:504; Rush to John Adams, October 31, 1807, 2:953.

27. Dagobert D. Runes, ed., *The Selected Writings of Benjamin Rush* (New York: The Philosophical Library, 1947; reprint, Omaha: The Classics of Liberty Library, 2012), "The Bible as a School Book," 1791, 117–21, 128.

28. Butterfield, *Letters of Benjamin Rush*, Rush to Charles Nisbet, Mary 15, 1784, 1:335; Rush to John Montgomery, June 21, 1799, 2:812; February 9, 1804, 2:878; Rush to Ashbel Green, December 9, 1802, 2:853–54.

29. Ibid., Rush to Jeremy Belknap, January 5, 1791, 1:573–74; Rush to Elhanan Winchester, May 11, 1791, 1:581; Rush to William Graydon, March 24, 1813, 2:1191; Nathan G. Goodman, *Benjamin Rush: Physician and Citizen, 1746–1813* (Philadelphia: University of Pennsylvania Press, 1934), 319.

30. W. B. Allen, ed., *The Works of Fisher Ames* (Indianapolis, IN: Liberty Classics, 1983), School Books, *The Palladium*, January 27, 1801, 1:12.

31. John C. Fitzpatrick, ed., *The Writings of George Washington* (Washington, DC: Government Printing Office, 1931–1940), "Speech to the Delaware Chiefs," May 2, 1779, 15:55; Washington to Reverend John Etwein, May 2, 1788, 29:489; W. W. Abbot, ed., *The Papers of George Washington: Presidential Series* (Charlottesville: University Press of Virginia, 1987–), Washington to the Moravian Society for Propagating the Gospel, August 15, 1789, 3:466; John Elliott Jr. to Washington, August 18, 1789, 3:491n; Washington to the Commissioners to the Southern Indians, August 29, 1789, 3:557–58.

32. Saul K. Padover, ed., *The Complete Jefferson: Containing His Major Writings, Published and Unpublished, Except His Letters* (New York: Duell, Sloan, and Pearce, 1943), "Education for a Lawyer," 1767, 1043–44; Looney, *Papers of Thomas Jefferson*, Jefferson to James Fishback, September 27, 1809, 1:566; Bergh and Lipscomb, *Writings of Thomas Jefferson*, Jefferson to Samuel Greenhow, January 31, 1814, 14:81; Jefferson to Michael Megear, May 29, 1823, 15:434; Sanford, *Religious Life of Thomas Jefferson*, 5, 25.

33. William Peden, ed., *Notes on the State of Virginia* (Chapel Hill: University of North Carolina Press, 1955), 147.

34. Bergh and Lipscomb, *Writings of Thomas Jefferson*, Jefferson to Isaac Engelbrecht, February 25, 1824, 16:16; Jefferson to Thomas Jefferson Smith, February 21, 1825, 16:110.

3. HEROES AND VILLAINS

1. Leonard W. Labaree et al., eds., *The Papers of Benjamin Franklin* (New Haven, CT: Yale University Press, 1959–), "Appeal for the Hospital," *Pennsylvania Gazette*, August 8, 1751, 4:147–48.

2. L. H. Butterfield, ed., *The Letters of Benjamin Rush* (Princeton, NJ: Princeton University Press, 1951), Rush to Julia Rush, September 18, 1793, 2:668.

3. Julian P. Boyd, ed., *The Papers of Thomas Jefferson* (Princeton, NJ: Princeton University Press, 1950–), Jefferson to Samuel Adams, March 29, 1801, 33:487.

4. Labaree et al., *Papers of Benjamin Franklin*, "Poor Richard," 1756 and 1765, 6:328; 12:4; Thomas J. Woody, ed., *Educational Views of Benjamin Franklin* (New York: McGraw-Hill, 1931), *Poor Richard*, 81.

5. Labaree et al., *Papers of Benjamin Franklin*, *Poor Richard Improved*, 1758, 7:326.

6. Eran Shalev, *American Zion: The Old Testament as a Political Text from the Revolution to the Civil War* (New Haven, CT: Yale University Press, 2013), 19; L. H. Butterfield, ed., *The Adams Family Correspondence* (Cambridge, MA: Harvard University Press, 1963), John to Abigail Adams, May 17, 1776, 1:410.

7. Boyd, *Papers of Thomas Jefferson*, "Report on a Seal for the United States," August 20, 1776, 1:494–95.

8. John P. Kaminsky et al., eds., *The Documentary History of the Ratification of the Constitution* (Madison: State Historical Society of Wisconsin, 1976–2008), Massachusetts Convention Debates, January 22, 1788, 6:1301; Butterfield, *Letters of Benjamin Rush*, Rush to the Trustees of Dickinson College, April 1786, 1:383; Robert Green McCloskey, ed., *The Collected Works of James Wilson* (Cambridge, MA: Harvard University Press, 1967), *Lectures on Law, 1790–1791*, 2:494.

9. Kaminsky et al., *Documentary History*, "A Plain Citizen to the Convention of the State of Pennsylvania," *Independent Gazette*, November 22, 1787, 2:290; Richard Walsh, ed., *The Writings of Christopher Gadsden, 1746–1805* (Columbia: University of South Carolina Press, 1966), "A Few Observations on Some Late Public Transactions," January 30, 1797, 276.

10. Albert Ellery Bergh and Andrew A. Lipscomb, eds., *The Writings of Thomas Jefferson* (Washington, DC: Thomas Jefferson Memorial Association, 1904), Jefferson to George Flower, September 12, 1817, 15:141.

11. Robert P. Hay, "George Washington: American Moses," *American Quarterly* 21 (Winter 1969): 782–88; Linda K. Kerber, *Federalists in Dissent: Imagery and Ideology in Jeffersonian America* (Ithaca, NY: Cornell University Press, 1970), 6–8; Edwin S. Gaustad, *Faith of Our Fathers: Religion and the New Nation* (San Francisco: Harper and Row, 1987), 75.

12. Carl E. Prince, ed., *The Papers of William Livingston* (Trenton: New Jersey Historical Commission, 1979–1988), De Lisle, *New York Gazette*, March 25, 1778, 2:274.

13. Labaree et al., *Papers of Benjamin Franklin*, "A Dialogue between X, Y, and Z," *Pennsylvania Gazette*, December 18, 1755, 6:305; Paul Leicester Ford, ed., *The Political Writings of John Dickinson, 1764–1774* (New York: Da Capo Press, 1970), "Speech on a Petition for a Change of Government of the Colony of Pennsylvania," May 24, 1764, 42.

14. Moncure Daniel Conway, ed., *The Writings of Thomas Paine* (New York: Burt Franklin, 1969), *Common Sense*, 1776, 1:76–77.

15. Labaree et al., *Papers of Benjamin Franklin*, Franklin to James Bowdoin, February 25, 1775, 21:507; Thomas Miller, ed., *The Selected Writings of John Witherspoon* (Carbondale: Southern Illinois University Press, 1990), "The Dominion of Providence over the Passions of Men," May 17, 1776, 139; Derek H.

Davis, *Religion and the Continental Congress, 1774–1789: Contributions to Original Intent* (Oxford: Oxford University Press, 2000), 88.

16. Saul K. Padover, ed., *The Complete Jefferson: Containing His Major Writings, Published and Unpublished, Except His Letters* (New York: Duell, Sloan, and Pearce, 1943), Jefferson to Walter Jones, January 2, 1814, 926.

17. Robert J. Taylor, ed., The *Papers of John Adams* (Cambridge, MA: Harvard University Press, 1977–), Adams to Jonathan Sewall, Spring 1763, 1:62–63.

18. Ibid., "Humphrey Ploughjogger to the *Boston Evening-Post*," June 20, 1763, 1:64; Alfred Owen Aldridge, *Benjamin Franklin and Nature's God* (Durham, NC: Duke University Press, 1967), 68; Robert A. Rutland et al., eds., *The Papers of James Madison* (Chicago: University of Chicago Press, 1962–1977; Charlottesville: University Press of Virginia, 1977–), "Notes on Commentary of the Bible," 1770–1773, 1:57–58.

19. Labaree et al., *Papers of Benjamin Franklin*, Franklin to Mary Fisher, July 31, 1758, 8:118.

20. Ibid., Franklin to Edward Bridgen, October 2, 1779, 30:430; Franklin to Henry Laurens, May 25, 1782, 37:415–16; Franklin to Samuel Cooper Johonnot, January 7, 1783, 38:558; L. Jesse Lemisch, ed., *Benjamin Franklin: The Autobiography and Other Writings* (New York: Penguin, 1961), *Autobiography*, 97, 108; "The Way to Wealth," 1757, 196.

21. Labaree et al., *Papers of Benjamin Franklin*, David Hume to Franklin, May 10, 1762, 10:81–82; Franklin to David Hume, May 19, 1762, 10:83–84.

22. Frederick Rudolph, ed., *Essays on Education in the Early Republic* (Cambridge, MA: Harvard University Press, 1965), Benjamin Rush, "Thoughts upon Female Education," 1787, 35–36.

23. J. Jefferson Looney, ed., *The Papers of Thomas Jefferson: Retirement Series* (Princeton, NJ: Princeton University Press, 2004–), Jefferson to the Inhabitants of Albemarle County, April 3, 1809, 1:103; Harry Alonzo Cushing, ed., *The Writings of Samuel Adams* (New York: Octagon, 1968), "Candidus," November 11, 1771, 2:273; Gaustad, *Faith of Our Fathers*, 73; Butterfield, *Letters of Benjamin Rush*, Rush to Elhannan Winchester, November 12, 1791, 1:611; Rush to John Adams, December 26, 1811, 2:1115–16.

24. Lemisch, *Benjamin Franklin*, *Autobiography*, 58–60.

25. Labaree et al., *Papers of Benjamin Franklin*, Franklin to Thomas Viny, May 4, 1779, 29:431; Richard B. Morris, ed., *John Jay: The Making of a Revolutionary, Unpublished Papers, 1745–1780* (New York: Harper and Row, 1975), Jay to Charles Thomson, April 23, 1781, 2:69.

26. Daniel L. Dreisbach, "The Bible in the Political Rhetoric of the American Founding," *Politics and Religion* 4 (2011): 408; John C. Fitzpatrick, ed., *The Writings of George Washington* (Washington, DC: Government Printing Office, 1931–1940), Washington to the Marquis de Lafayette, June 18, 1788, 18:184;

W. W. Abbot, ed., *The Papers of George Washington: Presidential Series* (Charlottesville: University Press of Virginia, 1987–), To the Hebrew Congregation in Newport, Rhode Island, August 18, 1790, 6:285; W. W. Abbot, ed., *The Papers of George Washington: Retirement Series* (Charlottesville: University Press of Virginia, 1998–1999), Washington to Oliver Wolcott Jr., May 15, 1797, 1:142–43; Washington to Thomas Pinckney, May 28, 1797, 1:157; Washington to John Quincy Adams, June 25, 1797, 1:211; Washington to Rufus King, June 25, 1797, 1:213; Washington to David Humphreys, June 26, 1797, 1:218; Washington to Randnor, July 8, 1797, 1:291.

27. For the statistic regarding Washington eulogies, see Mark A. Noll, "The United States as a Biblical Nation, 1776–1865," in Nathan O. Hatch, ed., *The Bible in America: Essays in Cultural History* (Oxford: Oxford University Press, 1982), 45.

28. Labaree et al., *Papers of Benjamin Franklin*, Franklin to Robert R. Livingston, December 5, 1782, 38:416–17; Kaminsky et al., *Documentary History*, Christopher Gadsden to Thomas Jefferson, October 29, 1787, 13:508; Charles B. Sanford, *The Religious Life of Thomas Jefferson* (Charlottesville: University Press of Virginia, 1984), 172.

29. Ford, *Political Writings of John Dickinson*, *Letters from a Farmer in Pennsylvania*, 1767–1768, 308; John C. Fitzpatrick, ed., *The Writings of George Washington* (Washington, DC: Government Printing Office, 1931–1940), Washington to Bushrod Washington, January 15, 1783, 26:40.

30. Butterfield, *Letters of Benjamin Rush*, Rush to John Adams, July 20, 1811, 2:1091.

31. Boyd, *Papers of Thomas Jefferson*, Jefferson to Nicholas Davies, August 6, 1794, 28:110; Looney, *Papers of Thomas Jefferson*, Jefferson to John Hollins, May 5, 1811, 3:606.

32. Miller, *Selected Writings of John Witherspoon*, "Lectures on Eloquence," 1782, 298; Labaree et al., *Papers of Benjamin Franklin*, Henry Laurens to Franklin, June 24, 1782, 37:525.

33. Kaminsky et al., *Documentary History*, Fabius III, *Pennsylvania Mercury*, April 17, 1788, 17:171.

34. Labaree et al., *Papers of Benjamin Franklin*, "Poor Richard," 1756, 6:326.

35. Butterfield, *Letters of Benjamin Rush*, To His Fellow Countrymen: On Patriotism, October 20, 1773, 1:83.

36. Taylor, *Papers of John Adams*, "Governor Winthrop to Governor Bradford," February 9, 1767, 1:200; Cushing, *Writings of Samuel Adams*, Adams to Christopher Gadsden, December 11, 1766, 1:109–10; "A Puritan," April 11, 1768, 1:203.

37. Labaree et al., *Papers of Benjamin Franklin*, Franklin to Sir William Browne, 1772, 19:444; Franklin to George Washington, April 8, 1782, 37:116.

38. W. W. Abbot, ed., *The Papers of George Washington: Revolutionary War Series* (Charlottesville: University Press of Virginia, 1985–), Charles Lee to Washington, February 19, 1776, 3:340; Conway, *Writings of Thomas Paine*, "The Crisis II," January 13, 1777, 1:180; *Letters to the Citizens of the United States V*, 1803, 3:406; Morris, *John Jay*, Edward Rutledge to Jay, December 25, 1778, 1:515; Prince, *Papers of William Livingston*, Livingston to Henry Laurens, October 9, 1778, 2:458; Robert A. Rutland, ed., *The Papers of George Mason* (Chapel Hill: University of North Carolina Press, 1970), Mason to Unidentified Correspondent, October 2, 1778, 1:435; James Curtis Ballagh, ed., *The Letters of Richard Henry Lee* (New York: Macmillan, 1911–1914; reprint, New York: Da Capo Press, 1970), Lee to Thomas Jefferson, October 13, 1779, 2:158.

39. Walsh, *Writings of Christopher Gadsden*, xxiii; Ballagh, *Letters of Richard Henry Lee*, Lee to Samuel Adams, November 18, 1784, 2:294.

40. Kaminsky et al., *Documentary History*, Joseph Barrell to Nathaniel Barrell, December 20, 1787, 5:491; America, *New York Daily Advertiser*, December 31, 1787, 15:194.

41. Butterfield, *Letters of Benjamin Rush*, Rush to Julia Rush, August 22, 1793, 2:638; Dagobert D. Runes, ed., *The Selected Writings of Benjamin Rush* (New York: The Philosophical Library, 1947; reprint, Omaha: The Classics of Liberty Library, 2012), "The Effects of Ardent Spirits upon Man," 1805, 339; Richard B. Mattern, ed., *James Madison's "Advice to My Country"* (Charlottesville: University Press of Virginia, 1997), 104–5.

42. David A. McCants, *Patrick Henry, The Orator* (Westport, CT: Greenwood, 1990), 60; Labaree et al., *Papers of Benjamin Franklin*, Franklin to the Marquis de Lafayette, May 14, 1781, 35:65.

43. Boyd, *Papers of Thomas Jefferson*, John Adams to Jefferson, October 9, 1787, 12:220.

44. Kaminsky et al., *Documentary History*, Benjamin Franklin's Speech, reprinted in the *Boston Gazette*, December 3, 1787, 4:372–73.

45. Conway, *Writings of Thomas Paine*, "The Crisis VI," October 20, 1778, 1:266.

46. Herbert J. Storing, ed., *The Complete Anti-Federalist* (Chicago: University of Chicago Press, 1981), 6:109; Looney, *Papers of Thomas Jefferson*, Jefferson to William Duane, July 25, 1811, 4:56–57.

47. Taylor, *Papers of John Adams*, "To the Inhabitants of the Colony of Massachusetts-Bay," February 13, 1775, 2:258.

48. Labaree et al., *Papers of Benjamin Franklin*, "Humorous Reasons for Restoring Canada," *London Chronicle*, December 25–27, 1759, 8:450; *The Colonist's Advocate* VII, February 1, 1770, 17:54; The American Commissioners to the Committee for Foreign Affairs, February 28, 1778, 25:727.

49. Cushing, *Writings of Samuel Adams*, Adams to Arthur Lee, September 27, 1771, 2:231; Adams to Joseph Hawley, April 15, 1776, 3:281.

50. William Wirt Henry, ed., *Patrick Henry: Life, Correspondence, and Speeches* (New York: Charles Scribner's Sons, 1891; reprint, New York: Burt Franklin, 1969), 1:280–81, 565; Rutland et al., *Papers of James Madison*, Edmund Randolph to Madison, August 6, 1782, 5:29.

51. Kaminsky et al., *Documentary History*, Unicus, *Maryland Journal*, November 9, 1787, 14:80; Luther Martin, "Address No. IV," *Maryland Journal*, April 4, 1788, 17:21.

52. Ellis Sandoz, *A Government of Laws: Political Theory, Religion, and the American Founding* (Baton Rouge: Louisiana State University Press, 1990), 107; Prince, *Papers of William Livingston*, De Lisle, *New York Gazette*, March 25, 1778, 2:275; Cushing, *Writings of Samuel Adams*, Adams to Arthur Lee, November 21, 1782, 4:276; Labaree et al., *Papers of Benjamin Franklin*, Robert R. Livingston to Franklin, September 5, 1782, 38:71.

53. Kaminsky et al., *Documentary History*, K, *Philadelphia Federal Gazette*, April 8, 1788, 17:37–39.

54. Labaree et al., *Papers of Benjamin Franklin*, Franklin to John Adams, February 12, 1782, 36:561; Kaminsky et al., *Documentary History*, The Connecticut Convention, January 4, 1787, 3:541.

55. Cushing, *Writings of Samuel Adams*, Adams to Arthur Lee, November 13, 1771, 2:276; Conway, *Writings of Thomas Paine*, "The Crisis VII," November 21, 1778, 1:281; Prince, *Papers of William Livingston*, Livingston to Joseph Reed, October 22, 1778, 2:471.

56. Kaminsky et al., *Documentary History*, Massachusetts Convention Debates, February 6, 1788, 6:1459; Boyd, *Papers of Thomas Jefferson*, Jefferson to Philip Mazzei, April 24, 1796, 29:82.

57. Douglas L. Wilson, ed., *Jefferson's Literary Commonplace Book* (Princeton, NJ: Princeton University Press, 1989), 20, 123–27.

58. Cushing, *Writings of Samuel Adams*, "Candidus," August 19, 1771, 2:201; Conway, *Writings of Thomas Paine*, *The Rights of Man*, 1792, 2:471.

59. Nathan R. Perl-Rosenthal, "The 'divine right of republics': Hebraic Republicanism and the Debate over Kingless Government in Revolutionary America," *William and Mary Quarterly* 66 (July 2009): 536, 550, 553; Eric Nelson, *The Hebrew Republic: Jewish Sources and the Transformation of European Political Thought* (Cambridge, MA: Harvard University Press, 2010), 3; Conway, *Writings of Thomas Paine*, *Common Sense*, 1776, 1:75–79, 99.

60. Kaminsky et al., *Documentary History*, A Columbian Patriot, "Observations on the Constitution," February 1788, 16:285; A Countryman III, *New York Journal*, December 20, 1787, 19:451–52; Storing, *Complete Anti-Federalist*,

Speeches by Melancton Smith, New York Ratifying Convention, June 20, 1788, 6:152.

61. Jonathan Elliot, ed., *Debates in the Several State Conventions on the Adoption of the Federal Constitution*, 2nd ed. (Washington, DC: Elliot, 1836), 2:405.

62. Labaree et al., *Papers of Benjamin Franklin*, "Pennsylvania Assembly Committee Report on the Proprietors' Answer," September 11, 1753, 5:57.

63. Cushing, *Writings of Samuel Adams*, "Candidus," November 11, 1771, 2:271–73.

64. Henry, *Patrick Henry*, 1:261.

65. Labaree et al., *Papers of Benjamin Franklin*, "The Somersett Case and the Slave Trade," *London Chronicle*, June 18–20, 1772, 19:187–88; Kaminsky et al., *Documentary History*, Samuel Osgood to Samuel Adams, January 5, 1788, 5:618; A Friend to Honesty, *Independent Chronicle*, January 10, 1788, 5:689; Elliot, *Debates*, 2:399–400.

66. Lester J. Cappon, ed., *The Adams-Jefferson Letters: The Complete Correspondence between Thomas Jefferson and Abigail and John Adams* (Chapel Hill: University of North Carolina Press, 1959), Jefferson to John Adams, January 24, 1814, 2:423.

67. Ibid., John Adams to Jefferson, June 30, 1813, 2:347.

68. Labaree et al., *Papers of Benjamin Franklin*, "Appeal for the Hospital," *Pennsylvania Gazette*, August 8, 1751, 4:149.

69. George Adams Boyd, *Elias Boudinot: Patriot and Statesman, 1740–1821* (Princeton, NJ: Princeton University Press, 1952), 253–54.

4. DIVINE INTERVENTION

1. For a much fuller discussion of the Greco-Roman gods and of the divine entities posited by classical philosophers, see Carl J. Richard, *Why We're All Romans: The Roman Contribution to the Western World* (Lanham, MD: Rowman & Littlefield, 2010), 135–63, 239–43, 260–68.

2. Leonard W. Labaree et al., eds., *The Papers of Benjamin Franklin* (New Haven, CT: Yale University Press, 1959–), "On the Providence of God in the Government of the World," 1732, 1:265–68; "Poor Richard," 1757, 7:91; Franklin to unidentified correspondent, December 13, 1757, 7:294.

3. L. Jesse Lemisch, ed., *Benjamin Franklin: The Autobiography and Other Writings* (New York: Penguin Books, 1961), *Autobiography*, 69–71, 92–93; Franklin to Ezra Stiles, March 9, 1790, 337.

4. Albert Ellery Bergh and Andrew A. Lipscomb, eds., *The Writings of Thomas Jefferson* (Washington, DC: Thomas Jefferson Memorial Association,

1904), Jefferson to Benjamin Rush, April 21, 1803, 10:382; Jefferson to William Short, October 31, 1819, 10:219, 223. For reference to Federalist accusations against Jefferson, see Douglass Adair and John A. Schutz, eds., *The Spur of Fame: Dialogues of John Adams and Benjamin Rush, 1805–1813* (San Marino, CA: Huntington Library, 1966), 121. For reference to my own mistaken belief in the past that Jefferson was a deist who embraced the Epicurean doctrine of divine noninterference, see Carl J. Richard, *The Battle for the American Mind: A Brief History of a Nation's Thought* (Lanham, MD: Rowman & Littlefield, 2004), xvi, 104. For a few other references to the alleged deism of Jefferson, Franklin, and Paine, see Merill D. Peterson, *Thomas Jefferson and the New Nation: A Biography* (Oxford: Oxford University Press, 1970), 50; Henry F. May, *The Enlightenment in America* (Oxford: Oxford University Press, 1976), 124, 137, 274; Gordon S. Wood, *The Radicalism of the American Revolution* (New York: Alfred A. Knopf, 1992), 158; Walter Isaacson, *Benjamin Franklin: An American Life* (New York: Simon and Schuster, 2003), 26. Since none of these historians defined deism, it is possible that they were employing a narrow definition of the term, such as the belief that reason rather than revelation should be used in uncovering religious truth, by which definition a few founders were indeed deists. My point is not to criticize these historians but to note that a widespread lack of precision in defining the term has created confusion in this field of study.

5. Lester J. Cappon, ed., *The Adams-Jefferson Letters: The Complete Correspondence between Thomas Jefferson and Abigail and John Adams* (Chapel Hill: University of North Carolina Press, 1959), Jefferson to John Adams, April 11, 1823, 2:592.

6. David McCullough, *John Adams* (New York: Simon and Schuster, 2001), 222; Edwin S. Gaustad, *Faith of Our Fathers: Religion and the New Nation* (San Francisco: Harper and Row, 1987), 92; Robert Green McCloskey, ed., *The Collected Works of James Wilson* (Cambridge, MA: Harvard University Press, 1967), *Lectures on Law*, 1790–1791, 1:97, 124.

7. William Wirt Henry, ed., *Patrick Henry: Life, Correspondence, and Speeches* (New York: Charles Scribner's Sons, 1891; reprint, New York: Burt Franklin, 1969), 2:570, 575; Thomas E. Buckley, "Patrick Henry, Religious Liberty, and the Search for Civic Virtue," in Daniel L. Dreisbach et al., eds., *The Forgotten Founders on Religion and Public Life* (South Bend, IN: University of Notre Dame Press, 2009), 136–37.

8. Dagobert Runes, ed., *The Selected Writings of Benjamin Rush* (New York: The Philosophical Library, 1947; reprint, Omaha: The Classics of Liberty Library, 2012), "On Manners," 1769, 381; "Lectures on Animal Life III," 1799, 179; Meyer Reinhold, *Classica Americana: The Greek and Roman Heritage in the United States* (Detroit: Wayne State University Press, 1984), 158.

9. Julian P. Boyd, ed., *The Papers of Thomas Jefferson* (Princeton, NJ: Princeton University Press, 1950–), Declaration of Independence, July 4, 1776, 1:432; Jeffrey H. Morrison, *John Witherspoon and the Founding of the American Republic* (South Bend, IN: University of Notre Dame Press, 2005), 77; Charles B. Sanford, *The Religious Life of Thomas Jefferson* (Charlottesville: University Press of Virginia, 1984), 93.

10. Paul K. Longmore, *The Invention of George Washington* (Berkeley: University of California Press, 1988), 29–30; John C. Fitzpatrick, ed., *The Writings of George Washington* (Washington, DC: Government Printing Office, 1931–1940), Washington to the Reverend William Gordon, May 3, 1776, 37:526.

11. W. W. Abbot, ed., *The Papers of George Washington: Colonial Series* (Charlottesville: University Press of Virginia, 1983–1995), Washington to Robert Jackson, August 2, 1755, 1:350; Washington to Robert Dinwiddie, November 9, 1756, 4:1.

12. W. W. Abbot, ed., *The Papers of George Washington: Revolutionary War Series* (Charlottesville: University Press of Virginia, 1985–), Washington to Martha Washington, June 18, 1775, 1:3–4; June 23, 1775, 1:27; Washington to Samuel Washington, September 30, 1775, 2:74; Paul F. Boller, *George Washington and Religion* (Dallas: Southern Methodist University Press, 1963), 107.

13. Boller, *George Washington and Religion*, 108–9.

14. W. W. Abbot, ed., *The Papers of George Washington: Presidential Series* (Charlottesville: University Press of Virginia, 1987–), Washington to the Citizens of Baltimore, April 17, 1789, 2:62; Washington to the Officials of Wilmington, Delaware, April 19, 1789, 2:77; Fitzpatrick, *Writings of George Washington*, Seventh Annual Address, December 8, 1795, 34:386; Washington to David Stuart, December 30, 1798, 37:78.

15. L. H. Butterfield, ed., *The Letters of Benjamin Rush* (Princeton, NJ: Princeton University Press, 1951), Rush to Ebenezer Hazard, September 27, 1762, 1:6; November 18, 1765, 1:20; Rush to John Bayard Smith, April 30, 1767, 1:42; Rush to David Ramsay, November 5, 1778, 1:219; Rush to Horatio Gates, November 30, 1797, 2:796; George W. Corner, ed., *The Autobiography of Benjamin Rush: His "Travels through Life" Together with His Commonplace Book, 1789–1813* (Princeton, NJ: Princeton University Press, 1948), *Autobiography*, 1800, 108; *Commonplace Book*, 1809, 286.

16. Thomas Miller, ed., *The Selected Writings of John Witherspoon* (Carbondale: Southern Illinois University Press, 1990), "The Dominion of Providence over the Passions of Men," May 17, 1776, 126, 133–35.

17. Lemisch, *Benjamin Franklin, Autobiography*, 17.

18. Harold C. Syrett, ed., *The Papers of Alexander Hamilton* (New York: Columbia University Press, 1961–1979), Hamilton to Elizabeth Hamilton, July 10, 1781, 2:647–48; George Washington to Hamilton, October 27, 1799, 23:574.

19. Gary Scott Smith, "Samuel Adams: America's Puritan Revolutionary," in Dreisbach, *Forgotten Founders on Religion and Public Life*, 46–47; Jonathan Den Hartog, "John Jay and 'the Great Plan of Providence,'" in Dreisbach, *Forgotten Founders on Religion and Public Life*, 160, 169n43; Stanislaus Murray Hamilton, ed., *The Writings of James Monroe* (New York: A.M.S., 1969), Second Inaugural Address, March 5, 1821, 6:174.

20. Labaree et al., *Papers of Benjamin Franklin*, Franklin to Jane Mecom, December 30, 1770, 17:315; Robert A. Rutland et al., eds., *The Papers of James Madison* (Chicago: University of Chicago Press, 1962–1977; Charlottesville: University Press of Virginia, 1977–), Madison to William Bradford, June 10, 1773, 1:89; Miller, *Selected Writings of John Witherspoon*, "The Dominion of Providence over the Passions of Men," May 17, 1776, 143; Richard B. Morris, ed., *John Jay: The Making of a Revolutionary, Unpublished Papers, 1745–1780* (New York: Harper and Row, 1975), Jay to Catherine W. Livingston, February 27–28, 1779, 1:568; Fitzpatrick, *Writings of George Washington*, Washington to Edmund Pendleton, November 1, 1779, 17:51.

21. Butterfield, *Letters of Benjamin Rush*, Rush to Julia Rush, August 25, 1793, 2:641; Boller, *George Washington and Religion*, 103–4; Bergh and Lipscomb, *Writings of Thomas Jefferson*, Jefferson to George Logan, October 3, 1813, 13:387; Gaustad, *Faith of Our Fathers*, 93.

22. Lemisch, *Benjamin Franklin*, Poor Richard, 1753, 235; Saul K. Padover, ed., *The Complete Jefferson: Containing His Major Writings, Published and Unpublished, Except His Letters* (New York: Duell, Sloan, and Pearce, 1943), Vice Presidential Inaugural Address, March 4, 1797, 383; Corner, *Autobiography of Benjamin Rush*, 96.

23. Moncure Daniel Conway, ed., *The Writings of Thomas Paine* (New York: Burt Franklin, 1969), *The Age of Reason*, 1794–1795, 4:33, 75–80, 167, 188.

24. Ibid., Address to the People of France, September 25, 1792, 3:99; Letter to the Citizens of the United States I, November 15, 1802, 3:381; *Prospect Papers*, 1806, 4:332.

25. Syrett, *Papers of Alexander Hamilton*, To the *Royal Danish American Gazette*, September 6, 1772, 1:36; Hamilton to Elizabeth Hamilton, August 12, 1794, 17:84; Miller, *Selected Writings of John Witherspoon, Lectures on Moral Philosophy*, 1774, 179; L. H. Butterfield, ed., *The Adams Family Correspondence* (Cambridge, MA: Harvard University Press, 1963), John to Abigail Adams, June 17, 1775, 1:216; Abbot, *Papers of George Washington: Revolutionary War Series*, Washington to Lund Washington, August 26, 1776, 6:137; Fitzpa-

trick, *Writings of George Washington*, Farewell Order to the Armies of the United States, November 2, 1783, 27:227.

26. James Curtis Ballagh, ed., *The Letters of Richard Henry Lee* (New York: Macmillan, 1911–1914; reprint, New York: Da Capo Press, 1970), Lee to Edmund Pendleton, May 22, 1788, 2:474; Charles F. Hobson, ed., *The Papers of John Marshall* (Chapel Hill: University of North Carolina Press, 1974–2006), Address, December 6, 1799, 4:41; John Edward Oster, ed., *The Political and Economic Doctrines of John Marshall: Letters and Speeches* (New York: Burt Franklin, 1967), Marshall to Joseph Story, June 26, 1831, 142; Hamilton, *Writings of James Monroe*, To the Speakers of the General Assembly, December 6, 1802, 3:376–77.

27. Butterfield, *Letters of Benjamin Rush*, Rush to Julia Rush, August 25, 1793, 2:641; August 30, 1793, 2:645; September 8, 1793, 2:656; September 9, 1793, 2:656; September 10, 1793, 2:658; September 12, 1793, 2:659; September 13, 1793, 2:663; September 18, 1793, 2:671; September 20, 1793, 2:672; September 21, 1793, 2:673; November 4, 1793, 2:739.

28. Boyd, *Papers of Thomas Jefferson*, Jefferson to the Marquis de Lafayette, November 21, 1791, 22:313; Jefferson to the Executive Directory of the Batavian Republic, May 30, 1801, 34:209; Padover, *Complete Jefferson*, Jefferson to the Republican Young Men of New London, February 24, 1809, 548; J. Jefferson Looney, ed., *The Papers of Thomas Jefferson: Retirement Series* (Princeton, NJ: Princeton University Press, 2004–), Jefferson to the Republicans of Essex County, March 28, 1809, 1:86.

29. J. C. A. Stagg, ed., *The Papers of James Madison: Presidential Series* (Charlottesville: University Press of Virginia, 1992–), Madison to the Chairman of the Republican Committee of Essex County, New Jersey, March 18, 1809, 1:66; Madison to Benjamin Rush, March 20, 1809, 1:88; Madison to the Mother Superior of the Ursuline Convent, April 24, 1809, 1:136; Madison to the Republican Committee of New York, September 24, 1809, 1:389.

30. Conway, *Writings of Thomas Paine*, Paine to Samuel Adams, January 1, 1803, 4:208; Answer to the Bishop of Llandaff, 1806, 4:275.

31. Labaree et al., *Papers of Benjamin Franklin*, "Poor Richard," 1749, 3:336–37.

32. Butterfield, *Adams Family Correspondence*, John to Abigail Adams, September 16, 1774, 1:156; John C. Miller, *Sam Adams: Pioneer in Propaganda* (Stanford, CA: Stanford University Press, 1936), 320.

33. Rutland et al., *Papers of James Madison*, Edmund Randolph to James Madison, May 15, 1783, 7:46–47n6.

34. Max Farrand, ed., *The Records of the Federal Convention of 1787*, 3rd ed. (New Haven, CT: Yale University Press, 1966), 1:451–52. Franklin, who was not classically trained and opposed the requirement of the classical languages in

the schools, prefaced his statement with a sneering reference to the plethora of classical allusions at the convention. Thus, his remarks can be interpreted as an attempt to advance the biblical influence in opposition to the classical. See E. Christian Kopff, "Open Shutters on the Past: Rome and the Founders," in Gary L. Gregg, ed., *Vital Remnants: America's Founding and the Western Tradition* (Wilmington, DE: ISI, 1999), 80–83.

35. John P. Kaminsky et al., eds., *The Documentary History of the Ratification of the Constitution* (Madison: State Historical Society of Wisconsin, 1976–2008), Newspaper Report of Proceedings and Debates, November 22, 1787, 2:328; Massachusetts Convention Journal, January 9, 1788, 6:1162.

36. Lemisch, *Benjamin Franklin, Autobiography*, 123.

37. Henry, *Patrick Henry*, 1:177–80; Paul Leicester Ford, ed., *The Political Writings of John Dickinson, 1764–1774* (New York: Da Capo, 1970), Letters to the Inhabitants of the British Colonies, May 1774, 496–97.

38. Carl E. Prince, ed., *The Papers of William Livingston* (Trenton, NJ: New Jersey Historical Commission, 1979–1988), Proclamation in Congress, March 16, 1776, 1:43–44; Proclamation, January 17, 1777, 1:200; Morrison, *John Witherspoon and the Founding of the American Republic*, 21, 40; Fitzpatrick, *Writings of George Washington*, General Orders, November 30, 1777, 10:123; Boyd, *Papers of Thomas Jefferson*, Proclamation Appointing a Day of Thanksgiving and Prayer, November 11, 1779, 3:177–78; Kaminsky et al., *Documentary History*, Governor John Hancock: Proclamation for a Day of Public Thanksgiving, October 25, 1787, 4:147; Harry Alonzo Cushing, ed., *The Writings of Samuel Adams* (New York: Octagon, 1968), Proclamation, February 19, 1794, 3:361–62; October 14, 1795, 4:383; Boller, *George Washington and Religion*, 62; Syrett, *Papers of Alexander Hamilton*, Draft of a Proclamation by George Washington, January 1, 1795, 18:2–3; Thomas Pickering to Hamilton, March 25, 1798, 21:370n1; Stagg, *Papers of James Madison*, Presidential Proclamation, July 9, 1812, 4:581–82; Vincent Phillip Munoz, *God and the Founders: Madison, Washington, and Jefferson* (Cambridge: Cambridge University Press, 2009), 42; Marvin Meyers, ed., *The Mind of the Founder: Sources of the Political Thought of James Madison* (Indianapolis, IN: Bobbs-Merrill, 1973), Madison to Edward Livingston, July 10, 1822, 432.

39. Boyd, *Papers of Thomas Jefferson*, Declaration of Independence, July 4, 1776, 1:429.

40. Maryanne Cline Horowitz, "The Stoic Synthesis of the Idea of Natural Law in Man: Four Themes," *Journal of the History of Ideas* 35 (January–March 1974):6, 9–10, 12–15.

41. Augustine, *On Free Choice of the Will*, trans. Anna S. Benjamin and L. H. Hackstaff (New York: Bobbs-Merrill, 1964), 49, 155.

42. Thomas Aquinas, *Summa Theologica*, trans. Fathers of the English Dominican Province (New York: Benziger Brothers, 1947), 1:398–99, 422–23, 851, 989; Alister McGrath, *The Intellectual Origins of the European Reformation* (Oxford: Basil Blackwell, 1987), 140; John Dillenberger, ed., *Martin Luther: Selections from His Writings* (Garden City, NY: Doubleday, 1961), Preface to the Epistle of St. Paul to the Romans, 1522, p. 20; John Calvin, *Institutes of the Christian Religion*, trans. Henry Beveridge (Grand Rapids, MI: Eerdmans, 1970), 1:64, 72; William J. Bouwsma, *John Calvin: A Sixteenth-Century Portrait* (Oxford: Oxford University Press, 1988), 139, 142, 147–48, 155.

43. Paul K. Conkin, *Self-Evident Truths* (Bloomington: Indiana University Press, 1974), 92, 95; Paul A. Rahe, *Republics, Ancient and Modern: Classical Republicanism and the American Revolution* (Chapel Hill: University of North Carolina Press, 1992), 509.

44. Barry Alan Shain, *The Myth of American Individualism: The Protestant Origins of American Political Thought* (Princeton, NJ: Princeton University Press, 1994), 132; Adrienne Koch and William Peden, eds., *The Selected Writings of John and John Quincy Adams* (New York: Alfred A. Knopf, 1946), "Dissertation on the Canon and the Feudal Law," 1765, 18, 22; Ford, *Political Writings of John Dickinson*, An Address to the Committee of Correspondence in Barbados, 1766, 262; *Letters from a Farmer in Pennsylvania to the Inhabitants of the British Colonies*, 1767–8, 322, 405.

45. Cushing, *Writings of Samuel Adams*, Vindex, December 19, 1768, 1:269; December 26, 1768, 1:277; The House of Representatives to the Lieutenant-Governor, August 3, 1770, 2:22; Adams to James Warren, March 31, 1774, 3:93; Adams to Elizabeth Adams, December 19, 1776, 3:328; Sanford, *Religious Life of Thomas Jefferson*, 88.

46. Syrett, *Papers of Alexander Hamilton*, "The Farmer Refuted," February 23, 1775, 1:87–88, 104, 122; Boyd, *Papers of Thomas Jefferson*, "Declaration of the Causes and Necessity for Taking Up Arms," June–July 1775, 1:202; Conway, *Writings of Thomas Paine*, "Thoughts on Defensive War," July 1775, 1:57; Ballagh, *Letters of Richard Henry Lee*, Lee to Samuel Adams, February 4, 1775, 1:128; McCloskey, *Collected Works of James Wilson*, Speech Delivered in the Convention for the Province of Pennsylvania, January 1775, 2:753.

47. Labaree et al., *Papers of Benjamin Franklin*, Franklin to Newenham, May 27, 1779, 29:565; Richard Walsh, ed., *The Writings of Christopher Gadsden* (Columbia: University of South Carolina Press, 1966), Gadsden to Morton Wilkinson, September 1781, 174; McCloskey, *Collected Works of James Wilson*, *Lectures on Law*, 1790–1791, 1:124; 2:585; "On the History of Property," 2:711; Boyd, *Papers of Thomas Jefferson*, Jefferson to Tench Coxe, June 1, 1795, 28:373; Hartog, "John Jay," 166.

48. L. H. Butterfield, ed., *The Diary and Autobiography of John Adams* (Cambridge, MA: Harvard University Press, 1962), Diary, July 22, 1756, 1:36; August 14, 1756, 1:41–42; Butterfield, *Adams Family Correspondence*, John to Abigail Adams, July 5, 1774, 1:124.

49. Butterfield, *Letters of Benjamin Rush*, Rush to John Dunlap, July 3, 1779, 1:233; Rush to Julia Rush, October 30, 1793, 2:733.

50. Labaree et al., *Papers of Benjamin Franklin*, "Poor Richard," 1757, 7:87; "A Narrative of the Late Massacres," 1764, 11:53, 68.

51. Fitzpatrick, *Writings of George Washington*, Circular to the States, June 8, 1783, 26:490.

52. Hartog, "John Jay," 158, 163.

53. Oster, *Political and Economic Doctrines of John Marshall*, Speech at Virginia Ratifying Convention, 282.

54. Kaminsky et al., *Documentary History*, Connecticut Convention, January 9, 1788, 3:558; James Madison to Edmund Pendleton, October 28, 1787, 8:125. Pennsylvania passed a law in 1772 allowing oaths to be accompanied by the raising of a right hand rather than the kissing of a Bible for those who had a religious objection to the latter procedure. See Labaree et al., *Papers of Benjamin Franklin*, William Marshall to Franklin, October 30, 1772, 19:354, 356.

55. Thomas O'Brien Hanley, *Charles Carroll of Carrollton: The Making of a Revolutionary Gentleman* (Washington, DC: Catholic University of America Press, 1970), 161.

56. Butterfield, *Letters of Benjamin Rush*, Rush to Thomas Bradford, June 3, 1768, 1:60; Rush to Elizabeth Graene Ferguson, December 24, 1777, 1:178; Rush to David Patteson, June 19, 1806, 2:921; Daniel Boorstin, *The Lost World of Thomas Jefferson* (New York: Henry Holt, 1948), 50.

57. Miller, *Selected Writings of John Witherspoon*, "The Dominion of Providence over the Passions of Men," May 17, 1776, 131–32.

58. Gordon S. Wood, *The Creation of the American Republic, 1776–1787* (Chapel Hill: University of North Carolina Press, 1969), 117; Jean M. Yarbrough, *American Virtues: Thomas Jefferson and the Character of a Free People* (Lawrence: University Press of Kansas, 1998), 180; Sanford, *Religious Life of Thomas Jefferson*, 156.

59. Hartog, "John Jay," 156.

60. Prince, *Papers of William Livingston*, Adolphus, *New York Gazette*, January 21, 1778, 2:188.

61. Fitzpatrick, *Writings of George Washington*, Washington to Bryan Fairfax, March 1, 1778, 11:3; Washington to Jonathan Trumbull, September 6, 1778, 12:406; Washington to Andrew Lewis, October 15, 1778, 13:79; Washington to Joseph Reed, November 27, 1778, 13:348; Washington to Lund Washington,

May 29, 1779, 15:180; Washington to General John Armstrong, March 26, 1781, 21:378.

62. Ibid., Washington to Jonathan Trumbull, June 11, 1780, 18:511; Washington to Henry Knox, September 12, 1782, 25:150n; Washington to Pierre Charles L'Enfant, April 28, 1788, 29:481.

63. Ibid., Washington to Thaddeus Kosciuszko, August 31, 1797, 36:22; Washington to William Augustine Washington, February 27, 1798, 36:171; Washington to Archibald Blair, June 24, 1799, 37:244; Abbot, *Papers of George Washington: Presidential Series*, Washington to Henry Lee, August 27, 1790, 6:347.

64. Labaree et al., *Papers of Benjamin Franklin*, Franklin to All Captains of American Armed Ships, February 7, 1781, 34:354–55; Alfred Owen Aldridge, *Benjamin Franklin and Nature's God* (Durham, NC: Duke University Press, 1967), 266.

65. Boyd, *Papers of Thomas Jefferson*, Jefferson to Benjamin Rush, September 23, 1800, 32:167; Sanford, *Religious Life of Thomas Jefferson*, 156.

66. Syrett, *Papers of Alexander Hamilton*, Hamilton to Unidentified Correspondent, April 13, 1804, 26:219; Douglass Adair, *Fame and the Founding Fathers*, ed. H. Trevor Colbourn (New York: W. W. Norton, 1974), 155–56.

67. Oster, *Political and Economic Doctrines of John Marshall*, Marshall to Joseph Story, June 26, 1831, 136; Eulogy for Mary Marshall, December 25, 1832, 203.

68. David B. Mattern, ed., *James Madison's "Advice to My Country"* (Charlottesville: University Press of Virginia, 1997), Madison to John G. Jackson, December 28, 1821, 10.

5. THE NEW ISRAEL

1. Gordon S. Wood, *The Radicalism of the American Revolution* (New York: Alfred A. Knopf, 1992), 191; Gordon S. Wood, *Revolutionary Characters: What Made the Founders Great* (New York: Penguin, 2006), 179; Leonard W. Labaree et al., eds., *The Papers of Benjamin Franklin* (New Haven, CT: Yale University Press, 1959–), Massachusetts Board of War to Franklin, May 8, 1778, 26: 420–21.

2. William Wirt Henry, ed., *Patrick Henry: Life, Correspondence, and Speeches* (New York: Charles Scribner's Sons, 1891; reprint, New York: Burt Franklin, 1969), 2:370, 373.

3. L. H. Butterfield, ed., *The Letters of Benjamin Rush* (Princeton, NJ: Princeton University Press, 1951), Rush to William Gordon, December 10, 1778, 1:221; Ellis Sandoz, *A Government of Laws: Political Theory, Religion, and the*

American Founding (Baton Rouge: Louisiana State University Press, 1990), 113; W. W. Abbot, ed., *The Papers of George Washington: Presidential Series* (Charlottesville: University Press of Virginia, 1987–), To the Savannah Hebrew Congregation, May 1790, 5:448–49.

4. Butterfield, *Letters of Benjamin Rush*, Rush to James Kidd, May 13, 1794, 2:748; Harold C. Syrett, ed., *The Papers of Alexander Hamilton* (New York: Columbia University Press, 1961–1979), John Jay to Hamilton, September 17, 1794, 17:240; Julian P. Boyd, ed., *The Papers of Thomas Jefferson* (Princeton, NJ: Princeton University Press, 1950–), John Dickinson to Jefferson, February 21, 1801, 33:32.

5. Eran Shalev, *American Zion: The Old Testament as a Political Text from the Revolution to the Civil War* (New Haven, CT: Yale University Press, 2013), 128–31, 135.

6. Harry Alonzo Cushing, ed., *The Writings of Samuel Adams* (New York: Octagon, 1968), Adams to Reverend Unidentified Correspondent, November 11, 1765, 1:27; Address of the House of Representatives of Massachusetts to the Governor, June 3, 1766, 1:74–75; Jonathan Den Hartog, "John Jay and the 'Great Plan of Providence,'" in Daniel L. Dreisbach et al., eds., *The Forgotten Founders on Religion and Public Life* (South Bend, IN: University of Notre Dame Press, 2009), 145; George Bancroft, *A History of the United States of America from the Discovery of the American Continent* (Boston: Little, Brown, 1854–1878).

7. John P. Kaminsky et al., eds., *The Documentary History of the Ratification of the Constitution* (Madison: State Historical Society of Wisconsin, 1976–2008), George Washington to the Executives of the States, *United States Chronicle*, March 1783, 13:62–63.

8. Boyd, *Papers of Thomas Jefferson*, First Inaugural Address, March 4, 1801, 33:150; Charles B. Sanford, *The Religious Life of Thomas Jefferson* (Charlottesville: University Press of Virginia, 1984), 95; Albert Ellery Bergh and Andrew A. Lipscomb, eds. *The Writings of Thomas Jefferson* (Washington, DC: Thomas Jefferson Memorial Association, 1904), Second Inaugural Address, 1805, 17:iv.

9. Stanislaus Murray Hamilton, ed., *The Writings of James Monroe* (New York: A.M.S., 1969), To the Speakers of the House of Delegates and the Senate, December 7, 1801, 3:304; Inaugural Address, March 4, 1817, 6:14; Fourth Annual Message, November 14, 1820, 6:156–57.

10. Henry, *Patrick Henry*, 2:195; Syrett, *Papers of Alexander Hamilton*, Tully No. IV, *American Daily Advertiser*, September 2, 1794, 17:180; John C. Fitzpatrick, ed., *The Writings of George Washington* (Washington, DC: Government Printing Office, 1931–1940), Sixth Annual Message to Congress, November 19, 1794, 34:37; Charles F. Hobson, ed., *The Papers of John Marshall* (Chapel Hill:

University of North Carolina Press, 1974–2006), Address, December 6, 1799, 4:40.

11. Moncure Daniel Conway, ed., *The Writings of Thomas Paine* (New York: Burt Franklin, 1969), The American Philosophical Society, February 14, 1780, 2:26; Hobson, *Papers of John Marshall*, Speech, December 19, 1799, 4:47.

12. Carl E. Prince, ed., *The Papers of William Livingston* (Trenton: New Jersey Historical Commission, 1979–1988), To the Legislature, September 11, 1776, 1:145; Butterfield, *Letters of Benjamin Rush*, Rush to John Adams, February 24, 1790, 1:534; Abbot, *Papers of George Washington: Presidential Series*, Washington to Samuel Langdon, September 28, 1789, 4:104.

13. Robert A. Rutland, ed., *The Papers of George Mason* (Chapel Hill: University of North Carolina Press, 1970), Letter of "Atticus," May 11, 1769, 1:107; Henry, *Patrick Henry*, 1:265; Cushing, *Writings of Samuel Adams*, Adams to Joseph Nye, February 21, 1775, 3:181–82; Adams to Joseph Palmer, April 2, 1776, 3:273.

14. W. W. Abbot, ed., *The Papers of George Washington: Revolutionary War Series* (Charlottesville: University Press of Virginia, 1985–), Address to the Massachusetts General Court, April 1, 1776, 4:9; General Orders, August 13, 1776, 6:1; August 14, 1776, 6:18.

15. Thomas Miller, ed., *The Selected Writings of John Witherspoon* (Carbondale: Southern Illinois University Press, 1990), "The Dominion of Providence over the Passions of Men," May 17, 1776, 138; Butterfield, *Letters of Benjamin Rush*, Rush to Julia Rush, May 29, 1776, 1:99; Rush to William Gordon, December 10, 1778, 1:222.

16. Prince, *Papers of William Livingston*, To the Assembly, October 5, 1776, 1:162; September 3, 1777, 2:52; Adolphus, *New York Gazette*, January 21, 1778, 2:189; Hortensius, *New York Gazette*, January 21, 1778, 2:201; Livingston to Baron van der Capellen, November 30, 1778, 2:490.

17. Fitzpatrick, *Writings of George Washington*, Washington to John Parke Custis, January 22, 1777, 7:53; Washington to General Samuel Holden Parsons, April 23, 1777, 7:456; General Orders, October 18, 1777, 9:391.

18. Ibid., General Orders, May 8, 1778, 11:342–43; Washington to Landon Carter, May 30, 1778, 11:492; Washington to John Augustine Washington, July 4, 1778, 12:156–57; Washington to General Thomas Nelson, August 20, 1778, 12:343; Washington to Benjamin Harrison, December 18, 1778, 13:468; Washington to Joseph Reed, July 29, 1779, 16:10.

19. Ibid., General Orders, September 26, 1780, 20:95; Washington to Henry Laurens, October 13, 1780, 20:173; L. H. Butterfield, ed., *The Letters of Benjamin Rush* (Princeton, NJ: Princeton University Press, 1951), Rush to John Adams, October 23, 1780, 1:255; Cushing, *Writings of Samuel Adams*, Adams to John Adams, December 17, 1780, 4:233.

20. Fitzpatrick, *Writings of George Washington*, Washington to the Reverend William Gordon, March 9, 1781, 21:332; Circular to New Jersey, Delaware, and Maryland, September 3, 1781, 23:81–82; Washington to James McHenry, July 18, 1782, 24:432.

21. Ibid., Washington to the Inhabitants of Princeton, August 25, 1783, 27:116; Washington to Comte de Rochambeau, October 15, 1783, 27:191; Farewell Orders to the Armies of the United States, November 2, 1783, 27:223.

22. Boyd, *Papers of Thomas Jefferson*, George Washington's Resignation as Commander-in-Chief, December 23, 1783, 6:406, 411–12; Paul F. Boller, *George Washington and Religion* (Dallas, TX: Southern Methodist University Press, 1963), 107; Fitzpatrick, *Writings of George Washington*, Washington to Jonathan Williams, March 2, 1795, 34:130.

23. Hartog, "John Jay," 157; Cushing, *Writings of Samuel Adams*, Adams to Horatio Gates, October 1777, 3:414; Kate M. Rowland, ed., *The Life and Correspondence of George Mason* (New York: Russell and Russell, 1964), 1:300; Boyd, *Papers of Thomas Jefferson*, Proclamation Appointing a Day of Thanksgiving and Prayer, November 11, 1779, 3:177–78.

24. Conway, *Writings of Thomas Paine*, "The Dream Interpreted," June 1775, 1:50; "Thoughts on Defensive War," July 1775, 1:55; "A Dialogue," 1776, 1:167; "Crisis I," December 19, 1776, 1:176; "Crisis II," January 13, 1777, 1:188.

25. Ibid., Preamble to the Act Passed by the Pennsylvania Assembly, March 1, 1780, 2:29; "Public Good," 1780, 2:33.

26. Henry, *Patrick Henry*, 2:550–51; 3:610–11; Kaminsky et al., *Documentary History*, Luther Martin, Address No. IV, *Maryland Journal*, April 4, 1788, 17:20.

27. Alfred Owen Aldridge, *Benjamin Franklin and Nature's God* (Durham, NC: Duke University Press, 1967), 43; Mark A. Noll, *Christians in the American Revolution* (Washington, DC: Christian University Press, 1977), 68; Boyd, *Papers of Thomas Jefferson*, Jefferson to Maria Cosway, October 12, 1786, 10:451; Response to the Address of Welcome, March 11, 1790, 16:225; Douglass Adair and John A. Schutz, eds., *The Spur of Fame: Dialogues of John Adams and Benjamin Rush, 1805–1813* (San Marino, CA: Huntington Library, 1966), Adams to Rush, August 28, 1811, 191; Rush to Adams, June 4, 1812, 223; George W. Corner, ed., *The Autobiography of Benjamin Rush: His "Travels Through Life" Together with His Commonplace Book for 1789–1813* (Princeton, NJ: Princeton University Press, 1948), 155.

28. Boller, *George Washington and Religion*, 98, 147; Kaminsky et al., *Documentary History*, George Washington to the Marquis de Lafayette, May 28, 1788, 18:82–83; George Washington to Benjamin Lincoln, June 29, 1788, 18:208; George Washington to Jonathan Trumbull Jr., July 20, 1788, 18:274–75.

29. Abbot, *Papers of George Washington: Presidential Series*, To the Mayor, Recorder, Aldermen, and Common Council of Philadelphia, April 20, 1789, 2:83–84.

30. Ibid., First Inaugural Address, April 30, 1789, 2:174; Thanksgiving Proclamation, October 3, 1789, 4:132.

31. Ibid., Charles Thomson to Washington, December 25, 1789, 4:442.

32. Max Farrand, ed., *The Records of the Federal Convention of 1787*, 3rd ed. (New Haven, CT: Yale University Press, 1966), Benjamin Franklin to the Editor of the *Federal Gazette*, April 8, 1788, 3:297.

33. Kaminsky et al., *Documentary History*, The Pennsylvania Convention, December 12, 1787, 2:595; Benjamin Rush to Jeremy Belknap, May 6, 1788, 17:391; Benjamin Rush, Observations on the Fourth of July Procession in Philadelphia, *Pennsylvania Mercury*, July 15, 1788, 18:266.

34. Ibid., Publius, *Federalist* No. 2, *New York Independent Journal*, October 31, 1787, 13:518; David Ramsay Oration, *Charleston Columbian Herald*, June 5, 1788, 18:160; Hartog, "John Jay," 163; Syrett, *Papers of Alexander Hamilton*, New York Ratifying Convention, Second Speech of July 17, 1788, 5:177; George W. Carey and James McClellan, eds., *The Federalist* (Indianapolis, IN: Liberty Fund, 2001), *Federalist* No. 37, 184–85.

35. David B. Mattern, ed., *James Madison's "Advice to My Country"* (Charlottesville: University Press of Virginia, 1997), Madison to Thomas Jefferson, October 24, 1787, 27.

36. John Witte Jr., "'A Most Mild and Equitable Establishment of Religion': John Adams and the Massachusetts Experiment," in James H. Hutson, ed., *Religion in the New Republic: Faith in the Founding of America* (Lanham, MD: Rowman & Littlefield, 2000), 30.

37. Dagobert D. Runes, ed., *The Selected Writings of Benjamin Rush* (New York: The Philosophical Library, 1947; reprint, Omaha: The Classics of Liberty Library, 2012), "On Slave Keeping," 1773, 18.

38. Conway, *Writings of Thomas Paine*, African Slavery in America, March 8, 1775, 1:7–8; A Serious Political Thought, October 1775, 1:65–66.

39. William Peden, ed., *Notes on the State of Virginia* (Chapel Hill: University of North Carolina Press, 1955), 163; Bergh and Lipscomb, *Writings of Thomas Jefferson*, Jefferson to Jean Nicholas Demeunier, January 24, 1786, 17:103.

40. Richard B. Morris, ed., *John Jay: The Making of a Revolutionary, Unpublished Papers, 1745–1780* (New York: Harper and Row, 1975), Jay to Egbert Benson, September 18, 1780, 1:823.

41. Kaminsky et al., *Documentary History*, A Countryman II, *New York Journal*, December 13, 1787, 19:409.

42. Rutland, *Papers of George Mason*, Constitutional Convention, August 22, 1787, 3:966.

43. George Adams Boyd, *Elias Boudinot: Patriot and Statesman, 1740–1821* (Princeton, NJ: Princeton University Press, 1952), 182.

44. Shalev, *American Zion*, 189–90.

45. Robert G. Ferris, *Signers of the Declaration: Historic Places Commemorating the Signing of the Declaration of Independence* (Washington, DC: National Park Service, 1973), 31; Jeffry H. Morrison, *John Witherspoon and the Founding of the American Republic* (South Bend, IN: University of Notre Dame Press, 2005), 73.

6. RELIGION, MORALITY, AND REPUBLICANISM

1. Henry C. Montgomery, "Washington the Stoic," *Classical Journal* 31 (March 1936): 371–72; James Thomas Flexner, *George Washington* (Boston: Little, Brown, 1965–1969), 1:241.

2. Zoltan Haraszti, *John Adams and the Prophets of Progress* (Cambridge, MA: Harvard University Press, 1972), 60; L. Jesse Lemisch, ed., *Benjamin Franklin: The Autobiography and Other Writings* (New York: Penguin Books, 1961), *Autobiography*, 95. Franklin characterized his own youthful use of the Socratic method as "put[ting] on the humble enquirer" in order to draw people into self-contradiction, which demonstrates that on some level he recognized Socratic humility as a sham. See 30–31.

3. Wilson Smith, ed., *Theories of Education in Early America, 1655–1819* (New York: Bobbs-Merrill, 1973), John Witherspoon, *Letters on Education*, 1765, 219.

4. Thomas Miller, ed., *The Selected Writings of John Witherspoon* (Carbondale: Southern Illinois University Press, 1990), "Christian Magnanimity," 1775, 124–25.

5. Julian P. Boyd, ed., *The Papers of Thomas Jefferson* (Princeton, NJ: Princeton University Press, 1950–), "Notes on the Doctrine of Epicurus," 1799, 31:285; Albert Ellery Bergh and Andrew A. Lipscomb, eds., *The Writings of Thomas Jefferson* (Washington, DC: Thomas Jefferson Memorial Association, 1904), Jefferson to William Short, August 4, 1820, 15:259.

6. Gordon S. Wood, *Revolutionary Characters: What Made the Founders Different* (New York: Penguin, 2006), 37; Garry Wills, *Cincinnatus: George Washington and the Enlightenment* (Garden City, NY: Doubleday, 1984).

7. Boyd, *Papers of Thomas Jefferson*, Jefferson to Maria Cosway, October 12, 1786, 10:451; Jefferson to Moses Robinson, March 23, 1801, 33:424; Bergh and Lipscomb, *Writings of Thomas Jefferson*, Jefferson to Benjamin Rush, April

21, 1803, 10:383, 385; Jefferson to Samuel Kercheval, January 19, 1810, 12:345; Jefferson to Charles Thomson, January 9, 1816, 14:385; Jefferson to Ezra Stiles, June 25, 1819, 15:203; Jefferson to William Short, October 31, 1819, 15:219, 223–24; April 13, 1820, 15:244; Lester J. Cappon, ed., *The Adams-Jefferson Letters: The Complete Correspondence between Thomas Jefferson and Abigail and John Adams* (Chapel Hill: University of North Carolina Press, 1959), Jefferson to John Adams, October 12, 1813, 2:384; Merrill D. Peterson, *Thomas Jefferson and the New Nation: A Biography* (Oxford: Oxford University Press, 1970), 53; Jeffry H. Morrison, *John Witherspoon and the Founding of the American Republic* (South Bend, IN: University of Notre Dame Press, 2005), 37.

8. Lemisch, *Benjamin Franklin*, Franklin to Ezra Stiles, March 9, 1790, 337; Leonard W. Labaree et al., eds., *The Papers of Benjamin Franklin* (New Haven, CT: Yale University Press, 1959–), "The Busy-Body" Number 3, February 18, 1729, 1:120; Alfred Owen Aldridge, *Benjamin Franklin and Nature's God* (Durham, NC: Duke University Press, 1967), 135; Thomas J. Woody, ed., *Educational Views of Benjamin Franklin* (New York: McGraw-Hill, 1931), Franklin to Mary Hewson, June 11, 1760, 101.

9. L. H. Butterfield, ed., *The Letters of Benjamin Rush* (Princeton, NJ: Princeton University Press, 1951), Rush to Jeremy Belknap, April 5, 1791, 1:579; Rush to Julia Rush, September 30, 1793, 2:688; Dagobert D. Runes, ed., *The Selected Writings of Benjamin Rush* (New York: The Philosophical Library, 1947; reprint, Omaha: The Classics of Liberty Library, 2012), "A Plan of a Peace Office for the United States," 1799, 20; George W. Corner, ed., *The Autobiography of Benjamin Rush: His "Travels through Life" Together with His Commonplace Book for 1789–1813* (Princeton, NJ: Princeton University Press, 1948), *Autobiography*, 1800, 165; *Commonplace Book*, 1809, 334.

10. Moncure Daniel Conway, ed., *The Writings of Thomas Paine* (New York: Burt Franklin, 1969), *The Rights of Man*, 1791, 2:306.

11. L. H. Butterfield, ed., *The Diary and Autobiography of John Adams* (Cambridge, MA: Harvard University Press, 1962), Diary, February 22, 1756, 1:9; Haraszti, *John Adams and the Prophets of Progress*, 194, 218, 245–46.

12. Haraszti, *John Adams and the Prophets of Progress*, 302; Cappon, *Adams-Jefferson Letters*, John Adams to Jefferson, July 16, 1813, 2:359; February 2, 1816, 2:462; November 4, 1816, 2:494; Bergh and Lipscomb, *Writings of Thomas Jefferson*, John Adams to Jefferson, April 19, 1817, 15:106.

13. Labaree et al., *Papers of Benjamin Franklin*, John Adams to Franklin, April 16, 1781, 34:552; Haraszti, *John Adams and the Prophets of Progress*, 284; Butterfield, *Diary and Autobiography of John Adams*, *Autobiography*, 3:434–35; Broadus Mitchell, *Alexander Hamilton: The National Adventure, 1788–1804* (New York: Macmillan, 1962), 537.

14. Aldridge, *Benjamin Franklin and Nature's God*, 172; Lorraine Smith Pangle and Thomas L. Pangle, *The Learning of Liberty: The Educational Ideas of the American Founders* (Lawrence: University Press of Kansas, 1993), 275; Wood, *Revolutionary Characters*, 85; Walter Isaacson, *Benjamin Franklin: An American Life* (New York: Simon and Schuster, 2003), 471.

15. Butterfield, *Letters of Benjamin Rush*, Rush to John Adams, February 24, 1790, 1:533–34; Rush to Thomas Smith, February 26, 1790, 1:537; May 12, 1807, 2:944; Corner, *Autobiography of Benjamin Rush, Commonplace Book*, 1808, 323.

16. Butterfield, *Letters of Benjamin Rush*, Rush to John Adams, December 6, 1811, 2:1110.

17. Jean M. Yarbrough, *American Virtues: Thomas Jefferson and the Character of a Free People* (Lawrence: University Press of Kansas, 1998), 52.

18. William Wirt Henry, ed., *Patrick Henry: Life, Correspondence, and Speeches* (New York: Charles Scribner's Sons, 1891; reprint, New York: Burt Franklin, 1969), 3:606–7; David A. McCants, *Patrick Henry, The Orator* (Westport, CT: Greenwood, 1990), 72, 91.

19. Charles E. Prince, ed., *The Papers of William Livingston* (Trenton: New Jersey Historical Commission, 1979–1988), Livingston to Henry Laurens, May 7, 1778, 2:329; Livingston to the New Jersey Assembly, May 29, 1778, 2:351.

20. Ibid., Livingston to Samuel Allinson, July 25, 1778, 2:401.

21. Conway, *Writings of Thomas Paine, Common Sense*, 1776, 1:100.

22. James Curtis Ballagh, ed., *The Letters of Richard Henry Lee* (New York: Macmillan, 1911–1914; reprint, New York: Da Capo Press, 1970), Lee to Thomas Lee Shippen, April 15, 1793, 2:556–57.

23. Lemisch, *Benjamin Franklin, Autobiography*, 102.

24. Conway, *Writings of Thomas Paine, The Age of Reason*, 1794–1795, 4:26, 187–88.

25. W. W. Abbot, ed., *The Papers of George Washington: Presidential Series* (Charlottesville: University Press of Virginia, 1987–), Washington to the Congregational Ministers of New Haven, October 17, 1789, 4:198; Washington to the Synod of the Dutch Reformed Church in North America, October 1789, 4:264; Saul K. Padover, ed., *The Washington Papers: Basic Selections from the Public and Private Writings of George Washington* (New York: Grosset & Dunlap, 1967), Farewell Address, September 19, 1796, 318–19.

26. Miller, *Selected Writings of John Witherspoon*, "Christian Magnanimity," 1775, 144; *Lectures on Moral Philosophy*, 1774, 212; Milton E. Flower, *John Dickinson: Conservative Revolutionary* (Charlottesville: University Press of Virginia, 1983), 285; Ballagh, *Letters of Richard Henry Lee*, Lee to James Madison, November 26, 1784, 2:304.

27. Labaree et al., *Papers of Benjamin Franklin*, "Poor Richard," 1739 and 1751, 2:224; 4:96; "Appeal for the Hospital," August 8, 1751, 4:151; Franklin to Unidentified Correspondent, December 13, 1757, 7:294–95. Some have suggested that the unidentified correspondent was Thomas Paine, that the time was the 1780s, and that the manuscript was an early version of *The Age of Reason.* But the date of 1757 is fairly well attested, so that it could not have been Paine, who was only twenty years old then and not yet a writer. Furthermore, Franklin states that the author of the manuscript disbelieves in Providence, which was not true of Paine even in later years.

28. Lemisch, *Benjamin Franklin, Autobiography*, 37.

29. Edwin S. Gaustad, *Faith of Our Fathers: Religion and the New Nation* (San Francisco: Harper & Row, 1987), 79, 92; Linda K. Kerber, *Federalists in Dissent: Imagery and Ideology in Jeffersonian America* (Ithaca, NY: Cornell University Press, 1970), 208; Daniel Boorstin, *The Lost World of Thomas Jefferson* (New York: Henry Holt, 1948), 156; Haraszti, *John Adams and the Prophets of Progress*, 291.

30. Harry Alonzo Cushing, ed., *The Writings of Samuel Adams* (New York: Octagon, 1968), Adams to Richard Henry Lee, December 23, 1784, 4:311.

31. Frederick Rudolph, ed., *Essays on Education in the Early Republic* (Cambridge, MA: Harvard University Press, 1965), Benjamin Rush, "A Plan for the Establishment of Public Schools and the Diffusion of Knowledge in Pennsylvania," 1786, 11.

32. Butterfield, *Letters of Benjamin Rush*, Rush to John Coakley Lettsom, September 28, 1787, 1:441; "To the Ministers of the Gospel of All Denominations: An Address upon Subjects Interesting to Morals," June 21, 1788, 1:466.

33. Ibid., To American Farmers about to Settle in New Parts of the United States, March 1789, 1:505; Rush to James Kidd, November 25, 1793, 2:746; Rush to Noah Webster, July 20, 1798, 2:799; Runes, *Selected Writings of Benjamin Rush*, The Bible as a School Book, 1791, 130.

34. Corner, *Autobiography of Benjamin Rush*, *Autobiography*, 52; *Commonplace Book*, 1807, 272; Butterfield, *Letters of Benjamin Rush*, Rush to Ashbel Green, December 9, 1802, 2:854; Rush to John Adams, April 1, 1809, 2:1002; Rush to James Rush, October 4, 1810, 2:1069.

35. Butterfield, *Letters of Benjamin Rush*, Rush to John Adams, July 21, 1789, 1:523; Rush to Elhanan Winchester, November 12, 1791, 1:611; Rush to Jeremy Belknap, June 21, 1792, 1:620; Boyd, *Papers of Thomas Jefferson*, Benjamin Rush to Jefferson, August 22, 1800, 32:111.

36. Douglass Adair and John A. Schutz, eds., *The Spur of Fame: Dialogues of John Adams and Benjamin Rush, 1805–1813* (San Marino, CA: Huntington Library, 1966), Rush to Adams, August 20, 1811, 190.

37. Adair and Schutz, *Spur of Fame*, Adams to Rush, August 28, 1811, 192; Cappon, *Adams-Jefferson Letters*, John Adams to Jefferson, April 19, 1817, 2:509.

38. Robert Green McCloskey, ed., *The Works of James Wilson* (Cambridge, MA: Harvard University Press, 1967), *Lectures on Law*, 1790–1791, 1:143–44.

39. Boyd, *Papers of Thomas Jefferson*, Jefferson to Peter Carr, August 10, 1787, 12:16–17; Eleanor Davis Berman, *Thomas Jefferson among the Arts: An Essay in Early American Esthetics* (New York: Philosophical Library, 1947), 24; Charles B. Sanford, *The Religious Life of Thomas Jefferson* (Charlottesville: University Press of Virginia, 1984), 145.

40. Harold C. Syrett, ed., *The Papers of Alexander Hamilton* (New York: Columbia University Press, 1961–1979), "Views on the French Revolution," 1794, 26:738–39; "The Stand No. III," April 7, 1798, 21:403–5; Hamilton to James Bayard, April 1802, 25:606.

41. Henry, *Patrick Henry*, 2:591–92.

42. Eric Nelson, *The Hebrew Republic: Jewish Sources and the Transformation of European Political Thought* (Cambridge, MA: Harvard University Press, 2010), 138–39.

43. Henry, *Patrick Henry*, 2:632.

44. John P. Kaminsky et al., eds., *The Documentary History of the Ratification of the Constitution* (Madison: State Historical Society of Wisconsin, 1976–2008), James Madison to Thomas Jefferson, October 24, 1787, 13:448; Richard B. Mattern, ed., *James Madison's "Advice to My Country"* (Charlottesville: University Press of Virginia, 1997), Madison to Frederick Beasley, November 29, 1825, 51.

45. Conway, *Writings of Thomas Paine*, *The Age of Reason*, 1794–1795, 4:21, 184–85, 190.

7. OTHER SHARED BELIEFS

1. Henry Chadwick, *The Early Church* (Baltimore: Penguin, 1969), 58–59.

2. Ibid., 59–60.

3. David Brion Davis, *Challenging the Boundaries of Slavery* (Cambridge, MA: Harvard University Press, 2003), 10, 25.

4. Stanislaus Murray Hamilton, ed., *The Writings of James Monroe* (New York: A.M.S., 1969), To the Speakers of the House of Delegates and the Senate, December 7, 1801, 3:304.

5. John C. Miller, *The Wolf by the Ears: Thomas Jefferson and Slavery* (New York: Free Press, 1977), 14.

6. Thomas Miller, ed., *The Selected Writings of John Witherspoon* (Carbondale: Southern Illinois University Press, 1990), *Lectures on Moral Philosophy*, 1774, 192, 198; Jeffry H. Morrison, *John Witherspoon and the Founding of the American Republic* (South Bend, IN: University of Notre Dame Press, 2005), 76; Charles E. Prince, ed., *The Papers of William Livingston* (Trenton: New Jersey Historical Commission, 1979–1988), Livingston to Samuel Allinson, July 25, 1778, 2:403; Moncure Daniel Conway, ed., *The Writings of Thomas Paine* (New York: Burt Franklin, 1969), Preamble to the Act Passed by the Pennsylvania Assembly, March 1, 1780, 2:29–30; L. H. Butterfield, ed., *The Letters of Benjamin Rush* (Princeton, NJ: Princeton University Press, 1951), Rush to Jeremy Belknap, August 19, 1788, 1:483; Walter Isaacson, *Benjamin Franklin: An American Life* (New York: Simon and Schuster, 2003), 465; Jonathan Den Hartog, "John Jay and 'the Great Plan of Providence,'" in Daniel L. Dreisbach et al., eds., *The Forgotten Founders on Religion and Public Life* (South Bend, IN: University of Notre Dame Press, 2009), 164; David L. Holmes, *The Faiths of the Founding Fathers* (Oxford: Oxford University Press, 2006), 156.

7. Conway, *Writings of Thomas Paine*, *The Rights of Man*, 1791, 2:304–6.

8. Edmund S. Morgan, "The Puritan Ethic and the American Revolution," *William and Mary Quarterly* 24 (January 1967): 23; Miller, *Wolf by the Ears*, 5; Julian P. Boyd, ed., *The Papers of Thomas Jefferson* (Princeton, NJ: Princeton University Press, 1950–), "A Summary View of the Rights of British America," July 1774, 1:130.

9. William Peden, ed., *Notes on the State of Virginia* (Chapel Hill: University of North Carolina Press, 1955), 138–43, 162; Daniel Boorstin, *The Lost World of Thomas Jefferson* (New York: Henry Holt, 1948), 73–74; Charles B. Sanford, *The Religious Life of Thomas Jefferson* (Charlottesville: University Press of Virginia, 1984), 98.

10. Albert Ellery Bergh and Andrew A. Lipscomb, eds., *The Writings of Thomas Jefferson* (Washington, DC: Thomas Jefferson Memorial Association, 1904), Jefferson to Henri Gregoire, February 25, 1809, 12:255; Sanford, *Religious Life of Thomas Jefferson*, 70.

11. Gordon S. Wood, *Revolutionary Characters: What Made the Founders Different* (New York: Penguin, 2006), 39–40.

12. Peden, *Notes on the State of Virginia*, 93; David A. McCants, *Patrick Henry, The Orator* (Westport, CT: Greenwood, 1990), 72.

13. Conway, *Writings of Thomas Paine*, *The Rights of Man*, 1791, 2:304; *Agrarian Justice*, 1797, 3:327; Saul K. Padover, ed., *The Complete Jefferson: Containing His Major Writings, Published and Unpublished, Except His Letters* (New York: Duell, Sloan, and Pearce, 1943), Jefferson to John Cartwright, June 5, 1824, 296; Adrienne Koch, *Jefferson and Madison: The Great Collaboration* (Oxford: Oxford University Press, 1950), 70–75.

14. Leonard W. Labaree et al., eds., *The Papers of Benjamin Franklin* (New Haven, CT: Yale University Press, 1959–), "A Narrative of the Late Massacres," 1764, 11:55–56, 66.

15. Dagobert D. Runes, ed., *The Selected Writings of Benjamin Rush* (New York: The Philosophical Library, 1947; reprint, Omaha: The Classics of Liberty Library, 2012), "On Slave Keeping," 1773, 4–6.

16. Ibid., 8–9.

17. Ibid., 9.

18. Ibid., 10–11, 13.

19. Nathan G. Goodman, *Benjamin Rush: Physician and Citizen, 1746–1813* (Philadelphia: University of Pennsylvania Press, 1934), 298–99.

20. Conway, *Writings of Thomas Paine*, African Slavery in America, March 8, 1775, 1:5–6, 8–9.

21. Thomas J. Woody, ed., *Educational Views of Benjamin Franklin* (New York: McGraw-Hill, 1931), "On the Slave Trade," *Federal Gazette*, March 25, 1790, 241–44.

22. Boyd, *Papers of Thomas Jefferson*, A Bill for the Establishment of Religious Freedom, 1779, 2:545; Lester J. Cappon, ed., *The Adams-Jefferson Letters: The Complete Correspondence between Thomas Jefferson and Abigail and John Adams* (Chapel Hill: University of North Carolina Press, 1959), Jefferson to John Adams, April 11, 1823, 2:591; Bergh and Lipscomb, *Writings of Thomas Jefferson*, Jefferson to Benjamin Waterhouse, June 26, 1822, 15:384–85.

23. L. H. Butterfield, ed., *The Earliest Diary of John Adams* (Cambridge, MA: Harvard University Press, 1966), August 22, 1756, 338; L. H. Butterfield, ed., *The Diary and Autobiography of John Adams* (Cambridge, MA: Harvard University Press, 1961), *Autobiography*, 3:262.

24. Cappon, *Adams-Jefferson Letters*, Adams to Jefferson, September 14, 1813, 2:374; February 24, 1819, 2:534; Bergh and Lipscomb, *Writings of Thomas Jefferson*, John Adams to Jefferson, December 21, 1819, 15:236.

25. Isaacson, *Benjamin Franklin*, 45; Labaree et al., *Papers of Benjamin Franklin*, "A Dissertation on Liberty and Necessity," 1725, 57–71; "On the Providence of God in the Government of the World," 1732, 1:267, 269.

26. George W. Corner, ed., *The Autobiography of Benjamin Rush: His "Travels through Life" Together with His Commonplace Book for 1789–1813* (Princeton, NJ: Princeton University Press, 1948), *Commonplace Book*, 1791, 193.

27. Conway, *Writings of Thomas Paine*, "Examination of Prophecies," 1806, 4:358–59.

28. Barry Alan Shain, *The Myth of American Individualism: The Protestant Origins of American Political Thought* (Princeton, NJ: Princeton University Press, 1994), 130.

29. Charles Page Smith, *James Wilson: Founding Father, 1742–1799* (Chapel Hill: University of North Carolina Press, 1956), 28.

30. Mark A. Noll, *Christians in the American Revolution* (Washington, DC: Christian University Press, 1977), 66.

31. For a lengthier discussion of the advantages that Christianity possessed in its contest against paganism, see Carl J. Richard, *Why We're All Romans: The Roman Contribution to the Western World* (Lanham, MD: Rowman & Littlefield, 2010), 260–69.

32. Ibid., 159, 241.

33. Conway, *Writings of Thomas Paine, The Age of Reason*, 1791, 4:83, 179; "Examination of Prophecies," 1806, 4:419–20.

34. Douglas L. Wilson, ed., *Jefferson's Literary Commonplace Book* (Princeton, NJ: Princeton University Press, 1989), 123; Boyd, *Papers of Thomas Jefferson*, Jefferson to John Page, December 25, 1762, 1:5; July 17, 1763, 1:10.

35. Boyd, *Papers of Thomas Jefferson*, Jefferson to Francis Willis, July 15, 1796, 29:153; Bergh and Lipscomb, *Writings of Thomas Jefferson*, Jefferson to John Page, June 25, 1804, 11:31; Sanford, *Religious Life of Thomas Jefferson*, 146–47.

36. Bergh and Lipscomb, *Writings of Thomas Jefferson*, Jefferson to Abigail Adams, January 11, 1817, 15:96–97; Jefferson to John Adams, November 13, 1818, 15:174; April 11, 1823, 15:430; Sanford, *Religious Life of Thomas Jefferson*, 159.

37. Bergh and Lipscomb, *Writings of Thomas Jefferson*, Jefferson to Thomas Jefferson Smith, February 21, 1825, 16:110–11; Sanford, *Religious Life of Thomas Jefferson*, 159.

38. Sanford, *Religious Life of Thomas Jefferson*, 154; Jean M. Yarbrough, *American Virtues: Thomas Jefferson and the Character of a Free People* (Lawrence: University Press of Kansas, 1998), 186.

39. Labaree et al., *Papers of Benjamin Franklin*, Epitaph, 1728, 1:111; "Doctrine to Be Preached," 1731, 1:213.

40. Ibid., "Poor Richard," 1756, 6:320–21.

41. Ibid., Franklin to Elizabeth Hubbort, February 22, 1756, 6:406–7; "Poor Richard," 1757, 7:89; Franklin to George Whitefield, June 19, 1764, 11:232; Franklin to Madame Brillon, April 20, 1781, 34:562.

42. Ibid., Franklin to James Hutton, July 7, 1782, 37:586–88; L. Jesse Lemisch, ed., *Benjamin Franklin: The Autobiography and Other Writings* (New York: Penguin, 1961), Franklin to Jane Mecom, October 19, 1789, 337; Franklin to Ezra Stiles, March 9, 1790, 337.

43. Woody, *Educational Views of Benjamin Franklin*, 35; Holmes, *Faiths of the Founding Fathers*, 68; Alfred Owen Aldridge, *Benjamin Franklin and Nature's God* (Durham, NC: Duke University Press, 1967), 267–68.

44. Harry Alonzo Cushing, ed., *The Writings of Samuel Adams* (New York: Octagon, 1968), Vindex, December 17, 1770, 2:83; January 21, 1771, 2:143; Adams to Andrew Elton Wells, October 21, 1772, 2:338; Adams to Elizabeth Adams, January 29, 1777, 3:349.

45. Butterfield, *Diary and Autobiography of John Adams*, *Autobiography*, 3:265; Adrienne Koch and William Peden, eds., *The Selected Writings of John and John Quincy Adams* (New York: Alfred A. Knopf, 1946), *Diary of John Adams*, 1770 or 1771, 30; John Adams to F. A. Vanderkemp, July 13, 1815, 193; Boyd, *Papers of Thomas Jefferson*, John Adams to Jefferson, January 31, 1796, 28:600; Cappon, *Adams-Jefferson Letters*, John Adams to Jefferson, May 3, 1816, 2:471; December 8, 1818, 2:530; January 14, 1826, 2:613.

46. Robert Green McCloskey, ed., *The Works of James Wilson* (Cambridge, MA: Harvard University Press, 1967), *Lectures on Law*, 1790–1791, 1:124.

47. Paul F. Boller, *George Washington and Religion* (Dallas, TX: Southern Methodist University Press, 1963), 111–13; Harold C. Syrett, ed., *The Papers of Alexander Hamilton* (New York: Columbia University Press, 1961–1979), Draft of Washington's Farewell Address, July 30, 1796, 20:287; Edwin S. Gaustad, *Faith of Our Fathers: Religion and the New Nation* (San Francisco: Harper and Row, 1987), 81–83.

48. William Wirt Henry, ed., *Patrick Henry: Life, Correspondence, and Speeches* (New York: Charles Scribner's Sons, 1891; reprint New York: Burt Franklin, 1969), 2:252, 286–87.

49. Richard B. Morris, ed., *John Jay: The Making of a Revolutionary, Unpublished Papers, 1745–1780* (New York: Harper and Row, 1975), Jay to Robert R. Livingston, March 4, 1776, 1:232; October 6, 1780, 2:31; Jay to Silas Deane, November 1, 1780, 2:60.

50. Ibid., Jay to Robert R. Livingston, July 19, 1783, 2:563.

51. Hartog, "John Jay," 151.

52. Robert A. Rutland et al., eds., *The Papers of James Madison* (Chicago: University of Chicago Press, 1962–1977; Charlottesville: University Press of Virginia, 1977–), Madison to William Bradford, November 9, 1772, 1:75.

53. Holmes, *Faiths of the Founding Fathers*, 102.

54. John Edward Oster, ed., *The Political and Economic Doctrines of John Marshall* (New York: Burt Franklin, 1967), Eulogy for His Wife, December 25, 1832, 205.

55. Butterfield, *Letters of Benjamin Rush*, Rush to John Montgomery, April 9, 1788, 1:456; Corner, *Autobiography of Benjamin Rush*, *Autobiography*, 1800, 56; *Commonplace Book*, 1810, 287; Runes, *Selected Writings of Benjamin Rush*, "The Vices and Virtues of Physicians," 1801, 294, 296.

56. Corner, *Autobiography of Benjamin Rush, Autobiography*, 163–64; *Commonplace Book*, 1792, 226; 1810, 343–44; Butterfield, *Letters of Benjamin Rush*, Rush to Richard Price, October 15, 1785, 1:373n7.

57. Syrett, *Papers of Alexander Hamilton*, To the *Royal Danish American Gazette*, September 6, 1772, 1:36–37; "The Soul Ascending into Bliss, in Humble Imitation of Pope's 'Dying Christian to His Soul,'" October 17, 1772, 1:38–39; Hamilton to Elizabeth Hamilton, March 16, 1801, 25:349.

58. Ibid., Statement on Impending Duel with Aaron Burr, June–July, 1804, 26:278, 280; Hamilton to Elizabeth Hamilton, July 4, 1804, 26:293; July 10, 1804, 26:308; Benjamin Moore to William Coleman, July 12, 1804, 26:315–17; David Hosack to William Coleman, August 17, 1804, 26:347. For an excellent study of the political duels common in this age, few of which were fatal to the duelists, see Joanne Freeman, *Affairs of Honor: National Politics in the New Republic* (New Haven, CT: Yale University Press, 2001).

59. Syrett, *Papers of Alexander Hamilton*, The State of New Jersey vs. Aaron Burr: Indictment for Murder, October 23, 1804, 26:348.

8. DIFFERENCES

1. Robert G. Ferris, *Signers of the Declaration: Historic Places Commemorating the Signing of the Declaration of Independence* (Washington, DC: National Parks Service, 1973), 31, 45, 68, 77, 95, 115, 122, 149; Lawrence Cremin, *American Education: The Colonial Experience, 1607–1783* (New York: Harper and Row, 1970), 298–301; Thomas Miller, ed., *The Selected Writings of John Witherspoon* (Carbondale: Southern Illinois University Press, 1990), *Lectures on Moral Philosophy*, 1774, 229.

2. John P. Kaminsky et al., eds., *The Documentary History of the Ratification of the Constitution* (Madison: State Historical Society of Wisconsin, 1976–2008), *Massachusetts Gazette*, January 11, 1788, 5:696; *Massachusetts Convention Journal*, January 14, 1788, 6:1184; *Pennsylvania Mercury*, March 8, 1788, 7:1724; "A Hint, Providence," *United States Chronicle*, March 20, 1788, 7:1727; Aedanus Burke to John Lamb, June 23, 1788, 18:55.

3. L. H. Butterfield, ed., *The Letters of Benjamin Rush* (Princeton, NJ: Princeton University Press, 1951), Rush to Ebenezer Hazard, November 18, 1765, 1:20; Rush to Mary Stockton, September 7, 1788, 1:483–84; Rush to John Adams, January 23, 1807, 2:936; August 19, 1811, 2:1094.

4. George W. Corner, ed., *The Autobiography of Benjamin Rush: His "Travels through Life" Together with His Commonplace Books for 1789–1813* (Princeton, NJ: Princeton University Press, 1948), *Commonplace Book*, 1810, 294.

5. Robert Green McCloskey, ed., *The Works of James Wilson* (Cambridge, MA: Harvard University Press, 1967), *Lectures on Law*, 1790–1791, 1:133, 143–44.

6. Richard B. Morris, ed., *John Jay: The Making of a Revolutionary, Unpublished Papers, 1745–1780* (New York: Harper and Row, 1975), Jay to Peter Augustus Jay, April 8, 1784, 2:709; Jonathan Den Hartog, "John Jay and the 'Great Plan of Providence,'" in Daniel L. Dreisbach et al., eds., *The Forgotten Founders on Religion and Public Life* (South Bend, IN: University of Notre Dame Press, 2009), 150.

7. Mark David Hall, "Roger Sherman: An Old Puritan in a New Nation," in Dreisbach et al., *Forgotten Founders on Religion and Public Life*, 259.

8. Gregg L. Frazer, "Alexander Hamilton, Theistic Rationalist," in Dreisbach et al., *Forgotten Founders on Religion and Public Life*, 117.

9. Moncure Daniel Conway, ed., *The Writings of Thomas Paine* (New York: Burt Franklin, 1969), *The Age of Reason*, 1794–1795, 4:38, 45–48, 184.

10. Ibid., 4:30, 34, 90, 103.

11. Ibid., 4:27–28, 42, 65.

12. Ibid., 4:21, 84. Paine claimed erroneously that the Bible declared that Satan had been put in a pit immediately after his rebellion against God but had escaped from it, that Jesus's ministry lasted eighteen months (instead of forty-two), that His parents were so poor that they could not afford "to pay for a bed when he was born" (a mangling of the story of the full inn), that He "suspended preaching publicly" near the end of His life, that the last book of the Bible is called "Revelation*s*," and that Paul taught that the resurrection would involve returning to our current bodies. Paine also confused the Catholic doctrine of the immaculate conception with that of the virgin birth. See 30, 39–40, 42, 177.

13. Ibid., *Examination of Prophecies*, 1806, 4:410–11.

14. Gordon S. Wood, *Revolutionary Characters: What Made the Founders Different* (New York: Penguin, 2006), 208–9, 217–18, 220.

15. Ibid., 206; Merrill D. Peterson, *Thomas Jefferson and the New Nation: A Biography* (Oxford: Oxford University Press, 1970), 712–13; Thomas P. Slaughter, ed., *Common Sense and Related Writings* (Boston: Bedford, 2001), 56.

16. L. H. Butterfield, ed., *The Diary and Autobiography of John Adams* (Cambridge, MA: Harvard University Press, 1962), *Autobiography*, 3:333; Douglass Adair and John A. Schutz, eds., *The Spur of Fame: Dialogues of John Adams and Benjamin Rush, 1805–1813* (San Marino, CA: Huntington Library, 1966), Rush to Adams, June 27, 1812, 227; David McCullough, *John Adams* (New York: Simon and Schuster, 2001), 113; Richard B. Morris, *Seven Who Shaped Our Destiny: The Founding Fathers as Revolutionaries* (New York: Harper and Row, 1973), 80.

17. Adair and Schutz, *Spur of Fame*, Adams to Rush, August 14, 1805, 32; January 21, 1810, 160; Michael Novak, "The Influence of Judaism and Christianity on the American Founding," in James H. Hutson, ed., *Religion and the New Republic: Faith in the Founding of America* (Lanham, MD: Rowman & Littlefield, 2000), 170; Lester J. Cappon, ed., *The Adams-Jefferson Letters: The Complete Correspondence between Thomas Jefferson and Abigail and John Adams* (Chapel Hill: University of North Carolina Press, 1959), John Adams to Jefferson, June 28, 1813, 2:340; Adrienne Koch and William Peden, eds., *The Selected Writings of John and John Quincy Adams* (New York: Alfred A. Knopf, 1946), John Adams to Benjamin Rush, January 21, 1810, 157; John Adams to F. A. Vanderkemp, July 13, 1815, 193; Daniel L. Dreisbach, "The Bible in the Political Rhetoric of the American Founding," *Politics and Religion* 4 (2011): 421n10.

18. Albert Ellery Bergh and Andrew A. Lipscomb, eds., *The Writings of Thomas Jefferson* (Washington, DC: Thomas Jefferson Memorial Association, 1904), John Adams to Jefferson, November 15, 1813, 13:440.

19. Harry Alonzo Cushing, ed., *The Writings of Samuel Adams* (New York: Octagon, 1968), Adams to Thomas Paine, November 30, 1802, 4:412.

20. George Adams Boyd, *Elias Boudinot: Patriot and Statesman, 1740–1821* (Princeton, NJ: Princeton University Press, 1952), 252.

21. Douglas L. Wilson, ed., *Jefferson's Literary Commonplace Book* (Princeton, NJ: Princeton University Press, 1989), 55, 156.

22. Cappon, *Adams-Jefferson Letters*, Jefferson to John Adams, January 24, 1814, 2:421.

23. Julian P. Boyd, ed., *The Papers of Thomas Jefferson* (Princeton, NJ: Princeton University Press, 1950–), Jefferson to John Jay, January 25, 1786, 9:216; Jefferson to Peter Carr, August 10, 1787, 12:15–16; Linda K. Kerber, *Federalists in Dissent: Imagery and Ideology in Jeffersonian America* (Ithaca, NY: Cornell University Press, 1970), 90.

24. Daniel Boorstin, *The Lost World of Thomas Jefferson* (New York: Henry Holt, 1948), 41–42.

25. Bergh and Lipscomb, *Writings of Thomas Jefferson*, Jefferson to Benjamin Rush, April 21, 1803, 10:382; Jefferson to Ezra Stiles, June 25, 1819, 15:203.

26. Ibid., Jefferson to William Short, August 4, 1820, 15:259.

27. Cappon, *Adams-Jefferson Letters*, Jefferson to John Adams, January 24, 1814, 2:421; April 11, 1823, 2:594; Bergh and Lipscomb, *Writings of Thomas Jefferson*, Jefferson to Benjamin Rush, April 21, 1803, 10:384; Jefferson to William Short, August 4, 1820, 15:257; Jefferson to Benjamin Waterhouse, June 26, 1822, 15:385.

28. Dickinson W. Adams, ed., *Jefferson's Extracts from the Gospels* (Princeton, NJ: Princeton University Press, 1983), 37, 125, 297; Edwin S. Gaustad, *Faith of Our Fathers: Religion and the New Nation* (San Francisco: Harper & Row, 1987), 102–3.

29. Cappon, *Adams-Jefferson Letters*, Jefferson to John Adams, October 12, 1813, 2:384; Bergh and Lipscomb, *Writings of Thomas Jefferson*, Jefferson to F. A. Van der Kemp, April 25, 1816, 15:3; Jefferson to William Short, April 13, 1820, 15:244–45; August 4, 1820, 15:259–60.

30. Alfred Owen Aldridge, *Benjamin Franklin and Nature's God* (Durham, NC: Duke University Press, 1967), 91.

31. Kaminsky et al., *Documentary History*, George Washington to the Executives of the States, *United States Chronicle*, March 1783, 13:62–63; Paul F. Boller, *George Washington and Religion* (Dallas, TX: Southern Methodist University Press, 1963), 41.

32. Robert A. Rutland et al., eds., *The Papers of James Madison* (Chicago: University of Chicago Press, 1962–1977; Charlottesville: University Press of Virginia, 1977–), "Notes on Commentary of the Bible," 1770–1773, 1:59; Harold C. Syrett, ed., *The Papers of Alexander Hamilton* (New York: Columbia University Press, 1961–1979), To the *Royal Danish American Gazette*, September 6, 1772, 1:36–37; Hartog, "John Jay," 150, 152; McCloskey, *Works of James Wilson, Lectures on Law*, 1790–1791, 1:376; Corner, *Autobiography of Benjamin Rush, Commonplace Book*, 1809, 336–37; Holmes, *Faiths of the Founding Fathers*, 152.

33. Bergh and Lipscomb, *Writings of Thomas Jefferson*, John Adams to Jefferson, September 14, 1813, 13:369; Koch and Peden, *Selected Writings of John and John Quincy Adams*, John Quincy Adams to John Adams, January 3, 1817, 292; Matthew Stewart, *Nature's God: The Heretical Origins of the American Republic* (New York: W. W. Norton, 2014), 112; Paul K. Conkin, "The Religious Pilgrimage of Thomas Jefferson," in Peter S. Onuf, ed., *Jeffersonian Legacies* (Charlottesville: University Press of Virginia, 1993), 41; Holmes, *Faiths of the Founding Fathers*, 77.

34. Leonard W. Labaree et al., eds., *The Papers of Benjamin Franklin* (New Haven, CT: Yale University Press, 1959–), Franklin's Contributions to *An Abridgment of the Book of Common Prayer*, August 5, 1773, 20:345–48; L. Jesse Lemisch, ed., *Benjamin Franklin: The Autobiography and Other Writings* (New York: Penguin Books, 1961), Franklin to Ezra Stiles, March 9, 1790, 337–38.

35. Boyd, *Papers of Thomas Jefferson*, Jefferson to J. P. P. Derieux, July 25, 1788, 13:418.

36. Bergh and Lipscomb, *Writings of Thomas Jefferson*, Jefferson to Benjamin Rush, April 21, 1803, 10:380; Jefferson to William Short, August 4, 1820, 15:261; Conkin, "Religious Pilgrimage of Thomas Jefferson," 40.

37. Cappon, *Adams-Jefferson Letters*, Jefferson to John Adams, July 5, 1814, 2:432–33.

38. Boyd, *Papers of Thomas Jefferson*, Jefferson to Joseph Priestley, March 21, 1801, 33:393; Jefferson to Elbridge Gerry, March 29, 1801, 33:491–92; Bergh and Lipscomb, *Writings of Thomas Jefferson*, Jefferson to Jared Sparks, November 4, 1820, 15:288; Jefferson to James Smith, December 8, 1822, 15:408–9.

39. Conway, *Writings of Thomas Paine*, *The Age of Reason*, 1794–1795, 4:39, 58, 188.

40. Kaminsky et al., *Documentary History*, George Washington to the Executives of the States, *United States Chronicle*, March 1783, 13:70; Boller, *George Washington and Religion*, 71–75.

41. For Nelly Custis's statement, see Holmes, *Faiths of the Founding Fathers*, 70.

42. Ibid., 91–92, 97; Rutland et al., *Papers of James Madison*, "Notes on Commentary of the Bible," 1770–1773, 1:59; Madison to William Bradford, September 25, 1773, 1:96–97n2.

43. Robert A. Rutland, ed., *The Papers of George Mason* (Chapel Hill: University of North Carolina Press, 1970), Last Will and Testament, March 20, 1773, 1:147; Miller, *Selected Writings of John Witherspoon*, "The Dominion of Providence over the Passions of Men," May 17, 1776, 138; Cushing, *Writings of Samuel Adams*, Adams to Hannah Adams, August 17, 1780, 4:201; Gary Scott Smith, "Samuel Adams: America's Puritan Revolutionary," in Dreisbach et al., *Forgotten Founders on Religion and Public Life*, 46; William Wirt Henry, ed., *Patrick Henry: Life, Correspondence, and Speeches* (New York: Charles Scribner's Sons, 1891; reprint, New York: Burt Franklin, 1969), 2:287; Mark David Hall, "Roger Sherman: An Old Puritan in a New Nation," in Dreisbach et al., *Forgotten Founders on Religion and Public Life*, 247; Richard Walsh, ed., *The Writings of Christopher Gadsden* (Columbia: University of South Carolina Press, 1966), Will, June 5, 1804, 311.

44. Holmes, *Faiths of the Founding Fathers*, 152; Boyd, *Elias Boudinot*, 293.

45. Syrett, *Papers of Alexander Hamilton*, Hamilton to Elizabeth Hamilton, July 4, 1804, 26:293; Benjamin Moore to William Coleman, July 12, 1804, 26:316–17; Broadus Mitchell, *Alexander Hamilton: The National Adventure, 1788–1804* (New York: Macmillan, 1962), 537.

46. Butterfield, *Letters of Benjamin Rush*, Rush to Ebenezer Hazard, November 7, 1764, 1:9; June 27, 1765, 1:16; Corner, *Autobiography of Benjamin Rush*, *Autobiography*, 1800, 167; *Commonplace Book*, 1797, 238–39; 1810, 343; Nathan G. Goodman, *Benjamin Rush: Physician and Citizen, 1746–1813* (Philadelphia: University of Pennsylvania Press, 1934), 299; Adams, *Jefferson's Extracts from the Gospels*, Benjamin Rush to Jefferson, August 29, 1804, 29.

47. Labaree et al., *Papers of Benjamin Franklin,* "Articles of Belief and Acts of Religion," 1728, 1:101–9; "Dialogue between Two Presbyterians," *Pennsylvania Gazette*, April 10, 1735, 2:27–30; "A Defence of the Reverend Mr. Hemphill's Observations," 1735, 2:114; Franklin to Jane Mecom, July 28, 1743, 2:385.

48. Ibid., Franklin to Joseph Huey, June 6, 1753, 4:505–6.

49. Ibid., Franklin to Lord Kames, May 3, 1760, 9:105.

50. Ibid., A New Version of the Lord's Prayer, probably late 1768, 15:301–3.

51. Lemisch, *Benjamin Franklin,* Franklin to Ezra Stiles, March 9, 1790, 337–38.

52. Boyd, *Papers of Thomas Jefferson,* "A Bill for Establishing Religious Freedom," 1779, 2:545.

53. Ibid., Jefferson to Martha Jefferson, December 11, 1783, 6:380–81.

54. Ibid., Jefferson to Peter Carr, August 10, 1787, 12:17; Boorstin, *Lost World of Thomas Jefferson,* 263n24; Bergh and Lipscomb, *Writings of Thomas Jefferson,* Jefferson to William Canby, September 18, 1813, 13:377–78; Adams, *Jefferson's Extracts from the Gospels,* Jefferson to Thomas B. Parker, May 15, 1819, 386.

55. Conway, *Writings of Thomas Paine, The Age of Reason,* 1794–1795, 4:166, 188; "Prospect Papers," 1806, 4:321.

9. HUMAN NATURE AND BALANCED GOVERNMENT

1. For the erroneous theory that Augustine was the originator of the doctrine of original sin, see, for instance, Elaine Pagels, *Adam, Eve, and the Serpent* (New York: Random House, 1988).

2. Harold C. Syrett, ed., *The Papers of Alexander Hamilton* (New York: Columbia University Press, 1961–1979), "The Farmer Refuted," February 23, 1775, 1:126; Thomas Miller, ed., *The Selected Writings of John Witherspoon* (Carbondale: Southern Illinois University Press, 1990), "The Dominion of Providence over the Passions of Men," May 17, 1776, 128–29, 141.

3. Robert J. Taylor, ed., *The Papers of John Adams* (Cambridge, MA: Harvard University Press, 1977–), "An Essay on Man's Lust for Power," August 29, 1763, 1:83; L. H. Butterfield, ed., *The Diary and Autobiography of John Adams* (Cambridge, MA: Harvard University Press, 1962), Diary, December 31, 1772, 2:75; John Adams, *A Defence of the Constitutions of Government of the United States of America* (1787–1788; reprint, New York: Da Capo, 1971), 1:322–24; Albert Ellery Bergh and Andrew A. Lipscomb, eds., *The Writings of Thomas Jefferson* (Washington, DC: Thomas Jefferson Memorial Association, 1904), John Adams to Jefferson, February 1814, 4:109.

4. Max Farrand, ed., *The Records of the Federal Convention of 1787*, 3rd ed. (New Haven, CT: Yale University Press, 1966), 1:299–300, 308, 424, 432; James H. Smylie, "Madison and Witherspoon: Theological Roots of American Political Thought," *American Presbyterians* 73 (Fall 1995): 156–57, 161.

5. Mark David Hall, "Roger Sherman: An Old Puritan in a New Nation," in Daniel L. Dreisbach et al., eds., *The Forgotten Founders on Religion and Public Life* (South Bend, IN: University of Notre Dame Press, 2009), 247, 259.

6. Richard B. Mattern, ed., *James Madison's "Advice to My Country"* (Charlottesville: University Press of Virginia, 1997), Speech to the Constitutional Convention, July 11, 1787, 79; Edward M. Burns, "The Philosophy of History of the Founding Fathers," *The Historian* 16 (Spring 1954): 168; Jeffry H. Morrison, *John Witherspoon and the Founding of the American Republic* (South Bend, IN: University of Notre Dame Press, 2005), 39; Julian P. Boyd, ed., *The Papers of Thomas Jefferson* (Princeton, NJ: Princeton University Press, 1950–), James Madison to Jefferson, October 17, 1788, 14:19; Syrett, *Papers of Alexander Hamilton, Federalist* No. 51, February 6, 1788, 4:498–99; *Federalist* No. 75, March 26, 1788, 4:630. Although Syrett provides the text of *Federalist* No. 51, he concludes that Madison, not Hamilton, was almost certainly the author.

7. Syrett, *Papers of Alexander Hamilton,* The Continentalist No. III, August 9, 1781, 2:660; *Federalist* No. 6, November 4, 1787, 4:310, 313; *Federalist* No. 15, December 1, 1787, 4:362; *Federalist* No. 34, January 5, 1788, 4:473.

8. W. W. Abbot, ed., *The Papers of George Washington: Confederation Series* (Charlottesville: University Press of Virginia, 1992–1997), Washington to John Jay, August 15, 1786, 4:212.

9. John P. Kaminsky et al., eds., *The Documentary History of the Ratification of the Constitution* (Madison: State Historical Society of Wisconsin, 1976–2008), Massachusetts Convention Debates, January 17, 1788, 6:1227–28.

10. Bernard Bailyn, *The Ideological Origins of the American Revolution,* 2nd ed. (Cambridge, MA: Harvard University Press, 1992), 345–46; Burns, "Philosophy of History of the Founding Fathers," 155.

11. For reference to Madison's alarm at and response to the Nullification Crisis, see Adrienne Koch, *Madison's "Advice to My Country"* (Princeton, NJ: Princeton University Press, 1966), 128–32.

12. Alexander Hamilton, John Jay, and James Madison, *The Federalist: A Commentary on the Constitution of the United States* (New York: Modern Library, 1941), No. 10, 58–59.

13. Syrett, *Papers of Alexander Hamilton,* "Views on the French Revolution," 1794, 26:740–41.

14. Ibid., Hamilton to James Bayard, April 1804, 25:605–6.

15. John C. Fitzpatrick, ed., *The Writings of George Washington* (Washington, DC: Government Printing Office, 1931–1940), Washington to Dr. James Anderson, December 24, 1795, 34:407.

16. Zoltan Haraszti, *John Adams and the Prophets of Progress* (Cambridge, MA: Harvard University Press, 1952), 218; John Witte Jr., "'A Most Mild and Equitable Establishment of Religion': John Adams and the Massachusetts Experiment," in James H. Hutson, ed., *Religion and the New Republic: Faith in the Founding of America* (Lanham, MD: Rowman & Littlefield, 2000), 4.

17. Mattern, *James Madison's "Advice to My Country,"* Madison to Thomas Ritchie, December 18, 1825, 80; Ralph Ketcham, *From Colony to Country: The Revolution in American Thought, 1750–1820* (New York: Macmillan, 1974), 144.

18. Adams, *A Defence*, 1:vi, 99, 181–82; 3:505.

19. Douglass Adair and John A. Schutz, eds., *The Spur of Fame: Dialogues of John Adams and Benjamin Rush, 1805–1813* (San Marino, CA: Huntington Library, 1966), Adams to Rush, September 9, 1806, 66–67.

20. Bailyn, *Ideological Origins of the American Revolution*, 369; Morrison, *John Witherspoon and the Founding of the American Republic*, 39; Smylie, "Madison and Witherspoon," 157–58.

21. Clinton Rossiter, *Seedtime of the Republic: The Origin of the American Tradition of Liberty* (New York: Harcourt, Brace, 1953), 372; Harry Alonzo Cushing, ed., *The Writings of Samuel Adams* (New York: G. P. Putnam's Sons, 1908; reprint, New York: Octagon, 1968), Adams to Elbridge Gerry, April 23, 1784, 4:302; Adams to John Adams, October 4, 1790, 4:341–43.

22. Cushing, *Writings of Samuel Adams*, Adams to John Adams, October 4, 1790, 4:343; November 25, 1790, 4:347–48; Nathan O. Hatch, *The Sacred Cause of Liberty: Republican Thought and the Millennium in Revolutionary New England* (New Haven, CT: Yale University Press, 1977), 28.

23. Dagobert D. Runes, ed., *The Selected Writings of Benjamin Rush* (New York: The Philosophical Library, 1947; reprint, Omaha: The Classics of Liberty Library, 2012), "The Influence of Physical Causes upon the Moral Faculty," 1786, 209; L. H. Butterfield, ed., *The Letters of Benjamin Rush* (Princeton, NJ: Princeton University Press, 1951), Rush to John Adams, April 13, 1790, 1:545; Rush to Jeremy Belknap, June 21, 1792, 1:620.

24. Butterfield, *Letters of Benjamin Rush*, Rush to John Montgomery, August 5, 1801, 2:837; Rush to John Adams, June 10, 1806, 2:919–20; November 7, 1812, 2:1168; Adair and Schutz, *Spur of Fame*, Rush to Adams, January 13, 1809, 127.

25. Robert Green McCloskey, ed., *The Works of James Wilson* (Cambridge, MA: Harvard University Press, 1967), *Lectures on Law*, 1790–1791, 1:376.

26. Thomas P. Slaughter, ed., *Common Sense and Related Writings* (Boston: Bedford, 2001), 74–75, 84, 113; Robert Middlekauff, *The Glorious Cause: The American Revolution, 1763–1789* (Oxford: Oxford University Press, 1982), 320; John Locke, *An Essay Concerning Human Understanding*, ed. A. D. Woozley (New York: Penguin, 1964), 12, 16–20, 89; Eric Foner, *Thomas Paine and Revolutionary America* (Oxford: Oxford University Press, 1976), 91.

27. Gordon S. Wood, *The Creation of the American Republic* (Chapel Hill: University of North Carolina Press, 1969), 201, 213, 215, 436; William Peden, ed., *Notes on the State of Virginia* (Chapel Hill: University of North Carolina Press, 1955), 165; Bergh and Lipscomb, *Writings of Thomas Jefferson*, Memoranda Taken on a Journey from Paris into the Southern Parts of France and Northern of Italy, 1787, 17:153; Richard K. Matthews, *The Radical Politics of Thomas Jefferson: A Revisionist View* (Lawrence: University Press of Kansas, 1984), 43; A. Whitney Griswold, "Jefferson's Agrarian Democracy," in Henry C. Dethloff, ed., *Thomas Jefferson and American Democracy* (Lexington, MA: D. C. Heath, 1971), 46–47.

28. Eleanor Davidson Berman, *Thomas Jefferson among the Arts: An Essay in Early American Esthetics* (New York: Philosophical Library, 1947), 25; Bergh and Lipscomb, *Writings of Thomas Jefferson*, Jefferson to DuPont de Nemours, April 24, 1816, 14:491–92; Wilson Smith, ed., *Theories on Education in Early America, 1655–1819* (New York: Bobbs-Merrill, 1973), Report of the Commissioners Appointed to Fix the Site of the University of Virginia, 1818, 326.

29. Leonard W. Labaree et al., eds., *The Papers of Benjamin Franklin* (New Haven, CT: Yale University Press, 1959–), "A Defence of the Reverend Hemphill's Observations," 1735, 2:114.

30. Ibid., Franklin to Lord Kames, May 3, 1760, 9:104n9; L. Jesse Lemisch, ed., *Benjamin Franklin: The Autobiography and Other Writings* (New York: Penguin Books, 1961), *Autobiography*, 94–105.

31. Lemisch, *Benjamin Franklin*, *Autobiography*, 99.

10. CHURCH AND STATE

1. For a more in-depth discussion of the differences between Judaic and pagan concepts of deity and their varying implications, see Carl J. Richard, *Why We're All Romans: The Roman Contribution to the Western World* (Lanham, MD: Rowman & Littlefield, 2010), 251–55.

2. Peter Brown, *Augustine of Hippo: A Biography* (Berkeley: University of California Press, 1967), 234, 237, 241; Frederick B. Artz, *The Mind of the Middle Ages, A.D. 200–1500: An Historical Survey*, 3rd ed. (New York: Alfred A. Knopf, 1962), 269; Mary Martin McLaughlin and James Bruce Ross, eds.,

The Portable Medieval Reader (New York: Viking Press, 1949), Jacob von Konigshofen, "The Cremation of the Strasbourg Jewry," 174; Bernard Gui, "The Waldensian Heretics," 215; Jeffrey Burton Russell, *A History of Medieval Christianity: Prophecy and Order* (New York: Thomas Y. Crowell, 1968), 153–57; Steven Ozment, *The Age of Reform, 1250–1550: An Intellectual and Religious History of Late Medieval and Reformation Europe* (New Haven, CT: Yale University Press, 1980), 14, 371; Mark U. Edwards Jr., *Luther's Last Battles: Politics and Polemics, 1531–1546* (Ithaca, NY: Cornell University Press, 1983), 137; Roland H. Bainton, *Here I Stand: A Life of Martin Luther* (New York: Abingdon-Cokesbury Press, 1950), 314, 379; William J. Bouwsma, *John Calvin: A Sixteenth-Century Portrait* (Oxford: Oxford University Press, 1988), 211.

3. Perry Miller, *The New England Mind* (New York: Macmillan, 1939), 1:457.

4. Perry Miller, *Errand into the Wilderness* (Cambridge, MA: Harvard University Press, 1956), 151–52; Miller, *New England Mind*, 2:129; Kenneth Lockridge, *A New England Town: The First Hundred Years* (New York: W. W. Norton, 1970), 88; Paul K. Conkin, *Puritans and Pragmatists: Eight Eminent American Thinkers* (Bloomington: Indiana University Press, 1968), 21.

5. Randall Balmer, *A Perfect Babel of Confusion: Dutch Religion and English Culture in the Middle Colonies* (Oxford: Oxford University Press, 1989), vii, 3–4; William Warren Sweet, *Religion in Colonial America* (New York: Charles Scribner's Sons, 1943), 35–38.

6. Melvin B. Endy Jr., *William Penn and Early Quakerism* (Princeton, NJ: Princeton University Press, 1973), 351–52.

7. E. Digby Baltzell, *Puritan Boston and Quaker Philadelphia: Two Protestant Ethics and the Spirit of Class Authority and Leadership* (New York: Free Press, 1979), 117–18; Sweet, *Religion in Colonial America*, 163.

8. Edwin B. Bronner, *William Penn's "Holy Experiment": The Founding of Pennsylvania, 1681–1701* (Westport, CT: Greenwood, 1978), 38.

9. Frederick Woolverton, *Colonial Anglicanism in North America* (Detroit: Wayne State University Press, 1984), 37, 41, 64; Miller, *Errand into the Wilderness*, 105–6, 108; Jon Butler, *Awash in a Sea of Faith: Christianizing the American People* (Cambridge, MA: Harvard University Press, 1990), 38–39; Sweet, *Religion in Colonial America*, 33.

10. Woolverton, *Colonial Anglicanism in North America*, 22, 52–53, 84, 87, 136, 157, 171.

11. Ibid., 189–90; Balmer, *Perfect Babel of Confusion*, 138–39; Alfred Owen Aldridge, *Benjamin Franklin and Nature's God* (Durham, NC: Duke University Press, 1967), 115; George William Pilcher, *Samuel Davies: Apostle of Dissent in Colonial Virginia* (Knoxville: University of Tennessee Press, 1971), 56.

12. Lawrence Cremin, *American Education: The Colonial Experience, 1607–1783* (New York: Harper and Row, 1970), 497; Edgar W. Knight, ed., *A Documentary History of Education in the South Before 1860* (Chapel Hill: University of North Carolina Press, 1949–1953), "In Georgia," 2:42–43; "In South Carolina," 2:45–46; John P. Kaminsky et al., eds., *The Documentary History of the Ratification of the Constitution* (Madison: State Historical Society of Wisconsin, 1976–2008), Ordinance for the Government of the Territory of the United States Northwest of the River Ohio, July 13, 1787, 1:172.

13. Thomas Miller, ed., *The Selected Writings of John Witherspoon* (Carbondale: Southern Illinois University Press, 1990), *Lectures on Moral Philosophy*, 1774, 212; Jeffry H. Morrison, *John Witherspoon and the Founding of the American Republic* (South Bend, IN: University of Notre Dame Press, 2005), 107–8; Moncure Daniel Conway, ed., *The Writings of Thomas Paine* (New York: Burt Franklin, 1969), *Common Sense*, 1776, 1:108–9; Robert A. Rutland, ed., *The Papers of George Mason* (Chapel Hill: University of North Carolina Press, 1970), Final Draft of the Virginia Declaration of Rights, June 12, 1776, 1:288.

14. Julian P. Boyd, ed., *The Papers of Thomas Jefferson* (Princeton, NJ: Princeton University Press, 1950–), Jefferson's Outline of Argument in Support of His Resolutions, 1776, 1:537; Notes on Locke and Shaftesbury, 1776, 1:544; A Bill for the Establishment of Religious Freedom, 1779, 2:545–46.

15. L. Jesse Lemsich, ed., *Benjamin Franklin: The Autobiography and Other Writings* (New York: Penguin, 1961), *Autobiography*, 21–22; Leonard W. Labaree et al., eds., *The Papers of Benjamin Franklin* (New Haven, CT: Yale University Press, 1959–), Franklin to Richard Price, October 9, 1780, 33:390; Aldridge, *Benjamin Franklin and Nature's God*, 229–30, 247–49.

16. Eric Foner, *Thomas Paine and Revolutionary America* (Oxford: Oxford University Press, 1976), 129; L. H. Butterfield, ed., *The Letters of Benjamin Rush* (Princeton, NJ: Princeton University Press, 1951), To the Citizens of Pennsylvania of German Birth and Extraction: Proposal of a German College, August 31, 1785, 1:367.

17. Robert A. Rutland et al., eds., *The Papers of James Madison* (Chicago: University of Chicago Press, 1962–1977; Charlottesville: University Press of Virginia, 1977–), Madison to William Bradford, January 24, 1774, 1:106–7n9; William Lee Miller, *The First Liberty: Religion and the American Republic* (New York: Alfred A. Knopf, 1986), 6.

18. Rutland et al., *Papers of James Madison*, "Memorial and Remonstrance against Religious Assessments," June 20, 1785, 8:299–304.

19. Rutland, *Papers of George Mason*, George Washington to Mason, October 3, 1785, 2:832.

20. Robert Douthat Meade, *Patrick Henry: Patriot in the Making* (Philadelphia: J. B. Lippincott, 1957), 247; Richard R. Beeman, *Patrick Henry: A Biogra-*

phy (New York: McGraw-Hill, 1974), 113; Thomas E. Buckley, "Patrick Henry, Religious Liberty, and the Search for Civic Virtue," in Daniel L. Dreisbach et al., eds., *The Forgotten Founders on Religion and Public Life* (South Bend, IN: University of Notre Dame Press, 2009), 132–34; David A. McCants, *Patrick Henry, The Orator* (Westport, CT: Greenwood, 1990), 23, 98–99, 344; Edwin S. Gaustad, *Faith of Our Fathers: Religion and the New Nation* (San Francisco: Harper & Row, 1987), 39; Victor Phillip Munoz, *God and the Founders: Madison, Washington, and Jefferson* (Cambridge: Cambridge University Press, 2009), 21.

21. Drew R. McCoy, *The Last of the Fathers: James Madison and the Republican Legacy* (Cambridge: Cambridge University Press, 1986), 228–29; Leonard W. Levy, *The Establishment Clause: Religion and the First Amendment* (New York: Macmillan, 1986), 55.

22. Derek H. Davis, *Religion and the Continental Congress, 1774–1789: Contributions to Original Intent* (Oxford: Oxford University Press, 2000), 65, 67–68, 77, 147, 195.

23. W. W. Abbot, ed., *The Papers of George Washington: Revolutionary War Series* (Charlottesville: University Press of Virginia, 1985–), Washington to General William Smallwood, May 26, 1777, 8:129; General Orders, June 28, 1777, 8:308; February 15, 1783, 26:135–36; March 22, 1783, 25:250; "General Instructions for the Colonels and Commanding Officers of Regiments in the Continental Service," 1777, 10:242; Munoz, *God and the Founders*, 58; Paul F. Boller, *George Washington and Religion* (Dallas, TX: Southern Methodist University Press, 1963), 49–51, 54–55.

24. Fitzpatrick, *Writings of George Washington*, General Orders, August 3, 1776, 5:551; May 31, 1777, 8:152–53; July 29, 1779, 16:13.

25. Abbot, *Papers of George Washington: Revolutionary War Series*, Instructions to Colonel Benedict Arnold, September 14, 1775, 1:459; General Orders, November 5, 1775, 2:300; Boller, *George Washington and Religion*, 124–26; John C. Miller, *Sam Adams: Pioneer in Propaganda* (Stanford, CA: Stanford University Press, 1936), 68–69.

26. Max Farrand, ed., *The Records of the Federal Convention of 1787*, 3rd ed. (New Haven, CT: Yale University Press, 1966), 2:461; Jonathan Elliot, ed., *Debates in the Several State Conventions on the Adoption of the Federal Constitution*, 2nd ed. (Washington, DC: Elliot, 1836), 4:194; Boller, *George Washington and Religion*, 149.

27. Kaminsky et al., *Documentary History*, Richard Henry Lee to Samuel Adams, October 27, 1787, 13:485; Thomas Jefferson to James Madison, December 20, 1787, 14:482.

28. Levy, *Establishment Clause*, xvi, 65, 84, 95.

29. Lorraine Smith Pangle and Thomas L. Pangle, *The Learning of Liberty: The Educational Ideas of the American Founders* (Lawrence: University Press of Kansas, 1993), 198–99; Clifford S. Griffin, *Their Brothers' Keepers: Moral Stewardship in the United States, 1800–1865* (New Brunswick, NJ: Rutgers University Press, 1981), 138.

30. Munoz, *God and the Founders*, 43; Levy, *Establishment Clause*, 118.

31. Boyd, *Papers of Thomas Jefferson*, Proclamation Appointing a Day of Prayer and Thanksgiving, November 11, 1779, 3:178; Jefferson's Policy Concerning Presents to Foreign Diplomats, April 1790, 16:358; Jefferson to the Delaware Baptist Association, July 2, 1801, 34:490; Daniel L. Dreisbach, "Thomas Jefferson, a Mammoth Cheese, and the 'Wall of Separation between Church and State,'" in James H. Hutson, ed., *Religion and the New Republic: Faith in the Founding of America* (Lanham, MD: Rowman & Littlefield, 2000), 77; Marie Kimball, *Jefferson: The Road to Glory, 1743–1776* (New York: Coward-McCann, 1943), 235; Albert Ellery Bergh and Andrew A. Lipscomb, eds., *The Writings of Thomas Jefferson* (Washington, DC: Thomas Jefferson Memorial Association, 1904), Jefferson to the Danbury Baptist Association, January 1, 1802, 16:282; Jefferson to Samuel Miller, January 23, 1808, 11:428–30.

32. Bergh and Lipscomb, *Writings of Thomas Jefferson*, Meeting of the Visitors of the University of Virginia, October 7, 1822, 19:414–15; Jefferson to Thomas Cooper, November 2, 1822, 15:405; Editor's Note, 18:iii.

33. James H. Hutson, "Thomas Jefferson's Letter to the Danbury Baptists: A Controversy Rejoined," *William and Mary Quarterly* 56 (October 1999): 785–88.

34. Thomas E. Buckley, "Reflections on a Wall," *William and Mary Quarterly* 56 (October 1999): 799.

35. Ibid., 799.

36. Richard B. Mattern, ed., *James Madison's "Advice to My Country"* (Charlottesville: University Press of Virginia, 1997), Detached Memorandum, post 1817, 87–88, 94; Levy, *Establishment Clause*, 96, 105–6, 122.

37. Lester J. Cappon, ed., *The Adams-Jefferson Letters: The Complete Correspondence between Thomas Jefferson and Abigail and John Adams* (Chapel Hill: University of North Carolina Press, 1959), John Adams to Jefferson, January 23, 1825, 2:608.

38. Butterfield, *Letters of Benjamin Rush*, Observations on the Federal Procession in Philadelphia, July 9, 1788, 1:474; "Information to Europeans Who Are Disposed to Migrate to the United States," April 16, 1790, 1:556; Boyd, *Papers of Thomas Jefferson*, Benjamin Rush to Jefferson, October 6, 1800, 32:205; George W. Corner, ed., *The Autobiography of Benjamin Rush: His "Travels through Life" Together with His Commonplace Books for 1789–1813* (Princeton, NJ: Princeton University Press, 1948), *Commonplace Book*, 1810, 339–40.

39. W. W. Abbot, ed., *The Papers of George Washington: Presidential Series* (Charlottesville: University Press of Virginia, 1987–), Washington to the Protestant Episcopalian Church, August 19, 1789, 3:497; Washington to the Society of Quakers, October 1789, 4:266; Boller, *George Washington and Religion*, 112.

40. Conway, *Writings of Thomas Paine, The Rights of Man*, 1791, 2:325–26, 515–16.

41. Kaminsky et al., *Documentary History*, Federal Farmer, Letter VI, December 25, 1787, 17:275; Editors' Note, 20:670n17; Morrison, *John Witherspoon and the Founding of the American Republic*, 24, 39; Boyd, *Papers of Thomas Jefferson*, Jefferson to Jeremiah Moore, August 14, 1800, 32:103; Munoz, *God and the Founders*, 112.

42. Miller, *First Liberty*, 37; Gaustad, *Faith of Our Fathers*, 114–17; Farrand, *Records of the Federal Convention*, 3:78; Forrest McDonald, *Novus Ordo Seclorum: The Intellectual Origins of the Constitution* (Lawrence: University Press of Kansas, 1985), 43.

43. Thomas J. Curry, *The First Freedoms: Church and State in America to the Passage of the First Amendment* (Oxford: Oxford University Press, 1986), 218–19.

44. Merrill D. Peterson, *Thomas Jefferson and the New Nation: A Biography* (Oxford: Oxford University Press, 1970), 144; Gaustad, *Faith of Our Fathers*, 120; Garry Wills, *Under God: Religion and American Politics* (New York: Simon & Schuster, 1990), 16, 25.

EPILOGUE

1. For a lengthier discussion of the interplay between Christianity and the classics in antebellum America, see Carl J. Richard, *The Golden Age of the Classics in America: Greece, Rome, and the Antebellum United States* (Cambridge, MA: Harvard University Press, 2009), 152–80.

2. John B. Boles, *The Great Revival, 1787–1805* (Lexington: University Press of Kentucky, 1972), 47, 70, 113–14, 124; Milton Rugoff, *The Beechers: An American Family in the Nineteenth Century* (New York: Harper & Row, 1981), 9.

3. Paul K. Conkin, *The Uneasy Center: Reformed Christianity in Antebellum America* (Chapel Hill: University of North Carolina Press, 1995), 45, 59, 82, 145, 277; Albert J. Raboteau, *Slave Religion: The "Invisible Institution" in the Antebellum South* (Oxford: Oxford University Press, 1978), 133; Timothy L. Smith, *Revivalism and Social Reform: American Protestantism on the Eve of the Civil War*, 2nd ed. (Baltimore: Johns Hopkins University Press, 1980), 19, 22, 36, 86, 114–15, 167; William G. McLoughlin, *Revivals, Awakenings, and Re-*

form: An Essay on Religion and Social Change in America, 1607–1977 (Chicago: University of Chicago Press, 1978), 130, 134–35; Boles, *Great Revival*, 41, 146–47; Whitney R. Cross, *The Burned-Over District: The Social and Intellectual History of Enthusiastic Religion in Western New York, 1800–1850* (New York: Octagon, 1981), 40; Rugoff, *Beechers*, 21, 23; Daniel Walker Howe, *The Political Culture of the American Whigs* (Chicago: University of Chicago Press, 1979), 157; Charles Capper and David A. Hollinger, eds., *The American Intellectual Tradition*, 3rd ed. (Oxford: Oxford University Press, 1997), Charles G. Finney, "What a Revival of Religion Is," 1835, 1:194; Sarah Grimké, *Letters on the Equality of the Sexes and the Condition of Woman*, 1838, 1:214–15, 218, 222, 225; Ronald G. Walters, *American Reformers, 1815–1860* (New York: Hill & Wang, 1978), 108, 127, 129, 137, 174–75, 195–97, 200–202, 204, 207–9; Clifford S. Griffin, *Their Brothers' Keepers: Moral Stewardship in the United States, 1800–1865* (New Brunswick, NJ: Rutgers University Press, 1981), 138; Helen E. Marshall, *Dorothea Dix: Forgotten Samaritan* (New York: Russell & Russell, 1937), 65–66.

4. Walters, *American Reformers*, 78–80; John L. Thomas, *The Liberator: William Lloyd Garrison, a Biography* (Boston: Little, Brown, 1963), 98–99, 128, 203; William R. Merrill, *Against the Tide: A Biography of William Lloyd Garrison* (Cambridge, MA: Harvard University Press, 1963), 54; Leon F. Litwack, *North of Slavery: The Negro in the Free States, 1790–1860* (Chicago: University of Chicago Press, 1961), 70–71, 75–87, 97, 114.

5. Rugoff, *Beechers*, 141, 146, 150; Griffin, *Their Brothers' Keepers*, 86–88; Cross, *Burned-Over District*, 196.

INDEX

ABOUT THE AUTHOR

Carl J. Richard is professor of history at the University of Louisiana at Lafayette. He received his PhD in history from Vanderbilt University in 1988. He is the author of eight books, including *The Founders and the Classics: Greece, Rome, and the American Enlightenment* (1994) and *Greeks and Romans Bearing Gifts: How the Ancients Inspired the Founding Fathers* (2008).